1965

University of St. Francis
GEN 873.1 O86
Otis
Virgil, a study in civilized p

3 0301 00035218 3

W9-ABR-563

This book may be kept

VIRGIL

A STUDY IN CIVILIZED POETRY

Oxford University Press, Amen House, London E.C.4
GLASGOW NEW YORK TORONTO MELBOURNE WELLINGTON
BOMBAY CALCUTTA MADRAS KARACHI LAHORE DACCA
CAPE TOWN SALISBURY NAIROBI IBADAN ACCRA
KUALA LUMPUR HONG KONG

VIRGIL

A STUDY IN CIVILIZED POETRY

BY

BROOKS OTIS

CLARENDON PRESS·OXFORD
1963

LIBRARY
College of St. Francis
JOLIET, ILL.

© *Oxford University Press*, 1964

PRINTED IN GREAT BRITAIN AT
THE UNIVERSITY PRESS
ABERDEEN

873.1
O86

3.22.65 Offord $6.28

37751

SORORIBUS FAXONIANIS

PREFACE

THIS book has a history about which I must say a few words. Some fifteen years ago I shared with my friend Paul J. Alexander the responsibility for imparting a little knowledge of the whole ancient world to a large group of undergraduates at Hobart College. Such a task had certainly its humdrum aspects but it had also the somewhat startling result of making me see familiar problems in an unfamiliar perspective. In particular the necessity of dealing with the early Christian period called my attention to a cultural phenomenon I had never really noticed before. This was the evident rift between the Greek and Roman worlds in the later empire. That this rift was not merely political or economic became more and more apparent to me as (largely in consequence of Paul Alexander's inspiration) I began to study the Latin and Greek Fathers of the fourth century. I began to see that the startling differences between Ambrose or Augustine and the Cappadocian Fathers were after all to be explained in much the same way as those between Greeks and Romans of the earlier and so-called 'classical' periods. However closely a Roman might keep his eye on a Greek model, he could not really succeed in hellenizing either his thought or his sensibility.

The Christian fourth century in fact renewed my interest in a very familiar problem,—that of the rise of a great Latin literature amid the evident decadence of Hellenic culture. The Latin writers of the late Republic and of the Augustan era for the most part revered and imitated the Greeks of the great or 'classical' period and as a result themselves produced 'classics' of comparable importance. But these Romans still lived in what was largely a Hellenistic or post-classical culture. How could they do what no contemporary Greek could do? What was the magic in the Latin language and milieu that made it possible? I turned to the available answers of classical scholarship and it seemed to me that they were at best vague and at worst misleading. So, to cut a long story very short, I tried to reach a much more precise answer by applying the question to a selection of specific but crucial materials.

One result was an enormous manuscript on the 'Augustan Epic', whose major sections were devoted to Virgil and Ovid. I have now, on the wise advice of Sir Ronald Syme, reduced a portion of this MS to the present volume. Later on and *dis volentibus*, I hope to reduce another portion to a book on Ovid and, above all, to reformulate my discussion of the more general and more important question of Roman narrative style as distinct from the quite different narrative style of the Greeks. It is obviously an advantage to treat Virgil by and for himself. But there is also some loss in the more limited perspective—a loss that I may later be able to make good.

For the present this book must stand on its own feet. In itself, it is an effort to say some new things about Virgil. It is not an attempt to repeat the familiar data that can be found in many other works. In this sense it needs no particular apology for its existence. Reduction and compression have, I think, decidedly improved it. But this has meant, among other things, the elimination of rather more than nine-tenths of its original notes and scholarly apparatus. I do not regret this but I do regret one corollary of it : the disappearance of most of my references to other scholars. I have in fact only recorded direct indebtedness, a few major differences of opinion, and the most indispensable references, though I have tried in the appendices to indicate where I stand in relation to the major trends of Virgilian scholarship. I think I have been reasonably conscientious in making use of the admirable bibliographies of Mambelli, Duckworth, and Marouzeau. Inevitably I have missed many items in the ample tide of *Virgiliana*. Still, my omissions are for the most part deliberate and indeed required by the size and character of the present volume. (The considerable hiatus between the completion of the final manuscript in June 1962 and the actual date of publication explains the omission of all very recent material.) The text of Virgil used in the quotations may be described as my own compromise between Hirzel and Sabbadini with considerably more weight given to the latter than the former. In the last analysis, I could not settle for either alone.

So much for the scholar. I hope also that the unprofessional Virgilian will find this book readable, at least in part. I have translated almost all the Greek: I have not translated the

numerous Virgilian quotations; but there now exists a spate of
excellent modern versions. Aside from at most a very few pages,
there is little that the non-specialist cannot follow. But he must
bear in mind that Virgil is pre-eminently an author who can be
read at several levels of comprehension. To understand him, we
must not only accomplish the easy descent to Avernus. We must
also return to the upper air: *hoc opus, hic labor est.*

My obligations to colleagues, scholars, friends, and students
(also friends) are very great and extend far beyond North
America. I have enjoyed the generous hospitality of the libraries
of Harvard, Cornell, Stanford, and Berkeley (University of
California), and of Hobart College and the American University of Beirut. I have been awarded Fulbright, Guggenheim,
and Smith-Mundt fellowships, and received research grants
from the American Philosophical Society and Stanford University: the former gave me time; the latter material assistance
in the typing and preparation of this book. The interest of the
Clarendon Press has made possible the present form and character of the work. I am very grateful to all. Without them this
book, such as it is, would not exist.

Stanford, California   BROOKS OTIS
18 *June,* 1963

CONTENTS

ABBREVIATIONS

AJP American Journal of Philology.

CQ Classical Quarterly.

HSCP Harvard Studies in Classical Philology.

Mus. Helv. Museum Helveticum.

PW Pauly-Wissowa-Kroll, *Realenenzyklopädie der Klassischen Altertumswissenschaft.*

REL Revue des Études Latines.

Rh. Mus. Rheinisches Museum.

TAPA Transactions of the American Philological Association.

Büchner Karl Büchner, *P. Vergilius Maro, Der Dichter der Römer* (1955) = PW, 'Vergilius'.

Cartault A. Cartault, *L'Art de Virgile dans l'Énéide* (1926).

Conington J. Conington, H. Nettleship & F. Haverfield, *Commentary:* Vol. I, *Bucolics, Georgics* (1898); Vols. II–III, *Aeneid* (1872).

Constans L. A. Constans, *L'Énéide de Virgile* (no date).

Heinze R. Heinze, *Vergils Epische Technik* (1st ed., 1902; 4th ed., 1957).

Morel W. Morel, *Fragmenta poetarum Latinorum* (Biblioteca Teubneriana, 1927).

Norden E. Norden, *Aeneis VI* (4th ed., 1957).

Pease A. S. Pease, ed., *Publii Vergili Maronis Aeneidos Liber Quartus* (1935).

Perret J. Perret, *Virgile, l'homme et l'oeuvre* (1952).

Pöschl Viktor Pöschl, *Die Dichtkunst Virgils* (1950).

CHAPTER I

THE MYSTERY OF THE *AENEID*

Virgil died at the seaport of Brundisium on 21 September 19 B.C. All his plans for a prolonged residence abroad had been interrupted by his meeting with Augustus at Athens, his subsequent sunstroke at Megara and his hasty return to Italy and death. His projected three-year revision of the *Aeneid* in the retirement of Greece and Asia had been disastrously cut short. Yet Virgil had either foreseen or provided for the contingency: on leaving Italy for Greece, he had instructed Varius to burn the *Aeneid* 'if anything should happen to him'. On his death-bed, he seems to have wavered a little: he asked for the manuscript in order to burn it, yet he did not insist when no one complied with his request.[1] We must, I think, see in this instruction and this uncertainty more than the morbid doubts of a perfectionist or the ostentatious modesty of one who secretly expected his wish to be ignored. The *Aeneid* was a colossal *tour de force*, unprecedented in both its aim and its execution. Virgil felt he could not let it out into the world without the most elaborate revision.

We can gather as much from the little we know about its composition. When Augustus once requested a sample of the poem, Virgil replied that he had nothing to show that was worthy of Augustus' attention: the very attempt had begun to look like madness, such was its scope, such the preliminary studies that it required.[2] Finally, after reiterated requests,

---

[1] Cf. *Vita Donati* (35): Anno aetatis quinquagesimo secundo inpositurus Aeneidi summam manum statuit in Graeciam et in Asiam secedere triennioque continuo nihil amplius quam emendare, ut reliqua vita tantum philosophiae vacaret. Sed cum ingressus iter Athenis occurrisset Augusto ab oriente Romam revertenti destinaretque non absistere atque etiam una redire, dum Megara vicinum oppidum ferventissimo sole cognoscit, languorem nactus est eumque non intermissa navigatione auxit ita, ut gravior aliquanto Brundisium appelleret, ubi diebus paucis obiit XI Kal. Octobr. Cn. Sentio Q. Lucretio coss. (39): Egerat cum Vario, priusquam Italia decederet, ut, si quid sibi accidisset, Aeneida combureret; at is facturum se pernegarat; igitur in extrema valetudine assidue scrinia desideravit crematurus ipse; verum nemine offerente nihil quidem nominatim de ea cavit.

[2] Letter to Augustus (Macrobius, *Sat.* I. 24. 11): De Aenea quidem meo, si mehercle iam dignum auribus haberem tuis, libenter mitterem, sed tanta inchoata res est, ut paene vitio mentis tantum opus ingressus mihi videar cum praesertim, ut scis, alia quoque studia ad id opus multoque potiora impendam.

Virgil did read Augustus three books (2, 4, 6) but it seems quite clear from Donatus' account that the requests had to be very pressing indeed.[1] We do not even require Donatus' famous description of Virgil's method of composition—the prose outline, the utter lack of continuity in the actual writing, the tiny daily quota of verses, the constant revision—to understand the terrible difficulty of the task.[2] It was not, to judge by all the appearances, the kind of reluctance that delayed the completion of *Faust*—a sheer inability to come to terms with the poetic *daimon*—but the very magnitude and scope of the work itself.

Yet no one, surely, can seriously doubt the wisdom of Augustus, Varius and Tucca in publishing the *Aeneid*. Whatever its difficulties and its rough spots, it had actually reached a stage of sufficient completion to reveal the poet's intention, and more —his conquest of those difficulties that had so baffled him, and his attainment of that magnitude, that poetic ὕψος, which he had thought so presumptuous. This has been vaguely sensed by generations of readers and critics, though Virgil has had his detractors, especially among romantically inclined nineteenth-century Germans; but it has not yet been clearly understood. It is only when one tries to grasp the self-imposed difficulties, the almost preposterous ambition of the Augustan poet, that one can begin to appreciate the poem and perhaps to see *how* it was after all possible.

We can state at once the character of his task by saying that Virgil did what no one else had done before him and no one was able to do after him. The *Aeneid* is, in one sense, an imitation of Homer: it is based on the *Iliad* and *Odyssey* not only in its Homeric plot and incidents but in its choice of an Heroic date and milieu. Virgil was thus the first and only poet truly to recreate the heroic-age epic in an urban civilization. There had been many—there were to be more—second-rate imitations of Homeric or Homeric-style epic. But these were all anachronisms betraying at every joint their obsolete and imitative substance. There were to be other great and authentic epics but these, like the Germanic eddas, are themselves the original products of other heroic ages or, like the *Divine Comedy* and *Paradise Lost*, are deliberate departures from the theme and the mood of heroic-age epic. Only the *Aeneid* aspired to be both

---

[1] *Vita Donati,* 31–32.   [2] *Vita Donati,* 22–24

heroic and civilized, both remote and contemporary, both Homeric and Augustan. This was precisely the 'mad' undertaking in which Virgil succeeded. It is our task and problem to explain how it was possible.

The fact with which previous attempts to explain this achievement have not really reckoned is quite simply the law of obsolescence in literature. In all literature, but most especially in Greek literature, the literary genre or form is inseparably attached to a particular age. The age of epic yielded to the age of personal and choral lyric, this to tragedy, tragedy to comedy and the prose forms. There were overlappings and transitions but no essential reversals: apart from learned and uninspired imitations, the course of literary development was quite as definite as that in any other field. The change from the rudimentary *polis* of Homer to the democratic-imperialistic *polis* of Pericles and the vast *metropolis* of the Ptolemies was no less great than the change from the *Iliad* to Thucydides, or from Pindar to Callimachus, and no less irreversible. It is thus wholly false to account for Virgil's achievement in terms of his imitative predecessors—the fact that many before him tried and miserably failed to write like Homer—or to 'explain' the *Aeneid* by the Augustans' proclaimed desire to revive the classical Greek genres (as if the thought could guarantee the deed) or by their ardent wish to praise Augustus in true Homeric fashion (again the thought and the deed). None of these 'reasons' explains anything. Nor does it help to declare that the *Aeneid* is a different kind of epic from Homer's, if one does not also explain how the difference accounts for Virgil's success. What did he do that Homer did not do, so that in the doing an obvious 'imitation' of Homer could become the true epic of a metropolis that has vastly more in common with contemporary New York than with Mycenae or Tiryns?

This is a question to which modern classical scholarship has produced no satisfactory answer. It has been relatively easy to show the un-Homeric character of Virgil's technique (though even here it was not until 1902 that Richard Heinze really collected and analysed the evidence). We can now see the difference between Homer's *oral* and Virgil's *literary* or written style. We can understand, at least partially, the devices by which Virgil connected his two ages; his use of prophecy and prophetic revelation, his combination of Homeric and old Roman legend. We can also see the evident influence of Stoic philosophy and allegory on both the human and the divine sections of the poem. But all this says little about the essential problem—the use of Homer to produce a genuine Roman epic or the very fact that this *imitation* is also a great poem in its own right.

Nor can the problem be disposed of by an easy submission to the inexplicable ways of genius. Any great literary work is bound to contain a residue of mystery, but the mystery of the *Aeneid* is much more than a residue. Virgil was not just another genius. Shakespeare, Sophocles, Homer himself took their form, their *genre* fresh from the hands of a line of predecessors: they added the master's touch, but only to a vital tradition which was in fact ripe for them. Virgil had no such living genre to work on. He was, indeed, reviving, giving new breath and life to a form some seven hundred years obsolete. This was a quite new thing in literature. We ought to be able to penetrate part of the secret by which this unexampled metamorphosis was accomplished.

CHAPTER II

FROM HOMER TO VIRGIL:
THE OBSOLESCENCE OF EPIC

THE first step toward understanding the *Aeneid* is understanding the status of epic in Virgil's own day. We must see exactly what he inherited—what forms, ideas, poetical criteria—before we can see what he himself contributed. Only so can we appreciate the novelty and the audacity of his undertaking.

No name in any other literature really corresponds to Homer. He was not only the source, the father of what came after him: he was also a figure of unapproachable magnitude in his own right. He both attracted and repelled the imitator and finally achieved a position of solitary grandeur. This was undoubtedly due to his own great literary merits. Yet these very merits were all but inseparably attached to his age and milieu. His poems (and we need not here redebate the reality of the 'his') belong, presumably, to the end or close to the end of a long epic tradition reaching back, perhaps, to the very heart of the Mycenaean age. The *Iliad*, if we accept Miss Lorimer's dating,[1] was composed about the middle of the eighth century B.C. and the *Odyssey* somewhat later. The Heroic Age of Greece had passed; yet its ideals and beliefs had not been wholly superseded by those of another age. The world of gods and heroes was still a thing which a poet could accept with 'natural piety'. More exactly, the Homeric simplicity and objectivity—the straightforward rapid narrative of action, the direct discourse of both gods and men, the inimitable combination of familiarity and nobility—reflected an era and milieu which could accept the heroic and the divine with no great, disturbing reservations. The objective style of Homer mirrored a real world in which the poet believed: he was, as the later Greeks put it, imitating life and imitating it in a great but also a direct and simple way. This was hardly possible for later writers to whom both gods and heroes were not only remote but actually 'irrational', unbelievable or unreal. In this sense Homer belonged to his time: the

---

[1] Cf. H. L. Lorimer, *Homer and the Monuments* (1950), esp. pp. 452 f.

very fact that he made the heroic and divine seem so 'human' and so real was what isolated him from later generations who lacked his easy access to such a *Weltanschauung*. It was not only the genius of Homer which made him unapproachable: it was also his age and his ideas.

Yet Homer left one legacy which largely determined the character of all later ancient poetry. This was his mythical subject-matter—more exactly, his limitation of poetry's proper content to a cycle of heroic myths in which men were almost inextricably mingled with gods and other divinities. Thus Posidonius' definition [1] of poetry (ποίησις) as a significant poem (ποίημα, i.e. metrical or rhythmic statement) which imitates or represents *things human and divine* (μίμησις ... θείων καὶ ἀνθρωπείων) undoubtedly reflects the prevailing idea or ideal of Greek poetry: its almost axiomatic acceptance by so scientific a thinker, as late as the first century B.C., is an evident proof of its hold on the Greek world. The Greeks even defined the content of poetry chronologically as the deeds of men who lived in the heroic or Homeric age. The author of the Pseudo-Demosthenic *Epitaphios* [2] carefully distinguished between the 'recent' exploits of the Persian War and the 'heroic' past which is the true content of poetry: the former is just as great in itself but belonged to history and prose since '*it had not yet been mythologized*' (οὔπω μεμυθολόγηται). We need not here inquire why and how this remarkable limitation of poetical content took place. As a matter of fact the whole thing is still rather obscure, but we must accept the event itself: Homer's influence and reputation had in effect fixed heroic myth as the proper subject of poetry.

It is thus plain that post-Homeric poetry was involved in a great dilemma or, better, tension of opposed forces. On the one hand, it could not accept Homer's world, his *mythos*, with his own 'natural piety': on the other, it was bound to that world by an all but unbreakable tradition. We cannot here hope to trace the multifarious workings of this dilemma or tension: this would amount to nothing less than the rewriting of all Greek literary history. Yet we can see at least some major lines of development. The significant thing, perhaps, is that narrative

---

[1] Quoted by Diogenes Laertius VII. 60 from Posidonius' περὶ λέξεως.
[2] Demosthenes, 1391.

poetry was replaced by choral lyric and tragedy. The myth ceased to be taken as a simple reflection of life or actuality—truth in the sense of history or narrative—and became instead *exemplum*, a kind of paradigm of the values upheld by a particular poet. Pindar, for example, uses the myth to illustrate the heroic ideal or golden 'moment' (καιρός) or to bring out the full force of a gnomic saying or aphorism. Aeschylus uses the myth to explain the emergence of a theodicy and an ethic which the fifth-century Athenian could accept. We need not of course suppose that either Pindar or Aeschylus would have used just these words to account for their poetry or, indeed, that they were consciously aware of what they were actually doing. Nevertheless it is hardly to be gainsaid that myth in their hands was made to reflect a reality far beyond its literal meaning and was, in the process, radically transformed. Its exemplary or, in the fullest sense, *symbolic* significance largely replaced its factual or historical content. Thus the shift from a narrative to a lyrical or dramatic form and style implied a shift in the poetical function of myth itself: myth was no longer a story that could be told in a direct and simple way but had become the lyric expression or dramatic re-enactment of quite contemporary feelings and ideas.

Yet even the Pindaric and Aeschylean transformation of myth was possible only so long as myth retained its power over men's minds and feelings and kept something of its nobility and holiness. As has been so often remarked, the very labelling of myths as 'myths' is a sign that they have lost symbolic power. This is why Hesiod's attempt (in his *Theogony*) not to tell 'myths like the truth but the truth itself' [1] had such fatal results for myth. For Hesiod's mythological inquiries eventually led to a quite 'demythologized' philosophy or science. We need not subscribe to the nineteenth-century view of the Pre-Socratics as mere forerunners of Galileo and Newton, but we must certainly admit that the Pre-Socratics marked a sharp break with previous 'mythical thinking': Xenophanes was doubtless a religious man but his God was not the old Zeus. The great Sophistic movement only made this 'demythologizing' explicit and radical. When it finally impinged on tragedy in the dramas of Euripides, the dilemma or tension to which we have referred

---

[1] *Theogony*, 27–28.

became articulate in poetry itself and therefore all but lethal to
poetry. For Euripides, whatever else he may or may not have
done, obviously broke the barrier by which myth had been kept
separate from prosaic reality. His ordinary men, ordinary
heroes and even ordinary gods were all deliberate violations of
the convention by which an heroic, mythical past had been
equated with more or less sacred values. The initial act of
iconoclasm was effective (and in its way poetical) but it could
not be repeated. Here Euripides was probably only the agent of
a *Zeitgeist* that was increasingly anti-mythical. Myth had
finally lost its capacity to activate great poetry: in becoming
incredible, it had also become symbolically irrelevant.

It is only in terms of this general development of Greek
literature and thought that the special case of post-Homeric
epic can be explained or understood. 'Homeric' epic, as we have
just seen, was myth or *mythos* in pure, narrative form. It was thus
the direct opposite of prose *historia*, which was non-poetical narrative applied to a *non-mythical, non-mythologized* subject-matter.
Even in comparison with other poetic forms that used myth,
epic was archaic since it was after all narrative and could not,
by its very nature, subject myth to the symbolic and dramatic
transformations of lyric and tragedy. Yet there were in fact
many epics written after Homer and right down to Hellenistic
and Roman times. Here undoubtedly there is a real literary
problem. How are the later epics to be explained? What was
their *status*, their literary importance, in their own time?

These questions can be answered only in terms of what went
on in Alexandria between about 270 and 250 B.C. The importance of the great Alexandrians of that time lies in the fact that
they fixed the limits, set the aims, of all subsequent *serious*
poetry written in Greek. The key word here, of course, is
serious: much, indeed the great bulk, of the verse or poetry
written in Hellenistic and Roman times was directly opposed
to the canons of such Alexandrine writers as Callimachus and
Theocritus, but this poetry was not *serious*, either in the sense
that it was intrinsically worthwhile or in the sense that it was
really an available model for any later original poet.

The reason why Callimachus and Theocritus were of such
influence (at least on all later poets who counted) was that they
alone seem to have understood the possibilities of poetry in the

Hellenistic age. They lived and worked in a great research centre and library, itself set in a great new metropolis. Their surroundings thus indicated at every turn the obsolescence of the old *polis* and the old *paideia*. Yet the change of poetic milieu would in itself have been of little effect, had they been only librarians, scholars or professors and not also sensitive artists and true poets. But because they combined these two rather incompatible functions they were able to see the poetical problem of their age with a quite unexampled clarity of vision. They did not set themselves against the traditional forms—least of all the Homeric canon which decreed a mythical content for poetry—but they did try to adapt the forms and the canon to the quite new conditions of poetry in their era. Unlike Euripides, they had no new, inconoclastic ideas, but at least they were willing to accept the results of his inconoclasm and to acknowledge the almost complete obsolescence of the heroic-mythical world view.

The specific problem that confronted them was the validity of post-Homeric epic as this had been 'revived' by the late fifth-century poet, Antimachus of Colophon, and exemplified in their own literary circle by Apollonius of Rhodes. Antimachus shares with Choerilus of Samos the distinction of having given epic a new lease of life at the exact moment, the second half of the fifth century, when it seemed to be almost extinct. Homer had been followed in the seventh and sixth centuries by a number of lesser writers: the authors of the so-called Cyclic Epics—the *Thebais, Cypria, Aithiopis, Iliupersis, Telegonia, Nostoi,* &c.—which 'completed' the *Iliad* and *Odyssey* by narrating the whole 'cycle' of saga belonging to the Mycenaean age. These are obvious *epigoni* who showed their inferiority to Homer by the peripheral and disunified character of their plots and by the imitative nature of their style. Their inspiration seems to have run out well before 450: we can see the transition in the change from the epic preoccupations of Herodotus' uncle, Panyassis (he wrote a *Heracleia* in fourteen books) to Herodotus' own *historia*, a painstaking exposition of contemporary events in narrative prose. This clearly is the situation that Choerilus and Antimachus recognized in trying to find a new goal or method for epic.

Choerilus of Samos (after 450 B.C.) innovated by dropping

the 'Homeric canon' and choosing a non-mythical subject, the
Persian Wars. His *Persika* was, in short, an Homeric epic on a
contemporary historical theme. His excuse, as he explains in
his proem, was the pre-emption of other topics by his predecessors: he came at a time when the epic field had been
already claimed and occupied and new poets had nowhere to
take their chariots. Hence his turning to 'another theme'
(λόγον ἄλλον) and to poetry modelled on recent history.[1] But
this daring innovation was too much for his contemporaries.
Though he had some later influence (as we shall see), he was not
able to renew epic by changing its content. So Antimachus of
Colophon, at the end of the century, based his own renewal of
epic not on any novelty of subject-matter—he wrote in fact
another *Thebais*—but on the novelty of his style and diction.
He seems to have been the first writer of epic who sought to
'rival' Homer by outdoing Homer 'at his own game', so to
speak, or by applying a more refined technique to the traditional matter and manner of Homeric epic. The scanty fragments of Antimachus' *Thebais* hardly permit us to grasp the
true character of his stylistic innovations but the important
thing is that he tried to renew epic without abandoning its
traditional content.[2]   His attempt seems to have been much
more successful in its time than the quite opposite programme of
Choerilus. At any rate he sets the terms of the great Alexandrian
debate.

We can, I think, see quite plainly why Callimachus and
Theocritus rejected Antimachean epic. Their criticism may in
itself be obscure or elusive. Taken in conjunction with their
actual poetical practice, however, it is relatively easy to understand. Callimachus tells us he was attacked by certain people
whom he calls *Telchines* because he refused to write a single
continuous poem (ἕν ἄεισμα διηνεκές) and insisted on writing
little poems (ἔπη τυτθά). It is quite clear that by *one continuous
poem* he meant, mainly, Cyclic or Antimachean epic: a single
poem in thousands of verses in a 'big sounding' style on kings,
heroes and gods (the 'thunder of Zeus'). As against this kind of
poem, he advocates the 'little epic' (ἔπος τυτθόν) and the
'light style' (μοῦσαν λεπταλέην). In concrete terms this meant

---

[1] Cf. Kinkel, *Epicorum Graecorum Fragmenta* I, pp. 266–7 (frag. 1, 1a).
[2] Cf. B. Wyss, *Antimachi Colophonii Reliquiae* (1936), esp. the Introduction.

either a single short poem (at longest an *epos* of four or five hundred lines, like his *Hecale*) *or* the *discontinuous* 'Hesiodic' epic. Here Callimachus clearly referred either to *didactic* epic (like, e.g. Aratus' *Phainomena*) or to a 'collective' poem (i.e. a *collection* of separate short poems, sometimes united by a narrative thread: in the first two books of his *Aitia*, for example, many of the separate episodes are told as 'answers' that the Muses give to the poet's questions about various puzzling customs or rites). It is thus evident that both the *Hecale* and the *Aitia* are set up as alternatives to Antimachean epic: Callimachus is setting the *short* against the *long* poem, the *light* against the heavy or *grandiose* style, the discontinuous *Hesiodic* against the continuous *Homeric epos*.[1]

What all this implied about his conception of poetry and of the content of poetry is revealed in what he actually wrote. Though he had no desire to break with the 'Homeric canon' itself, the traditionally mythical subject-matter of epic and lyric, he obviously felt it was necessary to give this subject-matter a quite new tone and emphasis. This explains his interest in unusual or recondite myths and his insistence on variety (πολυείδεια) in his verse forms.[2] He knew poets in his age could not go on doing the same old thing. But what is most important is his narrative style itself: this shows four major characteristics: a special kind of *realism* (a deliberate *modernizing* of the mythical element); a *familiar* or, often, *familiar-ironical* tone; a striking *subjectivism* of approach (the use of the 'I' or first person and the direct appeal of poet to reader); and, perhaps most important of all, a marked *brevity and asymmetry* of the narrative proper. There is a difference between the style of the *Hymns* and of the *Aitia* (the latter is far lighter and even at times frivolous) but both alike manifest these four characteristics, as indeed does the more epic *Hecale* also.

The novelty of Callimachus' approach to poetry really consists in his quite new treatment of myth. This is perhaps most obvious in his familiar tone, use of the first person and direct

---

[1] Cf. here R. Pfeiffer, *Callimachus* I (1949), pp. 1–8 and the two fragments 398 (p. 325), 465 (p. 353); also Pfeiffer II (1953), Epigram VI (p. 82); *Hymn to Apollo* (ll. 105–13). Callimachus' tribute to Hesiod is in Epigram XXVII (Pfeiffer II, p. 88); this should be taken with XXVIII.

[2] Cf. Pfeiffer, *Callimachus* I, Iambus XIII (203), pp. 205 f. (esp. ll. 30 f. and *Diegesis* on p. 205).

appeals to his characters. When, for example, he tells Acontius (the mythical hero of the Cydippe episode of the *Aitia*) that he got his story out of a mythological handbook [1] or (in the *Hymn to Zeus*) carries on a conversational and politely sceptical dialogue with Zeus himself, he is obviously discounting the credibility of his mythical material in a most radical way. His modernization of myth has nothing in common with the well-known 'anthropomorphism' of Homer: Callimachus' gods and heroes are more than human; they are bourgeois Alexandrines also, like the precocious Artemis and the hypocritical Heracles of the *Artemis Hymn*, or the status-conscious parents of Erysichthon (in the *Demeter Hymn*), or the curiously defensive Pallas of the *Loutra Pallados*. But it is above all the brevity and asymmetry of his narratives that reveal his true attitude to myth. He never tells any story or action in a symmetrical or balanced fashion: even the shortest piece of narrative is asymmetrically pointed at a particular scene and a particular effect. He is not interested (in the *Loutra Pallados*) in the blinding of Tiresias as such but in the goddess's defence of her action and the grieving mother; he is not really concerned (in the *Demeter Hymn*) with Erysichthon's *act* but only with the parents' reaction to it. In other words, Callimachus *avoids* the myth proper by emphasizing a realistic or sentimental detail which is really not the myth itself but his own invention.

We can thus see why he avoided the imitation of Homer. His Alexandrian or sceptically sophisticated conception of myth was admirably suited to his light, familiar, subjective and truncated narrative but it would have been utterly unsuited to the continuous and high style of Homeric epic. We must here try to grasp what this really meant: it was not just that Callimachus treated myth in a new way (though in a sense he did so) but that, in so doing, he cut short the development of all narrative poetry. For he had no idea of recreating truly narrative poetry on the basis of a new, non-mythical subject-matter. Here he was quite traditional, quite bound to the 'Homeric canon'. His only recourse, therefore, was to cut down his mythical narrative so as to fit his very limited conception of myth: the result was an exceedingly slight and peripheral thing that was in fact neither true myth nor true narrative.

[1] Cf. Pfeiffer, *Callimachus* I, *Aitia* III (fr. 75), p. 81, ll. 53 f.

The reason why Callimachus could not handle full length narrative or 'true' myth is also evident enough from the case of his contemporary, Apollonius of Rhodes. We need not attempt here to discuss the famous 'quarrel' between Apollonius and Callimachus: its details and chronology are rather obscure but there seems no good reason to doubt its existence or its cause— an obvious difference of opinion as to epic in general and as to Apollonius' *Argonautica* in particular. In any event, we have quite positive evidence as to what Callimachus and his partisans disliked in the *Argonautica*. Theocritus, who in his seventh Idyll indicated clearly his Callimachean allegiance, his disdain for poets who senselessly tried to rival Homer, has left us two poems (Idylls XIII and XXII) which treat two episodes of Apollonius' *Argonautica* in the new Callimachean fashion. There can be, I think, little doubt that Theocritus was here deliberately 'rewriting' Apollonius, showing in effect the 'right' way to treat themes that Apollonius, as he thought, had bungled.[1] But whatever view may be taken on this point, it is still the case that Theocritus' poems do show quite concretely the difference between two approaches to myth and to epic narrative.

In the *Argonautica* (I, 1153–1362 and II, 1–163) Apollonius relates two episodes: the story of the separation of Heracles and Hylas and the story of the fight between Polydeuces and Amycus. Obviously both episodes belong to a continuous narrative. Heracles is the great hero who is left behind by the Argonautic expedition; the Argonauts' attempt to turn back and find him is barred by the interposition of the sea-god Glaucus. The love episode—Hylas' abduction by the spring nymph and Heracles' consequent grief—is only a small part of the whole story. The problem with which Apollonius is mainly concerned is the continuation of the voyage after Heracles' separation from the other Argonauts. Similarly the fight between Polydeuces and the insolent Bebrycian king Amycus is but a prelude to the general conflict between all the Argonauts and the Bebrycians. Theocritus, on the other hand, has almost eliminated the Argonauts and Bebrycians as such: his emphasis is solely on the love of Heracles for Hylas, on the skill and modesty of Polydeuces in vanquishing an arrogant 'strongman'. Even the locale of each of the two episodes is a distant

---

[1] See Appendix 3.

spring, obviously and intentionally kept remote from the locale
(the shore) of the other Argonauts. He has thus abstracted two
isolated themes from a continuous narrative. Naturally he
thereby achieved far greater unity and concentration of effect.
But why did he aim at such unity? What was his artistic
purpose?

   We can only answer these questions by pointing to his
different characterization of Heracles and Polydeuces. In
Apollonius, Heracles is the epic hero, the hero who outrows
everybody else, pulls up a whole tree for an oar, overwhelms
all the Argonauts by his absence, and is finally abandoned
only after the epiphany of a god unveils what is fated for all
concerned. Actually, Heracles' love for Hylas plays but a minor
role in the whole episode. Again Apollonius' Polydeuces is a
true hero and demi-god: his victory over Amycus is represented
as that of Right and Piety over sheer Evil; the boxing is related
in epic fashion, with similes and lordly epithets. It all leads into
an Homeric battle, at the end of which the Argonauts hymn the
glory of their divine champion. The contrast with Theocritus'
Heracles and Polydeuces is striking indeed! Theocritus does
tell us that Heracles is 'brazen-hearted' ($\chi\alpha\lambda\kappa\epsilon o\kappa\acute{\alpha}\rho\delta\iota o\varsigma$) but
the epithet is about all that is left of the old hero. Instead,
Theocritus' Heracles is a lover and a pederast simply, one who
shows, as the narrating Nikias insists, that the gods could love
'just like us'. All that detracts our attention from Heracles'
love for Hylas is omitted: the oar, Polyphemus and the other
Argonauts, Glaucus, &c. All that is heroic, in short, has made
way for a love-agony utterly devoid of epic restraint. In the
Polydeuces Idyll, the contrast with Apollonius is equally
striking: what we have is the story not of a demi-god but of an
extremely clever boxer whose manners and boxing technique
are suavely superior to those of his rude and boorish opponent.
The idyll is told by the use of dialogue (stichomythia) and an
almost 'sports-page' reportage. At the end there is only the
expertise and courtesy of a skilful and gentlemanly victor: this
boxing contest is obviously no prelude to an epic battle!

   There is no point in debating the merits of Theocritus and
Apollonius here. Obviously each was striving for a different
effect, with a different kind of narrative and poetry. But no
reader can deny the effectiveness of Theocritus—the wonderful

harmony of style, plot, characterization, mood—or the relative woodenness of Apollonius. The latter aims for the Homeric elevation and charm but he cannot bring it off: Homer (as in the Epeius-Euryalus fight of *Iliad* 23. 653–99, for example) could depict heroes with human characteristics but Apollonius cannot quite take his heroes so easily; he cannot combine the elevation of epic with the naturalness of life. His gods are either awkward and bathetic (as in the case of Glaucus) or incongruously frivolous (as in the case of Aphrodite and Cupid in the third book). His similes (unlike Homer's) are too often laboured and otiose. But obviously he could not have done what Theocritus and Callimachus did without utterly relinquishing his epic. Theocritus' Heracles and Polydeuces are not traditional, truly mythical heroes but modernized quasi-Alexandrine figures who can only exist in the most cleverly stage-managed isolation. We catch just a glimpse, a vignette of their full story and, even so, a glimpse through a particular aperture and with a very special lighting. Otherwise the disparity between the myth they come from and the modern role they are made to play would be all but unbearable. In short Theocritus achieves his effect by his very brevity as well as by a most marked asymmetry. What he writes is, really, neither true myth nor true narrative but only an artful semblance of both.

But we need not disparage Apollonius' whole epic in order to show the correctness of Callimachus' and Theocritus' criticism of it. There are passages in the *Argonautica*, especially the love episode of the third book, which are masterpieces of psychological analysis but, as we shall see in detail later on, they are not integral parts of an Homeric epos; they in fact clash rather violently with their heroic and divine context. But the essential point is that Apollonius had tried to 'rival' Homer on Homer's own ground—the differences between him and Homer do not affect the imitative substance of his work—and had been unable to achieve an original or aesthetically successful result. In contrast, the short poems of Callimachus and Theocritus, limited and 'light' as they may be, are poetical successes because they effectively transmit an original and contemporary feeling for life. In a word: the heroic age had passed and no later poet could revive it without subjecting it to a very profound metamorphosis.

The fact that long epics still continued to be written did not in the least alter this general situation. That the *Argonautica* is the only complete epic to survive from the whole post-Homeric period before Virgil, is surely no accident: whatever its own demerits, it was manifestly much superior to any of its later rivals. It is indeed difficult to write any sort of account of these lost epics, so complete has been their disappearance and so total the oblivion into which they have sunk.[1] Yet we can find enough evidence to indicate fairly clearly what their general quality and character was. We can perhaps distinguish three basic types here: the panegyric-historical, the regional-historical and the Antimachean or Apollonian.

The first type, the panegyric-historical, seems to go back to a poet-follower of Alexander the Great: this is another Choerilus (perhaps a century later than the first Choerilus of the *Persika*) who came from the island of Iasos. He, along with his contemporaries and associates, Agis the Argive and Cleo the Sicilian, wrote epics on Alexander's campaigns. Quintus Curtius tells us that their flattery was extreme: they are said to have represented Alexander as a new god to whom Heracles, Bacchus and Castor were glad to yield precedence. Perhaps, as has been suggested, the deification of Alexander and the 'epic' scale of his actions provided an excuse for the employment of divine machinery and the raising of contemporary battles to heroic-Homeric proportions. In any event, all that we know of Choerilus and his friends is depreciatory: Porphyrio refers to him as the *pessimus poeta* about whom Alexander was wont to joke; Horace talks of his *inculti versus*.[2] What is evident is that Choerilus was the first of a long line of eulogizing poets attached to royal and wealthy patrons: they were expected to flatter and they did. There is no indication at all that their work was more than imitative and mediocre. After Alexander, the Macedonian diadochi and the Hellenistic monarchs had also their epic eulogists: we know, for example, of Simonides of Magnesia at the court of Antiochus Soter, of Leschides and Musaios with the Attalids, of Theodoros with Cleopatra. The custom was also continued by Roman patrons of Greek poets: Boethos sang of Antony, and the famous Archias of Marius

---

[1] See Appendix 2.
[2] See Q. Curtius, *Hist. Alex.* 8. 5. 8; Porph. *Art. Poet.* 357; Horace, *Ep.* II. 1, 233.

and the Mithradatic war. There were without doubt a great many such epics.[1]

Seemingly more important was the regional or regional-historical epic. Here the principal name is clearly Rhianos of the third century (possibly a contemporary of Apollonius and Callimachus, though he seems to have no connection with Alexandria). He wrote a series of epics about the history of various regions or cities (*Achaika*, *Thessalika*, and *Eliaka* in addition to the better known *Messeniaka*) as well as an Antimachean or mythological epic, the *Heracleia* in fourteen books. Though we have only a minimum of actual fragments, we have considerable information about the *Messeniaka* in Pausanias (IV, 17–22 or 23). This epic was about the second Messenian War and had a hero, Aristomenes. So far as we can tell it lacked any divine machinery: though its general style was epic, its plan was historical, possibly following the war from the Trench disaster (Pausanias IV, 17. 10) to its end. It made much of Aristomenes' hairbreadth escapes: he was obviously a kind of Messenian David and corresponded in epic terms to Achilles.[2] There were later a number of similar epics (in addition to the other *three* of Rhianos) such as Phaistos' *Lakedamonika*, Apollonius' *Ktisis Rhodou* and *Alexandreias*, and the Jewish epics of Philo the Elder.

The distinction between regional epics and epics on separate wars (usually more aptly labelled *panegryic-historical*) is often hard to maintain. But there does seem to be a difference between the strictly historical or historical-regional *epos* (of which the first Choerilus' *Persika* was perhaps the model though the *Messeniaka* is the best known) and the more definitely panegyrical epic of Choerilus of Iasos and his followers. The latter type seems, for example, to have introduced the gods while the former probably avoided them. In any event there is little reason to suppose the one type of epic was markedly

---

[1] See Susemihl, *Geschichte der Griechischen Litteratur in der Alexandrinerzeit* (1891), I, pp. 404–9 and notes.

[2] See Powell, *Collectanea Alexandrina*, pp. 9–21. Presumably Pausanias follows Rhianos' order since he stipulates (IV. 6) where he follows Rhianos as distinct from his other source for Messenian history, Myron of Priene. This would *apparently* indicate that, apart from oracles and portents (cf. IV. 20, 21), there is no divine machinery as such. Clearly Aristomenes' escape from the *Ceadas* (18), from his captors by the help of the Messenian girl (19, 5–6), and the adulterous treachery of Neda with the Laconian herdsman (20, 5–10) are the central episodes of the epic.

C

superior to the other. The very productivity of Rhianos (five big epics) is hard to reconcile with a high degree of art.

It is tempting at first sight to see in the choice of an historical, non-mythical subject-matter a true renewal of the content of poetry. But there is every reason to believe that the very contrary was the case. Though rejecting the mythical subject-matter of Antimachus and Apollonius, the two Choerili had not changed either the language, the style or the spirit of epic. They had on the contrary tried to force new, prosaic material into an old poetical mould. But their 'history' had not, like the heroic legends, been habituated to poetry. The Homeric style was but the reflex of an heroic way of life and of a society in which heroes quite naturally consorted with gods. It was only, therefore, by raising their contemporary characters to a legendary status that the Choerili could fit them to the Homeric pattern. But in so doing these poets increased rather than mitigated the anachronism of their undertaking. Apollonius had at least tried to write of real Homeric heroes, of Jason, Heracles and the Dioscuri, of Homeric gods and goddesses, and of the Homeric era and society. Choerilus and Rhianos could only make an Alexander talk like Zeus or an Aristomenes like Achilles. Theirs was the very reverse of the procedure by which the great Alexandrians had given new, contemporary vitality to Homeric subjects: instead of modernizing the old, they archaized the new.

On the other hand, there is nothing to indicate anything distinctive about the *Antimachean* or mythological Greek epics of the Hellenistic and Roman periods. We have mentioned Rhianos' fourteen-book *Heracleia*: but there was also Theodoros' twenty-one-book epic on Heracles, the *Heracleia* of Phaidimos of Bisanthe and the *Athla Herakleous* of Diotimos of Adramyttion. In addition Menelaos of Aigai wrote an eleven-book *Thebais*; Theolytos of Methymna, the *Bacchica Epe*; Neoptolemos of Parium a *Dionysias*. And there were more *Argonautica* by Theolytos and Cleon of Kurion. We need not prolong the list. If there was any advance beyond Antimachus or Apollonius, there is absolutely no indication of it on the record. The overwhelming probability is that all this work was markedly inferior to that of either.[1]

---

[1] Cf. references in Appendix 1; see also Appendix 2.

What is important, however, about this mass of Hellenistic epic is simply the fact that it was written and had some sort of popularity in its time. The notion that Callimachus dominated the whole Hellenistic and Roman eras is manifestly false. Callimachus in fact affected a very restricted circle of poets. But Callimachean influence, though limited and selective, was highly strategic. For the line that includes Euphorion, Moschus, Bion, the *Megara* and Parthenius was continued in the 'new poets' around Cinna and Catullus and by their poetical successors Gallus, Virgil, Varius and the Maecenas group. But such a line must be envisaged as a very thin thread traversing a great mass of more or less popular literature. Not until the first century were Romans at all prepared to accept Callimachean doctrine or practice. But this is equivalent to saying that no group of poets or critics between the time of Callimachus and the time of Cinna had either the critical acumen or the poetical sensitivity to grasp the defects of Hellenistic epic. Nothing had happened to change the judgement that Callimachus and Theocritus had passed on Antimachus and Apollonius, though much—indeed the whole enormous output of historical and mythological epic—had happened to confirm it.[1]

On the other hand, the positive heritage of Callimachus and Theocritus, the ἔπος τυτθόν and the Hesiodic collective poem, had hardly been an unqualified success. Moschus' *Europa* is a worthy successor of Theocritus' *Hylas*. But Euphorion [2] seems to have lacked both the directness and the charm of the great Alexandrines, and Parthenius, so far as we can judge, was only a second-rate poet. Furthermore the increasingly amatory or erotic content of the ἔπος τυτθόν in the later Hellenistic period, the preference for pathological and outré topics (such as the amours of Pasiphae, Medea, Scylla, Myrrha and Byblis), was an evident sign of decline. The genre, in so far as it can be called a genre, had always been limited and difficult (it was, as we have seen, neither true myth nor true narrative), but it now tended to become overspecialized and monotonous. The gap

---

[1] Cf. Appendix 2.
[2] Cf. Euphorion's *Thrax* (most conveniently accessible in D. L. Page, *Greek Literary Papyri* (Loeb edn.) I (1942), pp. 494 f.). Cf. also Kurt Latte, 'Der Thrax des Euphorion' (*Philologus*, 90, 1935), esp. pp. 152–3. There is no doubt that Euphorion followed Callimachus and Theocritus in such features of style as brevity, asymmetry, and the familiar appeals to a character.

between it and the mighty genres to which it was the self-proclaimed alternative, loomed disturbingly immense.

It was thus quite clear that poetry had reached a definite *impasse* in Hellenistic society. Callimachus and Theocritus had not so much met the problem of poetry as avoided it. They had rejected continuous epic for quite sound reasons, but their discontinuous long poems and their 'short epics' had really evacuated both myth and narrative from poetry. By their brevity, asymmetry and use of a light, familiar style they had achieved contemporary freshness, but at an enormous price: the reduction of the huge canvas of epic to a few pretty or piquant vignettes. The need, obviously, was to drop the Homeric content and style altogether or to transform them into material usable once more for serious poetry. But no Greek or Greek-speaking poet was prepared or able to do either. The Romans were different. Yet even the Romans could only approach the problem by a Greek route. That is to say, they also had to write anachronistic and unsuccessful epics and they also had to achieve a critical awareness of both the anachronism and the failure. It was not simply by copying a Greek *or* Roman model that Virgil learned to write the *Aeneid*. His first problem was to appreciate the defects, the poetical unavailability, of his Roman epic predecessors. This fact has as yet been quite insufficiently appreciated.

The first Roman epic (apart from Livius Andronicus' crude version of Homer) was the *Bellum Punicum* of Naevius (written toward the end of the third century B.C.). This was, as Ennius somewhat rudely declared, the poetry of fauns and fortune-tellers (*Fauni vatesque*), a highly unsophisticated composition in the native Saturnian measure. It was quite clearly indebted to Choerilus and the historical epic he had fathered. But it was indebted also to Roman sources. The arrangement of its seven books (the division was not due to Naevius) is not certain, but it is plain that it recounted the events of the first Punic War in chronological order, the order of Roman *annales*, after a considerable proem or introduction on the mythical or legendary causes of the war. Here Naevius brought in the gods and the Dido-Aeneas story as a prophetic prelude to his contemporary theme. There is no good reason to doubt Macrobius' flat statement that Virgil here found the original of the storm and the

colloquy of Jove and Venus with which he began the *Aeneid*.
There was probably a formal *concilium deorum* in it as well. The
juxtaposition of an Homeric mythology:

> dein pollens sagittis inclutus arquitenens
> sanctus Iove prognatus Pythius Apollo

and rather bald history:

> Marius Valerius
> consul partem exerciti in expeditionem
> ducit

would not have bothered Naevius or his contemporaries. We
cannot expect at that era any special sensitivity to style, any
strong sense of the incongruity between annalistic history and
Homeric narrative. And the poem had its merits and originality:
unlike the work of Rhianos and Choerilus, it was a real
national epic, full of crude but genuine Roman feeling.

But it was Ennius' *Annales* (probably written during the
decade before his death in 169 B.C.) which really set the decisive
precedent for later Roman epic before Virgil. It was obviously
indebted to Naevius' *Bellum Punicum* but it was obviously also
an explicit and avowed attempt to create an Homeric epic on a
Roman theme. Its hexameter metre is itself an index of its
Homeric pretensions. The dream introduction, which has been
so much discussed, can be understood only as a deliberate
declaration of Ennius' intention to be an *alter Homerus*, the
Homer of Rome. His encounter with the Muses at Helicon, his
dream on Parnassus, his vision of Homer and the Pythagorean
explanation of how he came to be Homer's Roman reincarnation, are only devices for expressing this intention. Ennius
almost certainly imitated here the introduction of Callimachus'
Aitia, which is also a dream involving the Muses and Helicon,
but he used it in order to make apparent the very different
character of his own epic: where Callimachus dreamed of
Hesiod (and the beginning of the *Theogony*), Ennius dreamed of
Homer; this is a clear sign that he wants to be taken as the rival
of Homer, not Hesiod; as the author of Homeric, not Hesiodic
epic.[1]

---

[1] Cf. Skutsch on Ennius in PW. Both E. Reitzenstein (*Festschrift R. Reitzenstein*,
pp. 63 f.) and Pfeiffer (*Callimachus*, I, pp. 9–11) deny Ennius' dependance on Callimachus but the comparison of the digest of the *Aitia* in the *Scholia Florentina*
(Pfeiffer I, p. 11) with Lucretius. I, 112–26 and Propertius III. 3, 1–12 seems to me

In any event, the Homeric intention is obvious enough in the poem. Ennius clearly 'Homerizes' the early legends of Rome. He not only retells, after Naevius, the story of Aeneas but he gives a divine-heroic, an Homeric aura, to the founding of Rome. The story of Mars and Ilia is related with true epic solemnity. A *concilium deorum* is called to propose Romulus' divinization and his very obsequies are magnified by the awe his apotheosis excites:

> O Romule Romule die
> Qualem te patriae custodem di genuerunt . . .

> Romulus in caelo cum dis genitalibus aevum
> degit.

But Ennius did not choose to linger long in the realm of legend. The eighteen books of the poem recorded the Roman *res gestae* down to his own time in straight chronological order, with far more space allotted to recent or contemporary history than to ancient legend. Thus the Punic Wars began in Book 7; the Macedonian War in 10; the War with Antiochus in 13; the Istrian War in 16. Obviously such subject-matter was far less epical or Homeric. Ennius, however, still used the gods as much as he could: Jupiter was brought in to predict the destruction of Carthage and Juno's wrath was appeased in order to implement the prophecy. Yet such epic episodes could not overcome the obviously unepic character of the vast bulk of the poem. The discrepancy between the Homeric and the historical aspects of the *Annales* is glaring. He begins the first book with:

> Musae quae pedibus magnum pulsatis Olympum

and the tenth book with:

> Insece, Musa, manu Romanorum induperator
> Quod quisque in bello gessit cum rege Philippo.

We find such epic passages as the Ilia-complaint (Vahlen 35 ff.) and such prosaic descriptions as that of Gellius (V. 234 f.); such lines as:

> postquam Discordia taetra
> Belli ferratos postes portasque refregit

---

decisive: Hesiod did not meet the Muses *in a dream* but Callimachus and (in imitation of him) Ennius did. Cf. J. H. Waszink, 'The Proem of the *Annales* of Ennius' (*Mnemosyne*, 1950, pp. 215–40).

and such lines as:

> Appius indixit Karthaginiensibus bellum.

There is no apparent effort to maintain any uniformity of style or content: myth and history, poetry and prose, the elevated and the pedestrian are not so much combined as baldly juxtaposed. We can well understand Horace's complaint that this *alter Homerus* had taken his Pythagorean dreams and promises rather lightly.[1]

There can be no doubt that Ennius had in some sense created a true national epic, far more inclusive than, and poetically far superior to, Naevius' *Punic War*. But he had not overcome the defects of Greek historical epic: on the contrary, no Greek could ever have combined history and myth in quite so jarring a manner. Ennius had simply ignored the problem of 'Homerizing' history: he had crudely joined Homeric mythology to an annalistic historical narrative (prosaic except for its hexameter rhythm) without apparently any feeling for the consequent clash of styles, epochs and ideas.

There is sufficient evidence to show that the first important Roman literary critic, Lucilius, who lived *circa* 170–102 B.C., was aware of Ennius' major defects. The meaning of the strictly literary part of his *Saturae*, the twenty-sixth book, is still rather obscure. We know that he criticized some of Ennius' verses as of less than epic gravity (*gravitate minores*) and that he attacked all the older poets to at least some extent. But, despite Mario Puelma Piwonka,[2] it is not yet certain that he was a consistent follower of Callimachus. Probably he objected to historical epic or at least to contemporaries who contemplated writing it. He certainly did not like the 'portents and winged snakes' that some poets fancied, that is, the purely imitative use of far-fetched conceits and images. His parody of an epic *concilium deorum* in the first book of the *Satires* is, however, the most definite evidence of his attitude toward the Homeric treatment of a Roman, contemporary theme. This has been admirably interpreted by Marx, Cichorius and Terzaghi:[3] all their guesses may not be right but they have surely caught its main drift. It is a burlesque of serious epic; the object of the gods' debate is

---

[1] *Ep.* II. 1. 50–52.   [2] *Lucilius und Kallimachos* (1949), esp. pp. 137 f.
[3] Cf. esp. C. Cichorius, *Untersuchungen zu Lucilius* (1908), pp. 219 f.; N. Terzaghi, *Lucilio* (1934), pp. 261 f.

the deceased *princeps senatus*, L. Cornelius Lentulus Lupus, and the divine council is really a mock-senate. Romulus talks of the *concilium* he missed: this is almost surely a reference to the Ennian *concilium* which decreed Romulus' deification before his actual decease; the scene is thus an evident parody of its Ennian original. It is hard to believe that the satirist who wrote this passage could have failed to grasp the incongruity of the whole *Annales*, the general futility of Ennius' Homeric ambitions. Lucilius' brand of humour was the natural foe of such pretences.

But Lucilius' satire did not seem to affect the development of Roman epic. Ennius had many followers. We probably lack even the names of most of them but we have enough to show the trend. Accius (his dates are approximately 170–86 B.C.) wrote twenty-seven, or possibly seven books of *Annales*:[1] we know little about them but they were certainly historical epic in the Ennian vein. Hostius wrote in the late second century an epic on the Istrian War of 129 B.C.: we know that it contained at least three books. Furius of Antium wrote *Annales*, probably on the Marian campaign of 101 B.C. By the middle of the first century B.C. at least five writers of historical epic were or shortly would be at work. Furius Bibaculus on a *Bellum Gallicum* of at least eleven books; P. Terentius Varro on a *Bellum Sequanicum* (Caesar's campaign against Ariovistus); Volusius, Catullus' foe, on *Annales* (we have no idea of their historical limits but they were extensive); Hortensius also on *Annales* (Catullus refers to his 50,000 verses); and Cicero on three major epics: the *Marius*, the *De Consulatu Suo* and the *De Temporibus Meis*, each of three books.[2]

These epics, it seems all but certain, marked no aesthetic improvement on Ennius' *Annales*. The case of Cicero is surely indicative. He does not scruple to interlard his contemporary history (for the most part his own *facta*) with all the conventional devices of Homeric epic. In the *De Consulatu Suo* Cicero is

---

[1] There is no reason for supposing, as some do, that his *Annales* deal with 'festivals' just because the long fragment in Macrobius (*Sat.* I. 7. 36–37) is about the *Saturnalia*. The title *Annales* naturally refers to a work like that of Ennius.

[2] On Hostius, cf. Bardon, *La Littérature Latine Inconnue* I (1952), pp. 178–9; on Furius of Antium, ibid. pp. 179–81; on Furius Bibaculus (not to be confused with Furius of Antium), ibid. pp. 347–52. Bardon (pp. 249–50) denies that Hortensius wrote *Annales* in verse but his over-literal interpretation of Plutarch (*Lucullus* I. 5) cannot destroy Catullus' evidence (95). On Cicero's epics, the relevant evidence is collected in Morel.

addressed in most laudatory terms by the Muses, Urania and Calliope; and by Jupiter himself in a *concilium deorum*. Again in one of his letters he contemplates a wonderful addendum (mirificum ἐμβόλιον) to the second book of the *De Temporibus Meis*, a *concilium deorum* in which Apollo prophesies the unhappy returns of the generals Piso and Gabinius. He could have derived such scenes from Greek models (the *exemplaria Graeca* on which Quintilian blames them: XI. 1–24) but this is not at all certain: they were now a tradition of Roman epic as well. The bald disparity of historical and epic styles that we saw in Naevius and Ennius is perhaps less apparent (so at least the few fragments of these epics would indicate) but the greater smoothness of the style only conceals a much more fundamental failure of imagination. It is not simply that Cicero's egotism rose or sank to the grotesque *concilium deorum* of the *De Consulatu Suo* but that he saw no incongruity whatsoever in this kind of epic façade to what was, after all, political pamphleteering. He had not rethought the divine machinery of epic and invested it with any sort of symbolic depth: it was simply conventional decoration, a flashy frame for self-eulogy.

But we can see the reason for the superficiality of his epics in the very circumstances of their composition. In the year 54, for example, Cicero wrote to his brother Quintus, at that time with Caesar in Gaul. In the letter he urged Quintus to write an epic on Caesar's British campaign and took the occasion to ask anxiously about Caesar's reaction to his own *De Temporibus Meis*. He recalls that Caesar had already read the first book of this epic and thought it better than anything he had yet seen in Greek, at least the best parts of it; some of it seemed to Caesar a little négligé (ῥαθυμότερα). Quintus, however, was urging Cicero himself to do the epic on Caesar. But Cicero was doubtful: he was too busy, too distracted. Later he writes that he may finish it off in the coming holidays. These letters [1] and others like them tell us almost all we need to know about Cicero's attitude toward epic: his political motivation, the complete absence of any sensitivity to aesthetic problems, above all the ease, the flippant ease with which he contemplated and undertook such works.

---

[1] See *Ad. Q. Fr.* II. 15 (16) = Tyrrel and Purser, 147; ibid. III. 5 (= T. and P. 155), 4; ibid. III. 8 (= T. and P. 159), 3.

37751   LIBRARY
College of St. Francis
JOLIET, ILL.

But this kind of attitude was not peculiar to Cicero. It was clearly also that of such contemporary statesman-littérateurs as his rival Hortensius and it set the tone, of course, for the professional poets they patronized. Cicero's praise of Archias, obviously a very second-rate writer of Greek historical epic, and his querulous reaction to the *poetae novi*, his constant magnification of Ennius and the Roman 'ancients'—all reflect his literary sensibility and that of his circle as well. We can understand how they regarded poetry: how, on the one hand, they indulged a taste for it, for they were no philistines and were anxious not to be taken for such; and, on the other, insisted that it was only pleasant and decorative amusement for their holidays. Above all they saw no reason why literature could not be put to a good Roman and political use: they had no notion of a high aesthetic standard to which other aims must be subordinated.

This was the background, or at least the negative background, of the 'new poets', of Cinna, Catullus, Calvus and Valerius Cato. We need not think of them as an organized party so much as a group of friends with common literary ideals and a common programme. The New Poets seem, in retrospect, to represent a natural reaction to the prevailing state of poetry in Rome in the second quarter of the first century. But the direct impulse came from two men—the Greek emigré Parthenius and the Roman aristocrat C. Helvius Cinna. It was Parthenius who indoctrinated Cinna with Callimachean and Euphorian ideas; it was Cinna's *Zmyrna* that inspired his colleagues and friends with a new poetic ideal and example.

Parthenius lived through two generations of Roman literature: he was the mentor of Cinna and Catullus in the mid-first century and of Gallus, Varius and Virgil in the following decades. His importance consists in the fact that he was the principal representative of Callimachean doctrine in that era. Parthenius stood with Callimachus and Euphorion as the archopponent of the plagiarists of Homer, the Cyclic and Antimachean poets. He upheld the Callimachean *variety* (πολυείδεια) and wrote many types of verse but his principal works were, like those of Callimachus and Euphorion, elegies and short hexameter poems (the ἔπος τυτθόν). His style was highly Euphorionic as was his subject-matter.[1]

[1] See Appendix I.

Cinna's *Zmyrna*, an intricate work of nine years duration, was obviously derived from the Parthenian ἔπος τυτθόν. It was *the* work of art which the New Poets opposed to the voluminous *Annales* of Volusius and the 50,000 verses of Hortensius. Catullus, who tells us this (poem 95), adds that he rejoices in the prospective immortality of his friend's 'slender monument': he will let the mob (populus) continue to take pleasure in 'tumid Antimachus'. In other words, Roman poets had at last begun to take the same line against their local Roman epics as Callimachus had taken against Antimachus and Apollonius. And they had also, like Callimachus, countered the opposition in a positive way by writing the esoteric kind of Alexandrine 'little epic' that illustrated their new ideal of poetry.

The example of the *Zmyrna* was thus very important. The New Poets wrote many kinds of poetry in several metres: they, too, employed the Callimachean *variety*. But their chief claim to literary importance, their model for a masterpiece, was the 'short epic', the four or five-hundred-line hexameter poem, of which the *Zmyrna* was the prototype, and Catullus' *Peleus and Thetis* (64) is the sole surviving example. Cato's *Dictynna*, Caecilius' *Magna Mater*, Cornificius' *Glaucus*, Calvus' *Io* and the *Zmyrna* itself are, save for insignificant fragments,[1] lost: we can gain at best some faint idea of their content and nature from Ovid and, above all, from a much later poem (the *Ciris*) which partially imitated them—especially the *Io* and *Zmyrna*.[2] Catullus' *Attis* (63) also displays some characteristics of the genre. As a genre, it derived from Callimachus and Theocritus (though *via* Euphorion and Parthenius) but it also reveals some original traits.

All poems of this kind display in rather accentuated form the *asymmetry* we have already noted in their Greek analogues. In the *Peleus and Thetis* of Catullus the central episode, the story of the deserted Ariadne, is 'framed' within another episode, the marriage of Peleus and Thetis. The Ariadne episode is in fact ostensibly introduced as a description of the tapestried covering of the marriage couch. This somewhat awkward device of itself inhibits the narrative: in effect all we see is Ariadne at one moment, in one situation, as she wakes from sleep on the beach of Dia to find herself deserted by Theseus. Catullus *in fact* does

---

[1] All in Morel.　　　　[2] See Appendix i.

not observe the limits imposed by his setting: the entrance of Bacchus (theoretically depicted on the edge of the tapestry) is unreasonably deferred; the 'flash back' to Theseus' father, Aegeus, and to Theseus' departure from Athens, is a clear violation of his pictorial frame. But, even so, he has rigidly confined himself to a bare moment of *pathos*. There is only the illusion, not the reality of narrative; the centre of the Ariadne episode is occupied by her long declamatory lament, a lament which reiterates a single sensation and idea and actually stops the action. We find the same asymmetry in the *Attis*: an (expanded) moment of religious frenzy followed by a similar moment of repentance. Much the same thing must have been true of the *Io*, *Zmyrna*, *Dictynna*, &c. Probably we can see in the *Ciris* a reflection of the *Zmyrna*:[1] the expansion of the crucial moment—the moment of *pathos* preceding and motivating the decisive and horrible act—into a lengthy Euripidean dialogue (like that of the nurse and Phaedra in the *Hippolytus*) and the contraction of all that precedes and follows this expanded moment to the barest possible summary. Again at the end of the *Ciris*, another pathetic moment—Scylla's plight as she hangs in chains from Minos' ship—is 'expanded' by another declamatory complaint. What lies between the 'moments' is concentrated in fourteen lines (out of the total 541).

But this asymmetry has a rather different effect from that of Callimachus and Theocritus. These poets had, as we have seen, rejected continuity of narrative and thus separated their central figures (such as Heracles and Polydeuces) from their basic mythical setting: it was esential to isolate them in order to modernize them. Otherwise an unbearable incongruity could not have been avoided. But Catullus was not exactly 'modernizing' in the *Peleus and Thetis*. In fact he tries very hard to maintain a good deal of epic diction and style and even something of the epic gods and heroes. He uses the 'familiarity' and 'subjectivism' of Callimachus—for example in his direct invocation of Ariadne, his overt expressions of sympathy with her—not to lighten his style or to relieve it of epic solemnity, but to express his feeling for his heroine, his own participation in her *pathos*. Thus while he is using a technique derived from the Alexandrines and from Euphorion (doubtless also from

[1] Cf. Appendix 1.

Parthenius), he uses it in a very different way, to what clearly seems a quite different end. Yet his treatment of myth is also remote from that of Cicero or Ennius: myth is no longer to him mere convention, a required part of the epic style, but the index of a moral reality. He is trying to give real meaning to the relation of gods and men: his two mythical episodes are contrapuntal and symbolize two worlds, two conceptions of love and marriage. The gods sympathize with Ariadne as we do: it is human guilt, the betrayal of love and morality, such as Theseus' betrayal of Ariadne, which has brought about the cessation of that happy intercourse of gods and men depicted in the marriage of Peleus and Thetis.[1]

The *Ciris* is too crude to stand comparison with the *Peleus and Thetis* but in it we can see a similar reworking of Alexandrine subjectivism and familiarity, a similar (though very uneven and botchy) attempt to preserve the 'seriousness' of epic style. And Catullus' *Attis* (though not strictly an ἔπος τυτθόν: it is not 'epic' in metre or manner), reveals an almost lyric subjectivity of narrative that we can trace also in the *Peleus and Thetis*, but which has no parallel in similar Greek poetry.

The 'little epic' of the new poets thus seemed to reveal very interesting possibilities: a new use of the epic style and seriousness, a new application of Alexandrine familiarity, and a new feeling for myth. But it was a very limited and a very inchoate and imperfect thing: it quite failed to achieve the unity, the stylistic facility and the vivid characterizations of Callimachus or Theocritus. Despite all the empathy and sympathy he devoted to Ariadne, Catullus scarcely brought her to life: she is after all a tableau, the source of a monologue, a quite wooden figure with no individuality whatever. Nor is there any unity of style: the epic and the familiar (or Alexandrine) elements are not after all fused in an effective way; at times (this is especially true of the *Ciris*) the discontinuity is jarringly awkward. But above all there is no true narrative: the new poets had succeeded no more than the Alexandrines in presenting a real story. The rule of brevity and asymmetry was still carefully observed. In short, the *Ƶmyrna* and its offspring were splendid failures: but they had set at least a new standard of art. We are now

---

[1] Cf. F. Klingner's great monograph, *Catulls Peleus-Epos* (*Sitzungsberichte Bayerische Akad. Wiss. Phil.-Hist. Klasse*, 1956, 6).

in a quite different poetical world from that of Cicero's *De Consulatu Suo*.

The New Poets were, *from our point of view*, much more successful in their short elegiac and lyric pieces. These were obviously quite in the tradition of Callimachus and Parthenius: the Alexandrines prided themselves on *variety*, on running the gamut of poetical forms from epigrams to elegies, iambics, lyrics and the 'short epic'. But Catullus' *libellus* of short poems on personal topics (above all his Lesbia poems) reveals a directness of sensuous passion, a depth of self-revelation that explains their appeal to modern, and, above all, romantic taste. Here the difference from their Greek originals (such as the elegiac epigrams of Callimachus) or analogues is very striking. It is not only that Catullus here shows a subjectivity of feeling quite unexampled in any Greek poetry but that he connects his poems (sometimes by explicit cross reference) in what can almost be called a poetical autobiography or narrative of inner experience. The great importance of this we shall discuss later on:[1] here it is enough to note the achievement, the emergence of first-rate poetry, of poetry that is not merely aesthetically sophisticated but is also original in its sensibility and use of convention.

But the immediate and direct influence of the New Poets was not so much due to their originality (their unlikeness to any predecessors) as to their renewal of Alexandrine literary standards, their insistence that art, effort and painfully acquired knowledge (doctrina) were essential to poetical excellence. The historical epic was the most obvious target of their doctrine. But it is clear also that they objected to strictly Antimachean or mythological epic; indeed they included Volusius and Hortensius among the Antimachi. It may seem at first sight strange that one of the New Poets, Furius Bibaculus, could write an epic *Bellum Gallicum* and another, P. Terentius Varro of Atax, a Latin *Argonautica*, but it would probably be wrong to expect a rigid consistency.[2] There is no question about the main drive and influence of the whole neoteric movement: it was away

---

[1] See pp. 104–5.

[2] Cf. on this question Alfonsi, *Poetae Novi* (1945) pp. 41–46, 77–91. But I suspect hypotheses here: there was no 'party-line' among the New Poets, only a general agreement. Doubtless Cinna, Calvus, Cato and Catullus formed the 'hard core': none of these contemplated or wrote a long historical epic.

from long, pretentious and facile poetry toward the shorter forms such as lyric, elegy and the miniature epic. At the same time there is no evidence that this was because the New Poets ruled out epic on *a priori* grounds: rather they preferred to do only what they could do adequately and well, to avoid pretentious mediocrity at all costs.

The influence of the New Poets can be traced in three distinct movements or groups which had emerged by about the year 35 B.C. There were first of all the group of 'survivors', the Catullan generation, whose leader was Valerius Cato: they included Furius Bibaculus, Ticidas and Varro of Atax, with others—the Cassius, Tigellius Hermogenes, Demetrius, &c., referred to by Horace. All these harped on the example of Catullus and Calvus, insisted on Lucilius as the satiric model and made much of grecisms—the use of Greek words in their Latin verse. They were, in other words, true to the spirit and letter of the founders and had by 35 assumed the curiously reactionary role of ageing revolutionaries. Politically also they were republican and anti-Augustan, faithful to Brutus and the conspirators of 44.[1] But the future belonged to two quite different groups: the elegists, of which Gallus was leader, and whose 'mantle' then passed to Propertius, Tibullus and Ovid; and the original Maecenas group [2] that included Fundanius, Pollio, Varius, Virgil and Horace.

All three groups were neoteric in that they fully accepted the New Poets' protest against the kind of epic or poetry represented and fostered by Cicero and Hortensius. We must not, however, confuse their later reputation with their actual influence in their day. Epic on the Ennian model still continued to be written; patrons still wanted epical panegyrics of their *facta*. The dates here are somewhat uncertain but we know at least that there was an unbroken line of both historical and Antimachean epic: Ponticus, Propertius' friend, wrote a *Thebais*; Domitius Marsus an *Amazonis*; Cornelius Severus a *Carmen Regale* or *Res Romanae* (clearly an historical epic of some sort). Rabirius, Albinovanus Pedo, Iulius Montanus, Arbronius Silo, &c. seem to be post-Virgilian and, in part, post-Augustan.[3] But they

---

[1] Cf. here my article 'Horace and the Elegists' (*TAPA*, 76 (1945), pp. 177–90). The main data are provided by Horace in *Ser.* I. 10.   [2] Cf. n. 1 above.
[3] Cf. Bardon, op. cit. II (1956), pp. 11–77 for a good account of these writers. Surviving fragments are in Morel.

indicate a continuation of the trend. There was certainly a considerable number of poets relatively untouched by neotericism. This is important for we must not think of the elegists or the Maecenas group as more than extraordinary exceptions to the average of literary taste and performance.

The elegists were pre-eminently the direct Augustan successors of the new poets. Their Alexandrine inspiration was open and avowed. Ovid declares that his amatory elegies are Callimachean, not Homeric:

> Callimachi numeris non est dicendus Achilles.

Propertius paraphrases the proem of the *Aitia* in resigning his pretensions to epic.[1] Gallus was after Cinna the chief disciple of Parthenius. Propertius' and Ovid's narrative elegies are clearly and avowedly modelled on those of Callimachus. Yet the elegists owed at least as much to Catullus and Calvus as to the Alexandrines and even added a good deal of their own. Despite every effort, no Alexandrine model of the Lycoris, Cynthia, Delia or Corinna poems has been found. It is more and more apparent that Gallus was an innovator who expanded the briefer elegies and polymetra of Catullus and his associates into a connected series of standardized elegiac poems: he fused Catullus' subjective passion, the poet's own love-experience, with the stock themes of Hellenistic amatory epigram and the mythological learning of Alexandrine verse. The result was an odd blend of personal and conventional motifs that was altogether too disparate and artificial to last beyond a single generation: Ovid developed the *narrative* elegy to which Propertius finally passed and thus completed his strictly amatory elegies by the much more imitative *Heroides* and *Fasti*. The result was a considerable body of verse but also a revelation of elegy's limitations.[2]

For Augustan narrative elegy, as Richard Heinze [3] has demonstrated, was not only more asymmetrical than Alexandrine

---

[1] References are to Ovid, *Remedia Amoris* 381; *Propertius* III. 1 and esp. III. 3.13 f. Cf. also *Prop.* II. 34. W. Wimmel (*Kallimachos in Rom*, 1960) deals only with the *formal* side of the problem (i.e. overt declarations of Callimachean principles) *not* with Callimachus' actual influence (e.g. the influence of the *Aitia* on the narratives of Propertius IV and Ovid's *Fasti*).

[2] Despite all the huge literature on the subject, no definitive monograph on the origin of the Roman Love Elegy has yet been written.

[3] *Ovids Elegische Erzählung (Berichte . . . Sächs. Akad. Phil-Hist. Klasse*, 71, 1919, Heft 7).

and neoteric 'little epic' but was committed by its metre and spirit to a much lighter and more facile treatment of myth. In a few poems of Propertius and Ovid, it achieved charm and even brilliance: on the whole, it was monotonous, trivial and heartless. Its great achievement was formal: the reduction of the poetical variety of Catullus and the new poets to a smooth uniformity of metre, narrative and mood. Ovid in the *Fasti* had in a sense fulfilled neoteric ambition and latinized the *Aitia*: the result was a colder and far less amusing poem than its model. Elegy—one has to admit—was really a *pis aller*. It produced a few remarkable pieces, than quickly ran itself out. Here the neoteric ideal of artistic finish had finally led to the elimination of all the passion and seriousness that neotericism had also contributed to poetry.

The Maecenas group was in one sense just as committed to Alexandrine and neoteric ideals. Horace's objection to Valerius Cato and the older neoterics was in fact their failure to apply to themselves their own neoteric principle of polish and artistry or to appreciate their own crudities and that of their adored model, Lucilius. They were epigoni who had lost the spirit of their masters. In contrast, Horace and his friends thought themselves more, not less Callimachean in demanding a higher standard of workmanship and artistic finish. Horace emphatically condemns the Volusiuses of his day, those who think *length* the important thing in a poem, who, like old Lucilius himself, wrote too much and too fast and hastened to publish or recite their crude verse to a big audience. His own satires were mere talk, *sermo merus*, deliberately unpretentious conversations in verse that did not, in virtue of their metre alone, aspire to the rank of true poetry. He rejected Greek historical epic (Choerilus) and the Roman epic (Ennius *et al.*) alike: all lacked the true polish of the Classical Greeks.[1]

Virgil had originally, it seems, thought of writing a Roman epic (*res Romanae*) but gave up the attempt and turned instead to the *Bucolics*, imitations of the Alexandrine Theocritus. These are obviously the poems of a man thoroughly imbued with Callimachean and neoteric ideals. We cannot ever know exactly

---

[1] For Horace's views see esp. *Ser.* I. 4 and 10; *Ep.* II. 1. There is a direct paraphrase of Callimachus in *Ser.* II. 6, 14–15. F. Wehrli, 'Horaz und Kallimachos' (*Mus. Helv.* I (1944) pp. 69–76) has treated the subject in some detail,

D

what went on at Naples when in his youth he associated with Varius, Plotius Tucca and Quintilius Varus in Siro's epicurean fellowship.[1] It seems most probable that he knew Parthenius as well as Philodemus. At any rate he refers to Cinna as his literary master in his ninth eclogue (*circa* 40 B.C.) and, in his sixth, paraphrases Callimachus in declaring his preference for the thin, light style to the fat or heavy style of epic.[2] What he writes and can write about, he says, are low tamarisks and woods; poetry in a light vein (*deductum carmen*), not epic. Horace appropriately describes him in the tenth satire [3] (35 or earlier) as inspired by his rustic muses with a 'mild and pleasing' (*molle atque facetum*) song—obviously nothing epic. When after 39 or 38, he turned to didactic, he was still adhering, at least partly, to a Callimachean genre: the *Georgics* was an avowedly *Hesiodic* poem, exactly the kind of long poem that Callimachus admired.

Nor was the sole writer of epic in the Maecenas group at that time (i.e. 35 or shortly before) in any sense a follower of Ennius or Cicero or a writer of the usual Antimachean or historical kind of *epos*. Varius was praised by Horace (Satire 10), in the list that included Pollio, Virgil and Fundanius, for his *forte epos*. But Horace later contrasted Varius with Choerilus and his kind (*Ep.* II. 1. 229–47). The *epos* to which Horace refers was not, it is clear, a long epic in several books. It was probably the *De Morte* and was at best a 'short epic' of very slight if any narrative content. Varius turned to tragedy for his major poetical effort: he is not even listed by Quintilian as a writer of epic.[4]

But Varius' *epos* and tragedy at least indicate that the Maecenas circle was not satisfied with neotericism as a sufficient programme for poetry at this time. Horace, in those very satires (Book I: 4 and 10) where he deprecates crude and hasty writing, proclaims the excellence of the *Classical* Greek models. He exalts the 'intense spirit and force' (*acer spiritus ac vis*) of

---

[1] The available data on this are collected in Westendorp Boerma's *P. Vergilii Maronis Catalepton* I (1949), p. 10.

[2] See *Eclogue* 9. 30–36. Clearly Virgil is not disassociating himself from the views of Lycidas. In *Eclogue* 6. 1–12 he obviously paraphrases the *Aitia*, Pfeiffer I. 3–5.

[3] Lines 44–45.

[4] Cf. on Varius' epic Bardon, op. cit. II, pp. 28–30 and Alfonsi 'Studi di Poesia Augustea' (*Aevum* (1943), pp. 249 f.). Macrobius' manner of citing Varius shows that his *epos* cannot be long (i.e. in several books).

epic, even of Ennius at his best. He held no brief for elegy (*exigui elegi*) as the proper form for a true poet's genius to take: he saw its evident limitations.[1] The question then was not whether imitation of the Classical Greeks was desirable but whether it was possible. And this was pre-eminently a question that applied to epic. It is clear that Augustus wanted an epic that could be worthy of him: there was no letting up of official demand. But could anyone who was sensitive to the Callimachean and neoteric criteria of poetry actually write it?

The first point to be made here is a quite negative one to which indeed the whole argument of this chapter has contributed. Neither Virgil nor Horace nor, so far as we can tell, any close associate of theirs in the Maecenas circle, seriously believed that Choerilus or Ennius, or any of Ennius' followers down to Cicero and contemporary writers of *Bella* or *Annales*, had written an epic worthy of the proper model, Homer; or that imitation of Choerilus or Ennius was a proper way of fulfilling Horace's programme of a return to the Classical Greeks. The New Poets had established, at least in the eyes of Horace and Virgil, criteria of excellence and finish which had once more brought poetry back to the level of performance advocated by the doctrine and practice of Callimachus. Indeed Horace wanted to go beyond the new poets, to do more than babble of Catullus and Calvus [2] and to write poetry of an even superior finish. And actually the Horatian *doctrine* was exemplified in Horace's own odes and above all in Virgil's *Bucolics* and *Georgics*. It is most significant that Virgil abandoned his juvenile dreams of an epic on *res Romanae* [3] and turned instead to Theocritus, Hesiod, Aratus and Nicander as his poetical models—not to Homer. This does not mean that he had simply given up all his epic aspirations or his desire to praise Rome and Augustus in the high style they deserved; indeed, as we shall see later in detail, the *Bucolics* and *Georgics* reveal his growing devotion to these themes, his deepening sense of the *novus ordo* inaugurated by his *princeps*—but it does mean that he appreciated the incomparable difficulty of writing the kind of epic that could reach Horace's and his own exalted standard.

---

[1] On Horace's view of elegy, cf. my article (cited in note on p. 31).

[2] *Ser.* I. 10, 18–21.

[3] *Vita Donati* 19: Mox cum res Romanas inchoasset, offensus materia ad Bucolica transiit.

We have Horace's quite explicit statement of what this standard was and there is every reason to suppose that Horace, in making it, was fully aware of Virgil's example or intention and was completely reflecting the Virgilian point of view toward epic. But the *Ars Poetica*, which contains this statement, has met a curious fate from modern scholars and critics. Its bearing on the problem of the *Aeneid* has been minimized or misunderstood partly because it has been taken to be a rather unimaginative reflection of late Aristotelian poetical theory; in particular that of the relatively unimportant Neoptolemos, some of whose ideas on poetry we can with considerable difficulty recover from a few damaged fragments of a treatise on poetry by the Epicurean poet and philosopher, Philodemus. But the question of the poem's *sources* is in no sense identical with that of the genuineness or sincerity of Horace's own views. There is no reason to suppose that he did not mean what he said: indeed the *Ars Poetica* both expands and makes explicit the doctrine of the classical Greek model which he had stated as early as 35 B.C. (Satires 4 and 10) and had later reiterated, above all in his long letter to Augustus.[1]

The *leitmotif* of the *Ars Poetica* is *unity* and *simplicity* of style and plot:

23   denique sit quod vis, simplex dumtaxat et unum

he says of the kind of poem (be it epic or drama) that he advocates. There should be no incongruity of parts, no artificial conjunction of disparate elements, no human head on a horse's body, no 'purple patch' sewn on common cloth. Homer was excellent because he showed *consistency* of plot and style. He did not, like the author of a *Cyclic Epic*, promise more than he could perform (e.g. a history of the *whole* Trojan war) and then produce a mouse from his mountainous labour. Homer actually promises something much more limited: to sing of *one* man and *one* phase of his adventures—not a mass of uncoordinated myths and miracles. Homer thus presses right on to his narrative goal (*semper ad eventum festinat*), strikes at the outset the high note he wishes to maintain, leaves out all matter that will not give lustre to his style:

[1] See the reviews of the literature on the subject by Büchner (*Bursians Jahresbericht* 267, 1939) and Getty (*Classical World*, March 1959). I have profited here from discussion with Professor Charles Brink.

151   Atque ita mentitur, sic veris falsa remiscet,
                 primo ne medium, medio ne discrepet imum.

His fiction is such a blend of false and true, of *history* and *myth*,
that the whole—beginning, middle, end—is consistent and the
parts do not clash with each other. His celebrated commence-
ment of the *Odyssey—in medias res, non secus ac notas, auditorem
rapit*—is but the expression of this ideal: to start the epic
narrative at a supreme heroic moment that sets as it were the
tone of the whole.

There is no doubt that this description of the model epic,
Homer's epic, corresponds at every point to the Horatian and
Virgilian ideal. What is impressive is not just that the *Aeneid*
illustrates this ideal—a fact to which amazingly little attention
has been paid—but that Homer is here carefully set against his
opposite, cyclic epic. Horace was trying to establish the Greek
models for Roman poetry, not because the Greek models were
simply traditional but because in fact *they were not:* it was the
post-Homeric followers of Homer that had caused the decline
of epic and for the quite sufficient reason that, in departing
from Homer's consistency of plot and material, they had
thereby lost the consistency and elevation of his style. Horace's
Aristotelian theory of poetic unity, his celebrated doctrine of
decorum, his distinction of high and low styles of poetry, his
feeling for a hierarchy of genres, his apparent traditionalism in
the choice of plots and characters, all stem from his reaction to
the contemporary debasement of style, to its loss of unity and
consistency, and above all, elevation—its absurd mixture of
mythical-heroic with historical-contemporary material. It was
not wrong to write in a low style: what was wrong was to
pretend to the grandiose while violating the very things, consistency and maintenance of the high style, that made the
grandiose at all possible.

The date [1] of the *Ars Poetica* has been much disputed but
whether it is prior or subsequent to the publication of the *Aeneid*
is of little real importance. It clearly anticipates or recalls the
Aeneid: granting that a Roman poet wanted to write in the high
style, then the true model was Homer, the real Homer, not

---

[1] Cf. O. A. W. Dilke, 'When was the *Ars Poetica* written?' (Univ. London, Inst.
Classical Stud., *Bulletin* 5 (1958), pp. 49–57), esp. his table of dates given by various
scholars (p. 49).

Choerilus, Ennius, Cicero, Ponticus or Cornelius Severus. This was a viewpoint perfectly consistent with both neoteric and Callimachean doctrine, except indeed for the fact that neither the New Poets nor Callimachus had seriously believed such imitation of the real Homer to be possible. It was precisely because Creophylus, Antimachus, Apollonius, &c., were *not* Homers, did not maintain Homer's consistency of plot and style, could not reproduce the Homeric elevation, that Callimachus and Theocritus criticized them and turned, themselves, to other forms where they could at least achieve some sort of poetical success. Catullus had done much the same thing in attacking Volusius and Hortensius (*his* equivalents of Antimachus), praising the *Zmyrna* and writing his own *Peleus and Thetis* as an example of what could be done in his own place and time.

But how could Virgil hope to succeed where so many others had failed? How could a Roman and Augustan, at so much later a date, do what Callimachus had declared impossible and no one else had even attempted? Virgil had indulged in the traditional Callimachean refusal (*recusatio*) to write epic and had, like Horace and the elegists, insisted on the unpretentious lowliness of his own verse. His fleeting indication of an intent to sing Pollio's *facta* (*Eclogue* 8) or his wish, expressed in the fourth *eclogue*, to celebrate those of the *Wunderkind*,[1] cannot be taken as evidence of serious epic intentions: the projected *res Romanae* had been abandoned. But in the proem to the third *Georgic* (written, as in integral part of the book, about 30 B.C.) he declared his resolve to sing Caesar's (Octavian's) battles (*pugnas*) in a clear reference to the victory at Actium.[2] This statement has often been taken as showing Virgil's design to write an *historical* epic on Augustus' *Bella* or *Bellum*. But could Virgil really have had such an idea, on the very eve of the *Aeneid*, after almost two decades of work in a Theocritean and didactic vein? Did he really contemplate so un-Horatian, un-neoteric, and un-Callimachean a task? The answer is, I think, apparent to anyone who grasps the meaning of the *symbolic* description of the future epic given just a few verses before; it is, so Virgil declares, a great temple to Caesar (Augustus) that he (Virgil) will dedicate amid games in which

[1] *Eclogue* 8. 6–12; 4. 53–54.   [2] *Georgics* III. 46–48.

he will outvie all the Greeks—the Greeks who will desert their own country to be there. The temple's walls will be adorned with scenes of Augustus' triumphs and statues of his mythical ancestors, the great Trojans of old. Thus the contemplated epic was indeed to be a celebration of the victor of Actium but not simply a narrative of contemporary history. Rather, it was to be a thing which would outvie the Greeks, be the Roman equivalent of the *Iliad* and *Odyssey*. Propertius, even before the publication of the *Aeneid*, but with some advance knowledge of its content, recognizes this in mentioning the *Aeneid* as an Homeric poem greater than the *Iliad*, a poem which is at once the epic of Actium and of Aeneas (II. 34. 61–64).[1]

In short Virgil conceived of his epic as both Homeric and Augustan, *res Romanae* constructed on the principles laid down for epic in the *Ars Poetica*. As we shall see later in detail, he had in fact shown in both *Eclogues* and *Georgics* the essential Augustan themes (even something of their order and connection) that he wanted to use in his epic. The adoption of an Homeric framework, even much of the plot of the *Iliad* and the *Odyssey*, though an innovation—the Cyclics and their successors had, as we have seen, avoided *direct* imitation of the *Iliad* and *Odyssey* —was not in itself too astounding. But how was the juncture of two ages, two worlds—the Augustan and the Homeric—to be accomplished? Prophecy and prophetic scenes (the souls to be reincarnated in Book 6, the shield in Book 8) were obvious *devices* for bridging the gap between the two times and two milieux, but how was the real modernity of the whole poem to be accommodated to an Homeric setting? How was the divine machinery, the monsters, the heroes above all, to be given *Augustan* meaning and overtones? How was the artificiality of such a union, the obvious incongruity of the history and the myth, of the legendary and the contemporary, to be made bearable and poetically consistent? How was a continuous narrative to be recreated after both Callimachus and Catullus had declared it

---

[1] There has been much discussion of this proem (*Georgics* III. 1–48) most recently by Wimmel (op. cit. pp. 177–87), Richter (Commentary, ad loc.) and U. Fleischer (*Hermes* 88 (1960), pp. 280–331). Both Richter and Fleischer agree that the lines refer to Virgil's future epic (though Fleischer thinks that only the lines after *iam nunc*, l. 22, do so). Richter cites the analogy of *Georgics* II. 176 (where Virgil proclaims himself the Roman εὑρετής or discoverer of Hesiodic epic); hence the *novelty* of his claim here, to do Homeric epic. On Propertius' lines cf. Appendix 9, p. 419.

to be impossible? Alternatively, how was a neoterically oriented poet to violate the rule of brevity and asymmetry in narrative without violating also the artistic integrity, the devotion to poetical truth, which had established this rule? Here indeed we encounter the true mystery of the poem on which Horace's elucidation of the Homeric plot and style sheds no light at all.

The fact is that Virgil's epic would have been a most dismal failure had his attitude toward, his *envisagement* of, the Homeric material been that of Homer himself or the Cyclics or all other post-Homeric writers of epic. His innovations of theme and plot, the technical devices that he employs, are all subordinated to the general style or viewpoint of the narrative, and it is this that differs so signally from that of his epic predecessors. They were, broadly speaking, *objective* in their narrative and strove for at least the shadow of verisimilitude; Virgil was *subjective* and transmitted to his narrative the colour of his own purpose. The result was a quite new continuity of narrative, a quite new command of his mythical and legendary material, an ability to use it for, not against, his central Augustan theme. Once we appreciate the exact character and significance of this *subjective style* of his, we can see both its uniqueness and its origin, its essentially Roman and non-Hellenic origin. To this I shall turn in the next chapter.

So far we have established one important point: the *Aeneid* had no true precursors. The line of criticism and poetical practice which originated in third-century Alexandria and was introduced by Parthenius and Cinna into Rome had not stopped the flow of imitative epic but it had produced the taste and sensibility that made such epic poetically unavailable to Virgil. His neoteric and Callimachean heritage was thus largely negative. It had turned him from Antimachus, Choerilus and Ennius and from the contemporary Roman epic back once more to Homer. In cutting off all living and contemporary models, it had in fact immensely exacerbated his task. His achievement was as heroic and unusual as that of his own Aeneas.

CHAPTER III

THE SUBJECTIVE STYLE

So far our investigation has reached a largely negative result: we have tried to show the novelty of the *Aeneid*, the absence of a living epic tradition on which Virgil could draw. He was directed by Horace and others to return to Homer yet his Alexandrine and neoteric training had made clear the difficulty—perhaps the impossibility—of any such attempt. Yet somehow he did it: the *Aeneid* exists as the tangible proof of his achievement. Thus our problem is to see what the *Aeneid* is, by what innovations of thought or diction the old could be renewed, Homer could be made Roman and Augustan. Obviously, this can be no superficial task: we must look beneath all matters of technique and arrangement to the very texture of Virgil's style and language. Previous scholarship has gone a certain way—men like Heinze and Pöschl have pointed to some essential elements of the *Aeneid*'s style—but very much still remains to be done.

We must begin with some rather close textual analysis. Let us first consider a brief piece of narrative (the foot race: *Aeneid* 5. 315–42) and its Homeric model (*Iliad* 23. 757–83). The difference between the Virgilian and Homeric races is evident. We can see this best by looking closely at the accidental fall of Nisus and Ajax. In Homer, it is the result of Odysseus' prayer to his patron goddess, Athene. This is quite clear to Ajax (Oilean) whom the reader already knows as the companion of Telamonian Ajax, the ancient rival of Odysseus. It is all part of an old story of bad relations between Athene and the two Ajaxes. But Virgil's characters are unknowns: he has to create, as it were, a dramatic situation out of the race itself. So he makes Nisus' slip the means of Euryalus' victory: the defeat of the unimportant Salius is quite secondary to the demonstration of Nisus' affection for his friend. The race is thus *dramatic* (at least three of the participants seemed at one time possible winners) and above all a drama determined by the inner motivation (Nisus' love for Euryalus) of the main or deciding

Aeneid 5. 315–42

315 Haec ubi dicta, locum capiunt signoque repente
corripiunt spatia audito limenque relinquunt,
effusi nimbo similes; simul ultima signant.
Primus abit longeque ante omnia corpora Nisus
emicat, et ventis et fulminis ocior alis;
320 proximus huic, longo sed proximus intervallo,
insequitur Salius; spatio post deinde relicto
tertius Euryalus;
Euryalumque Helymus sequitur: quo deinde sub ipso
ecce volat calcemque terit iam calce Diores
325 incumbens umero; spatia et si plura supersint,
transeat elapsus prior ambiguumque relinquat.
Iamque fere spatio extremo fessique sub ipsam
finem adventabant, levi cum sanguine Nisus
labitur infelix, caesis ut forte iuvencis
330 fusus humum viridisque super madefecerat herbas.
Hic iuvenis iam victor ovans vestigia presso
haud tenuit titubata solo, sed pronus in ipso
concidit immundoque fimo sacroque cruore,
non tamen Euryali, non ille oblitus amorum:
335 nam sese opposuit Salio per lubrica surgens,
ille autem spissa iacuit revolutus harena.
Emicat Euryalus et munere victor amici
prima tenet plausuque volat fremituque secundo;
post Helymus subit et nunc tertia palma Diores.
340 Hic totum caveae consessum ingentis et ora
prima patrum magnis Salius clamoribus implet
342 ereptumque dolo reddi sibi poscit honorem.

---

participant. Homer's race is not dramatic in this sense: there is no true peripety or reversal arising out of the action itself; Athene is rather a quite extraneous figure who is introduced to decide the event by *force majeure*. Nor is there much dramatic suspense; we know that Odysseus wants to win and that his appeal to Athene will be heeded. In Virgil, the unexpected tripping of Salius completely changes the expected outcome: the friendship of Nisus and Euryalus, unlike the rivalry of Ajax and Odysseus, achieves a truly dramatic result. Virgil in brief has written a 'psycho-drama'; Homer a simple narrative.

315 This said, they take their place and quick at the signal's blast
They devour the course: and are well off the mark
Like a swift cloud burst: their eyes upon their goal.
First far beyond the other runners Nisus goes away.
He flashes faster than the winds or winged thunder bolt.
320 Next to him but next by a long interval
Follows Salius: finally then after another space
The third, Euryalus.
Helymus follows Euryalus: and then right on his track
Look! Diores flies and almost gets his heel
325 Straining upon him: and if there'd been more room
He would have gone ahead or left the race in doubt.
And now almost at the end and near exhaustion point
They were coming to the goal, when Nisus on slick ground
Slips, the unlucky, for a bullock's blood had there
330 Been shed and had made the grass slippery and wet.
Here the young man—so sure of victory—could not keep
His footing as he rocked and reeled, then headlong
Down he went in the foul mud and sacred gore.
334 Yet not Euryalus, yet not his love did he forget
335 For he threw himself on Salius, rising from where he slipped
And Salius now lay wallowing in the trodden sand.
Euryalus then flashes by, victor by his friend's gift,
And takes first place as he flies on to much applause and
    cheers.
Next Helymus comes in second; Diores is third.
340 Then the whole amphitheatre's broad expanse with Salius'
    cries
Is filled: with shouts he begs the chieftains to give back
342 The honour snatched from him only by deceitful trick.

All this is a familiar story ever since Richard Heinze's famous
analysis of Virgil's games.[1] What has *not* been so clearly seen is
the extent to which Virgil's psycho-dramatic approach governs
the smallest details of his language. Thus, comparing the
Homeric and Virgilian passages, we can note at once the
following differences:

1. The Virgilian narrative shifts the sentence subject as little
as possible. The subject of lines 315–17 is the *runners* (plural):
capiunt, corripiunt, relinquunt, signant. Then the subject shifts to
the individual runners in order: Nisus (318–19: abit, emicat),

[1] Heinze, Chapter 4.

757 Then they stood in a row and Achilles showed them the limits.
The course was laid out to the turn-point. Swiftly thereafter
Out started Oileus' son: right after him rushed Odysseus,
760 Close to him as the weaver's beam is close to the bosom
Of some woman fair-breasted as deftly with fingers she
draweth
The shuttle over the warps and very near does she hold it,
Near to her breast: so then did Odysseus run close and behind
He beat up the dust with his feet before it had settled
765 And on Ajax' head the noble Odysseus was breathing,
Ever swift running. And for him all the Achaeans did shout
As he strove for the victory and accosted him as he sped on-
ward.
But when they reached the final lap of the contest, straight-way
Odysseus
Prayed to Athene, the gleaming-eyed, in his bosom:
770 'Hear me, goddess, come aider benevolent, help now my feet!'
So he spoke praying. And Pallas Athene heard him.
Light made she his feet and his limbs and his hands above them.
But when they just were about to secure the prize,
Then Ajax slipped as he ran—for Athene upset him—
775 There where was spread the gore of the slaughtered, loud-
mouthed bulls
Which for Patroclus, the swift-footed Achilles had sacrificed,
777 And this was the gore Ajax' mouth and nostrils were filled with.
Thus gained the prize-bowl, the much-braving Odysseus,
As he came first in: but the ox seized glorious Ajax
780 And he stood holding its horn in his fingers,
Spewing forth gore as he spoke to the Argives as follows:
'Ah! fie! The goddess tripped me and always before this
783 Just like a mother she stands by Odysseus and helps him.'

Salius (320-1), Euryalus, Helymus, Diores. From 327–35 the subject is Nisus. In 336 it shifts logically enough to Salius (*ille*) and in 337 to Euryalus. In other words, we have as subject first the runners as a group, then each runner in his relative position at the start of the race, then Nisus again (quite logically since his fall shifts the race order), Salius (as Nisus trips him) and lastly Euryalus and the other two winners (Helymus, Diores) in the order of victory.

In contrast, Homer does not attempt to preserve any logical succession of subjects. Thus in line 757 the subject is plural

Homer, *Iliad* 23. 757–83

757 στὰν δὲ μεταστοιχί· σήμηνε δὲ τέρματ᾽ Ἀχιλλεύς.
τοῖσι δ᾽ ἀπὸ νύσσης τέτατο δρόμος· ὦκα δ᾽ ἔπειτα
ἔκφερ᾽ Ὀϊλιάδης· ἐπὶ δ᾽ ὤρνυτο δῖος Ὀδυσσεὺς
760 ἄγχι μάλ᾽, ὡς ὅτε τίς τε γυναικὸς ἐϋζώνοιο
στήθεός ἐστι κανών, ὅντ᾽ εὖ μάλα χερσὶ τανύσσῃ
πηνίον ἐξέλκουσα παρὲκ μίτον, ἀγχόθι δ᾽ ἴσχει
στήθεος· ὡς Ὀδυσεὺς θέεν ἐγγύθεν, αὐτὰρ ὄπισθεν
ἴχνια τύπτε πόδεσσι πάρος κόνιν ἀμφιχυθῆναι·
765 κὰδ δ᾽ ἄρα οἱ κεφαλῆς χέ᾽ ἀϋτμένα δῖος Ὀδυσσεὺς
αἰεὶ ῥίμφα θέων· ἴαχον δ᾽ ἐπὶ πάντες Ἀχαιοὶ
νίκης ἱεμένῳ, μάλα δὲ σπεύδοντι κέλευον.
ἀλλ᾽ ὅτε δὴ πύματον τέλεον δρόμον, αὐτίκ᾽ Ὀδυσσεὺς
εὔχετ᾽ Ἀθηναίῃ γλαυκώπιδι ὃν κατὰ θυμόν·
770 " κλῦθι, θεά, ἀγαθή μοι ἐπίρροθος ἐλθὲ ποδοῖιν."
ὡς ἔφατ᾽ εὐχόμενος· τοῦ δ᾽ ἔκλυε Παλλὰς Ἀθήνη,
γυῖα δ᾽ ἔθηκεν ἐλαφρά, πόδας καὶ χεῖρας ὕπερθεν.
ἀλλ᾽ ὅτε δὴ τάχ᾽ ἔμελλον ἐπαΐξασθαι ἄεθλον,
ἔνθ᾽ Αἴας μὲν ὄλισθε θέων—βλάψεν γὰρ Ἀθήνη—
775 τῇ ῥα βοῶν κέχυτ᾽ ὄνθος ἀποκταμένων ἐριμύκων,
οὓς ἐπὶ Πατρόκλῳ πέφνεν πόδας ὠκὺς Ἀχιλλεύς·
ἐν δ᾽ ὄνθου βοέου πλῆτο στόμα τε ῥῖνάς τε·
κρητῆρ᾽ αὖτ᾽ ἀνάειρε πολύτλας δῖος Ὀδυσσεύς,
ὡς ἦλθε φθάμενος· ὁ δὲ βοῦν ἕλε φαίδιμος Αἴας.
780 στῆ δὲ κέρας μετὰ χερσὶν ἔχων βοὸς ἀγραύλοιο,
ὄνθον ἀποπτύων, μετὰ δ᾽ Ἀργείοισιν ἔειπεν·
" ὢ πόποι, ἦ μ᾽ ἔβλαψε θεὰ πόδας, ἣ τὸ πάρος περ
783 μήτηρ ὡς Ὀδυσῆϊ παρίσταται ἠδ᾽ ἐπαρήγει."

(στὰν) but it shifts in the same line to Achilles; in the next to the impersonal δρόμος, then in 759 to the runners, Ajax and Odysseus. The simile (760–3) breaks the narrative but Odysseus is the grammatical subject of 765 though our attention is equally divided between him and Ajax. In 765 Ajax is referred to only by the pronoun οἱ while Odysseus is mentioned by name with the epithet δῖος. In 766 the subject shifts again, this time to the Achaeans (cheering on Odysseus). In 768 it is the runners again, then in the same line Odysseus. In 770 we have his single line prayer to Athene (with Athene as subject). It shifts, 773–7, from the runners (collective) to Ajax, to Athene again and (disregarding the relative clauses) to Ajax. Thereafter it alternates between Ajax and Odysseus with θεά (goddess) the subject of the two line quote of Ajax at the end (782–3).

2. The Homeric narrative is broken (as Virgil's is not) by two quotations (of one and two lines).

3. The Homeric narrative contains one (relatively) long simile (3–4 lines); the Virgilian, only brief phrase-similes in 317 (*nimbo similes*) and 319 (*ventis et fulminis ocior alis*).

4. The Homeric narrative contains a number of traditional epithets and patronymics (δῖος 'Οδυσσεύς (3 times)) πόδας ὠκὺς 'Αχιλλεύς, φαίδιμος Αἴας, &c. In Virgil Nisus is called *infelix*, *iuvenis*, *victor* but these are really descriptive adjectives rather than epithets.

5. All Homeric verbs are simple aorists or perfects and aoristic imperfects (στὰν, σήμηνε, ὄρνυτο, θέεν, τύπτε, ἴαχον). The only exception is ἴσχει (1. 762). There is obviously no exact temporal demarcation of the narrative. In Virgil the use of the tenses is most exact and telling: note, e.g. the presents of 315–17 (*capiunt, corripiunt, relinquunt*) and thereafter (*abit, emicat, insequitur, volat, terit*), the future-less-vivid condition of 325–26, the exact imperfect of 328 (to bring out the contrasted present, *labitur*, of 329). Finally there are the perfects of 332, 333–6 and again the presents (*emicat, tenet, volat, subit*) of 337–9. Here the vivid present of the actual running is contrasted with the imperfect (*adventabant* 328), explaining the incompleteness of the race, and the perfects (332–6), expressing the falls of Nisus and Salius (which of course abruptly remove them from the race).

6. The Virgilian passage is full of words which describe the feeling of the runners: note such verbs as *corripiunt spatia*, *emicat, volat*, such adjectives and adjectival phrases as *infelix*, *non ille oblitus amorum, iuvenis victor ovans*. In contrast the Homeric verbs and adjectives are quite ordinary and objective: στὰν, ὄρνυτο, θέεν, τέλεον, εὔχετο. The one indication of feeling is the phrase νίκης ἱεμένῳ of line 767 but this is pretty neutral: all know that Odysseus wants to win. As remarked, the epithets are strictly traditional. Phrases like ῥίμφα θέων and μάλα δὲ σπεύδοντι merely accent the *speed* of the race, not the emotion of the runners.

7. The use of subordinate clauses and participles is less immediately indicative. Homer uses three ὅτε clauses, a ὡς clause (for the simile) and a πάρος clause (with the infinitive).

There are ten participles though most of these are of the simplest kind (e.g. θέων used twice, ἔχων, ἀποπτύων, σπεύδοντι). In general the sentence structure is very simple (short sentences with concrete subjects and action verbs). The Virgilian narrative, as befits the rapid subject, has a number of verbs (*capiunt, corripiunt, emicat, volat, terit*, &c.) and short rapid sentences. But it also has a conditional subjunctive, an *ut* indicative clause and a number (4) of ablative absolutes. The difference here is not revealed by the statistics though Virgil uses fewer dependent clauses than Homer: the point is that the dependent clauses in Virgil are *deliberate* interruptions of the action as the clauses in Homer are not. Thus the condition of lines 325–6 expresses the unfulfilled intention of Diores, obviously an exception to the movement of the rest of the passage; the *ut* clause of line 329 is introduced to show by the pluperfect *madefecerat* that the blood had been shed on the ground *before* the race. (Note that Virgil has here an impersonal subject, *sanguis* (understood) rather than, as in Homer, a concrete individual. The slayer of the cattle is an unimportant detail which would merely distract the reader's attention.)

8. A metrical analysis of the two passages shows clearly that Virgil is using every device to focus the reader's attention on those aspects of the narrative he wants to emphasize: this is not so in Homer. Note, e.g. the line (320):

$$- \;\cup\;\cup\; / - \;-\; / - - / - \;\cup\;\cup\; / - - / - \;-$$
proximus huic longo sed proximus intervallo.

The striking fifth foot spondee here vividly expresses the distance between Salius and Nisus. The repetition of the *proximus* and the inclusion of the second *proximus* between *longo* and *intervallo* is very deliberate; so are the caesurae in the second and third feet which emphasize *longo* and the clash of prose and metrical stresses in *longo* as opposed to their agreement in the double *proximus*. In contrast to the fading Salius we have the gaining Diores:

$$- \;\cup\;\cup\; / - \;-\; / - \;\cup\;\cup\; / - - \quad - \;\cup\;\cup\; / - -$$
ecce volat calcemque terit iam calce Diores

Here the alternate dactyls and spondees, the tripartite division (caesurae in the second and fourth feet) and the repetition *calcem calce* produce the effect of rhythmic speed. Similar analyses could be made of, e.g. lines 319, 325, 328, 335, 336, 337. All this, however, is of less importance than the strictly psychological effect which Virgil gets through sound and rhythm. Note, e.g.

	$- \;\; \cup \cup / -- / -$
329	labitur infelix
	$- \;\;\; \cup \cup / -- \;\;\; / - \;\; \cup \;\; \cup -$
331	hic iuvenis iam victor ovans
	$- \;\; \cup \;\; \cup / - \cup\cup / - \;\; -/ \;\; - \;\; -/ - \cup \;\; \cup / - \cup$
334	non tamen Euryali, non ille oblitus amorum

It is clear that the three longs of *infelix* (329) with the following main caesura and the preceding diaeresis form a deliberate contrast to the rapid truncated *labitur*. Again line 331 expresses the triumphant feeling of Nisus. In 334 the metrical emphasis of *Euryali* and *ille*, the repetition of *non*, the two spondaic feet (3 and 4), the alliteration and the long *i* sounds in *Euryali* and *oblitus*, enhance the emotional effect. In its context the line is very striking for it slows up the rapid movement to focus a vivid light on the pathetic feeling which Virgil wishes to accent. In the Homeric passage, in contrast, I find it most difficult to be certain that any metrical effect is really intended. The frequency with which lines end in such ready-made phrases as δῖος 'Οδυσσεύς, Παλλὰς 'Αθήνη, φαίδιμος Αἴας seems to exclude the artful, Virgilian kind of onomatopoeia.[1]

These points of comparison suffice I think to bring out the striking differences between the two styles. Obviously Virgil's technique is far more deliberate and knowing than Homer's but this fact hardly needs demonstration. The point of interest is why and with what intent Virgil was so deliberate. Heinze has suggested the answer in saying that Virgil puts himself in the place of his characters and narrates through them. Virgil takes the point of view either of a specific character (Nisus, Diores, Euryalus, &c.) or of himself as interested spectator.

---

[1] Milman Parry, *L'epithète traditionelle dans Homère* (1928) has well shown the difference between a metric based on the ready-made patterns of the traditional *name-epithets* or *formulae* and the quite different *literary* metric of Apollonius (*Argonautica*) or Virgil. See esp. pp. 30–44 and the revealing tables on pp. 38–40, 50–51. But Parry does not discriminate between the metrics of Virgil and Apollonius: the important differences between them are in fact irrelevant to his purpose (to show the nature of *Homer's* oral style). Cf. note 1 on page 89 below. It may be said here that Parry's emphasis on the *difference* between *oral* and *literary* epic style *as such* has tended to obscure the equally important difference between Greek and Latin epic *as such*.

Actually he takes both at once in a very subtle and rather complicated way. As we have seen, his centre of interest is the friendship of Nisus and Euryalus. Thus his emphasis is not (as is Homer's) on the race as an objective event but on the psychological relation of Nisus and Euryalus.

All the points we have adduced—the relative continuity of grammatical subject, the absence of quotations, the shortness of the similes, the absence of traditional epithets, the abundance of words with feeling tone, the deliberateness of the grammatical structure, the artful onomatopoeia—receive their adequate explanation when we note that they are all necessitated by Virgil's subjective method and attitude. Virgil is constantly conscious of himself inside his characters; he thinks through them and for them. In the passage in question he identifies himself successively with the runners as a whole (315–17), with Nisus, then with the others (but specifically with Diores) and then again with Nisus though his attention reverts at the end to Euryalus, Salius and the rest. But he also makes it clear that he himself feels most deeply for Nisus and shares Nisus' noble affection for Euryalus: Nisus is *infelix* but he does not forget his friend. Virgil thus enters the *psyche* of each runner in turn to emerge with a final judgment or *parti pris*. Such a procedure supplies dramatic unity to the narrative as a whole. Each runner (at least all who interest Virgil at all) has his own view of the race but all these views are comprehended and unified in Virgil's view. He is doubly subjective—first in the *empathy* with which he shares the emotions of each runner, second in his own, *personal reaction* to their emotions. Such things as the shift of the subject and the use of tense are thus clues to the movement of the poet's feeling. There is a precise correspondence of grammatical structure and emotion which cannot be broken by direct quotations or relatively long similes (as in Homer). We can see, for example, the emotional content of tense differentiation when we consider a consecutive series of verbs in the passage, as, e.g. lines 327–33: iamque sub ipsum finem *adventabant* cum . . . Nisus . . . *labitur*. Hic iuvenis iam victor *ovans* vestigia haut *tenuit* . . . sed pronus *concidit*.

The most obvious key to Virgil's 'psychological identification' of himself with the characters is the tell-tale phrase or word which either describes the character's feelings or Virgil's

E

own feeling for him or—what is nearest to the fact—a subtle blend of both. These phrases also gain a large part of their effectiveness from their metrical position: the 'sound track' is always indispensable to the film proper. But the chief point to make about them is that they act as a means of *special* emphasis. Virgil's art is altogether too subtle to rely on them as the regular vehicles of his subjectivist method: his sympathy and personal feeling is in fact expressed by a series of devices far less obvious than overt editorializing such as e.g. the use of tenses, caesurae, vowel sounds, &c., as set forth above.

Let us consider in this connection lines 324–6:

> ecce volat calcemque terit iam calce Diores
> incumbens umero; spatia et si plura supersint
> transeat elapsus prior ambiguumque relinquat.

Is Virgil here describing the race of Diores objectively or does he identify himself with Diores? The latter is nearer the truth but we feel, nevertheless, that the identification is in no sense close or unambiguous. Thus the future-less-vivid clause can represent either Virgil's or Diores' point of view but neither is sharply discriminated. The *ecce* singles Diores out from the others for a moment only. What Virgil really wants us to grasp is that the race is close, that even the last might have been first. Diores is thus mainly a means of heightening the tension: it would have been quite distracting for Virgil to have identified himself with him too obviously. But Nisus is different: he is the true centre of attention and Virgil quite deliberately takes his point of view in the metrically impressive line 334:

> non tamen Euryali, non ille oblitus amorum

But he does more than this: he makes explicit his own feeling for Nisus in the obviously 'finger pointing' epithet *infelix* of line 329. The poet cannot at this point contain his own sympathy: it bursts out directly and thus gives climactic emphasis to the feeling in which the whole passage is drenched.

The radical difference between Homer and Virgil here is of course very obvious. Each is effective in his own way but each achieves a quite dissimilar effect. Homer is indifferent to the devices by which Virgil obtains subjective concentration of the narrative: he shifts his subjects almost at random, he relies on the relatively colourless aorist tense, his grammatical structure is loose and he puts in details (e.g. the relatively lengthy simile of weaving and the identification of the slayer of the cattle in line 776) which add nothing essential to the narrative. But his greater objectivity makes for much more vivid and clear characterizations. Thus even this brief passage brings out the feeling between Odysseus and Ajax and something of Ajax's character (cf. especially his two line speech 782–3). We grasp at once his sturdy independence of the gods and his attitude towards Athene's partiality to Odysseus. We have no doubt that here is a man with his own characteristic point of view though we in no sense identify ourselves with him or see him through the poet's emotions toward him. The *disadvantage*—if it can be called such—of Virgil's subjective approach is revealed in this contrast: his empathetic or sympathetic relation to his characters gives them a certain ambiguity; we are never sure when he is simply describing the character's feelings or putting his own feelings into the character—he actually seems to do both things—and we thus lose the sense of the character's objective reality. Homer's Ajax is real: he stands on his own feet and speaks his own thoughts. But Virgil's Nisus is much less real for he has not gotten fully away from his creator: he is a source of emotion (a pathetic instance) rather than a tangible human being in a tangible environment.

Broadly speaking the principles discovered in the analysis of Homer's and Virgil's foot-races hold for most of the other passages in which we can clearly identify the Homeric original or model of Virgil. We must of course allow for the special situations with which Virgil is dealing. Thus the fact that he avoids direct quotations in the account of the foot-race does not, of course, mean that he does not elsewhere make extensive use of quotation. But it is the very essence of his 'empathetic' and dramatico-psychological method to take the special dramatic situation into full account: there are places where the set speech of epic is appropriate and there are places (e.g. the foot-race) where it is not. This is apparent in a much longer episode that involves speeches and other elements more characteristic of Virgil's overall style.

In *Aeneid* 5 the account of the ship-race (114–243) obviously recalls Homer's chariot race (*Iliad* 23. 287–652) and is slightly more than five times the length of the narrative of the running contest. Here, however, as before, Virgil's account is far more condensed than Homer's.

We need not repeat Heinze's well known observations on Virgilian epic technique in this episode. Virgil brings all four contestants into dramatic relations with each other (especially at the *meta* or turning point), each having at a given moment the chance to win. In contrast, Homer's race is divided into two unrelated portions and does not constitute a single dramatic situation. We should note also the relative irrelevance of large parts of Homer. Thus the lengthy advice of Nestor to his son, Antilochus (ll. 306–48)—advice on how to make a close run around the turning post—has no direct relation to what happened later; in fact Antilochus' clever passing of Menelaos takes place long after the turn. It is also clear that, as Heinze has indicated, Virgil's narrative serves to point a moral (the ill-tempered Gyas loses, the pious Cloanthus wins) and is heavily centred on the mood and psychology of the ship-captains (not, as in Homer, primarily on non-human factors such as the horses and the capricious favouritism of the gods). Here again Homer's narrative is far more objective and far less tendentious.

But what the longer ship and chariot races reveal much more clearly than the shorter foot-races is the extent to which Virgil's editorial purpose and feeling almost completely de-objectify the events described. This is particularly evident in a comparison of Virgil 5, 124–38 and Homer, *Iliad* 23. 351–72. In Virgil our attention is first centred on the turning post—the rock which is also a favourite haunt of the seagulls (*statio gratissima mergis*), then on Father Aeneas' demarcation of it as *meta*, then on the leaders' lining up for the race and the glistening appearance and eager spirits of the crews as they await the starting signal. In Homer we have simply the start and a brief description of the first half of the race. Achilles shakes the lots which determine the starting order; he simply shows the runners the turning post (it is Nestor who *tells* his son *about it* in a speech which has no direct, dramatic relevance to the race) and then they are off, lashing and calling to their horses and raising the dust.

It is quite evident that Virgil is here directing the reader's attention to the crucial rock even before the narrative has properly begun. The detailed description of the rock—it is beaten by the waves when the storm winds blot the sky but it is now, in the summer calm, a grassy and favourite haunt of the sun-lit seagulls—puts us at once on the plane of vision and psychological concern that Virgil desires. Our physical point of view, looking down on rock, ships and bystanders from above, our emotional centre of attention and our general feeling for the mood of the occasion are set.

The passage as a whole bears out all the points I have made above. The use of the present tense, of emotive verbs, adjectives and phrases is striking. Thus, cf. Homer 370–1:

> ἔστασαν ἐν δίφροισι, πάτασσε δὲ θυμὸς ἑκάστου
> νίκης ἱεμένων· κέκλοντο δὲ οἷσιν ἕκαστος

> Stood in their seats, each one's heart aquiver
> As he yearns for the victory and each with a shout

with Virgil 137–8:

> *intenti exspectant* signum *exsultantiaque haurit*
> *corda pavor pulsans laudumque arrecta cupido*

where not merely the greater number of emotional words (*intenti, exspectant, exsultantia, pavor, pulsans,* &c.) but the meta-phorical force of *haurit* and the expectant spondees (broken by the initial dactyl of *corda pavor*) create a remarkable effect of tension. Secondly, the careful direction of attention by the orderly shift of subject (from all the racers, to the bystanders, to the individual participants) is evident. Lines 154–60 are here especially noteworthy with the dramatic subject shifts and the equally dramatic changes from the present to the imperfects of line 159 and back to the present of *compellat* (161).

Lines 162–82 are an admirable instance of Virgil's 'empathe-tic-sympathetic' method:

> 'Quo tantum mihi dexter abis? huc derige gressum;
> litus ama et laeva stringat sine palmula cautes;
> altum alii teneant.' dixit; sed caeca Menoetes
165 saxa timens proram pelagi detorquet ad undas.
> 'Quo diversus abis?' iterum 'pete saxa, Menoete!'
> cum clamore Gyas revocabat, et ecce Cloanthum
> respicit instantem tergo et propiora tenentem.
> Ille inter navemque Gyae scopulosque sonantis
170 radit iter laevum interior subitoque priorem
> praeterit et metis tenet aequora tuta relictis.

Tum vero exarsit iuveni dolor ossibus ingens
nec lacrimis caruere genae, segnemque Menoeten
oblitus decorisque sui sociumque salutis
175   in mare praecipitem puppi deturbat ab alta;
ipse gubernaclo rector subit, ipse magister
hortaturque viros clavumque ad litora torquet.
At gravis ut fundo vix tandem redditus imo est
iam senior madidaque fluens in veste Menoetes
180   summa petit scopuli siccaque in rupe resedit.
Illum et labentem Teucri et risere natantem
et salsos rident revomentem pectore fluctus.

Thus in the lines:

167   cum clamore Gyas *revocabat;* et *ecce* Cloanthum
respicit instantem tergo et propiora tenentem

the *ecce* with the present *respicit* (contrasting with the imperfect *revocabat*) not only points out Cloanthus to the reader: it also reflects Gyas' own surprise! But when Virgil comes to Gyas' violent rage at and consequent manhandling of Menoetes, he supplements empathy by obvious editorializing:

172   *Tum vero exarsit* iuveni *dolor* ossibus *ingens*
nec lacrimis caruere genae *segnemque* Menoeten
oblitus decorisque sui sociumque salutis
in mare praecipitem puppi *deturbat* ab alta.

To whom and for whom was Gyas forgetful of his dignity and his comrades' safety? Virgil is not here simply reproducing Gyas' own feelings but expressing a moral judgement, which is also borne out by the result of the race itself. With this, contrast the lines about the merely unfortunate Sergestus:

infelix saxis in procurrentibus haesit (204).

But a more instructive, because more subtle, passage is that of the final rivalry between Mnestheus and Cloanthus (ahead of the fast gaining Mnestheus):

229   Hi (i.e. Cloanthus and crew) proprium decus et partum indignantur honorem
ni *teneant* vitamque volunt pro laude pacisci;
hos successus alit: *possunt quia posse videntur.*
Et fors aequatis *cepissent* praemia rostris,
ni palmas ponto tendens utrasque Cloanthus
fudissetque preces divosque in vota vocasset.

Here the craving for glory and the impetus of success (note the editorial: *possunt quia posse videntur*) are balanced, but the latter would have won, had not Cloanthus turned to the Gods. Empathetic identification with the two rivals changes in the end to judgement in which Virgil gives the palm to Cloanthus' ambition and piety. The shift from the present subjunctive of *teneant* to the pluperfect subjunctive of *cepissent* skilfully measures the gap between the present desire and the imaginative forebodings of Cloanthus.

Let us now turn to the somewhat parallel lines of Homer (382–97). We note here, first of all, the entirely amoral character of the divine intervention: Apollo's wrath is merely spiteful and is quickly countered by Athene who then treats Eumelus much more disastrously than Apollo treated Diomedes. Noteworthy here is the contrast between Homer's:

382   καὶ νύ κεν ἢ παρέλασσ' ἢ ἀμφήριστον ἔθηκεν,
      εἰ μὴ Τυδέος υἱῖ κοτέσσατο Φοῖβος Ἀπόλλων

    And now Diomedes would have passed or made doubtful the outcome
    Had not Phoibos Apollo been angry with Tydeus' son

and Virgil's:

232   Et fors aequatis cepissent praemia rostris,
      ni palmas ponto tendens utrasque Cloanthus
      fudissetque preces.

The Homeric condition merely registers the result of divine intervention; the Virgilian expresses the piety which produced the result. But what is most striking in the whole passage is the completely objective and detached quality of Homer's narrative. There is a minimum of empathy or of moral judgement. His amoral conception of the gods goes with a cool acceptance of human destiny.

Yet here, even more clearly than in the foot-race, the objective reality of Homer's characters in contrast with Virgil's is very evident. Antilochus, the son of Nestor, is introduced to us first as the recipient of a long piece of advice (ll. 306–48) from his aged father. This as we have remarked, is quite irrelevant to the future narrative, but it is an extremely revealing indication of Nestor's character and of his fussy affection for Antilochus. It also gives us an insight into the 'cunning' (μῆτις) which Nestor expects Antilochus to show. We get a brief but revealing glimpse of his reputation in Menelaos' words: (l. 440)

ἔρρ', ἐπεὶ οὔ σ' ἔτυμόν γε φάμεν πεπνῦσθαι 'Αχαιοί
Go then since we Achaians are wrong in calling you clever.

After the race, the by-play between Antilochus, Achilles and Menelaos makes it quite clear how 'wise' or 'clever' Antilochus really is. Rightly sensing the mood of Menelaos, he surrenders the prize only to get it back along with Menelaos' good will. Evidently Antilochus' cleverness is supported by youthful charm. Yet this rather remarkable piece of characterization sheds absolutely no light on Homer's feelings: the whole thing comes out in speeches and in the bare recital of action. Consider the lines:

596   'Η ῥα, καὶ ἵππον ἄγων μεγαθύμου Νέστορος υἱὸς
ἐν χείρεσσι τίθει Μενελάου· τοῖο δὲ θυμὸς
ἰάνθη ὡς εἴ τε περὶ σταχύεσσιν ἐέρση
ληΐου ἀλδήσκοντος, ὅτε φρίσσουσιν ἄρουραι·
ὣς ἄρα σοί, Μενέλαε, μετὰ φρεσὶ θυμὸς ἰάνθη·

So he spoke and the son of great-hearted Nestor
Leads out his horse and offers it to Menelaos,
Whose heart then melted away, as the dew on the wheat-stalks
In the time of the growing of crops when the wheat fields all
    bristle:
So for you, Menelaos, did your heart melt in your bosom.

Line 600 is one of the rare instances where Homer addresses a character, yet this device has here no subjectivizing effect; all we know is that Menelaos is softened by Antilochus' offer, as indeed he immediately indicates himself. The simile of the ripened corn does not in the least detract from the objective reality of the situation.

Indeed the Homeric episode is so objective in its characterization that only by careful study can we penetrate the high art of the apparently simple—even seemingly *naïve*—narrative. It is precisely by leaving out the comment—the empathetic, sympathetic and editorial elements—that Homer achieves his most brilliant effects. Thus when Antilochus overtakes Menelaos by the shabby trick of trying to pass on the alternative route which Menelaos has taken precisely to avoid collision with him, we are given the exasperated protests of Menelaos but nothing from Antilochus, merely the statement:

429   Ὡς ἔφατ', Ἀντίλοχος δ' ἔτι καὶ πολὺ μᾶλλον ἔλαυνε
    κέντρῳ ἐπισπέρχων ὡς οὐκ ἀΐοντι ἐοικώς.
   So he spoke but Antilochus drove even faster
   Using his goad exactly as if he'd not heard the warning.

The silence of Antilochus—fully conscious of his guilt but determined to have his way—is here very eloquent. We are not told what his emotions were in so many words but we are given all the narrative cues necessary to make the telling superfluous.

  The catastrophe of Eumelus is handled with equal restraint and effectiveness. We note first (ll. 376–97) that the catastrophe itself is described (even to the quite amoral or immoral roles of Apollo and Athene) with complete objectivity and is told in its proper position in the race-narrative, then seems to yield place completely to the rivalry of Menelaos and Antilochus. But in:

448   Ἀργεῖοι δ' ἐν ἀγῶνι καθήμενοι εἰσορόωντο
   But the Argives in assembly seated kept all on the watch

Homer turns back to Eumelus though with characteristic indirection: the Cretan Idomeneus sees not Eumelus but Menelaos in the lead. This first intimation that Eumelus has suffered disaster rouses his partisan, Ajax (we are not, however, told that Ajax was his partisan: we only *see* him rebuking Idomeneus for his officious attempt to anticipate the news). Then after the detailed account of the arrival of the other contestants (Diomedes, Antilochus, Menelaos) we are simply told

532   υἱὸς δ' Ἀδμήτοιο πανύστατος ἤλυθεν ἄλλων
    ἕλκων ἄρματα καλά, ἐλαύνων πρόσσοθεν ἵππους
   Last behind all the rest came in the son of Admetus
   Dragging his beautiful chariot and driving before it his horses.

  The pathos of Eumelus is not described or commented upon: we merely see the reaction of Achilles and the Argives.

  From this the transition back to Menelaos and Antilochus is managed with the art which conceals art: it is Achilles' attempt to compensate poor Eumelus by the second prize which rouses

Antilochus, adds the final straw which breaks Menelaos' patience and sets the stage for the magnificent demonstration of Antilochus' superb mastery of human character for his own advantage. We *now* can look back and see how deliciously unnecessary Nestor's long speech of advice really was though, in literary terms, it sets the tone for this shrewd story of the conflict between μῆτις, the cleverness of Antilochus, and the ἀρετή of Menelaos. In all this, the principal media of Homer's characterizations are the speech, the quoted words of his character, and the simple narrative of action: we are seldom told—beyond the simplest indication of rage, pain, &c.—how a character feels and never told how to evaluate his emotions and actions.

Virgil, in contrast, uses only very abbreviated speeches and these add absolutely nothing to the characterization already achieved in the narrative. The remarks of Gyas to his pilot Menoetes, the hortatory speech of Mnestheus to his men, the prayer of Cloanthus, are all typical of general situations, not (like the quoted words of Nestor, Menelaos, Antilochus) of specific characters. Consider the words of Mnestheus:

189   'Nunc nunc insurgite remis,
Hectorei socii, Troiae quos sorte suprema
delegi comites: nunc illas promite vires,
nunc animos, quibus in Gaetulis Syrtibus usi
Ionioque mari Maleaeque sequacibus undis.
Non iam prima peto Mnestheus neque vincere certo;
quamquam o!—sed superent, quibus hoc, Neptune, dedisti;
extremos pudeat rediisse. Hoc vincite, cives,
et prohibete nefas.'

The rhetoric here is apparent: Aeneas or almost any Trojan leader could have said these lines on any important occasion calling for effort and courage. Even the use of the first person (*quos sorte suprema delegi comites . . . non iam prima peto*) sheds absolutely no light on what Mnestheus is really like. But it is clear that such characterizations, as, e.g. Homer's of Antilochus, are here excluded by Virgil's style of narrative. The characteristic concentration of effect at which he aimed had no room for for the leisurely dialogue by which Homer brought out character. Character (in the Homeric sense) was, rather, sacrificed to feeling: the reader is not expected to realize Gyas, Mnestheus, Cloanthus, &c., as distinct individuals so much as participants in a dramatic race; the psychological drama and excitement is not conveyed by the *dramatis personae* so much as by the author himself as he feels for each of his rather poorly individualized contestants and conveys his empathy and sympathy to the readers.

We can see this in such lines as the following:

210 At *laetus* Mnestheus successuque *acrior* ipso
221 Sergestum brevibusque vadis *frustraque* vocantem
202 namque *furens animi* dum proram ad saxa suburguet

But the shared emotion is communicated by the very structure of each sentence, above all by the metrical movement. Consider the lines describing the 'dunking' of Menoetes:

181 Illum et labentem Teucri et risere natantem
   et salsos rident revomentem pectore fluctus.

Here the shift of tense (*risere* to *rident*) puts us immediately *en rapport* with the bystanders: their laughter began at his fall, continued with his scurry to the rock and still re-echoed after he reached the rock and spewed forth the salt water he had swallowed. The present *rident* brings the reader into the *tempo* of the narrative. We realize the keenness with which the race is being watched and we are made to see the fun of Menoetes' fall (which of course the metre, the repetitions of *-entem*, *-antem*, *risere*, *rident*, in a series of comical spondees concluding with equally comical dactyls, greatly enhance). The episode is not simply related (with the humour left to the reader) nor are we simply told that the Trojans laughed at Menoetes: we are shown exactly what it was they thought funny and in such a metrically comical way that we also share their mirth.

Virgil's use of simile to convey empathy and sympathy is also very striking. The simile in lines 213–19 describes the dove suddenly alarmed in her rocky cave: the clatter of her ruffled wings fills the narrow place but when she emerges into the open air, her flight is one of effortless and liquid ease: her feathers hardly move.

213 qualis spelunca subito commota columba,
   cui domus et dulces latebroso in pumice nidi,
   fertur in arva volans plausumque exterrita pinnis

dat tecto ingentem, mox aëre lapsa quieto
radit iter liquidum celeris neque commovet alas;
sic Mnestheus, sic ipsa fuga secat ultima Pristis
aequora, sic illam fert impetus ipse volantem.

Her situation is exactly analogous to that of Mnestheus finally in the clear after the confusion at the rocky turning post. The three *sics* drive this home:

218   sic Mnestheus, sic ipsa fuga secat ultima Pristis
          aequora, sic illam fert impetus ipse volantem.

The simile, in other words, conveys not so much a visual image as the sense of relief—of trouble overcome—which Mnestheus feels on rounding the rock. This release of bottled energy is admirably conveyed by the metre with its initial spondees and caesura (*sic Mnestheus*) and the rapid dactyls of the close. This of course reflects a quite similar movement in the simile (ll. 216–17). Note here especially how the *sic* and *fert* of line 219 are set off by diaeresis and caesura thus giving the final *impetus ipse volantem* a heightened sense of released rapidity. From then on the course of Mnestheus is unimpeded. None of the Homeric similes perform a similar function (cf. 516–23, the horse and the chariot-wheel).

Yet what Virgil almost certainly had in mind here is not Homer but Apollonius (*Arg.* 2. 933–5) where the hawk is compared to the Argo sailing out of harbour on a swift breeze:

ἠύτε τίς τε δι' ἠέρος ὑψόθι κίρκος
ταρσὸν ἐφεὶς πνοιῇ φέρεται ταχύς, οὐδὲ τινάσσει
ῥιπήν· εὐκήλοισιν ἐνευδιόων πτερύγεσσιν.

Just as a hawk high through the air
Its feathers spread to the breeze swiftly is carried along
Nor swerves its flight, poised in clear sky on quiet wings.

Yet how great the difference between Apollonius and Virgil's imitation! The Apollonian simile corresponds only to the Virgilian lines:

mox aere lapsa quieto
Radit iter liquidum, celeris neque commovet alas.

Apollonius' simile is effective but very simple and straightforward; it merely describes the swift motion of the ship in a fair wind. In Virgil the smooth speed of the dove gains all its effectiveness from the contrast of its noisy fluttering in the cave:

> plausumque exterrita pinnis
> Dat tecto ingentem.

Furthermore Virgil's dove is frightened—it fears for its home and nest (*domus et dulces latebroso in pumice nidi*). The smooth flight in the open air expresses its release from fear as well as from cramped quarters. It, like Mnestheus, has escaped the danger of ruin in a place where escape was not easy. Furthermore, Virgil's feeling for the dove (the *dulces . . . nidi* expresses a sentiment more than a fact) makes the transference of feeling to Mnestheus all the easier. There is no such empathy in Apollonius' simile. Virgil's transformation of hawk into dove is an eloquent indication of the difference in function between the two similes. A hawk is better than a dove for Apollonius, since his emphasis is simply on swift, high flight. But the dove is a far better vehicle both of the particular transition (from one to another type of motion) and the particular empathy which Virgil is trying to convey. Because we feel with and for the dove, we feel for Mnestheus. This is, in fact, the real poetic purpose behind the 'humanity' of so many of Virgil's animal similes. Compare for example the famous simile of *Georgics* 4 where Orpheus weeping for Eurydice is compared to a nightingale:

> 511 *maerens* philomela sub umbra
> amissos queritur fetus quos *durus* arator
> observans nido implumis detraxit; at illa
> flet noctem ramoque sedens *miserabile* carmen
> 515 integrat et *maestis* late loca questibus implet.

2

So far then we have uncovered certain characteristics of the Virgilian epic style: the empathy and sympathy revealed in sentence structure, tense differentiation, metric, and choice of words and similes; the 'editorial' intrusion of the author by 'finger-pointing' epithet, explicit declaration of *parti pris* and the implicit bias of his language; the relative absence of objective characters, speaking their own words and with emotions distinct from those of their author. This is a *subjective* style:

Homer's in contrast is *objective*. Virgil *concentrates* on an object or purpose which dominates his characters and, to some extent, his readers; Homer, though he actually tells his story with great art, always gives the illusion that he is letting his characters speak and act for themselves in a narrative big enough and leisurely enough to give them the scope and independence they need. We must now try to see how Virgil used this subjective style, how it enabled him to give a quite new content and meaning to Homeric material.

For this purpose we shall take the Dido story of the first and fourth *Aeneid* and compare it with its 'model' or at least inspiration, the Medea story of the third and fourth books of Apollonius' *Argonautica*. Virgil certainly had other sources besides Apollonius: Dido's role is closely analogous to Homer's Calypso (both women detain the hero from his goal) and Naevius had used Dido in the proem to his *Bellum Punicum*. But it seems plain that Virgil got the romantic or amatory coloration of the Dido episode from Apollonius and perhaps also from later authors whom Apollonius had influenced. But our chief concern is not with Virgil's use of Apollonius (his direct imitations are relatively few) but with the difference between the two narrative styles. Apollonius, unlike Homer, had a 'romantic' theme and a literary, rather than an 'oral' diction: he was in short 'hellenistic'. By using him, therefore, we can set Virgil's style in quite another light and see how it compares with the later as well as with the strictly Homeric epic and style. Furthermore the two episodes (Dido and Medea) are admirable examples of both authors at their best and show them engaged on a psychological subject demanding extensive analysis of human motivation and behaviour. Each author deals with a similar theme—the loves of Medea-Jason, Dido-Aeneas—but employs a quite different kind of narrative. The basic distinction is that Virgil's narrative is psychologically *continuous* in a way that Apollonius' narrative is not. We can see this quite clearly by a brief analysis of the contents of the two episodes (*Argonautica* III, IV ; *Aeneid* 1, 4).

The third book of the *Argonautica* contains twelve more or less clear-cut sections or parts:

1. The *colloquium* of Athene, Hera, Aphrodite and the consequent dispatch of Eros: this section ends (l. 166) with the

latter *on his way* to earth and Aeetes' palace (ἀν' αἰθέρα πολλὸν ἰόντι) (1–166)

2. The heroes disembark, decide to parley with Aeetes, and proceed to the palace (167–274)

3. Eros arrives and 'shoots' Medea: her passion grows like fire in brushwood (275–98)

4. Debate between Aeetes, Argus, Jason: the latter agrees to yoke the bulls, &c. (299–442)

5. The first stage of Medea's love (443–70)

6. The Argonauts' plan of campaign is debated and decided: Aeetes plans his own strategy (471–615)

7. Second stage of Medea's passion: she agrees to aid Chalciope and Jason (616–739)

8. Third stage of Medea's passion (night): she tries to resist it, contemplates suicide, finally gives in (740–824)

9. Her journey with her maids to the rendezvous place (Hecate's Temple) (825–912)

10. Journey thither of Jason, Argus, Mopsus (the crow's advice) (913–47)

11. The meeting, the lovers' parley, Medea's consent, her return home and emotional distraction (948–1162)

12. Yoking of the bulls, sowing of the fields, destruction of the earthborn men (1163–1407)

There is here, it is evident, no attempt to maintain strict continuity of narrative or feeling-tone. The relatively long scene on Olympus which opens the book is unique in the whole *Argonautica*: it seems clear that Apollonius was especially concerned to give motivation and epic status to his love story. But its incongruity with the rest of the book and poem is very obvious: the goddesses (Hera, Athene, Aphrodite) are treated in the semi-facetious Callimachean manner; emphasis is put on the social differences between them; the relationship of Aphrodite and Eros is that of a typical middle class mother to a spoiled and exceedingly naughty child. But this strange piece of divine machinery ends abruptly with Eros in mid-air on his downward flight to Colchis. The next part (2) has nothing about love or Medea: it merely takes the heroes to Aeetes under cover of a mist sent down by the goddess Hera. We then (3) see Eros arrive, aim and 'shoot' Medea: the wound *burns* like a brush fire. But the love story is again interrupted by the long conversation between Argus, Jason and Aeetes (4). A brief section (5) depicts the very first stage of Medea's passion but has no essential relation to Eros, the wound or the flame; it is, rather, a quite straightforward account of any girl's first love, the effect of Jason's looks, clothes and voice, her naïve realization that she does not want him to perish under the bulls. But the love story is once more interrupted, this time by the plans and disputes of the Argonauts (6). It is only at line 616 that we come to a consecutive account of Medea's emotions, the conflict in her of shame (αἰδώς) and desire (ἵμερος), her reluctance to aid her sister Chalciope, her final agreement to do so, her ensuing revulsion and meditation of suicide. But the dark *timbre* of these sections (7, 8)—the darkness of night is emphasized—is followed by a cheerful dawn and an exultant ride to the trysting place: Medea, with her maids and chariot, is likened to Artemis and her nymphs speeding to a hekatomb. The relatively long colloquy with Jason only reinforces this mood: it ends in a full understanding between the pair. Though Apollonius inserts two quite extraneous warnings of evil to come (835–8, 1133–6), they do not affect the tone of the narrative itself.

The taming of the bulls, ploughing, sowing, &c., which end the book, have no amatory content at all: they merely show that Medea is a very able and successful magician. It is not until the beginning of Book 4 that her emotions re-emerge, this time her dread of Aeetes and what he may do: she is now the doe who dreads the pursuing hounds. She re-emerges thereafter as the fiercely jealous defender of her rights, the betrayer of her brother Apsyrtus, and an anxious participant in her curious 'marriage' at Phaeacia. The sections of Book 3 (5, 7, 8, 9, 11) on the growth of her love and on her determination to yield to it are, in themselves, a remarkable description of a single psychological process in all its successive stages, but they are neither followed up nor integrated with the other sections save in respect to their quite superficial relation to the plot. Medea's dual role of passionate ingenue and experienced witch is very hard to understand or accept. So also is the insistence on Medea's chastity prior to a proper marriage in Greece and the elaborate explanation of why the hasty cave-marriage was necessary. We simply cannot picture this exceedingly resolute and clever murderess of her own brother as a demure virgin. Nor can we accept so gauche a termination to so passionate a beginning.

The *Aeneid*, on the other hand, seems to belong to another world. Once Dido is mentioned, once Venus gives Aeneas the exciting story of Dido's past, we are caught up in a continuous crescendo of emotion with no stoppings or interludes at all. The mist in which Venus veils her son (1.410 f.) is of course reproduced from Homer and, more immediately, from Apollonius himself. But Apollonius makes no real use of it: nor does his account of the wonders of Aeetes' palace as Jason and company see them on approaching, add anything to his hero or his story. But Virgil uses the mist to give dramatic structure to the approach—to the interval between Aeneas' first knowledge of Dido and their actual encounter—and he uses the approach, the sights that Aeneas admires on his way to Dido, to prepare the encounter. This entirely different point of view is evident even in the verbs used: where Apollonius has only ἵκοντο, ἔσταν, τεθηπότες, εὔκηλοι ὑπὲρ οὐδὸν ἔβαν, Virgil has: *corripuere viam, ascendebant collem, aspectat, miratur,* &c. Their empathetic content is evident. But Virgil, unlike Apollonius, is depicting an emotional process. He is concerned with Aeneas' reaction to the new city, with Aeneas' growing sense of the character and ethos of this *dux femina facti*. Venus has set, as it were, his mood, prepared him to look for every evidence of what this remarkable woman has done and is doing.

We grasp Aeneas' situation at his first sight of the city: *miratur portas strepitumque . . . instant ardentes Tyrii*. He is covered by the mist and thus can see without being seen. The emotional distance between himself—just escaped from a shipwreck, hardly as yet certain of completing his voyage to Italy, let alone founding his city—and the active Tyrians under Dido, is thus objectified and enhanced. The isolated observer is more than physically separated from what he observes: the mist is also a symbol of his spiritual removal from the scene. Here they are busy as bees storing up honey—the simile suggests all the sweetness of security and happy employment: *fervet opus redolentque thymo fragrantia mella*—and Aeneas can but contrast his own very different plight:

F

437   'O fortunati quorum iam moenia surgunt!'
          Aeneas ait, et fastigia suspicit urbis.
          Infert se saeptus nebula (mirabile dictu)
          per medios miscetque viris neque cernitur ulli.

The one brief remark concentrates the feeling of the whole passage, the difference between two fates or destinies.

Virgil is now ready to focus our and Aeneas' attention on one particular aspect of the new city: the grove and temple of Juno. But again the emphasis is on Aeneas' emotional reaction to it:

450   Hoc primum in luco nova res oblata timorem
          leniit, hic primum Aeneas sperare salutem
          ausus et adflictis melius confidere rebus.

For he sees in the temple frieze the evidence of Dido's humanity and of her prospective sympathy with himself. The famous *sunt lacrimae rerum* is really a tribute to the woman who pitied heroes like himself and caused her pity to be thus made public. The time is therefore ripe for Dido's own appearance: *regina ad templum, forma pulcherrima Dido, incessit.*

Aeneas is now almost able to meet Dido in visible reality, for the emotional distance between them has begun to close. It is of course closed even more by the sight of his men given up for lost (Aeneas is eager to grasp their hands) and is finally dissipated by Dido's manifest humanity and pity for them. Her exchange of speeches with Ilioneus (which of course emotionally prepares Dido herself for the sight of Aeneas yet invisible) and her conclusion: *utinam rex ipse . . . adforet Aeneas!* at last provides the right setting for revelation. The mist dissolves and Aeneas stands in clear daylight *os umerosque deo similis.* The scene at once marks the climax of Aeneas' emotional preparation for Dido and the stunning effect of the hero on Dido herself: *obstipuit primo aspectu Sidonia Dido.*

What we may call the preparatory phase of the *amour* has now passed: both Aeneas and Dido are ready for each other; Virgil has made the Homeric-Apollonian motifs—the mist and the hero's approach to the heroine's city—the setting for a drama of two souls moving from isolation to emotional encounter.

This encounter now inaugurates a new phase of the action though one wholly continuous with what has preceded. Aeneas is now of course invited to the palace and sends back to the ships

for Ascanius and suitable gifts for the queen. Appropriately the
most important of these is a cloak of Argive Helen, a cloak she
took with her when she made off with Paris to Troy *inconcessosque hymenaeos*. Another fateful 'marriage' is thus foreshadowed.

The time has therefore come for Venus' intervention. All
events have led to this point: even Aeneas' fatherly summons of
Ascanius is timely since this provides the opportunity for his
temporary abduction and the substitution of the disguised
Cupid. And the device itself it very apt: Aeneas' paternal
solicitude for Ascanius is used by the gods to excite Dido's
maternal instincts. She gets at the father through the son. But
she is now predisposed to admire and to love. We are in short
ready for the amour to begin: Venus and Cupid but mark, so to
speak, the result of the encounter which has already taken place.
The Venus-Cupid plot is in fact the almost necessary effect of
the train of events set up by Venus' meeting with Aeneas: she,
by filling his mind with Dido and her remarkable exploits, had
given the proper coloration to his observations of the city and
the temple; he thus sees Dido in them before he sees Dido
herself. At the same time, we, as well as Aeneas, have learned
of the warm nature of Dido, her humanity and pity and her
special interest in the man who is, in effect, her *alter ego: me
quoque ... similis fortuna ... hac ... voluit consistere terra*. Thus
the divine machinery is an integral part of a continuous narrative as it is not in Apollonius: it is brought into play only when
it has been called for by the dramatic and emotional situation.

Virgil, however, does not follow Apollonius in lingering over
the first stage of the amour. He strikes at once the note on which
he is to remain through all the succeeding narrative: Dido is
infelix pesti devota futurae. But she is still unaware, *inscia*. Her
demand for the story of Troy's fall and Aeneas' *errores* is the
strategy of an as yet unconscious passion. On the other hand
the shift at the end of Book 1 from Aeneas to Dido—for it is
clearly to her and her new love, not to Aeneas that our attention
is directed after line 637—foreshadows the emphasis of Book 4.
Yet the passivity of Aeneas in that book has been in fact
prepared for long before: he had been for some time the passive,
isolated observer—the one who is affected and is acted on
rather than acts—and he is in no condition to resist his own and
Dido's emotions.

Book 4, the climax and fatal end of the *amour*, consists of seven closely connected parts that form together one truly continuous narrative:

1. *Before the consummation:* Dido's struggle with *pudor*, her love yet unavowed to Aeneas or the public (1–89)
2. *The consummation* (90–172):
    (*a*) its divine preparation by Venus and June (90–128)
    (*b*) the hunt and the cave (129–72)
3. *The divine response:* the *amour*, falsely publicized by Dido as 'marriage', is spread by Rumour until it reaches the rest of Africa (Iarbas) and finally Jupiter himself. He responds by sending down Mercury to Carthage: Aeneas hears and sees the god (173–278)
4. *The confrontation:* Aeneas proposes to leave; Dido calls him to account without avail (279–407)
5. *Dido's last appeal:* her plea through Anna is rejected (408–49)
6. *Dido prepares to die; Aeneas departs* (450–583):
    (*a*) Preparation: false appeal to Anna (450–521)
    (*b*) The last night (522–83)
        (i) Dido's sleeplessness (522–53)
        (ii) Aeneas' sleep, vision, departure (554–83)
7. *Dido's death* (584–705)

As we shall see presently, parts 6 and 7 'recapitulate' parts 1 and 2 but only to mark the extent to which the *amour* has changed, has in effect reached the tragic climax foreshadowed in parts 1 and 2 and even, before that, at the very close of Book 1. The action thus rises steadily to the dénouement in part 7. The first part describes the *amour* in the period when Dido is as yet uncertain, torn by conflicting emotions and, above all, unable to admit her love to Aeneas. It corresponds to sections 3, 5, 7, and 8 of the third book of the *Argonautica*. The hunt, the storm, and the consummation in the cave (part 2) are, like the Venus-Cupid plot, the ostensible result of divine intervention (2a) but of course follow naturally from 1. The storm and the reappearance of Juno as its motivating agent 'recapitulate' the storm that began Book 1: we are thus forced to connect the two storms and to realize the 'symbolic' function of both; they are *furor*, chafing at and seeming to overwhelm the *pietas* of the hero.

They also indicate the superhuman and demonic character of such *furor*, just as Jupiter (aided by Neptune and Mercury) indicates the calming and restraining character of supreme fate. The amour is so given a truly ecumenical and a fatal-historical significance. But the cave episode in itself marks a shift in Dido's whole conception of her passion: she brazenly calls it marriage and openly lives with Aeneas. The next part (3) thus brings *Fama* (Rumour) into action: the size of the drama is fantastically magnified until the heavens and Jupiter himself are involved. Then we return to earth with Mercury's down-ward flight. But it is not interrupted (as was Eros' flight in Apollonius, part 1) and leads us right back to Aeneas whom we now see through the eyes of divine wrath in the first flush of his *uxorious* neglect of all higher obligations.

So our attention once more (and for the first time in the book) swings to Aeneas himself as a man with his own destiny and duty: *at vero Aeneas*. His reaction to Mercury is as immediate as the vision was terrible. The 'showdown' with Dido is thus bound to end in her defeat (4), though her hopeless attempt to buy delay (5) only indicates the depth of her infatuation. But with part 6, she is finally *fatis exterrita* and thinks only of death. Her love has now turned to hate. The last night of her life and of Aeneas' stay at Carthage finds her sleepless in her palace, Aeneas dreaming on his ship. A vision of Mercury is needed to send him finally on his way. So Dido sees at dawn (7), as she looks down at the harbour, the whole Trojan fleet under sail. There is nothing more for her to do but to die. The book appropriately ends with her fatal curse and suicide. The whole of Carthage rings with the shouts of citizens once more aroused by Fama to the second and final consummation of Dido's passion; her lingering death is ambiguously indicated to the departing Trojans in the flames of her self-built pyre (beginning of Book 5). So up to the very end, the inexorable continuity of the whole narrative is maintained.

But we cannot get at the true meaning of either Virgilian 'continuity' of narrative or Apollonian 'discontinuity' until we grasp what their *function* is in both authors. The 'subjective' style of Virgil is necessarily associated with a continuous narrative because he wants to maintain a single feeling-tone, expound a single moral and point of view which will dominate the reader, and cause his empathy and sympathy to run on the single track that he (Virgil) has carefully laid out. He is not, like Apollonius, concerned with more or less objective or 'real' characters seemingly enacting their own drama. It does not really matter so much to the story when Apollonius shifts from Medea to the Argonauts and back again. But such shifts would be quite fatal to Virgil's style since it would destroy the feeling-tone and break the empathetic-sympathetic identifica-tion of reader and character, reader and author. Virgil's style is, so to speak, all of a piece and has to be so.

This is what makes it so complex. Every incident, epithet, simile, motif, &c., is embedded in a *coherent structure* of motifs: their effect is thus cumulative since each one 'recalls' the other in an intricately reciprocal arrangement. Thus the fourth book opens with the lines:

> *At* regina gravi iamdudum *saucia* cura
> *vulnus* alit venis et *caeco* carpitur *igni*.

The *at* marks the contrast with Aeneas (who has just finished his narrative), with the past, with the effect of the past (e.g. Anchises), with all that is not Dido and love. The *iamdudum* takes us at once back to Book 1 where we left Dido drinking the long draughts of love (longumque *bibebat* amorem, 749). We are now reverting to a process that has been insensibly at work all through the telling of Aeneas' narrative: *But Dido for some time now* &c. *Our emotional connection with Book 1* is thus re-established. There we learned that the newly amorous Dido was *infelix pesti devota futurae* (712), *inscia insidat quantus miserae deus* (718–19). *Infelix* is a key word—a finger-pointing word— that foreshadows future tragedy and at the same time expresses sympathy: it is the word for those who oppose fate or whom fate opposes but are yet worthy of true pity.[1] It will recur at crucial moments of the narrative. *Inscia* expresses a leitmotif of this section of Book 4 (1). Both epithets are contrasted with the happy (*laeta*) Dido whom Aeneas first saw at the Juno temple (1. 503) and who was there compared with Diana, the goddess

---

[1] On *infelix*, see Pease, pp. 145–6. The best treatment of this word, perhaps, is that of Rebert (*TAPA* 59 (1928), pp. 57–71). Apollonius' σχέτλιος is really quite different from *infelix:* it lacks the nuance of serious sympathy. Its nearest approach to *infelix* is at *Arg.* III. 1133 (of Medea) but even this use of σχέτλιος is quite distinct from *infelix.*

at whose sight her mother's *silent* (tacitum) heart was full of joy. Dido by the end of 1 and beginning of 4 is *misera* and *infelix*, not *laeta*; the emotion is no *tacit* joy, but a *hidden* fire. Furthermore the happy huntress (Diana) to whom she was likened at first view, is to change her tonality altogether: hunting is an extremely ominous motif for Dido. The description and simile of line 503 mark a high point of joy and sanity from which Dido was steadily to decline: the tragedy starts (l. 503) from a brief moment of self-command and joyous exaltation that marks as it were the depth of the fall to come. But (at) we are *now* (beginning of 4) confronted with a *wounded* Dido, eaten by a *hidden flame*.

The dominant motifs of Dido's amour at this stage (beginning of 4) are thus the *wound*, the *fire*, and treacherous ignorance or *unawareness*. They recur in lines 66 f.

> *Est mollis flamma medullas*
> interea et *tacitum* vivit sub pectore *vulnus*.

And they are then embodied in a remarkable simile:

68   *Uritur* infelix Dido totaque vagatur
            urbe furens qualis coniecta cerva sagitta
            quam procul *incautam* nemora inter Cresia *fixit*
            pastor agens telis, liquitque volatile ferrum
            nescius; illa fuga silvas saltusque peragrat
            Dictaeos, haeret lateri *letalis* harundo.

This, as Pöschl [1] has well said, goes far beyond the single-significance similes of Homer and Apollonius. It expresses (1) the present physical situation of Dido (her aimless wanderings), (2) her psychological state (the love wound and her tragic ignorance, *incautam*) and (3) her future doom. The weapon clings to her side (*haeret lateri* letalis harundo) as the features of Aeneas clung to her breast (*haerent infixi pectore* vultus—4). And he, like the hunter, is ignorant (nescius) of his terrible shot. In short the *wound* and the *flame*, the *unawareness* or *blindness* have now reached a note of quite tragic intensity. The simile is an integral—indeed a crucial—part of the motif structure.

But Virgil has also integrated his motifs with the very framework of his plot. It is with Aeneas' sword (ensem recludit Dardanium, 647) that Dido inflicts the fatal suicide-*wound* at the end: it is

---

[1] Op. cit. pp. 130–5.

the *flames* of her pyre that she wants him to see from the ocean (hauriat hunc oculis ignem, 661). We have but to compare the passages:

689   (Dido's death-agony) *infixum* stridit *sub pectore vulnus*.
67   (the love wound) tacitum vivit *sub pectore vulnus*
4   (Aeneas' features infixed in Dido's heart) haerent *infixi pectore vultus*

The wound and the flames that mark Dido's end, and proleptically Carthage's end as well (flammae furentes, 670), are thus the visible signs of an inner tragedy: the course of the book has developed Dido's *private* wound and *private* conflagration into a *public* catastrophe, foreshadowing a greater one to come. We shall see presently how Virgil makes the transition from the private to the public spheres of action.

This is a most instructive use of *motifs* for it illustrates the quite radical way in which Virgil has transformed a rather conventional episode of *Argonautica* III and how utterly his narrative style is unlike that of Apollonius. In part 3 of *Argonautica* III, Eros shoots at and wounds Medea with his arrow; her love is then likened to the rapid flame that devours the brushwood which a poor spinning woman has lit to illuminate her task in the darkness of early dawn. The *flame* and the *wound* seem at one point so like Virgil's that we can hardly doubt the latter's use of Apollonius here [1] (e.g. βέλος δ'ἐνεδαίετο κούρῃ νέρθεν ὑπὸ κραδίῃ φλογὶ εἴκελον). But Apollonius has no further use for the *wound* and the *flame*. His subsequent description of Medea's love is not in the least mythological but quite realistic. The simile of the spinning woman has no relation to any recurrent motif. Indeed all Apollonius' similes simply explicate the immediate theme or action. They do not forebode the future, indicate a contrast with or a reinforcement of a recurrent motif.

But in Virgil the simile is a device for heightening or placing his motifs. The wounded doe simile is an excellent case in point. Its origin, despite the doubts of some commentators, seems clear enough. Virgil here, as elsewhere, is reworking Apollonius by combining him with Homer and by adapting both to his own purpose. If we examine the similes *which involve*

[1] *Arg.* III. 286–7.

a direct comparison with Jason-Medea or Aeneas-Dido, we can at
once see what has happened. The list of parallels below follows
the Virgilian order of priority:

AENEID	APOLLONIUS	HOMER
1. 498–504 *Dido* (first appearance) compared to Diana with nymphs: talis erat Dido.	III. 876–85 *Medea* (riding with her maids to the tryst with Jason) compared to Artemis and her nymphs.	*Odyssey* 6. 102–9 *Nausikaa* compared to Artemis and her nymphs. Note esp. ll. 106–7.
4. 69–73 *Dido* (now deep in her as yet hidden passion) compared to a wounded doe.	IV. 12–13 *Medea* (afraid of her father after her successful assistance of Jason) compared to a light doe in the woods, pursued by dogs.	*Iliad* 11. 473–81 *Odysseus* (pursued by Trojans) is compared to a wounded stag attacked by jackals.
4. 143–50 *Aeneas* (at the start of the hunt) compared to Apollo.	I. 307–10 *Jason* (at departure) compared to Apollo.	*Iliad* 1. 46–7 The clang of *Apollo's* arrows on his shoulders.
4. 441–9 *Aeneas* unmoved by Anna's and Dido's pleas is compared to an oak vainly beaten by the winds.	III. 968–72 *Jason* and *Medea* at their first meeting compared to oaks or tall pines, first still, then stirred by the wind.	*Iliad* 12. 131–6 *Pirithous* and *Leontes* (defending the Achaian wall-gate) compared to oaks withstanding wind and rain.

There can thus be no doubt that Virgil is primarily indebted
to Apollonius: all his direct similes for Dido and Aeneas
correspond in some degree to the Apollonian similes for Medea
and Jason.[1] But he has added many Homeric touches to
Apollonius: the supereminence of Artemis, Leto's joy in her

[1] Virgil thus used all of Apollonius' Medea-Jason similes save that at III. 957–9
(the comparison of Jason with Sirius) and those at III. 656–63 and IV. 35–40
(Medea compared in the very first stage of love to a premature widow mourning
her new husband and ashamed to face her maids; Medea, departing, compared
to a girl leaving her country for harsh servitude under a new mistress).

daughter, in the Dido-Diana simile; the *wounded* deer, in the Dido-doe simile; the clang of Apollo's arms in the Aeneas-Apollo simile; the ferocity and attempt to uproot, of the winds, in the Aeneas-oak simile. Yet he obviously went *from* Apollonius *back to* Homer; the mere fact that *all* his Aeneas-Dido similes correspond, to at least some extent, with the Apollonian similes of this particular episode (the Medea-Jason amour), precludes coincidence. He has, however, rearranged and changed their Apollonian order and colour. Thus the Medea-Artemis simile is used only for Dido's first, happy appearance (*before* she has seen Aeneas). The Medea-deer simile (plus the Homeric touches) is used for the period of Dido's *unacknowledged* passion (the hunter is ignorant, *nescius*, of his deed) before the wound and flame have become overt and public. The Aeneas-Apollo simile is taken from the first book of the *Argonautica* (in the third book Jason is likened to the dog-star, Sirius) because it is obviously designed to be a pendant to the Dido-Diana simile (Dido and Aeneas are each likened to a god or goddess); but to it is added the ominous overtones of the Homeric Apollo about to shoot his pestilential arrows. Aeneas is now himself the declared hunter whose divine appearance and stature have a nuance of Bacchic frenzy and death-dealing power. We are meant to contrast the:

4. 146   Cretesque Dryopesque *fremunt* pictique Agathyrsi;
        ipse iugis Cynthi graditur mollique fluentem
        fronde premit crinem fingens atque implicat auro,
        tela sonant umeris: haut illo segnior ibat
        Aeneas, tantum egregio decus enitet ore.

with the calm and happy employment of Diana-Dido:

1. 500   illa *pharetram*
     fert umero, gradiensque deas supereminet omnis
     (Latonae tacitum pertemptant gaudia pectus)
     talis erat Dido, talem se *laeta* ferebat
     per medios instans operi regnisque futuris.

These are obviously not suited to the particular situations of Aeneas or Dido. The Sirius simile was, however, used later of Aeneas (10. 272 f.). Thus if we bear in mind Virgil's obviously close study of this whole section of the *Argonautica* (Book III, and the Medea episodes of IV), it seems evident that it was his primary or initial model for the similes, though, of course, he supplemented them by many Homeric touches. In other words, he went to Homer only to complete and alter the similes or simile-ideas he found originally in Apollonius. Here his relation to Apollonius and Homer closely parallels that of Theocritus (see Appendix 3).

The Aeneas-tree simile again conveys the new firmness of his hero: the contrast between the rustling trees of Apollonius and the isolated, gigantic oak is particularly instructive.

In a word, Virgil has rearranged and altered Apollonius' similes to fit the emotional progression of his narrative: calm joy (simile 1), followed in turn by hidden and tragic pain (simile 2), frenzied and baleful power (simile 3), and immovable determination (simile 4). The wounded doe simile (2) is but faintly indebted to its 'sources': its placing in the narrative, its use of a motif already well established (the wound), and its triple significance, are all Virgilian, not Apollonian or Homeric.

But we have not even yet exhausted the 'wounded doe'. Medea was likened to a light doe (κούφη κεμάς) fleeing the hounds when she, long after the first phase of her amour and after her successful assistance of Jason, began to dread the consequences of her act and to fear her father's resentment and probable vengeance. There is no *wound*, no imminent death or fatality in the Apollonius simile. The *wounded* Medea—the victim of Eros' arrow—is far in the past: a very different emotion now excites her. Virgil thus took the wound and the distracted doe from two very different points in Apollonius' narrative and (with Homer's help) combined them into a central symbol of *tragic love*. He also dropped the conventional Eros-arrow motif of Apollonius (Cupid's action on Dido is entirely mental: *paulatim abolere Sychaeum* [Cupido] *incipit et vivo temptat praevertere amore iam pridem resides animos*) in order to give the love wound a quite non-mythological depth and connotation. Thus simile is substituted for pure myth: the latter cannot be integrated into the motif structure that Virgil wants; the whole psychological emphasis would have been distorted. Dido has indeed been 'shot' by a cruel hunter but he is Aeneas, not the light hearted Cupid. And not until the effect of Aeneas has had time to work—and she to forget Sychaeus and revive the long-disused feelings—can she be described as fatally stricken.

Virgil's Dido-Aeneas similes also serve to bring out two *other* crucial motifs. They are *hunting* similes and are part of a motif-structure that is based on hunting. In Book 1 Aeneas lands and kills seven huge stags with his arrows; he then meets Venus disguised as a huntress (1. 314 f). Dido (in the first simile) is Diana the huntress: pharetram fert umero. She then becomes the stricken deer whom the unwitting hunter (Aeneas) has fatally wounded. Then (as with the wound and the flame) the hunting motif becomes part of the plot itself: Dido comes in hunting costume (4. 136 f.); Aeneas is the hunter Apollo. The hunt culminates in the storm and the cave. Thus a motif that was originally calm and happy in its tonality is gradually given an ominous and ominously frenzied meaning. We now take up the Bacchic motif. Dido who once wandered in her hidden amorous excitement *urbe furens* (69) is now caught in the overt fury of consummated passion. This we see first in the Aeneas-Apollo simile and its *fremunt*. It becomes plainer in the storm and its wild accompaniments of howling nymphs (ulularunt). Then a new stage of *furor* (the *furor* of *rejected* love) appears in Dido's response to the first news of Aeneas' preparations to depart: saevit . . . incensa per *urbem bacchatur*, qualis commotis excita sacris *Thyias*, &c. But it is only after she has finally grasped the futility of all attempts at reconciliation that she herself realizes how *tragic* her madness is: Eumenidum veluti demens videt agmina Pentheus, &c. (469 f.). At the end Bacchic fury pervades the whole doomed and stricken city: *bacchatur* Fama . . . femineo *ululatu* tecta *fremunt*.

Virgil in short has taken Apollonian, Homeric, and even tragic materials to form the structure of a very complex and very un-Apollonian and un-Homeric epic. His similes are clearly modelled on those of Apollonius and Homer but, unlike theirs, are integrated with the whole poem in virtue of their association with *leitmotifs* that recur at pivotal moments of the action. Thus it is essential to see how Virgil uses these motifs in the structure of his poem, how they are combined in one continuous narrative.

The first part of Book 4 (1–89) describes, as we have seen, the hidden cause of Dido's amour, the period when she bears the wound and flame without as yet revealing them to Aeneas. *Everything is here seen through Dido*: we empathetically read her mind and share her feelings. The amatory symptoms of Medea are mainly physical: Dido's are far more psychic and intellectual. Lines such as:

83   Illum absens absentem auditque videtque:
       aut gremio Ascanium, *genitoris imagine capta*,
       detinet, *infandum si fallere possit amorem*.

reveal Dido's innermost thoughts, her effort to beguile the love she cannot utter by means of an inadequate substitute.

But the author's overt sympathy, his *editorial* intrusion, is even more characteristic of the style here than his empathy. The exchange of speeches between Dido and Anna (9–53) recall in their content the battle of shame (αἰδώς) and desire (ἵμερος) within Medea. But Apollonius relates this with almost visual objectivity: we actually see Medea approaching and retreating from Chalciope's door as the shifting gusts of desire and shame pull her one way and another.[1] It is nothing but the experience *she* goes through in one particular period of time and it has not, in itself, any special *moral* content: this is the way Medea, not the author, feels. But Dido's contest with *pudor* is seen by both her and Virgil as the moral issue it really is:

24   sed mihi vel tellus optem prius ima dehiscat
        vel Pater omnipotens abigat me fulmine ad umbras,
        pallentes umbras Erebi noctemque profundam,
        ante, Pudor, quam te violo, aut tua iura resolvo.

Nor—and this is a most important point—does her speech 'stand out' from the surrounding narrative as do the speeches in Homer and Apollonius.[2] We know what to expect. We have already been told that Dido is *saucia, male sana, infelix, pesti devota futurae* before she speaks. When she is convinced by Anna, we are offered the editorialized conclusion:

54   His dictis incensum animum flammavit amore
        Spemque dedit *dubiae* menti solvitque *pudorem*.

Obviously *pudor* means the same for Virgil as for Dido but Virgil can *also* see (as Dido does not) the peculiar delusion of one who sins in full consciousness of her *culpa*. He sees, for example, the futility of her superstitious attempts to falsify the future:

65   Heu vatum ignarae mentes! quid vota *furentem*,
        quid delubra iuvant? Est mollis flamma medullas.

Dido's moral lapse is deliberate; the real determinant of her future deliberately obscured. (We here see the moral significance of the action *as Virgil wants us to see it*.)

---

[1] *Arg.* III. 645–55.
[2] Cf. here the exchange of speeches between Medea and Chalciope at *Arg.* III. 664–739.

But Dido still reflects Virgil's own morality. In fact, Dido's speeches, as we can tell from their generalized, rhetorical diction (e.g. the apostrophe of *Pudor* with a capital P), their periodic sentences and subjunctive clauses, convey *not* her actual on-going emotions (like those in Medea's speeches) but a generalized analysis of the total moral-historical situation as both she and Virgil see it. And this is also true of the narrative proper: the line between the moralizing empathetic-sympathetic narrative and Dido's quoted words is very thin. To be sure Anna contradicts Dido (at least *pro forma*) but it is made quite plain that Anna is wrong in undermining Dido's declared (but not firmly held) resolve: she *enflames* an already kindled mind (the flame is destructive always in this book), gives hope to a bad cause, dissolves the sense of shame. And the *shame* here is not the temporary resistance of a reluctant ingenue such as Medea, but a moral reality on which a whole life and society depend. Virgil makes it all quite clear: the reader is always emotionally and morally clued in.

We thus start with a more or less generalized and detemporalized analysis of Dido's situation (as it stood on the day or days after Aeneas' reception in the palace). The symptoms described in lines 56 f. are those of love, the disease, and are bunched together in one succinct, quasi-clinical, paragraph (56–89): Apollonius, on the contrary, spreads the symptoms over the whole course of a long development. But here again Virgil is not so much concerned with the symptoms themselves as with their moral and emotive meaning: hence the force of the *wound* and *flame* motifs, the wounded-doe simile, the editorial remarks and epithets (*heu*, &c., *infelix, furens*).

Once this initial moral-emotional situation—Dido as *infelix, male sana*, wounded, aflame and therefore pitiable—is established the narrative can progress. The transition to a continuous chronology is almost imperceptible:

80   post ubi digressi, lumenque obscura vicissim
        luna premit, suadentque cadentia sidera somnos
        sola domo maeret vacua, &c.

In this a particular night or just the kind of night (in general) that Dido endured in this epoch of her amour? The next section (2a—the Venus-Juno colloquy) merely begins with a *quam simul*: *as soon as* she &c. But Juno makes it clear that Dido and Aeneas have planned a hunt for the *following day* (ubi primos crastinus ortus/extulerit Titan, 118–19). In fact the day breaks even before the end of the divine colloquy:

129   Oceanum *interea* surgens Aurora reliquit.

So emotionally at least the dawn follows the wakeful night of lines 80 f. The Venus-Juno colloquy does not really interrupt the clock which had begun to tick, so to speak, at that point.[1]

Up to line 128 (parts 1 and 2a), then, the amour has been hidden from Aeneas—a guilty secret shared only by Dido and her sister and by Venus and Juno, the 'sub-fates' or tutelary deities of Dido and Aeneas. The night of 80 f. aptly symbolizes the darkness of the hidden *culpa* as well as the emotional isolation of Dido from Aeneas and all other mortals (who unlike her can sleep). But by line 89, the time has come for the covert to be made overt, for the hidden to be revealed. The Venus-Juno colloquy bridges the transition to it.

The 'unholy alliance' of these goddesses at this juncture of the drama marks the fulfilment of the action so far undertaken by each in hostile opposition to each other: of the storm by which Juno had diverted Aeneas from Italy to Africa; of the amour by which Venus had sought to insure the 'hospitality' of Dido. The scene thus marks and emphasizes the new stage of the narrative, the passing as it were of a critical barrier. The collusion of Venus and Juno is in effect a coalescence of two key symbols or motifs: to the amatory and Roman element for which Venus stands is added the Junonian, Carthaginian element of fury, of demonic opposition to Jupiter, of irrational wrath and violence, an element already given high symbolic expression by the great storm with which the epic began. The 'recall' of this storm by the new storm that Juno now prepares for Aeneas and Dido is obvious enough and is underlined not only by the context but by the tone and even by identical phrases; compare:

1. 124   *interea magno misceri murmure pontum*

and:

4. 160   *interea magno misceri murmure caelum.*

---

[1] Note the time element has already been introduced at l. 77: nunc eadem *labente die* convivia quaerit. The original banquet and narrative of Book 1 is repeated, again at night-fall. It is after it breaks up (post ubi digressi) that Dido keeps her restless vigil in the deserted banquet hall.

This is, indeed, the result of Juno's driving of Aeneas to Africa and thus into the arms of Dido: now Juno herself appears to make this emphatically clear and, at the same time, lend her own furious accents to the passion that Venus has so callously instigated. Both these goddesses are far below the level of Jupiter or the fate for which he stands: the difference is clearly marked later on, as we shall see. It is quite unnecessary to underline the distinctions between Apollonius (part 1) and Virgil here.

The next section (2b, 129–172) indicates by its opening reference to Aurora (l. 129) the shift of tonality: the dark night of hidden passion is now invaded by morning sunshine. But the daylight is not cheering or calming: it does not dissipate the gloomy forebodings of the preceding night. Rather it introduces a new violence and frenzy. There is the excitement before the hunt begins: *it* portis... delecta iuventus... Massylique *ruunt*... reginam *exspectant*... *stat sonipes*... *frena ferox spumantia mandit*. There is a frenetic and ominous nuance to the Aeneas-Apollo simile, as we have already seen. There is the speed and violence of the hunt itself. And then the storm: the mighty murmuring, the rain and hail, the rush of the mountain streams, the lightning, the shriek of the nymphs. All this prepares us for the solemn editorial lines:

169   Ille dies primus leti primusque malorum
        causa fuit.

It is really difficult to describe the effect of this remarkable section of the poem because it is so subtle: but we must note at least the way in which the daylight is given an ominous and even baleful aspect. The empathy and sympathy that have been so prodigally used in describing Dido before (part 1) are now quite gone: she is *regina, Dido* only; we see her horse and attire, but not her heart. The emphasis is much more on Aeneas —to him a long and seemingly most honorific simile is now devoted—but this is only deliberate and ironical ambiguity. The *pulcherrimus* Aeneas (note the epithet) who is likened to Apollo, is like him also the wielder of terrible weapons that bring doom. There is no healthiness in his beauty here. Aside from his appearance, i.e. the charms which have undone Dido, he hardly seems to count: again we have no empathetic penetration of his psyche, not an atom of sympathy, merely the epithets *dux Troianus* as he goes to the cave. Only the young Ascanius is empathetically described:

156   at puer Ascanius mediis in vallibus acri
          gaudet equo, iamque hos cursu, iam praeterit illos,
          spumantemque dari pecora inter inertia votis
          optat aprum, aut fulvum descendere monte leonem.

Only his *psyche* is innocent and open, penetrable by a sympathetic reader: the others are encased in an armour of guilt that, for the moment, forbids the penetration of other minds and hearts.

Thus the daylight of this section is harshly objective as well as deceptive. But the storm finally reveals the true violence and fury of Dido and Aeneas. Here, as so often in Virgil, a physical stands for a psychological event but it stands also for more: for the fact that Dido and Aeneas have now given an open and public character to their *amores*, that an inner storm has acquired an outer dimension. This first *day* of consummated love thus begins a new phase of the *pestis*, the terrible malaise, of which Dido is the victim. Her love is no more hidden, no more simply nocturnal:

171   nec iam *furtivum* Dido meditatur amorem:
          coniugium vocat, hoc praetexit nomine *culpam*.

The next section (3) takes its departure from Dido's *culpa* in 172: she has now, by outraging public opinion, made herself the prey of *Fama*, and has thus set in motion the demonic and divine forces which are to cause her ruin. We rise from the isolated pair to Heaven itself: from this in turn comes the command that changes everything for both Dido and Aeneas. The local here becomes ecumenical: the human touches the divine and the divine touches the human. A small event is magnified and heightened until the very quick of Fate—of destiny itself—is reached. The figure of *Fama* is admirably calculated to mark the transition from the private to the public, from the human to the divine spheres of action. She is at once *Rumour*, a transparent hypostasis who is in no sense a true personality, and at the same time a demonic force that lifts the human to a superhuman level. Her décor—her multiple feathers, eyes, tongues, mouths, ears—are obvious reflections of her nature as are her nightly, owl-like flights, her terrible sleeplessness, her brooding stance on roofs and high towers. To scan these characteristics for pictorial consistency is, of course, to reduce them and *Fama* herself to absurdity: this is not a picture but a vaguely descried monster—monstrum horrendum ingens—who represents as it were the demonic ambiguity of the force, publicity and rumour, that Dido has now roused. Virgil uses Homer's *Ossa* and *Eris* [1] but combines them and magnifies them into a quite new being that sounds a new note in epic: the terrible publicity of private sin when it defies society and its *mores*. Thus Rumour is especially monstrous in its capacity for swift magnification, raising, as it were, human crime to the very eyes and ears of the gods:

176   parva metu primo, mox sese attollit in auras
         ingrediturque solo, et caput inter nubila condit.

The narrative continuity between Dido, Fama, Iarbas (her rejected African suitor) and Jupiter is thus preserved while, at the same time, the transition to a quite new stage and sphere of action is effected. It is Iarbas' prayer to Jupiter that puts fate once again into action. The descent of Mercury (238–58) recalls the descents of Hermes in Homer, of Eros in Apollonius, but here this motif has quite a different function: it measures the *distance* between Jupiter and Aeneas, between shortsighted men and the grand design of fate; even, by implication between fate (Jupiter) and those sub-fates (Venus, Juno, Mercury himself) who, unlike Jupiter, can *directly* intervene among men. Thus the levels of action—the fatal, the sub-fatal, the human— are discriminated and at the same time set in intelligible relation to each other. Man's sinful action becomes magnified as it spreads through society (Fama) and so eventually causes that divine reaction which corrects it and puts it to unforeseen uses: the divine and demonic are thus given a social and moral meaning that they quite lack in Homer or Apollonius.

This is why we *now* for the first time can see Aeneas *through divine eyes*, when Mercury, Jupiter's messenger, observes him

260   fundantem arces ac tecta novantem,

as if he were only the consort of the woman whose regalia he wears (dives quae munera Dido fecerat) and in effect, a Carthaginian, not a prospective Roman. For it is one thing to

---

[1] Esp. Ossa in *Od.* 24. 413 and Eris in *Il.* 4. 442–3.

see Aeneas on a human level; another to see him from the perspective of fate itself. Once this new aspect of his *culpa* (as seen so to speak, *sub specie fati*) is made clear to both reader and Aeneas himself, it cannot but be reflected in the action. So we come back to Aeneas. *Now for the first time in the book,* our full attention shifts to him, now also for the first time in the book we grasp, empathetically, his point of view and read his mind:

281   *Ardet* abire fuga *dulces*que relinquere terras
    attonitus tanto monitu imperioque deorum.
    Heu quid agat? quo nunc reginam ambire furentem
    audeat adfatu? quae prima exordia sumat?
    atque animum nunc huc celerem, nunc dividit illuc.

These are *Aeneas'* thoughts and sensations: we now stand as it were in his own quivering shoes and see how he is, finally, forced to act. The initiative has at last passed to him.

With line 296, however, (*at regina* dolos—quis fallere possit amantem?—praesensit) we return to Dido as we did at the beginning of the book (*at regina*, &c.): a new stage of *Dido*'s story has *also* begun. To her also *Fama* (eadem impia Fama) brings a rumour (armari classem cursumque parari). She also feels the impact of fate and now becomes the mad maenad who shows the frenzy of thwarted, not consummated passion: *saevit* inops animi, totamque *incensa* per urbem bacchatur. She is like the Theban women on Cithaeron, the Bacchae of Euripides raging to their own ruin.

We are ready for the 'show-down', for the terrible dialogue between the guilty and anguished pair. But Aeneas has now heard the voice of a god speaking the language of fate; he cannot give in; he is once more *pius*: At pius Aeneas quamquam lenire dolentem solando cupit... multa gemens magnoque animum labefactus amore, iussa tamen divum exsequitur (393–6). But Dido is still the prey of *improbus Amor* (412): she loses all her dignity and is for once only a woman in love. (Virgil editorially 'marks the spot', so to speak: it is the ultimate degradation of Dido's character by her passion and, conversely, the degradation that Aeneas—once more *pius*—has finally escaped.)[1] She tries to appeal for time, for delay, for

---

[1] Cf. l. 412 (Improbe Amor, quid non mortalia pectora cogis?) with *Arg.* III. 297 (οὖλος ἔρως) and IV. 445 (Σχέτλι' Ἔρως). Virgil is certainly indebted to Apollonius here, but note his *placing* and *use* of Apollonius' phrases!

anything: Aeneas is affected—his tears still flow—but he is now the immovable oak, proof against all such entreaty.

So we reach the final act of the drama: The section (6) that begins:

450   Tum vero infelix fatis exterrita Dido
             mortem orat; taedet caeli convexa tueri.

is the narrative not of love, but of hatred and death. Dido is by now diseased and maddened in a very different way from that of the first sections of the book. And Virgil shows this by *recapitulating* the motifs of these sections (1–2), thus underlining the horrible difference between these two phases of Dido's story and character. As in the first section, Dido once more visits the temples and soothsayers: but *now* the voices of doom are clear and unmistakable. Even her dreams are unambiguously terrible. Once more, she turns to Anna but, this time, not to *be deceived* by Anna's fatal advice (spemque dedit [Anna] dubiae menti, 55) but to *deceive* (500 f.) in her turn. Anna believes in Dido's false love charms.

Then we revert (6b) to the night motif of section 1 (80 f.). But this time, the motif is much more explicit and intense:

522   *Nox erat* et placidum carpebant fessa soporem
             corpora per terras, &c.

Furthermore Virgil uses the motif (night) much more explicitly to compare and contrast his two main characters; *on this same night*, Dido is sleepless though all other creatures sleep; Aeneas is slumbering on the high poop of his vessel. Dido now realizes her plight and her guilt (*En quid ago?* 534 f.), her helplessness and the criminal folly of her deed (non licuit thalami expertem sine crimine vitam degere more ferae . . . non servata fides cineri promissa Sychaei).[1] She is no longer the woman who accepted the easy scepticism of Anna: 'id cinerem aut manes credis curare sepultos?' (34). But Aeneas is sleeping the sleep of a once more easy conscience (iam certus eundi): yet this (as we shall see later) is a premature ease and he has to be roused to action by a *second* vision of Mercury. Once more the gods (as before in the cave scene) prepare the dénouement.

With line 584 (et iam prima novo spargebat lumine terras . . . Aurora) *another dawn* and another day (cf. the Aurora of 129)

─────────
[1] See note 2 on p. 269 below.

again reveal the hidden meaning of the night: we witness, as before, the manifestation and enactment in daylight of nocturnal thoughts and feelings. Dido now sees for herself the Trojan fleet under sail: she curses Aeneas and his Trojans and then enacts her suicide resolve with Aeneas' own sword. And *once again* Fama spreads the news: concussam bacchatur Fama per urbem. The uproar in the city, the flames of her pyre, are likened to the final conflagration of Carthage itself. The wound and the flame, Bacchic furor, Fama, Anna, Dido, Carthage are finally fused in a grand unity of disaster realized and disaster yet to come.

The difference between Virgil and Apollonius here seems vast indeed and yet much of Virgil's narrative structure is Apollonian in origin. Thus the night-day contrast whose double use, as we have seen, plays so important a role in the organization of the Virgilian narrative is taken from parts 8 and 9 of the *Argonautica*. In III. 744 f. just after the colloquy between Medea and Chalciope, we find the night passage that Virgil used in both 80 f. and 522 f.[1] Medea, unlike other creatures, cannot sleep (751). She hesitates between suicide and the fulfilment of her promise to Chalciope. Then with dawn (828), her doubts all dissipated, she drives gaily to her tryst with Jason. She is Artemis joyfully proceeding with her nymphs towards the savoury hekatomb (876–85).

It is evident that Virgil has separated the suicide and amatory motifs in his separate uses of the day-night theme. Dido's sleeplessness (when others sleep) is put to very different employments:

80   Post, ubi digressi, lumenque obscura vicissim
        luna premit, suadentque cadentia sidera somnos
        sola domo maeret vacua stratisque relictis
        incubat. Illum absens absentem auditque videtque ...
522   Nox erat et placidum carpebant fessa soporem
        corpora per terras silvaeque et saeva quierant
        aequora, cum medio volvontur sidera lapsu,
        cum tacet omnis ager, pecudes pictaeque volucres,
        quaeque lacus late liquidos quaeque aspera dumis
        rura tenent, somno positae sub nocte silenti.

---

[1] Cf. *Arg.* III. 744 (Νὺξ μὲν ἔπειτ' ἐπὶ γαῖαν ἄγεν κνέφας) with *Aeneid* 4. 522 and *Arg.* III. 751 (ἀλλὰ μάλ' οὐ Μήδειαν ἐπὶ γλυκερὸς λάβεν ὕπνος) with *Aeneid* 4. 529 (*at non infelix*, &c.). A metrical comparison of Virgil and Apollonius here is most instructive.

529 At non infelix animi Phoenissa neque umquam
solvitur in somnos oculisve aut pectore noctem
accipit: ingeminant curae rursusque resurgens
saevit amor magnoque irarum fluctuat aestu.
Sic adeo insistit secumque ita corde volutat:
'En quid ago? rursusne procos inrisa priores
experiar Nomadumque petam conubia supplex,
quos ego sim totiens iam dedignata maritos? &c.

In the first passage, we have the love-wounded woman before
the consummation; in the second, the final battle with her
passion, and, then, the perception of her moral fall and its sole
possible remedy. In each case the ensuing day brings the
catastrophe foreseen and yet hidden in the darkness of night.
Night and Day, in other words, become really the settings—in
part the symbols—of moral states, of the deceptive, doubtful,
ambiguous and guilty as opposed to a horrible manifest reality.
Inability to sleep[1] is the index of a lost innocence: it isolates the
dark passion or guilty conscience in a black world that reflects
a moral blackness within. But the two night-day sequences
represent also two *different stages* of Dido's *inner darkness* and *outer
fury*: the first prepares us for the second, just as the consummation in the cave sets in motion the train of events that end on the
pyre.

 In Apollonius, the sleeplessness of Medea is solely due to her
natural anxiety, her fear for her reputation and of her parents,
as opposed to her love and her commitment to Chalciope. Her
choice between life and suicide is almost a tangible choice: she
actually takes out her poisons and puts them back. But as soon
as Medea decides to live and love, she can hardly wait for the
dawn. When it comes, it is unambiguously welcome. The tone
is now light and joyous: though Apollonius warns of woe
ahead in lines 835–8, there is no sense or connotation of woe
in the ensuing narrative itself. In short Apollonius' night-day
contrast is only the setting of one vivid episode; Virgil's is a
richly emotional motif that binds the narrative together and
relates the two supreme moments of Dido's tragic amour. As in
a symphony, a minor theme is repeated in a major key and thus

---

[1] The late hour is indicated by the phrases *suadent cadentia sidera somnos* and
medio voluuntur sidera lapsu. Stratisque relictis incubat (ll. 82–83) indicates not sleep
but restless brooding over the abandoned couch on which Aeneas had sat.

spells the difference between expectation and fulfilment, between the initial cause and the final enactment of doom.

Perhaps the most striking difference between Virgil and Apollonius is revealed in their treatment of the desertion theme itself. In *Argonautica IV*. 338–481, Medea is threatened by the agreement that Jason and the Argonauts make with Apsyrtus and the Colchians: the Argonauts will keep the fleece but Medea is to await the decision of an arbitrator. He is to determine whether she returns to her father, Aeetes, or stays with Jason. Naturally she cannot wait to get Jason alone and pour forth her wrath (355–90). Her words are obviously the partial model of Dido's speeches at 305 f., 365 f., and 590 f. But when Medea's passion is met by Jason's soft excuse (it is all a ruse to catch Apsyrtus), she shifts her ground completely and becomes once more the willing sorceress, the chief designer of Apsyrtus' infamous murder. The emotional crisis seems to leave no permanent scar at all.

The difference between Dido's tragic transition from love to hate and Medea's temporary fury is so obvious as to need no underlining. The main point to be made is that Virgil's heroine is conceived *from the very start* as *infelix*, as fatally seized by a ruinous passion. The outcome is the result of fate impinging upon character: her love is doomed as soon as it begins and its hideous transformation is determined by its very origin. Medea's accusations of ingratitude, rehearsal of her pitiful plight (if deserted), and threats to become Jason's avenging fury (385 f.) are not at all the necessary result of a pre-determined process and are over as soon as they are pronounced. Her witch-like connivance in Apsyrtus' death is simply the price of the marriage that she so single-mindedly seeks. Apollonius, certainly, has no idea that Medea is a 'good thing' for either Jason or Greece (Hera is using her to even the score with Pelias) and he expressly comments on the iniquity of both the murder and the love that can instigate it (445 f.). But there is no 'foreshadowing', no recurrence or intensification of motifs, no designed juxtaposition of times, no dramatic progression of emotion in his actual narrative. Virgil uses the fury and the sorcery of Medea, even her murderous proclivities, to produce an effect of psychological culmination: this is what the happy and humane Dido of the Juno-temple could become; this is the outcome of the original wound and the flame. But Apollonius himself has no conception of this kind of continuous narrative, this kind of psychological development and symbolic unity.

We can now at last begin to see the true character of Virgil's narrative style. As compared with that of either Homer or Apollonius, it is *subjective* or more accurately, *empathetic-sympathetic*. Virgil not only reads the minds of his characters; he constantly communicates to us his own reactions to them and to their behaviour. Apollonius, in his long narrative of Medea's amour, certainly came far closer than Homer to psychological and introspective analysis but, for all that, he still depicts Medea objectively, from without. We see her physical symptoms, we mark her observations (as e.g. she looks at Jason), we are given her thoughts in explicitly demarcated ('quoted') soliloquies or monologues.[1] There is, of course, a certain amount of empathy in the description of her emotions. But by and large we see her and her amour as objective facts: Apollonius' isolated comments or editorial intrusions are never imbedded in the narrative context as Virgil's are. We do in some sense grasp Medea as a real character, an ingenue in her first love, gradually yielding to strange feelings she can hardly understand. The episode is sufficiently long and leisurely to follow the twists and turns of her changing impulses, to hold the numerous soliloquies and conversations by which a relatively objective characterization can be effected. We have no sensation of a planned, directed narrative but rather of actual events in process, happening so to speak under our very eyes. Virgil, on the other hand, condenses his story (ruthlessly eliminating the details that do not fit his purpose) and very clearly directs the reader toward the end he has in view.

His empathy and sympathy are included in an editorial framework that ranges from explicit to implicit comment on Dido and the amour. The result is a complete transformation of the usual epic devices of simile, *ekphrasis* and epithet: the similes not only reflect and intensify the feeling-tone of the narrative and foreshadow the tragedy to come, but also introduce or repeat a dominant motif; the *ekphraseis* (e.g. Fama, the

---

[1] This is a point of some importance. Apollonius, like Homer (cf. *Od*. 6. 119 f.), puts his characters' thoughts into formal soliloquies. Virgil, in general, prefers to read their thoughts into the narrative reserving formal soliloquy for special occasions.

storm) perform much the same function as the similes but also add to the events they accompany, a larger, more public, more ecumenical and even super-human emphasis; the epithets (e.g. *infelix, pius, pulcherrimus*, &c.) strike the particular note that will determine or reinforce the reader's moral reaction to the character involved at a given moment of the action. The similes of Apollonius, on the other hand, have a quite single, univocal function: they directly reflect the immediate action and no more. His epithets have no diffused tonality; his *ekphraseis* (e.g. the description of night) are descriptive rather than evocative and symbolic. All these differences, as we have seen, are manifested at the verbal level in sentence structure, tense differentiation, use of adjectives and participles, metric [1] and colometry. In the case of Virgil, we have the most deliberate conformation of language to a central design or tone; in the case of Apollonius, as of Homer, a much less self-conscious, a much more 'natural' style, that corresponds to the ease and naturalness of the narrative itself.

One result of all this is, as we have clearly seen, that Virgil's characters do not stand out as individuals, as real people in a real society, to anything like the same degree as do those of Apollonius or Homer. Despite the Virgilian empathy and in part because of it, neither Dido nor Aeneas—to say nothing of the lesser characters—impress us as objective human beings in the way that Medea, Chalciope, Aeetes, Jason or even the other Argonauts do. The speeches of Dido and Aeneas are abstract, rhetorically structured, generalized: furthermore the line between them and the empathetic narrative is often very thin indeed; both speeches and narrative are set within the same editorial frame. This does not mean that Dido is not a real character or individual or that we can not sympathize with her. But the fact is that we only see her through Virgilian spectacles, in a very special light and colour. She remains, so to speak, on a peculiar kind of pedestal that is not at all the ordinary ground on which Medea, Chalciope and Chalciope's children stand.

---

[1] A good way of seeing how Apollonius' metric differs from Virgil is to compare *Aeneid* 10. 274–6 with *Arg.* III. 957–9 (the Jason-Sirius simile). We find quite artful onomatopoeia in Apollonius (e.g. *Arg.* III. 967 f.) *but not the emotive effects of Virgil* (cf. e.g. *Arg.* III. 744 f. with *Aeneid* 4. 522 f. or the use of caesurae in *Arg.* III. 970 and *Aeneid* 4 . 76). In other words, *as compared with Virgil*, Apollonius is still Homeric (i.e. retains the Homeric objectivity).

Apollonius to be sure is much less able than Homer to combine familiarity with epic elevation but even he is far more terre à terre, more familiar than Virgil. He has nothing like Virgil's moral tone and purpose to maintain.

The deliberateness or self-consciousness of the Virgilian or 'subjective' style is thus in no sense an indication of poetical superiority or excellence *per se*. A very good case can, in fact, be made for the greater naturalness or spontaneity of Apollonius, to say nothing of Homer. The Medea episode is, in its way, a masterpiece of both narrative and poetry, possessing a freshness and vitality that Virgil never approached and which his style did not permit him to approach. But we must also admit that Virgil's style enabled him to change the whole character of epic and, above all to assimilate its archaic or anachronistic features, its outmoded conventions, to a radically modern, Augustan purpose. For here we finally come to the true meaning or function of the *subjective* style. It made possible the *continuity* and the *symbolic-structure* of his narrative and without these, the *Aeneid* would never have succeeded in combining Homeric material with an un-Homeric, contemporary ideology.

We have already partially seen what the *continuity* of his narrative meant and entailed. In one sense Apollonius gives us a reasonably continuous account of Medea's emotional progress from her first sight of Jason to her acceptance of his offer of marriage, but he does not really assimilate this account to his main narrative: the connection of the two, as we have seen, is superficial and extrinsic; his romantic episode and his heroic plot do not coalesce in an emotional or poetical unity. His gods are brought in to explain the role of Medea in the winning of the fleece but they 'explain' it in a way which makes it quite clear that the love scene is but an adjunct to the real plot. Virgil, on the contrary, is concerned with the love story *only* so far as it is in itself the main plot or is wholly integral to it. But this obviously implies a quite un-Apollonian and un-Homeric conception of the plot or the narrative. For the love story could not have been 'internal' to the plot if the plot itself had not been 'internal' to the characters concerned. Dido was a danger to Aeneas because Aeneas' *love for Dido* was a danger to himself and because Dido's *love for him* was a danger to both of them. In other words, the primary plot or narrative is psychological and subjective, not what the hero does or encounters (as in the *Argonautica*) but how he deals with his own emotions and with other people's emotions, how, in so dealing, he achieves the victory over the unheroical element in himself and in those others whose affection or hatred he engages.

We can now see why the Virgilian empathy and sympathy are so essential to this kind of narrative continuity. We have already indicated the main points and need only summarize them here. The *Aeneid* begins with Aeneas: he is the victim of Juno's wrath and the storm. It is *his* despair (O terque quaterque beati, 94 f.) and *his* revived courage (O socii, &c., 198) that attract our initial attention. After the Jupiter prophecy, it is to Aeneas that we return (at pius Aeneas 305) and with Aeneas that we are empathetically identified (per noctem plurima volvens, &c.). It is through Aeneas' eyes that we see Venus, and it is, particularly, Aeneas' reflections that we follow as he enters the rising city, and gazes at the frieze of the Juno temple. It is *through him* that we see Dido for the first time: right up to line 656 he is the 'empathetic center' of our attention.

Then the re-entry of Venus marks a definite shift from Aeneas to Dido: by line 712 Dido is the centre of empathy; she is the mind whose thoughts we read and around whom the narrative revolves (expleri mentem nequit ardescitque tuendo). But the movement of Aeneas' thoughts (ever since his meeting with Venus) had already led us to Dido: the transition is thus quite natural but it is also crucial since it is only through her ill-omened passion, her fatal love-wound, that Dido takes our full empathetic attention (praecipue infelix). This attention does not leave Dido until 4. 90 when the gods or rather goddesses once more intervene. The cave scene it itself quite neutral (it is written from neither Aeneas' nor Dido's point of view) until, at its end, we gain one brief moment of insight into Dido's thoughts: nec iam furtivum Dido meditatur amorem (171). The ensuing Fama-Iarbas-Jupiter-Mercury sequence (173–278) redirects our attention back to Aeneas so that in line 279 we once more become empathetically identified with him (Heu quid agat? &c.). The narrative has now passed from *love* to the feelings and reactions of a guilty conscience. At last the way is open for the direct confrontation (in direct speeches) of the two lovers (295–392). We then see at least enough of Aeneas' thoughts to realize his shocked reversion to *pietas* (at pius Aeneas, 393), we witness the renewed entreaties of Dido (408 f.), and once more glimpse the unyielding resistance of Aeneas (441 f.). The hopelessness of Dido then leads her steadily toward suicide: she naturally holds the empathetic centre (losing it only for the brief moment of Aeneas' final departure, 554–83) as her tragedy goes toward its climactic end with that of the Book (4) itself.

We have here, therefore, the following major shifts of empathetic focus: Aeneas (seeking security)—Dido (love)—Aeneas (guilt and resistance to love)—Dido-Aeneas (in confrontation) —Dido (despair and suicide). What causes and also gives continuity to the shifts is, essentially, the conflict between Dido's *amor* and Aeneas' *pietas*. He is at first passive, an observer, a recipient of Dido's passion: we see him as it were, through Dido, as the object of her passion and passionate initiative. He only regains the centre of empathetic attention when he takes the initiative himself by resisting her. After this her own initiative can only turn destructive, but this also takes all our attention for it is once again *her* initiative (all Aeneas can do is carry out his escape). The continuity of the whole narrative is thus an internal, or psychological one which at once reflects a conflict *between* two individuals and a conflict *within* each. We hardly need to re-emphasize the difference of all this from the *Argonautica*. Apollonius shifts his scenes almost arbitrarily as the time-schedule of his essentially non-psychological plot demands (thus, e.g. leaving Eros in mid-air in order to get the Argonauts to Aeetes' palace and again abandoning Medea at the very beginning of her amour, in order to hatch the plot of the Argonauts and Chalciope) but Virgil always prepares each shift of our attention (from Aeneas to Dido or vice versa) by a previous *psychological* development.

But the continuity of the Virgilian narrative is not *only* psychological. In one sense the Dido-Aeneas story is a strictly human one. The stranded and desolate hero learns of the remarkable heroine and finally meets her at the very height of her activity and power: their amour is an almost obvious consequence of their respective characters and situations. Its disastrous ending is in turn a consequence of destinies which, even on a quite human level, they cannot evade. All this Virgil shows: but he also shows much more, the broad *historical* and *cosmic* meaning of the human love story. Here his use of the traditional divine-machinery of epic is an integral part of his editorial or 'sympathetic' style. The human and the divine sectors of the poem are linked by a far-reaching system of *motifs*: the effect is to set up a diffused reaction between the human and the divine (or cosmic) so that the one takes on the colour of the other, the human is given cosmic depth, the cosmic is given human significance. We thus see a transformation of all the conventional epic devices—not merely epic gods but epic similes, *ekphraseis*, epithets and speeches—into a single editorial structure that does not intrude at certain special points but penetrates the poem with the same continuity as that of the narrative itself. It is only by understanding this most complicated and subtle editorial structure that we can understand Virgil's major achievement in epic, his fusion of Augustan and Homeric or Apollonian elements into a poetical unity.

The *Aeneid* begins by mentioning the many woes that its hero had to suffer at the hands of Juno, the goddess who never forgot (saevae memorem Iunonis ob iram). And to the question why a celestial mind should harbour such wrath, Virgil replies by an apparent digression: *Urbs antiqua fuit . . . Karthago*. It was in effect Juno's 'wounded love' for Carthage that was the main cause of her opposition to Aeneas. She stands for the losing side of the conflict on which all history was to depend, both for Carthage and for the *furor*, the ultimate irrationality that resists fate. The storm which she sends and which drives Aeneas to Carthage is, as it were, the *motif* or symbol of Juno, of *furor*, of anti-fate. On the other hand, Venus is the tutelary *daimon* of Rome, though also, like Juno, operating on a sub-fatal level: she too stands for an irrational force, that of sexual as well as maternal *amor*. Though she hears Jupiter's revelation of the 'secrets' of Fate, she quite fails to grasp his *modus operandi* and is in no sense his agent. In point of fact, the temporary alliance or collusion of the two goddesses in Book 4 and, proleptically in Book 1 (since in effect Juno sends Aeneas to Carthage by means of the storm and Venus promotes the actual amour there) is almost disruptive of Jupiter's or fate's intention and has to be countered by his direct intervention (the mission of Mercury).

We should indeed note that Jupiter had already sent Mercury
(in Book 1, 297–304) to insure Dido's hospitality to Aeneas:
Mercury's second mission (in Book 4) was only necessitated by
the quite officious and unnecessary interference of Venus that,
of course, brought back the maleficent Juno and thus produced
the disaster of the 'second storm' and the cave. We can say in
brief: *Amor* joined to *furor* threaten *pietas* and *fatum*; *fatum* then
reacts to set *pietas* once more on its course. In the end Dido,
Juno *and* Carthage (the cosmic and historical instances of
furor) are the losers.

But this fairly obvious symbolism would have been quite artificial, quite extrinsic to the narrative, had Virgil not also constructed his narrative to confirm to it at every point. The
introductory storm scene (through Jupiter's prophecy, i.e. to line
305 of Book 1) brings on all the forces that are to dominate the
epic but, in itself, it is only proleptic: the narrative proper, which
is to show the forces in action, has barely begun. The real 'storm'
is ahead and is human and psychological. What really threatens
Aeneas is his encounter with Dido at the exact moment when
he has once more begun to hope and has seemingly recovered
from the objective or physical storm. It is not *until then* that
Venus sends Cupid to play his fatal trick on Dido. That her *amor*
is *infelix*, fatal, impious is clearly indicated at the time of its
very inception (close of Book 1). Her human love story—and it
is a fully human one without the slightest need for divine
motivation—is from the start invested with the tonality of high
tragedy. All the motifs and editorialisms—the wound, the flame,
the dying doe, Virgil's pity for her blind attempt to get the
oracles on her side—indicate Dido's *furor* and point to the
impending calamity. Then Juno's re-entry, collaboration with
Venus and action (the storm) make overt the psychological
fury of Dido's and Aeneas' *amor*. The two storms have now been
linked: the inner nature of Junonian *furor* is revealed. But it is
only when *amor-furor* becomes a public calamity (Fama, Iarbas)
that the narrative reaches social-historical and cosmic (Jupiter)
dimensions. We now (via Jupiter-Mercury) see Aeneas and his
guilty submission to Dido in the perspective of fate itself, just as
Mercury sees him in Tyrian costume building the new Carthage.
But his contrition and his recovery of *pietas* are *also* human and
psychological: he sees he has been false to his father, his mission,

his men, Ascanius, &c. The old motifs then take on a new dimension in the new phase of the story: Dido's *amor* becomes, when thwarted, the *furor* of hatred and reckless malevolence (thus clearly resembling Juno's, and, like Juno's, wreaking eventual destruction on her own Carthage); the love *wound* becomes Dido's death *wound* and Carthage's as well; the *flames* (simile of 669–71) are now likened to those of the Third Punic War; the mad rage of Fama now spreads the news of consummated tragedy. Aeneas (once more *pius*) puts to sea in an atmosphere which repeats—on so much deeper a level—the *furor* of his arrival and yet measures the tremendous significance of his departure.

We can now grasp the real difference of Virgil and Apollonius, of the 'subjective' and 'objective' styles. Virgil's essential narrative is psychological and empathetic: this is why the symbols and motifs can 'correspond' to or be attached to affective or emotive elements of his narrative. Neither the narrative nor the symbol-structure are external or simply additive to each other. Apollonius could not achieve any such correlation because his love story is only a small part of an essentially non-psychological, non-empathetic plot—a plot of physical action and adventure—and it is solely with the latter element that his gods and goddesses are concerned. It is not the amour but its quite tangible result, the acquisition of Medea's magic, in which Hera and Athene are interested. The very basis of Virgil's symbol or motif structure is thus lacking and the result is an evident failure to assimilate the conventional epic elements of plot or style to the 'psychological' sections of the narrative. Without a *continuous* empathetic narrative, an editorialized symbol-structure was quite impossible.

But we have hardly as yet touched upon either the narrative or the symbol-structure of the whole *Aeneid*. Indeed we can scarcely understand the full meaning of *Aeneid* 1 and 4 until we have grasped their relation to the other books. There are, clearly, three major elements in the poem: the continuous psychological narrative, the essential *fatum-furor-pietas* complex, and the Homeric plot motifs (the storm, *nekuia*, games, detaining woman, &c.). (At least this is true of the first six books: the last six are, as we shall see, somewhat different.) The inter-relating or rather inter-diffusing of these three elements was a task of extraordinary complexity. No poet could have attempted it without much preliminary work if, that is, he lacked, as Virgil did, a long tradition of similar poetry on which to build. Nor can we ourselves understand the *Aeneid*'s difficult and elaborate structure without some knowledge of its predecessors, the *Eclogues* and *Georgics*. We must turn back to the simpler origins in order, finally, to comprehend the intricate masterpiece. All we have so far gained is a preliminary and necessarily inadequate idea of Virgil's subjective style. Only as we begin to see the basic difference between it and the 'objective style' of Homer or Apollonius or, presumably, all other Greek epic, can we begin to solve the extraordinary problem it presents.

CHAPTER IV

THE YOUNG VIRGIL

THE earliest work of Virgil that has come down to us is the
collection of ten short poems usually known as the
Bucolics or *Eclogues*. It was a work of his late twenties and
early thirties (42–39 B.C. or possibly, 38).[1] Undoubtedly he had
written much poetry before this—the *Bucolics* are no callow
beginning—but this poetry is not preserved: it is now reasonably
certain that the so-called *Appendix Virgiliana* is *not* a collection of
Virgil's *juvenilia* but the very inferior production of a Virgilianiz-
ing poet of the later Augustan age or thereafter.[2] The great
interest of the *Eclogues* for our present purpose is that they show
in embryo, so to speak, the two main features of the subjective
style of the *Aeneid* which were discussed in the last chapter:
the psychological *continuity* of narrative and the *symbolic
structure*. But these features appear in a quite peculiar guise:
the 'continuity' belongs to very brief narrative episodes—in
some cases, scarcely even narrative on any strict definition—in a
few individual poems (particularly *Eclogues* 2, 6, 8); and anything like a 'symbolic structure' is to be found only in the
arrangement of the ten poems as published together by Virgil in 38
or 37 B.C. We must therefore consider each feature quite
separately: Virgil did not begin to integrate them in one unified
whole until his next phase, that of the *Georgics*, which we shall
discuss in the next chapter.

I

We have seen that the *narrative continuity* of the first and fourth
books of the *Aeneid* was dependent upon the maintenance of an
'empathetic continuum' by means of which the emotional drama

---

[1] Full data on chronology are given in Schanz-Hosius, *Römische-Literatur-
Geschichte* ii, pp. 37–38, 49–50, 57–58. The sources do not permit us to say more
than that the *Eclogues* were written between 42–41 and 39–38 with some possibility
that *Eclogue* 10 is later (e.g. 37) though attempts to date Lycoris' Alpine trip
(referred to in 10) are highly conjectural. At any rate it seems safe to say that the
complete Eclogue Book is not later than the end of 37.

[2] See the discussions of the Appendix in Büchner, 70–160; Westendorp-Boerma,
P. Vergili Maronis Catalepton I (1949), introduction, *passim*.

of two people was taken from their first encounter to their final tragic separation. Virgil followed two souls through an intensely dramatic experience, and followed them not as an external observer but as a participant of their inmost thoughts and feelings. The two main characteristics of this kind of continuity are thus its *subjective* character and its *dramatic* content.

It is in these two aspects, precisely, that Virgil differed from both Homer and Apollonius. Their epic style was, in the largest sense, *objective* and *non-dramatic*. We have seen this in one long episode (comparison of the Dido and Medea stories) but it is equally evident in the shorter episodes. Both Homer and Apollonius, for instance, describe a boxing contest (*Iliad* 23. 653–99; *Argonautica* II. 1–163) and Virgil followed their example (*Aeneid* 5. 362–484), but he converted what was in them a simply physical action into something of a psychological drama. In Homer and Apollonius, as in Theocritus (*Idyll* 22), the contests (Epeius with Euryalus; Amycus with Polydeuces) are quite ordinary fights with no true climax except for the almost preordained victory of the stronger (Epeius) or cleverer (Polydeuces). Virgil typically *dramatizes* his fight: the old man, Entellus, is at the start no match for his younger and more agile opponent (Dares), and falls with a terrible crash: but this rouses his *pudor* and *ira* and he comes back to overwhelm Dares and finally force Aeneas to take him out of the contest. In the fight we share the old man's feelings and empathetically grasp the change of spirit, the renewed strength, caused by his fall. Just as in the foot-race, an emotional reaction (there Nisus' feeling for Euryalus; here the shame of the old ex-hero) determines the physical event and brings about a dramatic peripety. We have seen also how Virgil converted Homer's chariot race into a contest in which all the participants had some chance of winning and victory came dramatically at the very last moment of the race. Here too it is the feelings, the reactions of the contestants that counted and even determined the result (e.g. the hot temper of Gyas, the piety of Cloanthus).

Did Virgil have any precedent for this kind of narrative? It is certainly true that quâ Roman he was far more likely to write empathetically than a Greek. Consider the following lines of Ennius (Vahlen 1.82 ff.):

certabant urbem Romam Remoramque *vocarent.*
omnibus *cura* viris uter *esset* induperator.
expectant, veluti consul cum mittere signum
volt, omnes *avidi spectant* ad carceris oras,
quam mox emittat pictis e faucibus currus,
sic *expectabat* populus, &c.

Here the imperfects, the subjunctives, the vivid presents (*volt,*
spectant), the adjectives (*avidi*) all have an empathetic cast: we
see the aims of Romulus and Remus *as they struggle,* the concern
of the people, the terrible expectancy (the simile has a vividly
empathetic force). To come to a much later precursor of Virgil,
Lucretius also is full of empathy. Consider such lines as the
following description of Iphigenia:

I. 89   et *maestum simul* ante aras adstare *parentem*
            sensit et hunc propter ferrum *celare* ministros
            aspectuque suo lacrimas *effundere* civis.
            muta metu terram genibus summissa *petebat.*

We experience not only what she sees, but how she feels as she
sees it (hence the present infinitives and the imperfect). There
can be no doubt that such passages have a truly Roman ring:
Greek narrative verse is far more objective, far less internal to
the characters described in it, as is evident even in such a
strikingly psychological passage as Apollonius' description of
Medea's first love (*Arg.* III. 451 f.).[1]

But there is no evidence that any Roman before Virgil had
done what he did with empathy in narrative. It is plain, even
from its scattered fragments, that Ennius' *Annales* maintained
no continuous 'subjective' narrative on any kind of consistent
psychological scheme. Generally speaking, as we have seen in
Chapter I, Roman epic before Virgil was either annalistic and
chronological (Roman history or Roman wars told in verse) in
its arrangement or a more or less faithful imitation of an
Hellenistic model (like, e.g. the *Argonautica* of P. Terentius
Varro). Probably the kind of 'narrative' that influenced Virgil
most was the 'short epic' of his mentor, Cinna, and of the new
poets generally. In some ways, this is certainly closer to his own
style than that of any other *genre*, but it is, as we have seen,

---

[1] The difference between Greek and Roman narrative poetry is a subject far too
large to be discussed here. Actually no adequate treatment of it exists. See preface.

deficient in the most essential narrative quality, action, movement or dramatic progression. Here it carried on and even intensified the immobility of its Alexandrine and Hellenistic predecessors (see Chapter I).

Thus Catullus' *and Peleus Thetis* (64) is full of sympathetic remarks to the characters (most of all Ariadne) and, especially rich in empathetic feeling. The famous lines describing Ariadne as she wakes to find herself alone and deserted on the shore of Dia (52–75) permit us to feel with and through the heroine at every point:

53   Thesea cedentem celeri cum classe tuetur
      indomitos in corde gerens Ariadna furores,
      necdum etiam sese quae visit visere credit
      ut pote *fallaci* quae tunc primum excita somno
      desertam in sola *miseram se cernat* harena.

But though the empathy is all but complete, *it is put to no dramatic use*. The episode is frozen, so to speak, to its frame (the tapestry) and though there is a brief 'flash-back' to the beginning of her story and a brief account of Aegeus' death in the future, Ariadne herself is immobilized in one moment of pathos. Her long soliloquy reiterates and dwells on it; her pictorial setting forbids any true movement out of it. As for the actual Peleus and Thetis story, it is obviously more of a frame than a narrative in its own right; its function is to provide a bright, moral contrast (the happy association of men and gods at a happy marriage of a man and a goddess) to a sad tale of broken faith and disrupted love.

And though the *Peleus and Thetis* is, strictly speaking, the only instance of the neoteric 'short epic' that has come down to us, we can, with high probability, regard it as typical of the genre. Catullus' *Attis* (63) is no epic: its galliambic metre and lyric intensity put it in quite another category. But it shows also the same approach to narrative as the *Peleus and Thetis*. We see Attis in two pathetic moments (as the frenzied *galla* and the rueful penitent) each 'expanded' by a declamatory soliloquy, but there is no dramatic progression from one to the other (it is in fact the sleep induced by his emotional excesses which restores him to temporary sobriety). The empathy is intense but leads nowhere.

But it is the pseudo-Virgilian *Ciris* that provides, perhaps, our best evidence for taking the *Peleus and Thetis* as typical of the genre. The *Ciris* is probably a product of the later Augustan or early Tiberian era: it shows nonetheless an obvious and intimate knowledge of the neoteric short epic on which it is modelled, of the *Peleus and Thetis* but also of Calvus' *Io* and, above all, of Cinna's *Zmyrna*.[1] There is very strong evidence that it repeats the arrangement of the *Zmyrna* in the elaborate central dialogue between Scylla and her nurse, Carme. And this is important since the long dialogue in the *Ciris* in effect corresponds to the tapestry in the *Peleus and Thetis*: both are devices for 'expanding' and giving space to a single pathetic moment (in the *Ciris* *Scylla*'s indecision before cutting the lock; in the *Peleus and Thetis*, Ariadne's emotional reaction to her abandonment by Theseus). Furthermore, the *Ciris* also uses monologue (Scylla's on the eve of metamorphosis) or soliloquy in the same way as the *Attis* or *Peleus and Thetis*, to expand and develop a quite static *pathos* or pathetic moment. We can likewise draw, with somewhat greater reservations, the same conclusions as to the nature of neoteric short epic from Ovid's *Metamorphoses* and *Heroides* and from elegiac narrative generally. Ovid was clearly influenced by Virgil; and his empathetic narratives, in the *Metamorphoses* at least, do progress in a quasi-Virgilian manner (cf. e.g. his account of Scylla with the *Ciris*) but, even when we allow for this, we can still discern in places, the influence of neoteric sources.[2]

The neoteric *epos* was thus no model for the kind of narrative Virgil came to write in the *Aeneid*, but it did point the way for him. Its strong use of empathy as well as of editorial sympathy (here going far beyond the Alexandrine familiarity), its attempt to return to something of the old epic content and style (as opposed to the 'modernizing' and 'lightness' of Callimachus and Theocritus) and above all its *seriousness* (its almost total absence of frivolity) all represented a new and Roman spirit in a genre that was otherwise so Hellenistic. The trouble was that these elements of a new style had not as yet been fused together: the *Ciris* with its Alexandrine chattiness, its Roman

---

[1] See Appendix 1.
[2] I plan to treat the whole subject of Ovid's hexameter narrative elsewhere. See my remarks in the preface.

empathy and sympathy, its occasional epic flights, its odd descents into the didactic, is only an exaggeration of traits we also find in the *Peleus and Thetis*; the neoteric epic had not yet achieved a unified style. Virgil did achieve this, but not without radically recasting what the neoterics had provided. If then we want to find a more direct source of Virgil's empathetically continuous narrative, we must turn in quite another direction. It has not often been realized that Catullus' *libellus* and in particular his Lesbia poems constitute a kind of narrative—a narrative of emotional experience and dramatically contrasted feelings. The facts that the individual poems are lyric or elegiac in form, are not explicitly connected, and above all are autobiographical or confessional rather than normally 'objective' narrative, do not in themselves change the intrinsic character of Catullus' achievement. The line between the *autobiographical* first or third person of lyric and the *empathetic* first or third person of epic is often very thin: Catullus himself did not carry his lyric or elegiac style into his formal hexameter narrative but he had laid down no rule against such a procedure and his total *corpus* or body of work constituted a virtual invitation to it. At any rate this is the step that Virgil seems to have taken.

We can see the situation best by considering a few of Catullus' elegies.[1] Let us start with 70, one of the so-called 'epigrams' of the Lesbia cycle:

> Nulli se dicit mulier mea nubere malle
> Quam mihi, non si se Iuppiter ipse petat.
> Dicit: sed mulier cupido quod dicit amanti
> In vento et rapida scribere oportet aqua.

This at first sight does not seem particularly autobiographic and in fact is obviously based on a well-known epigram of Callimachus (Pfeiffer XXV):

> Ὤμοσε Καλλίγνωτος Ἰωνίδι μήποτ' ἐκείνης
> ἕξειν μήτε φίλον κρέσσονα μήτε φίλην.

---

[1] Probably the best monograph on Catullus' epigrams is that of Oskar Hezel, *Catull und das griechische Epigramm* (*Tübinger Beiträge zur Altertumswiss.* 17, 1932). Cf. also O. Weinreich, *Die Distichen des Catull* (1926); D. Braga, *Catullo e i Poeti Greci* (1950), pp. 138–54. None of these works, however, sees the crucial importance of *temporal continuity* in Catullus' epigrams (esp. where this is reinforced by clear cross references between poems) and they also, for the most part, miss the significance of Catullus' metric.

ὤμοσεν· ἀλλὰ λέγουσιν ἀληθέα τοὺς ἐν ἔρωτι
ὅρκους μὴ δύνειν οὔατ' ἐς ἀθανάτων.
νῦν δ' ὁμὲν ἀρσενικῷ θέρεται πυρί, τῆς δὲ ταλαίνης
νύμφης ὡς Μεγαρέων οὐ λόγος οὐδ' ἀριθμός.

Swore Callignotus to his Ionis
Never to leave her for boy or for girl.
He swore, but oaths of lovers, it's well said,
Do not reach up to the ears of the gods.
Now he's inflamed by a boy. Of the poor girl Ionis
His account is as nil as a bankrupt's.

Not only the similarity of ideas but the repeated ὤμοσε (=
Catullus' *dicit*) and the parallelism of ὤμοσεν ἀλλὰ and *dicit: sed*
make the derivation certain. The difference between Callimachus and Catullus is that the former uses generalities (the
suspiciously generic names, Callignotus and Ionis, the very
general oath in line 2, the vague τοὺς ἐν ἔρωτι or 'those in
love') and the latter uses concrete and personal terms: *mulier
mea, cupidus amans*, the specific oath, *non si se Iuppiter ipse petat*.
Callimachus seems to be giving us a quite conventional *topos*
(the gods' indifference to lovers' oaths) in a light and ironic
style; Catullus, a serious statement of his own disillusionment
with an unfaithful mistress whom he still loves (mea mulier).

This difference of tone comes through the rhythmic movement of the two poems perhaps even more clearly than through
the words and the sense. Catullus': *Nulli se dicit mulier mea
nubere malle* differs from Callimachus': Ὤμοσε Καλλίγνωτος
Ἰωνίδι μήποτ' ἐκείνης both by its slow spondaic beginning
and by its emphasis (through diaeresis and caesura) of *nulli, se
dicit*, as well as by the grammatical rearrangement and the shift
of the subject from the man to the mistress. Instead of a typical
oath between two unknowns, we have the emphasized solemnity
of the lover dwelling on what *his* mistress has promised. Again
the difference between the lines:

$$- \ - \ - \quad \cup \ \cup - \cup \ \cup \ - \quad - \quad - \cup \ \cup - \ -$$
dicit: sed mulier cupido quod dicit amanti
$$- \ \cup \ \cup \ - \ \cup \ \cup \ - \ \cup \ \cup \ - \cup \cup \ - \quad \cup \ \cup \ - \cup$$
ὤμοσεν ἀλλὰ λέγουσιν ἀληθέα τοὺς ἐν ἔρωτι

is even more revealing: Callimachus' line is all dactyls, with no
strong breaks except after the first ὤμοσεν; Catullus metrically
emphasizes *cupido* (between two strong caesurae) as well. His

repetition of *dicit* in the same line (but beginning a dactyl rather than a spondee) sets Lesbia's easy promise against the strong emotion of her lover (cupido, amanti). The difference in metres corresponds to a radical difference in feeling.

So we suspect even from this one 'imitation' of Callimachus that Catullus has a personal as well as a literary source for his 'epigram'. But does this 'oath' of Lesbia (if it is Lesbia) have any *dramatic* content or setting? It is a present-general or a specifically temporal phenomenon? Our answer is supplied by 72 which expressly recalls the language of 70:

> Dicebas quondam solum te nosse Catullum
> Lesbia, nec prae me velle tenere Iovem.

The imperfect *dicebas* suggests a past state—a certain period of the past, not a mere moment—but Catullus immediately differentiates his *new* experience and knowledge from this past in the following lines:

3   Dilexi *tum* te non tantum ut vulgus amicam
          Sed pater ut gnatos diligit et generos.

then he leaps to the present:

5   *Nunc* te *cognovi:* quare etsi impensius uror,
              Multo mi tamen es vilior et levior.
          Qui potis est? inquis. Quod amantem iniuria talis
              Cogit amare magis, sed bene velle minus.

Thus what may have seemed an exercise after Callimachus on the most commonplace of amatory *topoi* is really shown to be part of a dramatic continuum: the oath, the state of Catullus' affections at the time of the oath, and his subsequent (present) disillusionment that, however, cannot quench but rather increases his passion. But 76 introduces a *third* stage: it recalls the oath once more (though with emphasis on his *own* good-faith, ll. 1–4) but now admits that Lesbia's ingratitude has gone so far there is nothing but torture left for him and therefore the necessity of getting rid of the burden of love altogether—of the *pestis, pernicies* and *morbus* which have brought him to such misery.

One can, with perhaps somewhat less certainty, find more direct 'recalls' of one poem by another in Catullus.[1] It is at any

---

[1] Certainly 75. 3–4: *ut iam nec bene velle queat tibi, si optima fias, | nec desistere amare, omnia si facias* recalls or is recalled by ll. 7–8 of 72. 85 (Odi et amo) is also certainly associated with 76 (esp. l. 10). Cf. also 73 and 72. Poems 72, 73, 75, 76, 85 obviously form one interrelated cycle.

rate clear that the Lesbia poems as a whole—both elegies and lyric polymetra—describe an amour extending through several stages, from initial passion to both preliminary and final disillusionment. This is certainly a Roman phenomenon in that we can find no such continuity in Greek lyric or elegy: Sappho's emotions, for example, are intense but not, so far as we can tell, related in anything like a dramatic sequence of lyrics. The fact that such an approach to lyric and elegy was no monopoly of Catullus, is amply evidenced in the amatory elegies of Gallus, Tibullus, Propertius and Ovid. Here again we can descry a continuous narrative of personal experience, though it must be admitted that the dramatic force of Catullus has evaporated and that the love experience itself is so fused with conventional amatory *topoi* as to become at times nothing more than an artificial jeu d'esprit (it seems wholly so in Ovid).

At any rate we can now see that many of the elements of Virgil's subjective style were already present in his Roman and, particularly, in his neoteric background. But no one, so far as we can tell, had as yet written an empathetically continuous *narrative*—something that was at once more than the static pathos of neoteric 'little epic' and more than the autobiographic continuity of Catullan or neoteric lyric and elegy. Furthermore no neoteric poet had as yet perfected a unified hexameter narrative style, a style that could unite neoteric empathy and sympathy with epic dignity and seriousness in one integrated poetical whole. This was Virgil's situation when he started to write the *Eclogues*. His associations had been largely neoteric: Cinna was his mentor; Gallus his friend and patron; Callimachus and Theocritus his literary and literary-critical models. No past or present model really anticipated what he was to do.

We shall begin our analysis of the *Eclogues* with a poem (8) that contains perhaps the most finished narrative of the whole collection. The poem is divided between the songs of two shepherds, Damon and Alphesiboeus. Each is quite independent: it is with the former (Damon's, ll. 17–61) only that we are here concerned. This Damon-song consists of nine stanzas of 2–5 lines divided by a refrain (the model for the arrangement is obviously Theocritus 1).[1] They are delivered in the first person by a

---

[1] Curiously no previous critic has (to my knowledge) brought out the climactic and dramatic structure of this eclogue. Cartault *Étude sur les Bucoliques de Virgile*, (1897, pp. 307–8), for example, misses the childhood-adulthood contrast of Stanzas

shepherd-lover about to drown himself through anguish at the unfaithfulness of his false love, Nisa. She has deserted him to marry the unspeakable Mopsus. At first glance the narrative continuity seems slight; this, however, is a deceptive impression; actually the shepherd-lover tells a dramatic story of himself and his emotions, a story that leads him from love through disillusionment to suicide. We must look first at the poem's arrangement or plan: the strophic arrangement (the nine sections separated by the cry of *Incipe Maenalios mecum, mea tibia, versus*) is actually a most important part of its narrative structure. (See page 107).

It is thus clear that Stanzas II–III and VIII–IX correspond: the 'topsy-turvy' theme in Stanzas III and VIII *and* the reference to the countryside (silvae, nemus, pinusque loquentis) in Stanzas II and IX. Stanza I (addressed to the Gods) and introductory to the whole is likewise recalled at the end of Stanza IX (extrema moriens . . . hora—extremum hoc munus morientis). Finally Stanza IV is recalled by Stanza VII: Nisa by her fatal exemplar in love, Medea. The true kernel of the poem is thus constituted by Stanzas V and VI: love as it seemed to be when the shepherd conceived his childish passion for Nisa in the orchard and love as he *now* (*Nunc* scio quid sit Amor) knows it after bitter experience. But this new knowledge—as revealed in Stanzas V and VI—affects *also* Stanzas VII, VIII and IX: he *now* knows what a woman can do from love and *now* sees that Nisa, like Medea, is in no sense cleared of blame for responding to so wicked a teacher; *now* indeed the wolf can flee from the sheep, &c., i.e. he *now* finally sees the true topsy-turviness of the world in seeing how his own conception of love and Nisa has been reversed. So the correspondences between the earlier and later stanzas in no sense detract from the rising motion—the growing emotion—of the song: rather the later stanzas are given a heightened emphasis, a deeper pathos by their recall of the earlier, and the suicide comes as a true climax.

V and VI; Georg Rohde (*De Vergilii eclogarum forma et indole*, 1925) sees only a certain 'gradation of emotion' (gradatio quaedam, qua leniter et lente via ad culmen carminis munitur) and Pfeiffer (*Virgils Bukolika*, 1933) only a formal structure ('rahmentechnisch'). Büchner alone (211) talks of the poem as a 'drama' and seems to recognize its dramatic content but (despite his lengthy treatment of other poems) supplies no adequate analysis of its structure (the combination of balanced verses with climactic movement, the transition from the Nisa-Mopsus contrast of the beginning to the knowledge-error contrast of the close).

I. (ll. 17–20): The lover complains (of Nisa's treacherous deception) to the *Gods* at the hour just before dawn (Nascere, praeque diem veniens age, Lucifer, almum) and he declares that these are his last words (extrema moriens . . . hora).

II. (ll. 22–24): He refers to Arcadia (Maenalus) and its eloquent (argutum) *grove* and speaking *pines*; it is always ready to hear of the loves of shepherds and listen to Pan who first roused the sleeping pipes to life. (In effect, the lover addresses his Arcadian country-side right after the Gods: he will refer to it again at the end: *vivite silvae*. l. 58, *extremum hoc munus habeto*, l. 60.)

III. (ll. 26–30): The theme of the world turned topsy-turvy because: *Mopso Nisa datur* (omitting line 28a).

IV. (ll. 32–35): Ironical address to *Nisa*: O digno coniuncta viro, &c.

V. (ll. 37–41): The inception of his love in the orchard when he and Nisa were children (the lover speaks in the first person directly to Nisa).

VI. (ll. 43–45): *Nunc scio, quid sit Amor: nudis in cotibus illum*, &c. He *now* (i.e. at a mature age) knows the bitter truth about love.

VII. (ll. 47–50): Still on *Amor*: the wicked (improbus) teacher. Then *Medea* (the prime exhibit of what *amor* can do) is herself addressed along with *Amor*.

VIII. (ll. 52–56): *Nunc et ovis ultro fugiat lupus*, &c. Return to the theme of the world turned topsy-turvy.

IX. (ll. 58–60): End of the 'topsy-turvy' theme (*Omnia vel medium fiat mare*) and by it, transition to the last farewell to the *woods* and the explicit declaration of his (immediate) future suicide (*praeceps . . . deferar: extremum hoc munus morientis habeto*).

The real theme then of Virgil here is the *contrast* between the idyllic orgin and the later (present) reality of love which is also identified with the apparent (original) nature of Nisa and her later over-turning of it by her marriage to Mopsus. But in reality it is not Nisa's character but the lover's world which is turned upside down: he has been deceived (deceptus) from the start; Nisa's love is *indignus* (l. 18) and the unspeakable Mopsus is worthy of her (digno coniuncta viro, l. 32) because the lover has from the start been carried away by a *malus error* (l. 41). His world (as he once conceived it) has been turned upside down and that is why he can no longer endure to live in it. In fact, however, the change is in himself: he has until *now* (Nunc scio quid sit Amor) confused reality and appearance. The contrasts here (which make his world topsy-turvy) can be thus set forth:

The lover	vs.	Mopsus
Nisa (as his prospective coniunx)	vs.	Nisa (actually married to Mopsus)
symbolizing by implication		symbolizing
Medea (as Jason's love)	vs.	Medea (as unnatural monster)
His former love (in the orchard when Nisa was his childhood 'coniunx')	vs.	The *improbus Amor* that he knows *now*
Time (the Past: from age 12)	vs.	Time (Now: *Nunc. scio, nunc et ovis ultro fugiat lupus*)
The orchard (where he thought his love was born)	vs.	The rocks (where his love was really born)
The mother of little children at play	vs.	The *crudelis mater* who can kill her own children
The woods (where he sings) Vivite silvae/argutum nemus pinusque loquentes	vs.	The sea (where he drowns himself: omnia vel medium fiat mare)
Orpheus in silvis	vs.	inter delphinas Arion

The poignancy of the speaker's (lover's) present is that *in it* he grasps all these discontinuities, sees his own world turned upside down. This is why suicide seems the only possibility. Until we sense this tremendous revolution in the lover's soul and world, the hyperbolical language of Stanzas VIII and IX will seem only far fetched. In fact they express the lover's conversion of his internal peripety into universal terms. Thus this curious 'song' is really a continuous, dramatic narrative in which an event—Nisa's marriage to Mopsus—precipitates an emotional reaction that leads to suicide: the shepherd-lover now sees that he has confused appearance and reality, that his present has abolished his past, that his whole world has gone.

Here there is no static moment of pathos; an intense tragedy has taken place under our very eyes. The shepherd-lover is in one sense delivering a monologue, yet it is not the declamatory monologue of an Ariadne or an Attis but the record of his own thoughts and feelings in the very moment that he comes to a realization of what has happened and of its consequences to himself.

The remarkable thing about the poem is the way in which the young Virgil has built a wholly novel type of narrative—a narrative as unneoteric as it is unalexandrine—out of isolated scraps of Theocritus. It is worth while to see this in some detail. The following schema shows the parallels.

Virgil (*Eclogue* 8) (in stanzas)	Theocritus (*Idylls* 1, 2, 3, 11) (with citation of lines)
i Lover's appeal to the Gods	Daphnis' appeal to the gods in 1
ii Appeal to the whole Arcadian *countryside*	1. 123–6: Daphnis' appeal to Pan to come *from* Arcadia *to* Sicily
iii Nisa married to Mopsus: iungentur iam grypes equis aevoque sequenti cum canibus venient ad pocula dammae	1. 132–6: let brambles bear violets, &c. let all be changed . . . since Daphnis is dying: let the stag worry the hounds
iv Ironical address to Nisa: her fastidious rejection of the lover contrasted with her choice of Mopsus	3. 8–9: Amaryllis' disdain of the snub-nosed, bearded shepherd 11. 30–3: Polyphemus on Galatea's dislike of his eye, eyebrow, &c.
v The origin of love in the orchard (when the shepherd was 12 years old)	11. 25–29: Polyphemus and Galatea meet when she with his mother, picks hyacinths on the hill
ut vidi, ut perii, ut me malus abstulit error	2. 82: χὼς ἴδον, ὡς ἐμάνην So saw I, so went mad: ὥς μοι πυρὶ θυμὸς ἰάφθη my heart went up in flame (the love-sickness of Simaetha)

Virgil (*Eclogue* 8) (in stanzas)	Theocritus (*Idylls* 1, 2, 3, 11) (with citation of lines)
	3. 42: ὡς ἴδεν ὡς ἐμάνη, Thus saw she, thus went mad, ὡς ἐς βαθὺν ἅλατ᾽ ἔρωτα Thus deep in love she plunged (Atalanta's love for Hippomenes).
vi Nunc scio quid sit amor	3. 15: νῦν ἔγνων τὸν Ἔρωτα 'Now I know Eros; he sucked a lioness's dug': the speaker is Amaryllis' lover, the snubnosed shepherd
vii Cruel amor taught Medea to kill her children: both Medea and Amor are cruel	No Theocritean parallel
viii The topsy-turvy world: let the wolf flee the sheep, &c.	1. 132–6 (see above)
ix Farewell to the woods: the suicide	1. 115–18 (cf. 1. 138–41) Daphnis' farewell to the animals and woods 3. 25–28: the snub-nosed shepherd's suicide threat

Virgil has used three idylls of Theocritus (1, 3, 11). The first describes the lament and death (by drowning) of the neatherd Daphnis. The poem (song of Thyrsis) represents Daphnis as wasting away from love (the object of his love is very obscure); he is mourned by all the animals and visited in his affliction by all the shepherds and goatherds and also by the god Priapus and the goddess of love, Cypris (who mocks his plight). He replies to Cypris with cynical disdain, bids farewell to the animals, woods and streams of Sicily, and calls on Pan to come from Arcadia and take his pipe from him; finally, after telling all of nature to turn topsy-turvy 'since he is dying', he goes to the stream and the waters close over him. The poem is to us very obscure; we do not know what version of the Daphnis story

Theocritus is alluding to. The emphasis, at any rate, is on Daphnis' pathetic death (not his love) and on the effect that this has on all of nature (animals, men, gods). Daphnis is really a sort of wonder-man whose song has raised him to superhuman heights and whose dying has universal consequence. The other two idylls (3, 11) used by Virgil, describe a common theme: the fruitless wooing of a girl (or nymph) by a comic shepherd. The cyclops Polyphemus (in 11) is of course an obvious butt: his courtship of the nymph Galatea is both naïve and humorous. The shepherd of 3 (the *Komos*) is much like him (he is snub-nosed and bearded and woos Amaryllis with apples and nanny goats) and his hyperbolical language (suicide threats, denunciations of love) is not meant to be taken seriously. Virgil has obviously coloured the rejected-love motif of these two idylls with the cosmic pathos of Daphnis, but has himself added all the tragedy and drama. Theocritus' idylls are not serious narratives but rather disordered laments or entreaties, sentimental-pathetic or comic in mood and deliberately conversational in style. We can best see what Virgil did to them by considering five of his motifs: (1) the characters themselves, (2) the relation of past and present, (3) the treatment of *amor* or love, (4) the 'topsy-turvy' world, and (5) death by drowning.

1. The shepherd-lover of the eclogue is, unlike Polyphemus or the shepherd of the *Komos*, a serious and tragic, not a comic figure. This is perhaps most evident in Virgil's reworking of

3. 8: ἦ ῥά γέ τοι σιμὸς καταφαίνομαι ἐγγύθεν ἦμεν,
νύμφα, καὶ προγένειος;

Or do I seem too snub nosed on close view
my girl, and perhaps my beard sticks out?

and:

11. 30: γινώσκω, χαρίεσσα κόρα, τίνος οὕνεκα φεύγεις·
οὕνεκά μοι λασία μὲν ὀφρὺς ἐπὶ παντὶ μετώπῳ
ἐξ ὠτὸς τέταται ποτὶ θώτερον ὡς μία μακρά,
εἷς δ' ὀφθαλμὸς ὕπεστι, πλατεῖα δὲ ῥὶς ἐπὶ χείλει.
ἀλλ' οὗτος τοιοῦτος ἐὼν βοτὰ χίλια βόσκω.

I know, dear girl, the reason you run from me,
the reason is that eyebrow shaggy and going
from ear to ear, one big long track. And I
have but one eye and great thick nostril too.
Yet even so, I have a thousand cows.

With these compare Virgil:

32   O digno coniuncta viro, *dum* despicis omnis,
          dumque tibi est odio mea fistula *dumque* capellae
          hirsutumque supercilium promissaque barba
          nec *curare deum* credis *mortalia quemquam.*

Here the situation is wholly altered by the lover's final aliena-
tion from his girl (Nisa). Her fastidious distaste for the shepherd-
lover's appearance is now turned against her own treacherous
error in marrying the unspeakable Mopsus. Thus what was
naif and hence humorous in Theocritus has become bitterly and
tragically ironical in Virgil. The *digno* reflects not only on the
quality of Mopsus but on the character of Nisa which this
marriage has finally revealed. The shepherd-lover now sees
that Nisa was after all 'worthy' of Mopsus: for she now appears
in a quite new light.

And this utter transformation of meaning and tone, is
reflected in the language. The repetition of *dum, dumque* and
umque (hirsutumque) and the continuing echo of the *um* and
que sounds, as well as other alliteration and assonance (the *d's,*
long *a's*), all work to intensify the crescendo that breaks at line
34 in order to introduce the solemn pathos of line 35. The anaphora and the cumulative cola are all contrasted with—piled
up against—the initial *O digno coniuncta viro* and thus set Nisa's
foolish depreciation of the shepherd-lover against her incongruous marriage. All this makes for greater solemnity in the
language and style but it is a solemnity fully adapted to the
subject-matter. Theocritus' two lovers in contrast use a familiar,
naif, *conversational* tone. The contrast here is something like that
between the blank verse of Milton and of Robert Frost. I have
tried to render this in my translations (above) of Theocritus.
Perhaps Virgil might be put like this:

> O worthy then your spouse, since you despise
> all else, despise my pipes, my goats
> my shaggy eyebrows and my lengthened beard,
> nor deem that any god can care for men.

Nisa, in short, is an Amaryllis or a Galatea who has fallen
from grace and has, in so doing, restored the original lover's
dignity even if this is the dignity of tragedy to come. It is by
this *reversal* of the Theocritean relationship (the *Komos* shepherd's

to Amaryllis, Polyphemus' to Galatea) that Virgil has raised his eclogue to the level of serious tragedy: his style cannot but reflect the change.

2. The heart of Virgil's eclogue is the peripety or change produced by Nisa's betrayal. This has the effect of showing the shepherd-lover that all his past experience has been deceptive: his present knowledge of Nisa is true to her character as his past *error* was not. Thus a new juxtaposition of *past* and *present*, *then* and *now* is, as it were, necessitated by his new knowledge. Here Virgil has miraculously transformed a quite ordinary bit of Theocritus. In the 11th idyll Polyphemus reminds Galatea of their first meeting:

25   ἠράσθην μὲν ἔγωγε τεοῦς, κόρα, ἁνίκα πρᾶτον
      ἦνθες ἐμᾷ σὺν ματρὶ θέλοισ' ὑακίνθινα φύλλα
      ἐξ ὄρεος δρέψασθαι, ἐγὼ δ' ὁδὸν ἁγεμόνευον.
      παύσασθαι δ' ἐσιδών τυ καὶ ὕστερον οὐδ' ἔτι πᾳ νῦν
29   ἐκ τήνω δύναμαι.

    I fell in love with you, my girl, when first
    you came here with my mother wanting to pick
    the hyacinths from the hill, I led the way.
    After I saw you then, I could not stop
    from loving you and I still love you now.

Virgil changes this to

37   *Saepibus* in *nostris parvam* te *roscida mala*,
      dux ego vester eram, vidi *cum matre* legentem.
      Alter ab undecimo tum me iam acceperat annus,
      iam fragiles poteram ab terra contingere ramos.
41   Ut vidi, ut perii! Ut me malus abstulit error!

I have italicized the differences. Theocritus' Galatea is no child: there is no reference to a distant past in Polyphemus' account; the meeting presumably was quite recent and between adults. Virgil's lover, however, is contrasting the high moment of his childish past (the little girl, the boy of 12[1] scarce tall enough to reach the branches) with the present reality that has shown this moment and its consequences to be only a *malus error*. The orchard (not the hill) and red apples (not hyacinths), the boyish

---

[1] The boy (according to the Roman system of *inclusive* counting) is in his *twelfth year*, hence would (in normal English usage) be referred to as eleven or 'eleven years old'. But there are instances of 'exclusive' counting by Romans. In any event he could not be more than 'twelve years old'. Cf. Conington, *ad loc.*

I

eagerness, the accompanying mother (hers, not his, as in Theocritus) all preserve the homely-childish note. But Virgil ends the scene with a line (ut vidi, &c.) that comes not from Polyphemus' complaint but from Theocritus' description of Atalanta's infatuation for Hippomenes (3. 42) or Simaetha's passion for Delphis (2. 82):

2. 82   χὼς ἴδον, ὣς ἐμάνην. ὥς μοι πυρὶ θυμὸς ἰάφθη
       So saw I, so went mad: my heart went up in flame

3. 42   ὡς ἴδεν, ὡς ἐμάνη, ὡς ἐς βαθὺν ἅλατ' ἔρωτα.
       Thus saw she, thus went mad, thus deep in love she plunged

He needs at this point a harsher, more impassioned verse than any in the Polyphemus passage. But Virgil is *not* here referring to an infatuation like Atalanta's or Simaetha's: his accent is not on the *love* but on the tragic *error* (ut me malus abstulit error). The line thus points the bitter moral of the episode when seen in retrospect.

But it is not merely by the insertion of this one tragic line that Virgil has altered Theocritus' tonality. The peculiar vividness of the shepherd-lover's *memory* of this one crucial moment is shown in the very position of the words and the movement of the rhythm. In lines 37–39 (corresponding to Theocritus, ll. 26-27) Virgil emphasizes the *boy's seeing the girl* at a particular age in a particular situation; Theocritus simply recounts an episode as it happens. Virgil thus separates the *parvam te* and *roscida mala* from their verbs (vidi . . . legentem) in the next line: we are first met by the concrete impressions— orchard, little girl, red apples—that linger in the lover's thought; therefore the natural sentence order of Theocritus is reversed. The rather elaborate phrase of line 39 (alter ab undecimo . . . annus), the repetition of *iam* in two different metrical positions (ll. 39, 40), give a serious or solemn cadence to the passage, but the two synaloephae (iam acceperat, poteram ab) add a contrasting note of childish hesitation, the boy just reaching, barely able to grasp, the lowest, the most fragile boughs. Then the 'tear-jerking' synaloephae of *vidi ut, perii ut* are followed by the inexorable dactyls of *me malus abstulit error*. This passage, in other words, sets a golden memory—still vivid and concrete, half solemn, half childish— against a tragic present evaluation of it.

3. The next strophe:

43 Nunc scio quid sit Amor: nudis in cotibus illum
   aut Tmaros aut Rhodope aut extremi Garamantes
   nec generis nostri puerum nec sanguinis edunt.

pits, of course, the *nunc*—the terrible present knowledge of love
—against the childish past. Line 43 is an imitation of Theocritus'
Komos (νῦν ἔγνων τὸν "Ερωτα· βαρὺς θεός: Now I know Love
—a harsh god) but represents a very different mood from that
of the lover there. There it is a banal statement of love's cruelty;
here it is the new *amor*, the *indignus amor* by which Virgil's
lover has been deceived (l. 18). Virgil has thus abandoned
the tame description of the *Komos* (that love sucked a
lioness' dug and was reared in the woods) and drawn
on the *Thalysia* (*Idyll* 7. 77: the distant mountains—Athos,
Rhodope, Caucasus—beneath which the snow wastes away)
and Homer (*Iliad* 16. 34 f.: rocks and sea as the proper mother
of the *cruel* Achilles) to give depth and power to his account of
love's origin and so make an effective contrast with the orchard
of the preceding verse. Then the stanza on love and the cruel
mother:

47 Saevus Amor docuit natorum sanguine, matrem
   commaculare manus. Crudelis tu quoque, mater!
   Crudelis mater magis, an puer improbus ille?
50 Improbus ille puer, crudelis tu quoque, mater!

once more brings us back from *Amor* to Nisa. The lines have no
Theocritean parallel and are therefore an important index to
Virgil's intention. Why did he introduce them? There has been
much fruitless debate on this question but the answer is clear
if we take into account both the order of the strophes and the
sequence of the thought. The strophe obviously corresponds to
IV (ll. 32–35) which describes the criminal folly of Nisa. The
shepherd-lover now sees behind the cruelty of *Amor*, the
cruelty of women subject to (taught by) *Amor*. Medea, the
child-murderess, is of course the most terrible and appropriate
instance of all. But can the deeds of such women be blamed
wholly on Amor? Is Medea blameless? The question here (l. 49)
expresses the shepherd's excited reluctance to exculpate the
woman (the ultimate reference is certainly to Nisa) from her due
responsibility. The proper answer is, therefore, that both are to

blame; it is both his own passion and Nisa herself that have
deceived the shepherd and brought him to ruin. Thus the transition from *Amor* to Medea (the mythological surrogate for Nisa)
and back to Nisa herself is effected. Also the fact that Medea is
a *mater* is important. We have just encountered a normal *mater*
(Nisa's *mater*) in the orchard; the entrance now of the unnatural
or perverted *mater* is but another illustration of the complete
overturn in the shepherd's mind. The present reality which has
dispelled all his past illusions—the *indignus amor* he now sees
between Mopsus and Nisa—has made everything seem to be
the exact opposite of what he had thought it.[1]

4. The topsy-turvy theme of both Stanza III (26–30) and of
the corresponding Stanza VIII (52–56) is based on one passage
in the Daphnis idyll:

132   νῦν ἴα μὲν φορέοιτε βάτοι, φορέοιτε ἄκανθαι,
        ἁ δὲ καλὰ νάρκισσος ἐπ᾽ ἀρκεύθοισι κομάσαι,
        πάντα δ᾽ ἄναλλα γένοιτο, καὶ ἁ πίτυς ὄχνας ἐνείκαι,
        Δάφνις ἐπεὶ θνάσκει, καὶ τὰς κύνας ὤλαφος ἕλκοι,
        κἠξ ὀρέων τοὶ σκῶπες ἀηδόσι γαρύσαιντο.

Now let the brambles bear violets and also the thorn bush,
And on the junipers now let the narcissus bloom,
Let all things be transmuted. Let pears grow on the pine tree
For Daphnis is dying, dying: now let the deer worry dogs
And from the mountains let owls to the nightingales sing.

But this is used, first, not of the general topsy-turviness of all
nature but of the specific unnaturalness of Nisa's marriage:

26   Mopso Nisa datur: quid non speremus amantes?
        Iungentur iam grypes equis aevoque sequenti
        cum canibus timidi venient ad pocula dammae.
        Mopse, novas incide faces, tibi ducitur uxor!
        Sparge, marite, nuces, tibi deserit Hesperus Oetan!

The point of view is not, here, Nisa's own unworthiness but the
disparity between her and the dreadful Mopsus. Her marriage

---

[1] Cf. on ll. 47–50 Vahlen, *Opuscula* (II. 526 f.); Rohde, p. 43; Cartault, op. cit.
p. 309; J. Hubaux (*Musée Belge* XXV (1921), p. 154 f.); Pfeiffer, pp. 44–47; G.
Stegen (*Commentaire sur cinq Bucoliques de Virgile* (1957) pp. 75–77). Curiously most
critics have not seen *why* Virgil employs the question and answer arrangement in
ll. 49–50 and *what* Medea stands for in these verses. But it is not *until* we see that
the shepherd-lover is brought back from his new knowledge of his own error (his
own fatal *amor*) to the complicity and guilt of Nisa (she too is to blame); it is not,
in other words, until we see that *Medea* really symbolizes or 'stands for' *Nisa*, that
the question and answer make sense. Here the correspondence of strophes (IV and
VII) makes the symbolic identification of Nisa and Medea clear.

is like that of griffins and horses, or the association of dogs and deer. The theme is not developed but is confined to a scant two verses. Very different is the use of the theme in Stanzas VIII and IX:

52   Nunc et ovis ultro fugiat lupus, aurea durae
            mala ferant quercus, narcisso floreat alnus,
            pinguia corticibus sudent electra myricae,
            certent et cycnis ululae, sit Tityrus Orpheus,
56   Orpheus in silvis, inter delphinas Arion!
58   Omnia vel medium fiat mare! Vivite, silvae!

The piling up of *exempla* is designed to produce a climax. The tension drops a little in 54 (with the one long colon after the three short ones) but immediately rises with the harsh *certent et cycnis ululae* of 55, to reach (after the refrain which is here alone parenthetic and actually interrupts the sentence) a climactic finale in 58. The running over of the refrain (57) shows the emotion of the speaker: as he reaches his climax—the moment before or of his leap into the sea—he sees the Arcadian woods merging into the sea (i.e. his own death) and views this as the fitting consequence of all nature over-turned; the transition comes in the movement of his thought from Orpheus to Arion.

Thus the topsy-turvy theme now reflects a disorder far greater than the unnatural marriage of Nisa: it re-enters the poem (Stanzas VIII–IX) as the expression of the shepherd-lover's own transmutation of values, his feeling that *now* (i.e. now that he has grasped the true nature of love and of Nisa and of his own *error*) all is indeed changed. His woods, his Arcadian landscape can *now* indeed become sea: suicide by drowning is the final expression of the complete revolution in his soul and of his own immersion (the woods really stand for *himself*, for his rural way of life) in a wholly different element—water and death. The multiplication of *exempla* from lines 52–58 is solely designed to mark the climactic movement toward the consummation of the tragedy. As in *Aeneid* 4, Virgil repeats a minor theme in a major key, and at much greater length, to achieve a crashing conclusion. But this magnification of the topsy-turvy theme would have been impossible had not Virgil already shown us the development of ideas and feelings from the shepherd-lover's first reaction to Nisa's betrayal up to the full comparison of past and present in stanzas V, VI and VII.

In learning what Amor really is, the lover not only learns his own error about Nisa but his error about all his former values. The world is not as he thought: he can now only accept its topsy-turviness and die. The shepherd-lover has almost no identity with the wonder-man Daphnis: the latter is a force of nature whose death can almost cause a cataclysmic disturbance within it; the former is a simple rustic whose cataclysm is wholly personal and psychological.

5. The suicide of the shepherd-lover:

58   Vivite silvae!
59   Praeceps aërii specula de montis in undas
60   deferar; extremum hoc munus morientis habeto!

is most directly reminiscent of the 'threat' of Theocritus' shepherd of the *Komos* (25–28):

25   τὰν βαίταν ἀποδὺς ἐς κύματα τηνῶ ἁλεῦμαι,
        ὧπερ τὼς θύννως σκοπιάζεται Ὄλπις ὁ γριπεύς·
        καί κα δὴ 'ποθάνω, τό γε μὲν τεὸν ἁδὺ τέτυκται.
        I'll strip away my coat and leap into the waves
        From where the fisher Olpis looks for tunny!
        And if I die perhaps, it will be sweet to you.

But this shepherd is after all only boasting: his threat comes in the middle of his tirade and is followed by a song that ends not in drowning but in an equally rhetorical determination to lie down and die where he is. In Virgil it is the climactic end of the whole lament and is obviously meant to prelude a real suicide. The omission of the Theocritean detail (taking off the coat, the picturesque designation of the vantage point) also marks the far greater seriousness of the Virgilian paraphrase. The invocation of the woods (vivite silvae) recalls the second stanza (Arcadia and its woods, *argutumque nemus pinosque loquentis*) and the *extremum munus* recalls the *extrema hora* of the first stanza. Here the reference to Daphnis (Theocritus 1. 123–6, 116–17, 140–1) adds a quite different coloration to the *Komos* paraphrase. But Daphnis does not merge the woods in the sea (nowhere in his own farewell speech does he mention his own death in the stream) nor directly connect the topsy-turviness of nature with his own drowning. For Daphnis, as we have seen, does not psychologize his own misfortune: his relation to nature is not metaphorical but real for he himself is a very extraordinary man who has a very special connection with the forces of nature. Similarly, the shepherd-lover's Arcadia (Stanza II) is his own ideal world, the world of Maenalian song and of Pan: Daphnis actually summons Pan *from* Arcadia *to* Sicily (123–6). It is again the difference between myth and metaphor or between an objective and a subjective narrative.[1]

We have devoted so much space to this short episode because it is, for all its brevity, a quite new departure in poetry. It is to be sure a monologue in the first person, but this fact does not in the least affect its significance. The line between first-personal and empathetic third-personal narrative is very thin and elusive. What is important is its novelty as compared with the work of either Greeks (Theocritus' idylls) or previous Romans (the neoteric little epics). Virgil altered the content and style of Theocritus because he was writing a different kind of narrative, a subjective tragedy whose action takes place inside the psyche. This is what, in the last analysis, produced the unified and elevated tone. Precisely because he sees events as parts of a single dramatic situation, his style itself achieves concentration and uniformity. The result is as different from Theocritean objectivity as it is from neoteric subjectivism. There is here no human *object* that we contemplate for our amusement. There is no harping on a single emotion whose dramatic foreground and background we can hardly see. Rather we are abruptly introduced to a lover at the moment of supreme disillusionment and suicide. And we see—rather feel as he expresses his feelings —the swift shattering of an idyllic past by a terrible present experience and, with this, the complete inversion of his whole sensibility. The past does not need to be suppressed or fore-shortened in the interest of a single pathos or moment of pathos because it is precisely his sense of the past which makes his pathos. Or, better still, it is the setting of the past against the present—the tragic juxtaposition of the two—that works the drama. *Nunc scio quid sit amor* cries the shepherd-lover as Catullus

---

[1] Virgil's identification of bucolic life and poetry with Arcadia is clearly based on Pan's connection with that region. But, *unlike Theocritus*, he takes 'Arcadia' as an ideal, not a real place. Bruno Snell (*The Discovery of the Mind*, trans. T. G. Rosen-meyer (1953) pp. 281 f.) has correctly seen the *ideal* character of Virgil's Arcadia (p. 288) but has added (after Ernst Kapp) the quite unnecessary hypothesis that Virgil's ideal Arcadia came from his reading of Polybius 4. 20!

before him had cried *Nunc te cognovi*: this is the fatal moment of tragedy when man wakes to a terrible reality—compare the *tum* of the line from the fourth *Aeneid*: *tum* vero infelix fatis exterrita Dido mortem orat—and it is an utterly different kind of 'moment' from that of Ariadne's declamatory passion on the beach or Scylla's rhetorical argument with her nurse.

The Damon song thus prefigures a new kind of narrative and a new kind of style. But one swallow hardly makes a summer. We must now, therefore, consider an earlier and more conventional lover's monologue and a very brief bit of third-personal narrative: the one shows the new style of the Damon song in rather rudimentary or embryonic form; the other shows at least something of the style's narrative possibilities.

The second eclogue (Corydon's complaint) is relatively early and probably belongs to the year 42–41 (i.e. three years prior to the eighth eclogue). Its structure is certainly much simpler than the Damon song of that eclogue. It falls into fairly definite sections even though it is not divided into stanzas by a refrain:
1. *Introduction* (ll. 1–5): Corydon *alone* (solus) sings his unpremeditated (incondita) verses to the woods and mountains: it is a piece of empty zeal (montibus et silvis studio iactabat inani).
2. *First lament* (6–16): He reproaches his beloved Alexis for neglecting him and his song. Then he indicates the setting of his song: *now* it is noon, the hour when beasts and men seek the shade, *but* he alone braves the meridional sun *tua dum vestigia lustro*.
3. *The courtship song* (though Alexis cannot hear it):

> a (17–27). Appeal to Alexis (not to rely on colour as a criterion of beauty or worth; actually Corydon is rich in lambs, an excellent singer, and not ugly).
>
> b (28–44). Alexis should come and live with him: he can teach him music, given him a fine pipe, and two young goats.
>
> c (45–55). He can offer Alexis wonderful gifts of herbs and flowers.

4. *Second lament* (56–68):

> a (56–59). Corydon's own self-criticism. He is *rusticus*: Alexis does not want his gifts. Corydon has only been hurting himself. *But*

b (60–62): Alexis is mad (demens) to despise the woods *and*

c (63–65): Corydon's love is a natural impulse.

d (66–68): *Yet* all enjoy the peace of evening except himself (me tamen urit amor; quis enim modus adsit amori?).

e (69–73): Corydon renews his self criticism; what madness has seized him? Let him get back to his neglected work. He can always find another Alexis.

Here, as in 8, Virgil's debt to Theocritus is very extensive. The chief model is *Idyll* 11 (Polyphemus' courtship of Galatea) but he also makes use of the other courtship poems (3, the snub-nosed shepherd's appeal to Amaryllis and 6, on Galatea as courted by Polyphemus and the neatherd Damoetas) and a significant bit from the second idyll (the *Pharmaceutria*) where Simaetha compares her amorous torment with the calmness of the sea (38–41). With the exception of this last, all the passages of Theocritus used by Virgil in this eclogue are naif and comic in tone or effect.

Polyphemus' song (11), like that of Alexis, starts with a lament (19–29) and then proceeds on quite similar lines (he discusses his appearance, his wealth in dairy products, his nice cave, &c., and invites her to come and live with him). At the end, he turns on himself with the line:

ὦ Κύκλωψ, Κύκλωψ, πᾷ τάς φρένας ἐκπεπότασαι;
O Cyclops, Cyclops, where have your wits awandered?

imitated by Virgil (A Corydon, Corydon, quae te dementia cepit?), and declares he'd show more sense if he started tending to business. He is popular with girls; maybe he can get a fairer Galatea; on land, at least, he is somebody. Polyphemus' 'return to sense' is of course not to be taken seriously: actually he hopes that Galatea is listening to him,[1] and his belated boasting is a naif strategy for making her jealous or interested. In any event he is no tragic lover. The same, of course, is true of the lovers in *Idylls* 3 and 6.

One thing Virgil did to Theocritus was to tone down the comic side of the courtship and make Corydon a rustic who can be taken seriously as a man who understands and appreciates the countryside he lives in. But his most important innovation

---

[1] Cf. Theocritus 11. 17–18: ἐς πόντον ὁρῶν, Polyphemus sings from a high rock; obviously he is trying to catch Galatea's attention.

was to set the courtship in brackets or quotation marks, as it were, by showing Corydon's situation and attitude both *before* and *after* his courtship song.[1] Thus the 'laments' enclose the song at both ends as they do not in Theocritus 11 (where there is but one lament at the beginning). Each contains the same theme that Virgil perhaps took from the *Pharmaceutria* (Theocritus 2): external quiet and inner turmoil. The lines

9   *nunc* viridis etiam occultant spineta lacertas, &c.
12   *at mecum* raucis tua dum vestigia lustro
13   sole sub ardenti resonant arbusta cicadis.

are re-echoed by the lines:

66   aspice aratra iugo referunt suspensa iuvenci
           et *sol* crescentis *decedens duplicat umbras;*
68   *me tamen* urit amor.

Corydon is isolated by his passion from both man and beast: while all others seek the shade at noon, he *alone* braves the sun with the hoarse cicadas; while all seek home and peace at eventide and the sun itself begins to wane, he alone is burned by love. The contrast of noon and night was possibly taken from an elegy of Meleager (A.P. XII. 127) though the latter is a mere jeu d'esprit based on the double sense of fire (πῦρ) as both natural (the sun) and human (the boy's eyes).[2] At any rate what is important is Virgil's quite original use of noon and evening. This is not merely as Klingner[3] thought, a rounding off of the poem by a return to the mood of its beginning, but a definite indication that the time span is important in its own right. Something happens to Corydon as he goes over the song with himself (for Alexis is not there; the whole thing is an *inane studium*, a courtship in the void) and, in the interval (that the actual song would not last from noon to dusk is of course irrelevant; this is dramatic not real time), his feelings are changed: the 'external-quiet-internal-passion' motif is itself changed and reflects the change in Corydon.

---

[1] Pfeiffer (pp. 1–7) clearly brings out the difference here between Virgil and Theocritus 11. Klingner had already made it plain in his review of Georg Rohde's monograph (*Gnomon* 3 (1927), pp. 576–83). But the connection between the two 'laments' has none the less remained obscure. Büchner (168) sees the contrast and cites Catullus 51 as a parallel, but fails to explain the transition between ll. 68 and 69 (i.e. how the ending is related to the second lament).
[2] This point was made by Jean Hubaux, *Le Réalisme dans les Bucoliques de Virgile* (*Bibl. de Faculté de Phil. et Lettres de Liége*, XXXVII, 1927) but Meleager's epigram is utterly different in both tone and meaning from Virgil's poem.   [3] Op. cit.

The turning point of the eclogue comes, as Rohde and others have seen, at line 56:

Rusticus es Corydon: nec munera curat Alexis.

The latter part of the courtship-song, especially from line 45 (huc ades, o formose puer), has described the rustic gifts (munera) in a steady crescendo of cola rising to the final couplet:

54 et vos, o lauri, carpam et te, proxima myrte;
   sic positae quoniam suavis miscetis odores.

The repetition of *tibi* in lines 45–46, the *tum* of 49, then the stronger *ipse ego* of 51 (as Corydon joins Nais in heaping the baskets), the two *cola* of 53:

  Addam cerea pruna (honos erit huic quoque pomo)

all contribute to the effect. Thus the break at lines 55–56 is accentuated: Corydon now sees that he cannot hope to attract Alexis by such rural delights. He cannot hope to rival the rich (presumably urban) Iollas. And he himself has succumbed to a passion that is as destructive of his own flowers and rural springs as the scorching sirocco or the wild boar (58–59). He now sees, moreover, that Alexis' disdain for the 'woods' (the rural life) is itself madness (Alexis is *demens*): the gods themselves have lived in the woods. And though there is nothing unnatural in his own *voluptas* (he is obeying the same law of appetite that all of nature exhibits, lions, wolves, goats, 62–65), the generality of *voluptas* (trahit sua quemque voluptas) can be no comfort to him now. He thus returns to himself and his own situation: it is evening, the hot sun is setting and the bullocks are going home; he alone burns with love (me tamen urit amor). What limit can there be to love? The mere statement of the fact, however, shows its folly:

  A Corydon, Corydon, quae te dementia cepit?

His madness has made him neglect the daily work on which his whole way of life depends. He should be plying some useful task: he can find another Alexis, if the first does not want him.

 The unique feature of this eclogue is thus the final 'lament' (56–68) in which Corydon analyses his courtship song and realizes its folly. He had been imputing to Alexis a love of nature which Alexis did not possess. He had been *rusticus* in two ways: as a true countryman who loved his native milieu; and as a naif ignoramus or 'country bumpkin'. Alexis also was certainly foolish in disdaining the country (Corydon is fully aware that he cannot and should not apologize for the country) but this is no help to Corydon now. His *voluptas* is natural but also fatal: it has isolated him from both man and beast and he sees his experience of high noon repeated at eventide. But the mere exercise of 'empty zeal' in composing his fictitious courtship has made him aware of the true situation: he is wasting his time on one who can neither appreciate his way of life nor reciprocate his passion. This is madness: he must return to sanity. The final lines are almost an exact copy of Polyphemus' (Theocritus, ll. 72–76 corresponding to Virgil's 69–73) but Polyphemus, unlike Corydon, has not seen the folly of his courtship, recognized his own naiveté or become aware that he has betrayed his own dignity and his own way of life. He is still boastful and stupid—still trying to attract the attention of Galatea as he supplements overt solicitation by a transparent pretence of indifference. In short Corydon's words contain a little drama, a subjective, psychological drama in which self-awareness emerges and cures an irrational passion. It is both a serious drama and the drama of a serious person. The Polyphemus idyll, on the other hand, is a quite non-dramatic parody of a courtship and Polyphemus is himself a butt without either insight or dignity.

We can see in the Corydon eclogue therefore a rather primitive form of the Damon song: the drama of the latter is part and parcel of the whole, of all the stanzas; the drama of the former is confined to the 'frame', the preluding and concluding 'laments' that contain the courtship song itself. This difference is fully comprehensible. We should expect the *Corydon* to precede the Damon Song in time of composition (as it actually did), since the latter is clearly a much more complicated kind of narrative. At any rate both together indicate something of the difference between Virgil on the one hand, Theocritus and the Neoterics on the other. But we have not yet exhausted the evidence for Virgil's new style. A brief—indeed very brief passage from the sixth eclogue is important because it shows not so much how Virgil treated, but how he might have treated, the more normal or third-personal type of narrative.

In *Eclogue* 6, Silenus, starting from the creation, sings of various myths: the most space (though still only fifteen lines) is devoted to the story of Pasiphaë. It is essential that we have this short narrative before us:

45 Et fortunatam, si numquam armenta fuissent,
    Pasiphaen nivei solatur amore iuvenci.
    A, virgo infelix, quae te dementia cepit?
    Proetides implerunt falsis mugitibus agros;
    at non tam turpis pecudum tamen ulla secuta
50 concubitus, quamvis collo timuisset aratrum,
    et saepe in levi quaesissent cornua fronte.
    A, virgo infelix, tu nunc in montibus erras;
    ille, latus niveum molli fultus hyacintho,
    ilice sub nigra pallentis ruminat herbas
55 aut aliquam in magno sequitur grege. 'Claudite, Nymphae,
    Dictaeae Nymphae, nemorum iam claudite saltus,
    si qua forte ferant oculis sese obvia nostris
    errabunda bovis vestigia; forsitan illum,
    aut herba captum viridi aut armenta secutum,
60 perducant aliquae stabula ad Gortynia vaccae.'

In this narrative, short as it is, we can discern clear demarcations or sections.

1. (ll. 45–46): The theme introduced and briefly stated: the narrator's mood of mingled *sympathy and shock* is conveyed in the opening line:

> Et fortunatam, si numquam armenta fuissent.

2. (ll. 47–51): The pathos and shame of Pasiphaë. The line

> A, virgo *infelix*, quae te *dementia* cepit?

gives the cue: Pasiphaë is *infelix* because she has lost her sanity. The case of the daughters of Proetus (who fancied themselves cows) was not so shameful because, though they dreaded the plow and felt their foreheads for horns, they avoided Pasiphaë's fate.

3. (ll. 52–55): The narrator puts Pasiphaë before us in the *present* of her misfortune:

> A, virgo infelix, tu *nunc* in montibus erras;

The *A virgo infelix* links this passage of course with line 47: we now *see* the actuality for which we have been emotionally prepared and editorially 'briefed' in part 2 (47–51): Pasiphaë wandering in the mountains; the bull ruminating beneath the black oak or pursuing some cow.

The line: *ille, latus niveum molli fultus hyacintho* gives us in fact a sensation of the bull *as Pasiphaë must realize him: to her* he is beautiful. The contrast between Pasiphaë vainly trying to find him in the mountains, while he rests comfortably in a grove of trees or pursues some cow in pasture, accentuates the incongruity of her love: *Tu* ... *erras: ille* ... *ruminat* ... *aut aliquam in grege sequitur.*

4. (ll. 55–60): Here we have the actual words of Pasiphaë as she is searching for the bull. She bids the Cretan nymphs close the pasture gates so that the bull cannot get out. Perhaps she may see his tracks; perhaps some cow will lead him home to stable.

This bit of narrative is so brief, so truncated (for all Virgil wishes to give is but an indication or suggestion of the whole story) that we cannot treat it as anything like a complete whole. None the less it is clear that here also he is narrating by identifying himself with his character in a temporal-biographical way. The direct address to Pasiphaë, the 'finger-pointing' *infelix*, the comparison to the Proetides all have an empathetic effect. The narrator identifies himself with Pasiphaë, though at the same time he carefully distinguishes between the sane (and thus unfortunate) and the insane (or momentarily deluded) Pasiphaë. Here the parallel with Catullus' *Attis* (63) is very relevant. Catullus fully expressed his sympathy with Attis only when Attis had momentarily recovered from his madness and grasped its consequences. The two speeches of Attis (one in madness, the other in recovered sanity) represent and expand the two emotional moments of the poem. Here, however, Virgil tries to convey the distinction of sanity and delusion in a subtler and more dramatic way. We actually see Pasiphaë in the moment (*tu nunc in montibus erras*) of her delusion; her words do not directly comment on or explain her emotional situation (as do Attis') but are *themselves part of the drama going on.* We see her directing the nymphs to help her round up the bull; we now see, in other words, *through* her eyes as she enacts her own tragedy.

Probably, if Virgil had continued the narrative (instead of breaking off at mid-point) he would have also made her recovery of sanity part of the drama. The emotional moments would have been themselves dramatically linked: the *nunc* of line 52 would have been followed by a corresponding later *nunc* or some other indication of time exactly as was the *nunc etiam pecudes*, &c. (l. 8) of Corydon's song. Or at least this seems to be exceedingly probable. At any rate, these fifteen lines reveal a *dramatic intention* that could hardly have been carried out (had Virgil ever tried to write a full-length *Pasiphaë*) in the manner of the *Attis*, the *Peleus and Thetis* or the *Ciris*. And this fact (and it certainly seems to be a fact) should also make us wary of taking Virgil's Silenus song as a mere 'catalogue' or 'advertisement' of neoteric 'little epics'.

So far then we have seen that the *Eclogues* mark a very close approach to, if not the actual beginning of, the kind of continuous narrative we analysed in the fourth *Aeneid*. There can be no doubt, of course, that the difference between the two—between the Damon song, Corydon eclogue and brief Pasiphaë narrative, on the one hand; the Dido book on the other—is a very considerable difference indeed.[1] But compared with Theocritus or Catullus, these bucolic narratives do represent something distinctly closer to the *Aeneid*. For they are, in a rather unmistakable way, both dramatic and subjective; they no longer discriminate sharply between a truncated or assumed background and a momentary but artificially expanded pathos-scene: they at least give the impression of an action integrally related to its past. Recollection has been made dramatic; past affects present and future; something decisive happens (and is not just 'emotionalized' *after* it happens), even if the happening is chiefly subjective or psychological. Empathy is no longer static; monologue is no longer declamatory only; emotion does not revolve about a single spot but actually progresses toward a climax. On the other hand, the objectivity of the Theocritean idyll is wholly gone: Virgil's shepherds are but poorly discriminated characters when set beside their Theocritean originals. But they are no longer only objects of comedy or pathos; they are serious lovers or sufferers whom we can take seriously because we empathetically follow their feelings

---

[1] This difference is one both of scale and of style. Here the *Eclogues* are very like the *Georgics* (esp. in respect to the *Aristaeus-Orpheus* narrative of the latter) when compared to the *Aeneid*. For the stylistic difference see Appendix 7.

and participate in their tragedy. Last but certainly not least in importance, Virgil has in the *Eclogues* assimilated both the empathetic and the sympathetic components of his narrative to something of the high style and diction of epic. The result is a unity—a finished harmony—of style, radically different from the jarring juxtaposition of styles in the *Peleus and Thetis* or *Ciris*. This unity of style of course carried with it a considerable restriction of tone and topic: comedy, objective realism, the light, chatty, familiar and ironic moods of the Alexandrines, are all very much in abeyance. But the Virgilian sadness or melancholy represented a new note in poetry: it was also an excellent preparative for epic.

2

We must now consider briefly the general or over-all meaning of the collected *Eclogues*: here, as distinct from the individual poems, we find something like a symbolic scheme or structure. The key to this structure is the arrangement of the ten poems by Virgil when he finally published the whole collection in or about 38 B.C. Heretofore, scholars and critics of the *Bucolics* have paid most attention to their chronological order or dates of composition. This, however, is really a point of minor importance compared with their internal relation to each other in the complete *Eclogue Book*. There is indeed evidence (as we shall see) that Virgil wrote at least some of the poems (certainly 7, 8, 10) expressly in order to round out or balance an already formulated scheme. In any event the lapse of time between 42 and 38 (the probable period of their composition) is too slight to throw very much light on his poetical development. But their arrangement, their position in a total plan, is perhaps the single most important clue to their meaning.

The eclogues clearly fall into three main categories: the fully Theocritean poems (2, 3, 7, 8); the Theocritean poems with a specifically Roman, contemporary bearing (5, 10); and the non-Theocritean poems (1, 4, 6, 9). All, it is true, show Theocritean influence in that all are, to a greater or lesser degree, indebted to Theocritus' style or manner. And, conversely, even so markedly Theocritean a poem as 3 contains topical references to Pollio and Virgil's poetical rivals, Bavius and Maevius. But these considerations do not in the least alter the facts that 2, 3, 7, 8 are directly based on Theocritean models; that 5 and 10 use a Theocritean original (the first Idyll) in a very special, Roman way; and that 1, 4, 6, 9 are not based on actual Theocritean models (with perhaps some slight qualification for 9) but derive instead from obviously non-Theocritean sources or ideas.

The second primary fact about the *Eclogue Book* is that the three categories are arranged on a clearly reciprocal pattern. Thus the four fully Theocritean poems correspond, and of the four, 2 corresponds to 8, 3 to 7. Both 2 and 8 deal with love and both contain relatively long songs or pieces on a single theme (2 is a single whole, 8 contains two love episodes, the *Damon* and *Alphesiboeus*) whereas 3 and 7 are of the amoebaean or responsive type (the 'capping' of discrete verses by two rival singers). Again, in the special Theocritean category, 5 and 10 clearly correspond (both are based exclusively on the first idyll; both deal with a Roman theme; 5 by representing Daphnis as *Caesar*, 10 by representing *Gallus* as Daphnis). Of the non-Theocritean poems, 9 and 1 correspond in that they obviously refer to each other and involve in part at least a similar or identical theme: the recovery and loss of homesteads by *coloni* to alien masters or settlers. 4 and 6 correspond by explicit cross-reference, as we shall see. Thus we get the following schema or plan of arrangement.[1]

1	Roman: loss and recovery of a homestead
2	Love (Corydon) narrative
	Theocritean
3	Amoebaean dialogue
4	*non arbusta . . . iuvant . . . humilesque myricae*
5	Daphnis—Caesar
6	te, Vare, nostrae *myricae, nemus . . . canet*
7	Amoebaean dialogue
	Theocritean
8	Love (Damon, Alphesiboeus) narratives
9	Roman: recovery and loss of a homestead
10	Gallus—Daphnis

[1] This schema, to the best of my knowledge, was first clearly worked out (along, alas, with much else) by Paul Maury, 'Le Secret de Virgile et l'Architecture des Bucoliques' (*Lettres d'Humanité* III (1944), pp. 71–147). It is accepted by Perret and by Duckworth (*AJP* 75 (1954), pp. 1–15). But none of these have supplied a convincing *explanation* of the scheme.

K

The third major fact about the *Eclogue Book* is its division into two parts or halves (1–5, 6–10). If we except the four fully Theocritean poems, there is an obvious contrast between 1, 4, 5 and 6, 9, 10. The first set (1, 4, 5) is Roman and Julio-Augustan: they praise the new god, his restoration of peace and the good new age that is coming to realization. The second set (6, 9, 10) deals with non-Julian and non-Augustan themes or (in the case of 9) balances bucolic or Theocritean themes against Julio-Roman themes while treating the latter with considerable reservation and ambiguity. Furthermore we note the following differences of emphasis between *all* the first five and *all* the second five:[1]

1. Exile revoked: praise of the new god; bitterness assuaged by hospitality; complete fusion of bucolic and Roman-Augustan themes.	9. Exile revoked, then reimposed: pointed juxtaposition (without fusion) of Roman-Julian and bucolic themes; the future is in doubt.
2. The cure of unworthy love by the recovery of reason.	8. Death worked by unworthy love. Daphnis bound by a spell.
3. Amoebaean contest starting in crude abuse and *ending* in a peaceful non-decision by an umpire.	7. Amoebaean contest *ending in* defeat of the harsh Thyrsis, victory of the mild Corydon.
4. The new age: return of the *Saturnia regna.*	6. The former age: passing of the ancient *Saturnia regna* into a series of unnatural *amores* and *metamorphoses.*
5. Death and transfiguration of Daphnis-Caesar.	10. Gallus as the Daphnis of Idyll 1 (wasting away from *unworthy love*).

It is clear (whatever else may not be clear) that *Eclogues* 1–5 are relatively forward-looking, peaceful, conciliatory, and patriotic in a Julio-Augustan sense. *Eclogues* 6–10, on the contrary, are neoteric, ambiguous or polemic, concerned with the past and emotively dominated by *amor indignus*, love which

[1] Cf. Carl Becker 'Virgils Eklogenbuch' (*Hermes* 83 (1955), pp. 314–49).

is essentially destructive and irrational and is implicitly inconsistent with (if not hostile to) a strong Roman-patriotic orientation. The conclusion is irresistible that *Eclogues* 6–10 were in large part written to form a contrast with *Eclogues* 1–5 and that the general design of the complete *Eclogue Book* emerged *before* Virgil had completed the whole series of ten poems.

We can thus see how Virgil came to design the *Eclogue Book* as it is now and as it appeared on its final publication in 38 or perhaps 37 B.C. It is plain that he wrote *Eclogues* 2, 3, 5 first in that order (since 2 and 3, in that order, are explicitly referred to at the end of 5 and it is most unlikely that any other eclogues then existed: the clear implication of 5. 85–87 is that Virgil was then—at the time he wrote 5—the author of two and only two, previous eclogues, viz. 2 and 3). But is is also evident that 5 directly preceded 9 and 9 preceded 1. In referring to Daphnis' death and obsequies, 5 (Mopsus) says:

40   Spargite humum foliis, inducite fontibus umbras,
41   pastores: mandat fieri sibi talia Daphnis.

These lines are recalled in 9, as Lycidas bewails the narrow escape (from death) of Menalcas (Virgil) and refers to his (Menalcas') poetry by paraphrasing it:

9. 19   Quis caneret Nymphas? Quis humum florentibus herbis
           spargeret aut viridi fontis induceret umbra?

It is all but impossible to take 9 here as anything but a reference back to 5. There is nothing strange about this, since as we have seen, 5 had been preceded by only 2 and 3. But 9 *also* makes it clear that Virgil at the time of its composition was known only as a poet who, in addition to verses on such bucolic themes as Galatea and Amaryllis, had written chiefly an unfinished poem to Varus (quae Varo necdum perfecta canebat) and a laudation of the deified Caesar as divine patron of the countryside (as we shall see, another clear reference to 5). Thus it seems most improbable that any of the other (i.e. other than 2, 3, 5) eclogues existed at the time he wrote 9.

But 1 is obviously constructed as a counterpart to 9. Quite aside from the parallelism of theme, 1 recalls 9 in a clearly polemical way, almost as if to mark the difference of the two.[1]

---

[1] This point has been well made by Rudolf Hanslik (*Wiener Studien* 68 (1955), pp. 5–19).

Whereas 9, in 'quoting' Menalcas' 'Praise of Caesar', directs Daphnis to act under the patronage of the new god and to expect his posterity to reap the benefits:

9. 50   Insere, Daphni, piros; carpent tua poma nepotes!

1 makes the exiled Meliboeus repeat to himself the same words with obviously ironical bitterness:

1. 73   Insere *nunc*, Meliboee, piros, pone ordine vitis!

This is what the promised blessings of Caesar have come to! There is no need *now* to mention posterity; the *nunc* points to the difference between the original promise and the changed, present situation of farmers like Meliboeus and the Daphnis of 5. In the end, however, the natural spleen of Meliboeus is assuaged by the hospitality of Tityrus: the poem strikes a note of reconciliation quite unlike the ninth eclogue where the 'Praise of Caesar' is recollected as one of the songs that Menalcas had sung before the catastrophe and is quite separated from Menalcas' bucolic verses about Tityrus (9. 23–25). Both poems seem concerned with the events of 41 B.C. but 1 represents a quite different and later attitude toward them: the evils of exile are not minimized (however happy Tityrus may be, Meliboeus at least is not) but the beneficence of the 'god' or 'youth'—clearly Octavian—is paramount and the ending at least is tranquil and pacific.

Thus 1 is, as it were, the turning point in Virgil's composition of the *Eclogue Book*. He had now reaffirmed his positive attitude toward the Julian *gens*, adding to his praise of Caesar in 5 the praise of Octavian in 1. We cannot know or even construct a likely hypothesis about what happened to Virgil between 43–42 and the end of 41 but *something happened* and must indeed be posited to account for the difference between 9 and 1. At any rate he was now able to conceive of a related cycle of poems with 5 in or near the central position and 1 balancing 9. He had now, in other words, written his first pair of reciprocal eclogues and thus suggested its continuation in a series of *five* such pairs.

He did not, however, proceed at once to write eclogues to balance 2 and 3 (the later 7 and 8) but added another corresponding pair of eclogues, 4 and 6. These (4 and 6) certainly seem to belong to the year 40 (Pollio's consulship) and are obviously closely related (they refer to each other in a quite explicit fashion). They also assume the existence of 1 since 6. 8 is assuredly a 'programmatic' quotation of 1. 2. It is, I think, fruitless to debate whether 6 preceded 4 or vice versa as they are clearly designed to complement each other. After writing them, Virgil then proceeded to complete his plan by adding 7 and 8 (these are later as their technique shows: furthermore 8 refers to Pollio's Illyrian campaign of 39, and 7 'recalls' or is recalled by a phrase of 8: 8. 63 = 7. 23). Finally the addition of the last poem, 10, completed the design. This was written to correspond with 5: Virgil had now achieved his plan of two contrasting halves—one Augustan or Julio-Augustan and one neoteric and bucolic—with 5 in the middle and 10 at the end.

Obviously Virgil, after he wrote 1 and therein indicated his adherence to Octavian, conceived the idea of expanding the Theocritean kernel of his collection by two poems (4, 6) which would more directly indicate the two divergent elements of his poetical and political thought and would also make clear their relation to each other. But 7, 8, and 10 also assisted the scheme since they also balanced 2, 3, and 5 and completed the more general balance of themes between the two halves. The 'secret' of the whole *Eclogue Book*, therefore, cannot be clarified until we find the clue that will unravel three problems: the central position of 5, the relation of 4 and 6, and the meaning of the devotion to Octavian expressed in 1.

In 5 two shepherds, Menalcas and Mopsus, sing the death and apotheosis of the wonderful neatherd-singer Daphnis. The Mopsus portion, devoted to Daphnis' death and burial, is clearly indebted to the first idyll of Theocritus though the imitation is nothing like as exact as that of *Eclogue* 10. The Menalcas portion concerned with the apotheosis is not based on Theocritus (except in details). The identification of Daphnis with the recently assassinated and deified Julius Caesar has been doubted by several scholars but seems none the less quite certain (at least to me). Wholly aside from historico-religious considerations, the description of the deified Daphnis in 5. 60–61:

60   Nec lupus insidias pecori, nec retia cervis
61   ulla dolum meditantur: *amat* bonus *otia Daphnis*

corresponds to Octavian's earthly enforcement of the new god's pacific policy in 1. 6:

O, Meliboee, *deus* nobis haec *otia fecit*

and to the peace of the Julian dispensation described in 4. 21 f.

These suggestive parallels are however rather supererogatory since 9. 46 f. actually refers to the deified Caesar (Caesaris astrum) as bringing fruitfulness to the crops and colour to the vine. Caesar is here exactly the same god as the deified Daphnis of 5:

5. 52   Daphnim ad astra feremus
5. 57   sub pedibus . . . videt nubes et sidera Daphnis
5. 78–79   Ut *Baccho Cererique*, tibi [i.e. Daphnidi]
            sic *vota* quotannis/*agricolae* facient

Furthermore it is *Daphnis*, who in 9, regards the heavens and sees the *Caesaris astrum*.

It has indeed been suggested that a *living* Daphnis could hardly contemplate the star of the *dead and deified* Daphnis-Caesar of 5 or that, at any rate, Virgil would not have mixed the roles of Daphnis in so curious a fashion, but this assumes a consistency of characterization in the *Eclogue Book* which Virgil not only fails to observe but seems quite deliberately to avoid. Yet the recurrence of the name *Daphnis* in 9, after its use in 5, does indicate a connection of the two as well as a difference: in 5 Virgil is restricting himself to bucolic or Theocritean conventions (Rome, Caesar, or Octavian are carefully *not* mentioned); in 9 he is deliberately alternating bucolic and Roman themes, or even mixing them in an intentionally jarring or paradoxical way. The poem (9) is to be read as rather direct (as seen by a contemporary at least) comment on Virgil's life and poetry to date: the apparent mixup of roles and themes is designed. In 1 we get for the first time a true fusion of Roman and bucolic themes. But in 9 Virgil is talking of his poetry (even quoting it) in all its contrasted variety: the reference to 5 (*Caesar* in 9, corresponding to *Daphnis* in 5) is unmistakable in this special context.[1]

----

[1] Among recent scholars, Büchner (198–9) and H. J. Rose (*The Eclogues of Vergil*, 1942) deny the identification of Daphnis with Caesar. But such denials go with (among other things) an almost complete indifference to the whole scheme of the *Eclogue Book*. While not impugning the cogency of historical arguments for the identity (e.g. Pierre Grimal, 'La Ve Eclogue et le Culte de César' *Mélanges . . . à Charles Picard* I, 1955 = vol. 29 of the *Revue Archaeologique*, pp. 406–19), I think there is quite enough proof of it in the *Eclogue Book* itself.

The deified Daphnis of 5 is thus the rather thin mask of the deified Julius. But of course the new 'peace' that he brings to the world and the new security he bestows on the farmer points also toward Octavian, his living successor, *Divi filius*, though Octavian's future role in the state was quite unclear in 42–41 (the probable date of 5). At any rate Virgil could see in the death and deification of Caesar (perhaps in the great comet— the *Iulium sidus*—of 43) the possibility of a revival of peace and prosperity in Italy. This was endangered by the events of 41, and the repercussions of these events on Virgil is discernible in the ninth eclogue. By 40, however, the diplomacy of Pollio bore fruit at Brundisium: the new pact between Octavian and Antonius was sealed by the latter's marriage with Octavian's sister, Octavia. And even before that (probably by the end of 41 or a little later) Virgil had achieved a new confidence in Octavian: we cannot know whether or not he 'recovered' his 'farm' (though there is nothing improbable in the tradition) but it is fantastic to deny that the 'god' and 'youth' of *Eclogue* 1 is Octavian and that Virgil now looked on him as the restorer of his peace and security in some sense. Thus the Brundisium pact (in which his friend Pollio was so prominent) must have seemed to him like the beginning of a new era. His portrait of death and resurrection, of the change by which a brutal murder—*crudele funus*—had led to new *otia* and security, could now be made the centrepiece of his new *libellus*. But 1 had already (i.e. before the pact) shown the direction of his thoughts.

1 is remarkable in that here Virgil for the first time united the Theocritean-bucolic themes of 2 and 3 and the Roman theme (only symbolically present in 5, almost harshly juxtaposed to bucolic in 9) in one harmonious whole. Tityrus was simply equated with Amaryllis and Galatea in 9—a name for a bucolic subject (22–25): in 1, he is brought to see that his bucolic *otium* is both the victim and the beneficiary of historical, Roman forces. History had, as it were, burst into the inner recesses of the bucolic world: neither poet nor shepherd nor farmer could live, could have peace, let alone sing or work, except by coming to terms with a political and historical actuality. When Meliboeus asks for the name of Tityrus' saving god (the mere fact that Tityrus had been saved by *a* god was *in itself* no

anachronism, no abandonment of the conventions of the genre),
the apparently digressive 'answer' comes:

19   Urbem quam dicunt Romam, Meliboee, putavi
            stultus ego, huic nostrae similem quo saepe solemus
            pastores ovium teneros depellere fetus.

Thus Virgil prepares us—with what apparent naturalness!—
for the amazing change of scene, the journey to Rome, and for
the encounter there with an actual historical personality, the
deus, the *iuvenis*. At no point does he abandon the bucolic manner
and diction: the name Octavian or Caesar is most carefully not
pronounced, but the bucolic response: 'Pascite ut ante boves,
pueri, submittite tauros', is enough.[1] The deed has been done;
pastoral, that most unhistorical of genres, has been Romanized
and brought into history. The poet has now seen and said that
poetry itself cannot live except by coming to terms with its age.
To see in this poem only a recovery of specific property—a mere
biographical datum—is to miss its major significance: it
actually poses the plight of the poet in a world of violence and
draws the moral that he can be saved only be identifying himself with the historical source of safety, the man who can
restore peace and security (haec otia) to a society that has lost
both.

   We can now grasp the meaning of 6 and 4 and their relation
to 5. 6 is at once neoteric and of the past and it is concerned with
the past as essentially the story of man's fall from peace and
happiness and from the golden age or *Saturnia regna*. 4 is the
opposite—the rebirth or restoration of the *Saturnia regna* in the
new dispensation inaugurated by the consul Pollio and the new
pact between Antonius and Octavian. The designed relation of
6 and 4 is apparent from their introductions. 6 begins, as we
have seen, with a paraphrase of Callimachus' preface to the
Aitia, an explanation to Varus that Virgil cannot write epic,
that his genius can only compass light poetry (deductum
carmen), the bucolic or rustic muse, the rural theme, *myricae*,
nemus, tamarisks and woods. But 4 explicitly goes beyond such
limits: Virgil declares that he will now broaden his scope and
sing of somewhat greater things (paulo maiora); it is not all

---

[1] I am of course indebted here to F. Klingner's admirable article, 'Virgils
Erste Ekloge' (*Hermes* 62 (1927), pp. 129–53).

men that woods and lowly tamarisks (myricae) can suit; if he is to sing of woods, let them at least be worthy of a consul, of Pollio. The contrast between bucolic, neoteric or Callimachean verse and verse in a bigger, more epic vein, could hardly be indicated more explicitly. And this is obviously borne out in the styles of the two poems: 6 is hurried, varied, plaintive, curtly allusive; 4 is solemn, continuous, full of epic anaphora and phraseology.

But to what does this designed stylistic difference point? The subject matters of the two poems are obviously as diverse as the styles. One is neoteric (almost a catalogue of neoteric 'little epics'); the other is prophetic and inspired—almost like a prayer that is answered. 6, furthermore, puts its essential subject (the *song*, ll. 31–81) into the mouth of the Bacchic Silenus and invests it with the tonality of a Bacchanalian revel. 4 has no frame at all but proceeds from the brief three line invocation of the Muses directly to the solemn prophecy: the style shows the abrupt, apodeictic certainty of the poet turned seer; he needs no intermediary now. It seems obvious that there is more here than a simple contrast between literary styles or types of poetry.

Much of the discussion of the sixth eclogue has concerned its relation to Gallus, its bearing on the neoteric poetry of the day. A common view of its content (or rather of the Silenus song which constitutes its core) has been that it is in effect a catalogue—either of Gallus' own poetry, or of various neoteric 'little epics', or of different genres (didactic, aetiological epic, *metamorphoses, amores,* &c.).[1] All such criticism, however, ignores its evident plan, its deliberately hurried *continuity*. It, in fact, corresponds to a model that Virgil later set forth in the fourth *Georgic* (345–7) when describing the song sung by Clymene in the under-water palace of Cyrene:

> inter quas curam Clymene narrabat inanem
> Volcani, Martisque dolos et dulcia furta,
> aque *Chao densos* divum *numerabat amores.*

---

[1] Franz Skutsch (*Gallus und Vergil*, 128–55, *Aus Vergils Frühzeit*, 28–49) held that Virgil was listing the works or *epyllia* of Gallus; Denis van Berchem (*Mus. Helv.* 3, 1946) holds that he listed the neoteric works 'on sale' at the time; Zeph Stewart (*HCSP*, 64 (1959), pp. 176–205), that he is listing the main genres or types of poetry then in vogue. None of these theories, however, accounts for the order or continuity of the Silenus song as a whole. See Appendix 5.

We find the same idea several times in Ovid (*Ars.* II. 467–80, *Fasti* I. 101 f.) and of course most explicitly in the *Metamorphoses* itself where, after the philosophical beginning (from Chaos), we proceed to the Creation, the Fall (declension from the age of gold to the age of iron), the Flood, the new Creation of Pyrrha and then, from I, 434 on, to the long series of *amores* and *metamorphoses*, often superficially linked to be sure, but still carrying on a semblance of chronology as well as of continuity (the poem is a *carmen perpetuum*) and reaching a crescendo of horror in the terrible stories of pathological heroines like Scylla, Myrrha and Byblis. Such a 'Collective-Poem' (Martini invented the apt label: *Kollektivgedicht*) goes back in part to hellenistic originals like Callimachus' *Aitia* and Nicander's *Heteroioumena* or Parthenius' *Metamorphoses* and was almost certainly much discussed in neoteric circles.

But clearly Virgil, like Ovid, gave the idea a special form and style. The neoteric components were arranged in a meaningful sequence. We can outline the plan of the Silenus song as follows:

I (31–40): Creation from Chaos (Philosophic style).

II (41–2): *Saturnia Regna*, Fall, Flood, and Second Creation (Theft of Prometheus, Pyrrha).

III (43–4): *Hylas* (Episode of Age of Heroes and Argonautic Expedition and fallen man's *first* venture on the ocean, cf. Horace, *Carmina* I. 3. 21 f.).

IV (45–60): *Pasiphaë* (first tragic *dementia* caused by *amor*).

V (61–3): Transitional *Amores* and *Metamorphoses* (Atalanta, sisters of Phaethon).

VI (64–73): *Interlude*: Gallus and the Muses.

VII (74–81): *Metamorphoses* representing fully *criminal amor* (Scylla, Tereus and Philomela).

Thus except for the Gallus 'interlude' (64–73) the Silenus song falls into a quite recognizable chronological pattern: Creation, Golden Age, Fall and Flood (Prometheus, Pyrrha), Age of Heroes and first expedition on the Sea (Hylas); then a series of *amores* (Pasiphaë, Atalanta) and *amores-metamorphoses* (Phaethontiades, Scylla, Tereus, Philomela) all illustrative of *amor indignus*, love gone wrong, love *after* the golden age or *Saturnia Regna*.

If we now turn to the fourth eclogue, we find a clearly contrasting chronology, a movement back from the iron to the full golden age (Saturnia Regna) as the wonder-child grows up:

1. (9–17): The child at birth, prophecy of the change to come (in future).

2. (18–25): The child as *puer*: disappearance of natural evil, recovered spontaneity of the earth.

3. (26–36): The child at the point of knowledge and ethical understanding. Continuation of natural spontaneity but a few remains (pauca vestigia) of sin (fraus) in the reversed 'heroic age' of the second Argonautic expedition (32–35) and the second Trojan War (35–36).

4. (37–45): The child a mature man; complete natural spontaneity: no sailing on the sea, commerce, agriculture, or dye-stuffs.

There seems to be some vagueness as to the exact time of arrival of the golden age of natural spontaneity and innocence, but the difference between stage 3 (the stage of awakened ethical understanding) and stage 4 (complete manhood) is clear: in the first (3) the 'heroic age' is still not free of all crime and fear though there has been a great recovery of natural spontaneity; in the second (4), the complete golden age of fully spontaneous plenty and absolute innocence has finally arrived. In any event, the inverse relation of *Eclogues* 4 and 6 is clear beyond any doubt: in 6 we decline forward from the golden age (it is, characteristically, dismissed with a bare mention: Silenus is hastening to more appropriate topics), to the Age of Heroes (Hylas) and the iron-age *amores*; in 4 we progress backward from the iron age (sceleris vestigia nostri) to the Age of Heroes and the Age of Gold. The growing child—whoever he may be and whatever parents he may have—is the symbol of the promised renewal and recovery of virtue and peace which Virgil saw in the events of 40 or in the new truce that Pollio had made between Antonius and Octavian. The dark *amores* and *metamorphoses* of 6, are, conversely, symbolic of the moral decline (scelus) of the 'iron age' through which Rome had just passed. The child comes from the fruitful, beneficient *amor* of noble and patriotic parents: to this is opposed the *indignus amor* of Pasiphaë, Scylla and Tereus, the representatives of the *dementia* and *scelus* into which the iron age had sunk.

The difficulty so often experienced in comprehending or acknowledging this contrast (which both the design of the two poems and the design of the whole *Eclogue Book* should put beyond any doubt) resides in the apparent ambiguity of Virgil's neotericism. Did he really take such a stern, moralistic view of poems so much in vogue as the 'little epics' mentioned in 6? Did he really represent Gallus and his poetry as the 'bad' side of such a comparison? Is he not, on the contrary, being as complimentary to Gallus as he well can be? The answer assuredly is that Virgil is *not* sternly banishing neoteric poetry to a moral dog-house but that he is none the less indicating in a poetical way two alternative conceptions of human destiny as well as of literary purpose. The neoteric and elegiac poetry of Cinna, Parthenius, and Gallus was not adapted to an age in which violent and criminal disorder called for moral restoration. Virgil himself had been neoteric or Alexandrine in his poetical past: he, like his dear friend Gallus, had written and was writing of *amor indignus*; but a new situation was now demanding a broader, bigger, more serious kind of poetry (paulo maiora). Gallus and Pollio were alike his friends and, alike, combined poetical with political interests. We can see this divergence of literary and moral ideas somewhat more clearly, in another designed contrast, that between 5 and 10.

Eclogue 5 partially imitates Theocritus 1 in the Mopsus song of Daphnis' decease (exstinctum crudeli funere Daphnim). But there is no mention of Daphnis' *love* nor of love as the cause of his death, nor of his suicide. All that is taken from Theocritus is the lament of the animals (greatly changed and expanded) and the 'topsy-turvy' theme. The latter however (cf. *Theocritus* 1. 132–6) is not only altered in substance but is converted from a wish (in Theocritus, Daphnis' wish *before* his suicide) to a statement of fact (in the present indicative) and of course is described as a consequence of Daphnis' death represented as already taken place. Virgil thus sees in the death a natural catastrophe, a veritable devastation of nature and its powers (5. 34 f.). Daphnis was the civilizer who tamed lions and covered with soft leaves the sharp spears of the Bacchic *Thiasi*: at his demise all is once more given to waste and disorder (pro molli viola, pro purpureo narcisso/carduus, &c.). But Daphnis, become immortal (song of Menalcàs), reverses nature in a quite opposite sense: no wolf stalks the cattle; no nets trap the deer; *amat bonus otia Daphnis.* Here Virgil seems to have used part of Theocritus' 'topsy-turvy' theme (on the stag worrying the hounds) as well as a spurious couplet from his *Herakliskos* (24. 84 f.), but the idea of a *peaceful* reversal of this sort is completely un-Theocritean. The basic contrast made by Virgil is one between the revolutionary effect of death (Caesar's) and the even more revolutionary effect of new life, his apotheosis. The paradoxes of the golden age, as in 4 (cf. 4. 16, 21–25, 40 f.) will return with the divine victory over death and chaos. Menalcas' song is indeed a startling addition to Theocritus.

Yet Virgil uses the *love-death* of Daphnis in his tenth eclogue. Here, however, Virgil is dealing with quite another Daphnis. Or rather instead of suggesting Caesar (or some *theios aner* of cosmic power) by the name Daphnis, he suggests Daphnis by his manner of depicting Gallus. Thus the imitation of Theocritus 1 is far more literal and overt than in 5. The initial lines of the lament:

9   Quae nemora aut qui vos saltus habuere, puellae
      Naides, indigno cum Gallus amore peribat?

only somewhat generalize the Theocritean lines:

1. 66   πᾷ ποκ' ἄρ' ἦσθ', ὅκα Δάφνις ἐτάκετο, πᾷ ποκα, Νύμφαι
      Where were you then, when Daphnis wasting lay, where were
      you, Nymphs?

      ἦ κατὰ Πηνειῶ καλὰ τέμπεα, ἦ κατὰ Πίνδω;
      In Peneus' lovely vales, in Pindus then?

The theme of *amor indignus* (set forth also in 8: *indigno Nisae deceptus amore*) and of *crudelis amor*, as the cause of Gallus' anguish, occupies the first section (ll. 9–30) of the poem. It is followed (ll. 31–69) by Gallus' reply: he wants to lead the life of a simple Arcadian shepherd-poet but his own occupation (*amor duri Martis*) and Lycoris' unfaithfulness make any such attempt or indeed any kind of *medicina furoris* of no avail. There is no escape from love and to love accordingly he must submit:

71   omnia vincit Amor, et nos cedamus Amori.

This is, certainly, a tribute to Gallus, Virgil's good friend and poetical associate:

10. 73   Gallo, cuius amor tantum mihi crescit in horas,
      quantum vere novo viridis se subicit alnus.

But it is clearly more: Gallus' *servitium* to Lycoris is also seen as something *indignum*, a grievous burden that condemns him to misery. Anyone who knows of Propertius' *servitium* to Cynthia or Tibullus' to Delia and Nemesis can hardly take this *amor* of Gallus in full seriousness: it is literary at least as much as it is real, and Gallus is a dying Daphnis and would-be Arcadian mainly in the Elegiac *amores* which he has been writing and which Virgil is here referring to and perhaps, in part, paraphrasing. But for all that, the contrast between the love-sick Gallus and the auspicious saviour—between the Daphnis of 5 and the Daphnis of 10—is very plain. Virgil, in taking, in 10, his leave of Arethusa, that is, of Theocritus as a model—is taking his leave of *love*, of amatory sentiment such as Gallus used and he himself had used in his eighth eclogue, and takes leave also of the *deductum carmen* in which he had expressed himself up to now. The centre of his real devotion, the goal of his true poetic instinct is not *Amor* and its service but the new *Romanitas* represented by Octavian, the new spirit at work in the world under the star of the deified Caesar and that actual *praesens deus*, the divine youth of *Eclogue* 1.

Thus the contrast between 5 and 10 corresponds to that between 4 and 6: each pair opposes the ideas of resurrection, rebirth, renovation to the ideas of unworthy love, irrational *furor*, sin (fraus, scelus) and social unrest, all of which are associated with or lead to death or (as in 6) to the punitive metamorphosis of the human into the animal. 5 is the centre around which 4 and 6, 2 and 8, 3 and 7, 1 and 9 are grouped because 5 most directly expresses the moral and political agency that transforms death and sterile disorder into new life and peaceful innocence: this agency is the Julian house that had at last promised peace to Italy and the empire and was actually performing the essential work of resurrection and renewal. The contrast between 1 and 9 is less pointed than that of 4 and 6 or of 5 and 10 but is still unmistakable: 1 fuses the bucolic and Roman themes of the *Eclogue Book* around the figure of the *deus* and *iuvenis*, Octavian; 9 leaves these two themes in a discordant juxtaposition and also colours them with a pessimism that the singing close cannot quite dispel. Even the Theocritean poems re-echo the contrast: 8 shows the baneful consequences of *amor indignus* or resorts (with Alphesiboeus) to magic as the sole means of restoring Daphnis to his lover; 2 shows the conquest of such love by a renewed rationality, a revived appreciation of the rustic innocence that an unworthy passion had threatened. Even 3 and 7, the least overtly antithetic pair of the *Eclogue Book*, reveal a contrast between two kinds of singing contests—one (3) proceeding from petty wrangling to an harmonious conclusion; the other (7) ending only in the defeat of the bitter and harshly emphatic Thyrsis. One can, perhaps, overdo or exaggerate the separate antitheses: in sum, they are cumulatively impressive.

So Virgil had developed during the years 41–38 from a neoteric and Theocritean to at least a potentially Augustan poet. As yet he had only begun to elaborate a unified style and a psychologically continuous narrative; he had certainly not worked out all the implications and meanings of his new Julio-Roman symbolism or included it within a single integral text. But he had laid the foundations on which he was later to build.

CHAPTER V

THE *GEORGICS*

I

THE Roman and historical vein first revealed in the *Eclogues* only reached true Epic form some eight years later (29). The interval (37–29 B.C.) was devoted to a didactic poem on agriculture, the *Georgics*.[1] This was far more than a parergon, a side product of a genius already dedicated to epic: in its length (four books) and, above all, in its intricate symmetry and stylistic finish, it was a major work avowedly and actually engaging the full powers of the mature poet. Herein lies its mystery: why, indeed, did Virgil's genius take this direction; why the delay between the promise and the fulfilment of his Roman epic; why, above all, the adoption of the didactic form and the agricultural subject?

This mystery lies squarely athwart the present investigation of Virgil's epic narrative. For until we can reach some notion of what the *Georgics* meant in his development as a narrative poet, we cannot understand that development at all. Seemingly he abandoned narrative—at least narrative in its ordinary meaning of a story with human content, a story of men or of men and gods—after writing the *Eclogues*, and did not resume it until he added the *Aristaeus* episode to the Fourth *Georgic* or, to adopt another hypothesis, until he had started to compose the *Aeneid* itself. It seems evident he was not yet ready for epic even though he had no desire to continue the kind of poetry represented by the *Bucolics*. But in the choice of *didactic*, he still remained formally faithful to Callimachean and neoteric principles: *didactic* was not *one continuous narrative* in Callimachus' sense of that term.

Yet in fact the *Georgics* is didactic only in the most superficial sense. It represents in actuality a quite new kind of poem which

---

[1] See the data given in Schanz-Hosius, op. cit. pp. 49, 57. Both the 'Donatus' and 'Servius' *vitae* state that Virgil composed the *Georgics* in *seven*, the *Aeneid* in *eleven* years. This gives us the approximate dates: *Georgics* 37 or 36–30 or 29; *Aeneid* 29–19. The completed *Georgics* was read to Augustus *reverso post Actiacam victoriam*, i.e. probably just before Augustus' triumph on 12 or 14 August, 29 B.C.

has only the most tenuous connection with Nicander and Aratus and is different indeed from the philosophical didactic of Lucretius. Though not a narrative—that is, not a *story*—it is, when properly interpreted, a continuous whole concerned with the most central and serious themes of Augustan Rome. Seen in this light, the *Georgics* may be recognizable as a non-narrative propaedeutic to narrative: after writing it, Virgil perhaps was able to see his way clear to a form of epic which could embody his patriotic purpose without offending his 'neoteric sensibility'. This we must now try to find out.

The mystery of the *Georgics* lies in its form and its subject matter. On one level—that on which until quite recently most critics have preferred to remain—it is a metrical treatise on agriculture written at Maecenas' order to encourage a 'back to the farm' movement in Italy or even to teach the Italian farmer how to raise corn and grapes or rear cattle and bees. At another and somewhat more sophisticated level of interpretation, it seems an elaborate 'Kunstwerk' principally inspired by Augustus' message of peace and the rehabilitation of rural Italy from the anarchy and moral decay of the civil wars. But on both levels, it remains a poem about agriculture, however much its artistry and its moving 'digressions' on the death of Caesar, Italy, the happy farmer or the bees of Aristaeus may serve to exalt the prosaic subject matter. It is only very recently that some critics—I think especially of Burck, Klingner and Büchner—have refused to treat Virgil with such naïveté and have tried to penetrate the deeper meaning of the poem (they believed it *had* a deeper meaning!) by analysing the symbolic character of the agricultural images and the relation of the 'digressions' to their context.[1] Though something has been done in this direction, much more still remains to be done: in what follows I shall develop the points that seem to me most essential for an understanding of Virgil's development as a narrative poet. This means primarily an analysis and explanation of the Aristaeus episode which concludes the whole poem, though, as will be seen, this also demands consideration of the poem in its entirety.

We must start with a clear recognition of the *novel* character of the *Georgics*. It is not a Hellenistic didactic poem like the

[1] See Appendix 6.

Georgika and *Alexipharmaka* of Nicander or the *Phainomena* of
Aratus, that is to say a poetical treatise primarily designed to
exhibit the poet's cleverness in giving metrical form to a prosaic
subject-matter. It may have been partially indebted to such
poetry (perhaps Virgil took the name *Georgika* from Nicander)
but it is quite clear that Virgil was really going back to Hesiod
(the Hesiod of the *Works and Days*) for a model and that he was
most heavily influenced by the didactic of Lucretius, itself a
return to the philosophical verse of the Pre-Socratics. There
is of course also much agricultural lore in the *Georgics*: Virgil
drew on Varro and other Greek and Latin prose treatises when
he needed them. The essential point is that he was writing not
an Alexandrine curiosity in an Alexandrine way (not using a
prosaic subject to demonstrate his poetic cleverness) but
invoking the spirit and mood of original, serious didactic, the
utterance of an age which put its message in verse because
verse was the only available medium of communication. In
other words: he has something to say and summons the seriousness of Hesiod and Lucretius in order to say it.

On the other hand, he is not, like Lucretius, writing in verse
in order to make a hard subject attractive to his audience. He
is not trying to sweeten his agricultural medicine with poetical
honey. Nor is he really concerned, like Hesiod, to give practical
advice. The *Georgics* is not a metrical treatise at all, but a poem,
a work of art. We can hardly suppose that Virgil really wrote it
for actual farmers. There is no reason to doubt that he was
seriously concerned with the plight of the farmer and intended
his poem, in part at least, as an exaltation of the rural way of
life. But this was surely not his *main* purpose: the *Georgics* is a
true poem because it has *poetical* meaning expressed through
but not exhausted by the agricultural subject matter. It is in
fact (to boldly state an opinion which needs to be defended) a
most intricate structure of symbols and its major concerns are
those most central in both human life and Augustan Rome:
work, play and man's relation to nature in both, and, beyond
these, life, death and rebirth. It is the transformation of
Hesiodic and Lucretian didactic into a single homogeneous
poem.

All this will become clearer when we analyse the poem. But
the initial problem that besets any such analysis must first be

mentioned: how far was Virgil himself conscious of a 'deeper purpose'; how far was he himself aware of his symbolic style, if such his style actually is? In other words, does modern criticism of the poem here go 'beyond' the poet's conscious intention? Clearly, this is a question which cannot be answered with absolute assurance. But it can I think be said that Virgil intended a great deal more than he explicitly and overtly revealed: it was, so to speak, part of his plan—and of the literary convention in which he worked—to write as if he were actually concerned only with his ostensible subjects—the planting of cereals and vineyards, the raising of cattle and bees—and to mark off all 'other' topics as 'digressions' from his 'technical' subject-matter. But it is to me inconceivable that he was unaware of the underlying symbolism, at least in its broader and most obvious aspects.

Here, of course, it is possible, as in all poets, to 'read in' much that, for better or worse, was never in the poet's mind or to uncover what was at best only in its subconscious recesses. The present problem of Virgilian critics is to preserve a safe *via media* between what can only be called the obtuseness and crude literalism of most older commentary on the poem and a more recent tendency to find all manner of mystical meanings and numerical correspondences in it. Basically it makes little difference what the poet consciously intended—we cannot hope to read his mind—if we can in fact reveal what constitutes the 'true' character and meaning of his poetry. In any event, the problem is to find what is there—if symbols, for example, genuine symbols and not will-o'-the-wisps of an infatuated critic—and at all costs to avoid the 'reading in' of purely suppositious and extrinsic meanings. Our goal, in short, is not so much to recover Virgil's original purpose as to recognize the true structure of his poem without the use of far-fetched analogies or theories.

Let us start with a quite obvious fact which, 'obvious' as indeed it is, has often been by-passed or ignored. This fact is that the *Georgics* is only superficially a guide for farmers. While the information is generally accurate—given the prevailing state of knowledge—it is deliberately elliptical: this is evident when one sets Virgil beside Varro. In Book IV, for example, he omits all the little animals (the *pastio villatica* of Varro) and treats only the bees. In Book II he devotes several hundred lines to the vine and only five to the olive, thirty-two to other trees. In Book III he deals with farm animals, cattle, horses, sheep, goats: the agriculturally significant pig, the dog, &c., are simply ignored. That this ellipsis has no simple, mechanical explanation (such as, e.g. lack of space) is evident when we consider the single fact that exactly half of Book IV is taken up by the Aristaeus episode despite the obvious practical importance of the smaller fauna. It is indeed not necessary to belabour the evidence that Virgil is not in the least concerned with adequate coverage or, in fact, with any sort of practical utility: how actually helpful, for example, are even the most technical portions of the poem such as the analysis of soils in Book II or the section on irrigation and drainage in Book I?

We are thus forced at once to look for a plan or structure of the poem which *determines* and is not *determined by* the agricultural content. This I think emerges quite clearly from even the simplest analysis of the four books:

I. 1–42: Invocation to the gods and Augustus.
A. 43–203: The *Work of the Farmer*.
This falls into four relatively distinct parts:

   (*a*) 43–70: *The farmer's two prime requisites:* to make his plough gleam in the furrow (*work*), ll. 43–49; and to learn, *before he ploughs*, the nature of the soil and climate, the right time for each activity (*experientia*), ll. 50–63. Man is of a hard race (*durum genus*, l. 63) subject to nature's eternal laws: he must therefore *work* hard to acquire *experience* (*Ergo, age*, l. 63).

   (*b*) 71–117: The *Work itself*: rotation of crops and fertilizing, ll. 71–99; irrigation and drainage, ll. 100–17.

   (*c*) 118–59: The *Religious Justification of Work* (digression). Jupiter has deliberately made man's life hard (by ending the Age of Gold) so that man might discover the arts of civilization. Labor omnia vicit/improbus, ll. 145–6.

   (*d*) 160–203: The *Harsh Struggle*.
      (1) The *weapons of the tough farmers* (*duris agrestibus*): plough, waggon, winnowing fan, &c., ll. 160–75.

   (2) The *constant struggle against deterioration*: The threshing floor and its enemies, the degeneration of seeds, the universal tendency toward the worse (*in peius ruere*, l. 200).

B. 204–350: *The Farmer's Calendar.*
  (*a*) 204–30: Sowing Times.
  (*b*) 231–58: The Divine Origin of the Calendar.
  (*c*) 259–310: Proper Use of the Times.
  (*d*) 311–50: The Farmer's Duty to the Gods of the Sky.
    338: *in primis venerare deos.*

C. 351–514: *The Signs of Things to Come.*
  (*a*) 351–423: The Signs of Bad and Good Weather.
    (1) 351–92: Bad Weather.
    (2) 393–423: Good Weather.
  (*b*) 424–514: The Moon and Sun as Prophetic.
    (1) 424–37: The Moon.
    (2) 438–63: The Sun as a Weather Prophet.
    (3) 463–514: The Sun as Prophet of Doom: the portents at Caesar's death; the evil condition of Rome (digression).

II. 1–8: Invocation to Bacchus.

A. 9–259: *Variety.*
  (*a*) 9–82: *The Varied Character of Arboriculture: the co-operation of nature and man.*
    (1) 9–34: The *varia natura arboribus creandis.*
    (2) 35–82: The *work involved:* grafting, budding, &c., *scilicet omnibus est labor impendendus*, l. 61.
  (*b*) 83–176: *The Variety of Species and Climes: Italy as the Perfect Mean.*
    (1) 83–108: The variety of species.
    (2) 109–35: The variety of climates.
    (3) 136–76: Italy (digression).
  (*c*) 177–258: *The Variety of Field and Soil.*
    (1) 177–225: Three Italian landscapes: Tuscany, Mantua, Capua.
    (2) 226–58: The soils and how to tell them.

B. 259–419: *Planting and Care of the Vine.*
  (*a*) 259–87: Where and how to plant.
  (*b*) 288–314: The Good and Bad Supports: Oak and wild olive.

(*c*) 315–45: The Spring (digression).
(*d*) 346–96: Care of the vine.
  (1) 346–53: Use of Mud and Stones in Ploughing.
  (2) 354–96: Care of the growing vine: Homage to Bacchus.
(*e*) 397–419: The Farmer's laborious round. *Redit agricolis labor actus in orbem.*

C. 420–57: *Other trees*: Olive, Apples, Willows, &c.
(*a*) 420–5: Olive.
(*b*) 426–33: Apples, wild fruits, &c.
(*c*) 434–57: Other trees: cedar, cypress, box, &c.

D. 458–540: *The Happy Farmers* (digression).
  541–2: Conclusion.

III. 1–48: Invocation: Virgil's Marble Temple.
A. 49–283: *The Big Animals*, Cattle and Horses.
(*a*) 49–137: Mating.
(*b*) 138–208: Care and Training.
(*c*) 209–83: *Amor* (digression).
  amor omnibus idem, l. 244.

B. 284–566: *The Smaller Animals*: Sheep and Goats.
(*a*) 284–94: Invocation to Pales.
(*b*) 295–383: Pasturage.
  (1) 295–338: The seasons of pasturage.
  (2) 339–48: The Libyan Shepherds.
  (3) 349–83: The Scythian Shepherds.
(*c*) 384–469: The Pests.
  (1) 384–438: Weeds, Thieves, Snakes.
  (2) 439–69: Diseases.
(*d*) 470–566: *Plague* (digression).

IV. 1–7: Invocation to Maecenas.
A. 8–280: *The Bees*.
(*a*) 8–115: How to locate and maintain the hive.
  (1) 8–50: The *location* of the hive.
  (2) 51–66: Swarming.
  (3) 67–115: Selection and treatment of the King.
(*b*) 116–48: The Old Man of Tarentum (digression).
(*c*) 149–227: Nature of the Bees.
  (1) 149–96: The communal spirit of the bees.
    (*labor omnibus unus*, l. 184).
  (2) 197–227: The *spiritual* nature of the bee.

(*d*) 228–280: The Care of Bees.
   (1) 228–38: Taking the Honey.
   (2) 239–80: The Protection of the Bee: from cold, pests, diseases.
B. 281–314: *Resurrection of the Bees* (transitional).
C. 315–558: *The Resurrection Myth* (digression).
   (*a*) 315–452: Aristaeus' grief and appeal to Proteus.
   (*b*) 453–527: The *Oracle* of Proteus: Orpheus and Eurydice.
   (*c*) 528–58: Implementation of the Oracle: the Resurrection of the Bees.
   559–66: Conclusion of the whole work.

Even such truncated summary reveals at once important things about the structure of the whole poem. It is clear:

(1) That Books III and IV agree in their essential plan of arrangement (*vis-à-vis* I and II). Each (III and IV) falls into two equal sections of almost exactly the same number of verses: 283 and 283, and 280 and 286 (278 if the eight verses of the conclusion are subtracted). I and II, in contrast, are much more varied and divided into much shorter sections.

(2) There is also a designed correspondence in arrangement between I and III and between II and IV. Thus both I and III begin with relatively long invocations (42 verses in I; 48 in III) and end with relatively long 'digressions' (52 verses in I; 97 in III) whereas II and IV begin with quite short invocations (8 verses in II; 7 in IV) and end with very brief passages of conclusion (ll. 541–2 in II; 559–66 in IV) quite unlike I and III which do not *explicitly* mark their conclusions at all.

(3) These relatively superficial correspondences clearly go with much more fundamental correspondences of subject-matter and mood. The relative gaiety and lightness of Books II and IV, the sombre and heavy character of I and III are evident to all. We can almost put this in musical language:

       I—allegro maestoso
       II—scherzo
       III—adagio
       IV—allegro vivace

But even more important than this *variatio* of tone and mood between the even and uneven books is the difference between the first two books and the last two: I–II deal with man's relation to the landscape and to the vegetable world of the crops, the vine, and the useful trees; III–IV deal with animals and are much more concerned with the animals in themselves—with, so to speak, their own point of view—than with the men who raise, tend and use them.

We can express the dual interplay of relations between the books in the following diagram where the connecting lines represent relations of *similarity* or *congruity*:

Or, put differently, there are four main *contrasts* in the poem: that between I and II; that between III and IV; that between I–III and II–IV; and that between I–II and III–IV. Thus it follows that the maximum effect of contrast is concentrated in IV (or at the end of IV) since it is only here that all four contrasts are finally realized and evidenced, even that between I and II not achieving its full impact until that between III and IV has been established. This is also indicated by the very structure of IV which, unlike the analogously structured III, devotes its second half or section *not* to the didactic description of an agricultural or animal subject but to an emotionally heightened and dramatic *narrative* of *human* action. This departure from both the otherwise analogous structure of III and the style of didactic would seem to have something to do with the strategic location of the second half of IV in the whole poem. This, in other words, is precisely the section in which we would expect some sort of 'resolution' of the fourfold contrast between the books and the fact that it so significantly differs from all that precedes it would indicate that it has a special meaning or function corresponding to its special position.

These considerations are of course quite unimportant in themselves but they have the great value of being relatively objective and thus of providing a more or less secure guide to further and necessarily more 'subjective' interpretation. It may well be that the intricate numerical correspondences to which latterly Le Grelle has pointed [1] may have some interpretative

---

[1] Guy Le Grelle, S.J., 'Les Premières Géorgiques, Poème Pythagoricien' (*Les Études Classiques* 17 (1949), pp. 139–225).

value but it seems—at least to me—far safer to proceed from the relatively obvious than from the relatively obscure. I shall at any rate follow the quite simple—and also I think almost self-evident—lines of the schema just set forth.

The most obvious difference between I–II and III–IV is, as said above, that between an inanimate and an animate subject-matter, between cereals and vines on the one hand; cattle, horses, sheep, goats and bees on the other. But behind and beyond this obvious difference there is one less obvious but more interesting: in I and II Virgil looks at (better: addresses, exhorts, admonishes) man as he struggles *against* a recalcitrant natural environment or (II) as he works *with* a receptive and helpful environment but in III and IV (at least as far as l. 280) Virgil shifts his centre of attention from man to cattle, horses and bees. For here Virgil in virtue of his own empathy and sympathy (what we have called above the 'empathetic-sympathetic method') sees the cattle, horses and bees anthropo-morphically, as men writ large or small.

But his humanization of the animal is never pushed to an extreme; the cattle and bees do not 'stand for' men as in a kind of allegory. In fact, their animality—their non-human nature—is carefully emphasized. Rather Virgil uses their animality to give point to his anthropomorphism: they stand, so to speak, for nature (the nature common to both animal and man) as nature might seem if it had the emotional language with which to make us share its feelings and if it also shared some of our own feelings. The brutality of love and death in III is thus animal in its amorality and terrible insistence but human in the pity and even horror which it excites. Yet both the animality and the pity are equally 'human' (though in different senses of *human*) since man is also an animal. Similarly the sexless life, the rigid communism, the blind loyalty and the indifference to death of the bees are both human and inhuman (or animal) and never fully one or the other: Man is also a communal animal though he is certainly not sexless and selfless in the way a bee is. We can express the main contrasts here schematically thus:

I. *Man's* harsh struggle with inanimate nature (regarded as a bitter opponent).

II. *Man's* happy co-operation with inanimate nature (re-garded as a friendly helper).

III. *Nature* (and man as part of it) as the animate locus of an amoral Love and Death.

IV. (to l. 280) *Nature* (man as part of it) as the animate locus of an immortal, sexless, selfless, and divinely inspired community.

So the contrast between the harsh and happy aspects of man's work *in* nature is set beside the contrast between the disruptive and harmonious aspects of his own character when seen *sub specie naturae*. The resolution of the tensions here exhibited can only come (so one would presume) when man by some act of heroic atonement (e.g. the conquest of his passions or the payment of a just penalty for their past excesses) transcends his animal self and thus wins divine sanction for a new natural and social order. Then the Age of Gold will replace the Age of Iron; the happy community of the bees will rise again from the carcass of the bull. And the passion which spelled anarchy and death will yield to the tranquillity of a harmonious society reconciled to itself and to nature. But we must not, so to speak, put words in Virgil's mouth: the poem is, as we shall see, subtler and deeper than such a schema (which represents but a first approximation to Virgil's actual schema) and contains its own surprises. Before we can generalize further, we must analyse each book more closely.

I. The book starts with an appeal to the gods and to Augustus, the god to be, the *theios aner*. The first five lines clearly demarcate the topics of the four books: the cereal crops (*laetae segetes*), the vine (*vitis*), cattle (*cura boum*) and bees. The sombre tone of the book, as well as its special *humanitas*, is suggested by the line (41):

> *ignaros*que *viae* mecum *miseratus* agrestis

where the echo of Lucretius' pity for human ignorance:

II. 9   unde queas alios passimque videre
 10 errare atque *viam palantis quaerere* vitae

       .   .   .   .   .

 14 O *miseras* hominum mentis, o pectora caeca!
     qualibus in tenebris vitae, quantisque periclis
     degitur hoc aevi quodcumquest!

seems unmistakable. Virgil in close co-operation with Augustus is engaged on a mission of enlightenment to a generation that

has lost its way. The limitation of this poem to farmers—
agrestes—must not deceive us: the poem is, of course, concerned
with the *agrestes* as well as with the crops, the vine, cattle and bees
but the tone of this dedication, the indicated *audacitas* of the
enterprise (*audacibus adnue coeptis* reminiscent of Lucretius'
sanctos ausus recludere fontes), above all, perhaps, the concern for
human ignorance, suggest the broader purpose, the transformation of the Lucretian *Aufklärung* into a divinely sanctioned
mission of regeneration.

The first two sections of the Book (A, 43–203 and B, 204–350)
obviously correspond to Hesiod's *Works* and *Days*. Virgil not
only follows Hesiod's emphasis on the severity of bitter, unremitting toil, but, above all, reproduces Hesiod's moralizing
earnestness, holding so to speak a dialogue with his reader
somewhat reminiscent of Hesiod's with Perses. But Virgil's
audience is more universal: his message rises far beyond the
parochial-rustic scope of Hesiod.

The work of the farmer (the gleaming plough in the deep
furrow: four times a year must he plough!) demands a prior
knowledge of weather, locality and the life of the land. Man—
the *durum genus* sprung from Deucalion's stones—must observe
the eternal laws (aeterna foedera) of nature as impressed on
each region of the earth. His life is one of *labor* and *experientia*:
Ergo age terrae/pingue solum primis extemplo a mensibus
anni/fortes invortant tauri, &c. (43–70).

Man in fact is faced with an environment ever on the point of
exhaustion and relapse: the tired fields after harvest must be
left idle or the crops must be rotated. Flax, oats and poppies
can burn the life out of a field:

77   *Urit* enim lini campum seges, *urit* avenae,
        Urunt Lethaeo perfusa papavera somno.

Hence the need for manuring and scattering ash on the land,
for breaking up and ploughing across the clods. Though wet
summers and dry winters will help (the farmer must pray for
them indeed), irrigation and drainage go, so to speak, without
saying (71–117).

Virgil's attitude toward the land is here very significant.
Both men and the land are represented as engaged in a terrible
struggle, man coming to the relief of a tormented earth whose

fertility is constantly under attack. The language of such lines as:

72	segnem patiere situ durescere campum
77 f.	*Urit* enim, &c.
81	*effetos* cinerem immundum iactare per *agros*
87	sive *illis* omne per ignem
	excoquitur vitium atque exsudat inutilis umor
92	ne tenues pluviae *rapidive potentia solis*
	acrior aut boreae *penetrabile frigus adurat*
94	multum adeo, rastris glaebas qui frangit inertis
	vimineasque trahit cratis, *iuvat* arva
107	. . . cum *exustus* ager morientibus aestuat herbis
	(with the ensuing picture of the refreshing water stream which tempers the scorching fields: *arentia temperat arva*).

is both empathetic and sympathetic: the soil is seen as a suffering victim gladly welcoming man's help (iuvat arva) or else as itself an obstacle which (or whom) man must break and command:

99	*Exercet*que frequens tellurem atque *imperat* arvis.

The structure of the cola here, the metric, the use of synaloepha—all emphasize the harshness of the struggle or the weariness of earth and the relief (the only happy note) brought to it by the labour of man. Consider especially such lines as:

94	Multum adeo, rastris glaebas qui frangit inertis
	vimineasque trahit cratis, iuvat arva, neque illum
	flava Ceres alto nequiquam spectat Olympo,
	et qui, proscisso quae suscitat aequore terga,
	rursus in obliquom verso perrumpit aratro
99	exercetque frequens tellurem atque imperat arvis.

Here such words as *frangit, trahit, suscitat, perrumpit,* the harsh s and c sounds (proscisso, suscitat, exercetque), the laborious and momentarily anticlimactic second *qui* clause (97), the spondees of line 97, the caesura after *verso* (98), the synaloepha in line 99 (tellurem atque), the position of *iuvat* (l. 95: two shorts set off by caesura and diaresis) along with much else— all build up a towering impression of the *exertion*, the struggle by which the farmer finally dominates his fields.

Virgil has thus indicated the struggle of man and of the earth against the hostility or perversity of nature. He is now ready to explain it. In the next section (118–59) of this first part (see the outline on p. 148) he again draws on Hesiod, on Hesiod's description of the origin of Work in the Fall of Man. But not only does he partially reverse Hesiod's order (for Hesiod *starts* with the myths of Prometheus, the baneful woman and the five generations) but he omits Prometheus altogether and attributes Zeus' (Jupiter's) corruption of the Golden Age to an original, deliberate intention:

121   Pater ipse colendi
         haut facilem esse viam voluit primusque per artem
123   movit agros curis acuens mortalia corda.

Jupiter, in fear that man might grow torpid in his golden-age inertia, has introduced all the evils: private property, venomous snakes, marauding wolves, storms at sea. The honey no longer drips from the trees and the wine no longer flows in streams. But for this very reason, man has been forced to master the arts—including agriculture—and even to discover for himself the secret of fire. Civilization and work come together:

145   tum variae venere artes. Labor omnia vicit
146   improbus et duris urgens in rebus egestas.

It does not seem to me that *improbus* here can be wholly divested of its harsh and bitter connotations.[1] Work and poverty are extremely unpleasant: Virgil does not deny it. But is this unpleasantness nevertheless to be justified by the glory of civilization and the arts which came from it? Is this, in short, a

---

[1] There has been much discussion of *improbus* here. Servius (*ad loc.*) interprets it as *indefessus, adsiduus, sine moderatione*, i.e. as 'unremitting, untiring work'. L. P. Wilkinson (*Greece and Rome*, 19 (1950), pp. 19–28), Burck (*Hermes* 64 (1929), pp. 279–321, esp. p. 283), R. Beutler (*Hermes* 75 (1940), pp. 410–21) and Büchner (250–1) take *labor improbus* here in a good sense: Virgil is *praising* hard work. But H. Altevogt (*Labor Improbus, eine Vergilstudie*, 1952), rightly denies that *improbus* ever has a good sense. As Henry in *Aeneidea* (II. 175) correctly says: '*Improbus* is always a term of reprobation, always means simply wicked.' (Cf. Merguet, *Lexicon, ad. loc.*) Nor is it just that things are doomed to decay *unless* man keeps working against it (as Büchner, 252, says). There is, in any event, a fatal shadow on the whole picture: man's 'civilization' has a curse on it. The items in it that Virgil selects (135–44) involve at every point the rending and perversion of natural things (i.e. the discovery of fire, navigation, trapping, hunting and fishing, iron and steel tools, and—most important of all—private property). The work is *bad* because the farmer struggles as Altevogt says with the bad powers (unguter Mächte) but it is not just through such *labor* (as Altevogt also says) that the Golden Age is restored. Here Altevogt quite fails to see the true antithesis. See pp. 162 f.; 169 below.

version of man's beginnings which leaves out the Fall? Is this, so to speak, Virgil's palinode to the Creation myth of Silenus in *Eclogue* 6 (where the *furtum Promethei* is part of the story)? The full answer to such questions requires, I think, the context of the other Books (especially II). But even in I, Virgil's attitude toward civilization is anything but optimistic. If the Fall may be omitted from the passage under consideration, it over-shadows the whole closing section of the Book and re-emerges constantly thereafter. If the Age of Gold—the Saturnian earth—is thought of as a time of unproductive sloth, it is glorified and exalted at the end of Book II. Nor can we, I think, solve the problem by supposing that Virgil here meant only the innocent *work* of farmers and simple artisans and that he thought of such as veritably golden age men when compared to the corrupt and senselessly ambitious worldlings of his own time. Rather we must, I think, let this passage stand by itself as indicating but one aspect of the theme, one mood of the poet's mind. *Labor* and *egestas* have their place in Jove's scheme of things: civilization is *part* of the divine plan. But there is an intricate correspon-dence between men and the gods or between human life and the universal *logos* of Virgil's Stoic philosophy. Neither human wickedness nor the order of nature are finally independent of each other. Civilization is, so to speak, what civilization does and this also the whole course of nature reflects and symbolizes.

But the farmer, in present actuality, is struggling with a steadily deteriorating condition of things. His work is harsh and unremitting, because he cannot otherwise hope to live at all. His implements (the plough, waggon, winnowing fan, &c.) are but his *weapons* in a hard fight (duris agrestibus arma, l. 166). Even his threshing floor is continually being undermined by pests, moles, weevils and toads. He can do nothing about a poor crop if the signs (the blossoms on the walnut)—that is, the course of nature itself—are unfavourable. The farmer can indeed help himself by doping his seeds with nitre. But in the long run only the harsh toil of hand-picking them before sowing will insure a good crop since *everything fatally tends to decline*:

199   Sic omnia fatis
         in peius ruere ac retro sublapsa referri
         non aliter quam qui adverso vix flumine lembum

remigiis subigit, si bracchia forte remisit,
203   atque illum in praeceps prono rapit alveus amni.

Thus the pessimism of the section (A) is clear. It is a peculiar blend of Hesiod and Lucretius. The pictures of the origin of the arts and of the general decline of things—the movement towards the worse—are of course indebted to the corresponding passages in the second and fifth books of Lucretius. But Virgil moralizes Lucretius. The decline that Lucretius sees:

II. 1158   Sponte sua primum mortalibus ipsa (tellus) creavit,
ipsa dedit dulcis fetus et pabula laeta;
quae nunc vix nostro grandescunt aucta labore

and the *usus* and *experientia* behind human 'progress' are described by Virgil as part of Jupiter's design. Here we encounter the moralism of Hesiod denuded of his simple mythology. It seems clear that Virgil is trying to construct a theodicy which will do justice to the Augustan age. But so far, he has not revealed its true dimension: the work of the farmer is not, as we shall see, only a bitter struggle with nature; the earth has not lost all its spontaneity; and the Age of Iron is not just a device of Jupiter. Nature can co-operate with man but only when man knows and recognizes what is good for him.

The second part of this book (B: 204–350) corresponds, of course, to the Hesiodic *Days*: it is the farmer's calendar. And here we see at once the dimension of cosmic sympathy. It was precisely to demarcate the Farmer's Year—to establish the right time to do the right thing—that the sky has been zoned as it is:

231   *Idcirco* certis dimensum partibus orbem
per duodena regit mundi sol aureus astra.

The *idcirco* clearly refers to lines 204–30 where Virgil with all possible brevity (for he is not of course interested in the calendar *per se*) described the Farmer's *Days*. Thus the universe is established to be man's almanack.[1] But the net result of this divine concern for man is not exhilarating: it is, if anything, to make him work harder than ever. Every moment must be used: when it storms without, the farmer within must hew out the hard teeth of the ploughshare or make the other instruments of his craft. Even holidays should be used for hedging, ditching and

---

[1] So rightly Burck, op. cit. p. 287.

sheep-dipping. He must work at night and his wife must work
with him. And in the good weather he must once more deter-
minedly strip to his task:

299   nudus ara, sere nudus: hiems ignava colono.

But in winter also there are all manner of things to do. Nor is a
knowledge of times and seasons so much a means to prosperity
as an escape from disaster; the farmer's seasonal lore leaves him
without excuse when he has not harvested before the autumn
storms:

335   Hoc metuens caeli menses et sidera serva.

This is more a message of fear than of hope. Yet the section
ends with the pious advice: *in primis venerare deos* and a description of the Ambarvalia whereat Ceres is properly worshipped.
We shall revert to this later. It certainly strikes a novel note of
cheer but it in no sense alters the general tone and movement of
the Book.

Actually Virgil had only begun to describe the real meaning
of cosmic sympathy. For in the third and last section of this
Book (C: 351–514), we see that it is far more than an eternally
fixed relationship of man and the cosmos in the Farmer's Year,
more even than a contest between man's toil and a fated process
of deterioration grimly designed to make him work harder than
ever. Nature in fact is prophetic: the voice of the gods speaks
in the heavens and in the dumb animals and in the sputtering
lamp wicks as it foretells through them the approach of bad and
good weather. *But more than this, natural phenomena forebode
historical events.* The assassination of Caesar provokes a veritable
Walpurgisnacht and the whole cosmos is shaken by the civil
conflicts of the Roman people. Nature is thus much more than a
fate which man must passively endure, more than a part of
Jove's scheme to encourage the arts. It is also a fellow-sufferer, so
to speak, whom man can influence and has influenced to much
ill. But by the same token, salvation also lies in man's hands. It
is possible to succour even so evil an age and one can pray the
gods for a saviour:

498   Di patrii, Indigetes et Romule Vestaque mater
             quae Tuscum Tiberim et Romana Palatia servas,
             hunc saltem everso iuvenem succurrere saeclo
501   ne prohibete!

The central emphasis in this section, however, is not on the saviour but on the catastrophe which needs and demands the saviour. To the pessimistic picture of the farmer's bitter struggle (labor improbus) against exhausted earth and all manner of natural perversity in the first section (A: 43–203), corresponds the pessimistic picture here of a world ruined through man's own fratricidal actions and blindly committed to chaos. It is no accident—it is in fact with the most deliberate intention—that Virgil closes the last and first (A and C) of the three main sections of this book with similar images of a vehicle out of control. To the last words of section C (and of the whole book):

513   frustra retinacula tendens
     fertur equis auriga neque audit currus habenas

correspond the last words of section A (202–203):

             Si bracchia forte remisit,
   atque illum (lembum) in praeceps prono rapit alveus amni.

Man at best is a rower going upstream against a violent current: only the fiercest *labor* can keep him on his course; if he once relaxes and loses control he will be carried headlong to destruction. But man is also a charioteer who can no longer guide his *own* course and is consequently involved in moral chaos: tam multae scelerum facies.

We can now see more clearly the structure of the whole book. The first section (A) describes the *improbus labor* of the farmer as he struggles to aid the fertility of earth in the battle of both against a steady deterioration, a loss of spontaneity that is the general characteristic of Jove's new dispensation. This *egestas* in the new nature of things is the spur of the arts and of civilization but it is a harsh spur indeed. On the other hand Virgil depicts in the second section of the book (B: 204–350) the intimate workings of cosmic sympathy throughout the Farmer's Year: here, as we have seen, the emphasis is still on unremitting toil (no moment must be lost) but there is none the less a real co-operation between nature and man; the Farmer's Year is written in the very heavens. And at the section's end the rigour of the book for once relaxes as the Ambarvalia is described:

339   sacra refer Cereri laetis operatus in herbis
        extremae sub casum hiemis, iam vero sereno.

M

> Tum pingues agni et tum mollissima vina,
> tum somni dulces densaeque in montibus umbrae.
> Cuncta tibi Cererem pubes agrestis adoret;
> quoi tu lacte favos et miti dilue Baccho,
> terque novas circum felix eat hostia fruges
> omnis quam chorus et socii comitentur ovantes
> et Cererem clamore vocent in tecta; neque ante
> falcem maturis quisquam supponat aristis
> quam Cereri torta redimitus tempora quercu
> det motus incompositos et carmina dicat.

Thus the double-edged character of cosmic sympathy is in-dicated. Man must do his part if the gods are to help: *in primis venerare deos.*

But what if he does not? This idea is developed in the third (C: 351–514) section of the Book. The transition from the yearly cycle—the seasonal round—to the weather takes us from the expected to the unexpected, from calculation to prophecy. Here cosmic sympathy acquires a deeper and more lively connotation: we see it expressed in the motion and cries of birds and in their quasi-human behaviour.[1] Nature is supremely sensitive: all parts of it are 'members one of another'. This idea 'triggers', so to speak, the final peroration. Suddenly (463 f.) we see how man by his wickedness (fraus, operta bella, l. 465) can overturn, as it were, the normality of things (e.g. sistunt amnes terraeque dehiscunt, &c. 479 f.). This perversion of cosmic nature corresponds to a moral perversion: *fas versum atque nefas* (505). The world goes headlong to ruin—the horses run away with the helpless charioteer—because man has lost all moral control. The only possible remedy is moral atonement and man's only ground for hope is that he has been sufficiently punished:

> 501   Satis iam pridem sanguine nostro
> Laomedonteae luimus periuria Troiae.

Thus the deterioration and *labor* of the first section find their meaning: man's struggle is not *just* against the counter force of nature—the cosmically decreed deterioration of the earth—but against his own vice and anarchy. The omission of the Fall in the first section's account of man's *labor* is now made good. Cosmic sympathy, we now see, is double-edged indeed. Man

---

[1] See chap. viii, pp. 386–8.

must deserve and atone if he is to get the co-operation of nature. His only hope is that he *has* atoned sufficiently to receive his saviour.

II. The happy invocation to Bacchus faithfully shows the mood of the whole Book. The first sub-section (a: 9–82) is concerned ostensibly with the *variety* of shrubs and trees (principio arboribus varia est natura creandis, 9) but *variety* here is really an expression of the spontaneous productiveness of nature. Man can greatly assist and enrich this productiveness by his labour, but this is now seen as a *happy* co-operation, something quite different in feeling-tone from the *improbus labor* of Book I. First of all the *spontaneity* of nature is stressed:

10   aliae nullis hominum cogentibus ipsae
     sponte sua veniunt.

Even trees which need human aid to grow good fruit retain, nevertheless, a natural exuberance: *sponte sua* quae se tollunt in luminis oras/infecunda quidem, sed *laeta* et *fortia* surgunt. They need some work but this is now taken quite joyfully for granted:

61   *scilicet* omnibus est labor impendendus et omnes
     cogendae in sulcum ac multa mercede domandae.

The accent is not on the tribulations, the weeds and pests, but on the assistance of a happily co-operating nature. We can even see the joy of the grafted tree in its *new* leaves and apples:

80   ingens
     exiit ad caelum ramis *felicibus* arbos
     *miratast*que novas frondes et non sua poma.

This boundless fertility—this infinite variety—of nature is specially stressed in the next sub-section (b: 83–176), which opens with the typically Lucretian word of transition, *praeterea* (l. 83). The essential purpose of the sub-section is to raise the *theme of variety* from fruit trees to the whole wide earth in all its diversity and fullness of being. The progression from:

83   genus haud unum nec fortibus ulmis
     nec salici lotoque neque Idaeis cyparissis

to:

109   Nec vero terrae ferre omnes omnia possunt

prepares us for the succession of exotic products of exotic lands in lines 114–35. The tone is now steadily exalted to a climax which not only completes the variety theme but gives it a local habitation and a home: Italy is the *ideal* to which all that is exotic and peculiar must yield the palm; it is the golden mean which is only set off and high-lighted by the variety around it. Furthermore we have now proceeded from the specific topics of arboriculture to a universal view of the earth in its natural integrity. Italy—the perfect land—is not only the producer of fruit and wine, of sheep and cattle but the home of famous cities, of wonderful rivers and lakes, and above all of men: it is in short, a *Saturnian land*, a region befitting the Age of Gold.

The theme of *variety and spontaneity*—of happy co-operation between man and nature—is thus at last connected with the two other themes so dear to Virgil: the *Golden Age* and *Italy*. Italy, in short, is the actual realization of that mean or measure within the exuberant variety of nature which corresponds to the primal paradise before the Fall. As in other pictures of the Saturnian earth or age, we see the continual springtime, the exuberant fertility, the absence of all that is horrible and monstrous (tigers, lions, poisons, snakes). And man is not here pitted against his environment in a fierce struggle for existence but forms, along with his works, the climactic essence of it:

173   Salve, magna parens frugum, Saturnia tellus,
174   magna virum.

The contrast with the harsh picture of the Iron Age, in almost the exactly corresponding portion of Book I (118–59), is surely deliberate: here is the other side of the coin, the happy union of man and countryside, of nature and civilization, of myth and Roman history, of innocence and security which must be set against the bitter struggle and tension which dominate the preceding book.

Virgil deliberately lowers the tone when he leaves this climactic passage and proceeds on his ostensibly didactic way. He is once more concerned with agriculture in Italy and, specifically, with the choice of land for different crops and fruits. And here again the variety of terrain and soil is viewed as part of nature's adaptability to man. A difficult soil of steep grade, clayey and covered with stones and brush, is excellent for olives; a rich valley between hills, for grapes; the plains of Mantua or Tarentum, for sheep. Here Virgil gives us, in a most concrete fashion, the actual feel of man's co-operation with his environment. The following passage:

184 At quae *pinguis* humus *dulci*que uligine *laeta*
    quique frequens herbis et *fertilis ubere* campus
    (qualem saepe cava montis convalle solemus
    despicere; huc summis liquontur rupibus amnes
    *felicem*que trahunt limum) quique editus austro
    et filicem curvis *invisam* pascit aratris,
190 hic tibi praevalidas olim multoque fluentis
    sufficiet Baccho vitis, hic fertilis uvae,
    hic laticis, qualem pateris libamus et auro,
    inflavit cum *pinguis* ebur Tyrrhenus ad aras,
    lancibus et pandis fumantia reddimus exta.

is an exact picture. He visualizes the fertile, moist valley full of ferns to block the plough but fine for vineyards. The wine from it will fill the golden mixing bowls from which 'we pour libation as the fat Tuscan blows his ivory flute to the offering of smoking entrails on bending platter'. The attitude of man is here answered by the attitude of the land itself: the earth is *fat, rejoices* in the *sweet* moisture; the streams bring the *blessed* mud. (See the italicized words in the passage.) The sentence is so structured that the triple *hic*s depend on three relatives (quae, quique, quique) and a more or less parenthetic *qualem*: thus the two parts of the sentence balance each other (ll. 184–9 and 190–4: 6 to 5 lines) and symbolize, so to speak, man's enjoyment (191–4) of nature's happy fertility (184–9) and the fitting dedication of both to the gods.

There is a suitable site for every agricultural purpose but man must know his land and soil: Virgil ends this section (A) with rules for testing different types of soil. In their almost technical precision and deliberate concreteness (not to say earthiness) these lines (226–58) form a contrast to the exalted Praise of Italy. Virgil here, as before, shows not so much his practicality as his realism: the co-operation of man and nature involves necessarily direct contact with the dirt.

The next section (B: 259–419) is the true centre of the Book and deals with its central topic: the planting and care of the vine. This is not so much because the vine is *per se* more important than all other shrubs and trees but because viticulture is the 'ideal-type', so to speak, of co-operation between man and nature. The olive can be summarily disposed of in six lines—other trees in thirty-two lines—because these, unlike the vine, need no *cultura* and grow of themselves: ad sidera raptim *via propria* nituntur. But grapes demand the thoughtful care of man: here we see the perfect association of the human and the natural and the happy result. The section falls into *three* main parts with a brief passage of conclusion:

1. 259–314: Planting the Vine.
2. 315–45: Spring (digression).
3. 346–96: The Care of the Vine.

Conclusion, 397–419: The Farmer's Laborious Round.

The key to the section is the central portion or the 'digression' on spring. With the labour of man in parts 1 and 3 co-operates the wonderful warmth and freshness of spring-time nature (2). The farmer tests and works the soil, selects the right spot for planting or transplanting his vines, spaces them properly so they can get ample nourishment from the earth and room wherein to spread their branches (284–7). He chooses for supporting tree the immobile and lofty oak, not the inflammable olive. At each point he must intelligently select the advantages which nature offers the vine. But Nature is ever ready to help. Thus the *Spring* (in which he must plant his vines; never in the cold winter or hot summer) is the season naturally intended for original growth:

323   Ver adeo frondi nemorum, ver *utile* silvis;
        Vere tument terrae et *genitalia semina poscunt.*

And in the following *laus veris* we see and feel this genital force at work. It is the proper season of creation whose anniversary it is:

336   Non alios prima crescentis origine mundi
        inluxisse dies aliumve habuisse tenorem
        crediderim: ver illud erat, ver magnus agebat
339   orbis.

The reminiscence here of the Golden or Saturnian age is unmistakable: *Hic ver adsiduum* he says of Italy in the *laus Italiae* preceding (149) and both these passages (i.e. both the *laus veris* and the *laus Italiae*) unmistakably recall the traditional pictures of the earthly paradise. The renewal of the order of the ages in *Eclogue* 4 (magnus ab integro saeclorum *nascitur* ordo) corresponds to the 'first beginning of the waxing world' (prima crescentis origo mundi) mentioned here (l. 336). Again Virgil sounds the *motif* of *Saturnia tellus*, the place and era wherein man is not the harsh exploiter but the cherished child of his mother Earth. After this, Virgil, as is his custom, returns abruptly to an intense realism:

346   Quod superest, quaecumque premes virgulta per agros,
        sparge fimo pingui.

The new plants must be carefully supported and later pruned: they must be protected from wild animals and cattle, from goats above all. The mention of *goat* suggests his fitness as victim to Bacchus: appropriately this part (346–96) closes with the description of a Bacchic festival in the country, a pendant to the Ambarvalia or Ceres festival of I. 338–50. But its mood is far more joyful and carefree.

A *coda* or brief conclusion to this whole section (259–419): goes from line 397 to line 419 and recalls the vineworker's year:

401   Redit agricolis labor actus in orbem
        atque in se sua per vestigia volvitur annus.

It is laborious (Est etiam ille labor curandis vitibus, &c. 397) and even hard but it is happy and crowned with fruition:

417   iam canit effectos extremus vinitor antes.

Virgil now turns to the olive and other trees. They, as we have seen, need no culture and can be disposed of briefly. But this very brevity, as Büchner points out, is intended, and marks the contrast between their easy cultivation and the lengthy and laborious care of the vine. Again the motif of *spontaneity*, of natural exuberance, of the Saturnian earth, recurs, for surely

430   sanguineis inculta rubent aviaria bacis

recalls the uncultivated vegetation of the *messianic Eclogue*:

4. 29   incultisque rubens pendebit sentibus uva.

But the moral which Virgil here draws is not quietistic; the very helpfulness of nature recognizes human effort:

433   Et dubitant homines serere atque impendere curam?

We now find a list of trees (cedar, willow, box, pine, &c.) which grow wild—non rastris, hominum vel ulli obnoxia curae —but have innumerable human uses. They are arranged to reach a skilful climax, marked at the end by the repeated *nec, nec non, nec non* and the rhetorical question:

454   Quid memorandum aeque Baccheia dona tulerunt?

which brings on the splendid conclusion:

455   Bacchus et ad culpam causas dedit; ille furentis
       Centauros leto domuit, Rhoetumque Pholumque
       et magno Hylaeum Lapithis cratere minantem.

Again, just as before the *laus Italiae*, Virgil has deliberately worked up a climax so that the great 'digression' which starts

458   O fortunatos nimium, &c.

comes on a high and exultant note. Enough surely has been said of the farmer's happy life—his wonderful support by a nature which invites his co-operation—to make this final peroration come with something like inevitability. The brief mention of the excesses of the drunken Centaurs, Rhoetus, &c., provides an immediate transition: when so much has been given, how can man so greatly abuse it? Fortunatos nimium *sua si bona norint:* too happy, indeed, *if they but knew their own blessings!* But, alas, civilization has taken a wrong turn and nature's gifts have been put to bad use: *casia liquidi corrumpitur usus olivi.* The problem is to make men understand what the good life is.

This famous finale of Book II has been finely analysed by Friedrich Klingner [1] who has shown how the contrasting themes interweave to reach a succession of climaxes. But the point I would stress here is the way in which it sums up the whole book and stands in firm contrast to the finale of I. The earth in its perfection of justice has indeed offered man an *easy* living:

460   fundit humo *facilem* victum *iustissima* tellus

But man has not accepted the offer: the ambitions of civilization have corrupted him. Only the farmer now knows the secure ease (secura quies) which nature intended for man. His is the *securitas* which is the philosopher's goal: those who cannot realize the βίος θεωρητικός—which is of course the absolute ideal—can at least choose the countryside: fortunatus et ille

[1] In *Hermes* 66 (1931), pp. 159–89.

deos qui novit agrestis. Against all the turmoil of urban life—its
wars, enmities, luxuries, ambitions—can be set the simple fact
of the farmer's ordinary occupation:

513   Agricola incurvo terram dimovit aratro.

This is at once the life by which Rome became the wonder of the
world (rerum facta est pulcherrima Roma) and Saturn maintained his golden age:

538   aureus hanc vitam in terris Saturnus agebat.

What then does this great passage finally mean? It sums up,
of course, the morality of Book II: nature offers man its full
co-operation and through this, the good life. His natural lot is
not one of terrible toil (labor improbus) but of peaceful security
(secura quies). The grim struggle of Book I seems far removed.
The farmer seems to have changed his outlook. The golden age
has exorcized the iron age altogether. But in fact the Fall of
man is quite as evident here as in the peroration of I: man will
not choose the good life and the farmer himself ceases to be
honoured. Yet a real contrast—an evident opposition—
remains: the *Saturnia tellus* seems impossible even for farmers or
especially for farmers in Book I; in Book II it seems a realizable
ideal. The degeneration of the earth and the contumacy of the
physical environment were in I the background and *raison
d'être* of man's harsh and laborious life; in II nature smiles and
in spontaneous fertility meets man more than halfway. Between
the differing views of nature and of man there is a tension
which has not yet been resolved.

But this tension is surely deliberate. Man can still have his
golden age—especially in Italy, that natural mean, that true
Saturnia tellus—if he realizes his own good (sua si bona norint).
Nature and Man are not independent of each other: the cosmos
reflects man's innocence *and* man's Fall. Book II expresses, so to
speak, the bright side, Book I the dark side of a reciprocal
relationship. But there are hints of light in I (e.g. the account
of the Ambarvalia in ll. 338–50) and darker tones in II (the
peritura regna, l. 498).

III. The forty-eight line invocation of III corresponds to the
forty-two line invocation of I: both are addressed to Maecenas
and Augustus. This fact indicates quite clearly the *correspondence
between the two books* (I to III). Furthermore each invocation

quite deliberately goes beyond the agricultural theme: that of I
is primarily concerned with the divine status of Augustus; that
of III with Virgil's future glorification of him in some new and
greater work. None the less III is also a quite new departure:
unlike the two preceding books, it is divided into two explicitly
demarcated halves. In fact the second half is even provided with
a separate introduction and an invocation to Pales (ll. 284–94).
(This is, as we shall see, true also of Book IV.) Each half is also
closed with a 'digression' dealing with its appropriate 'theme'
(love, death). Virgil, in other words, has here taken some pains
to mark and underline his arrangement, whereas in I and II the
different sections are more or less artfully concealed by the use of
connectives (*praeterea, his adversis, atque*, &c.) and careful transitions.

It seems quite clear that he is much concerned to emphasize
the contrast between the two parts of the book. This is not done
only by the explicit sectioning but by the careful differentiation
of the subject-matter: the first half (A) deals with the *big*
animals, horses and cattle; the second (B) with the *small* animals;
sheep and goats. As he says:

286   Hoc satis armentis; superat pars altera curae,
               lanigeros agitare greges hirtasque capellas.
               Hic labor, hinc laudem fortes sperate coloni.
               Nec sum animi dubius, verbis ea vincere magnum
290   quam sit et angustis hunc addere rebus honorem.

I think that we can hardly interpret these lines as a simple
confession of the poetic difficulty of dealing with such *small*
matters. Virgil made no excuses for mentioning moles, weevils
and toads or dirt and manure in I and II. To be sure he did
not treat them at such length as the sheep and goats of III but
the poetic incongruity (assuming a relatively conventional
ideal of poetry) was fully as great. We must rather look for
some symbolic significance in this emphasis of *size*. The descent
from bull and steer to the bee of IV seems quite intentional. At
the beginning of IV he again emphasizes the smallness or
tenuousness of his subject:

4. 6   In tenui labor; at tenuis non gloria.

In other words: cattle, sheep, bees 'stand for' *motifs* or *ideas*
arranged according to a scheme or series. This book (III)

corresponds to I in its tone and mood but to IV in its structure and symbolic meaning. We must not, however, anticipate our analysis further: interpretation here as always depends on exact elucidation of the text.

The description of cattle and horses starts with the choice of cows and mares for a successful mating:

49   Seu quis Olympiacae miratus praemia palmae
        pascit equos seu quis fortis ad aratra iuvencos,
        corpora praecipue *matrum* legat.

His description of the right brood-cow at once strikes the note of *bigness, uncouthness* and *power:*

51   Optuma *torvae*
        forma bovis, cui *turpe* caput, cui *plurima* cervix
        et *crurum tenus* a mento palearia pendent;
        tum *longo nullus* lateri *modus*; omnia magna,
        pes etiam; et *camuris hirtae* sub cornibus aures.

The brood-cow in fact is almost a bull in her appearance: *faciem tauro propior*. It is above all important that mating take place *while the animals are young* for the best days of a mortal's life are the first to go:

66   Optima quaeque dies miseris mortalibus aevi
        prima fugit; subeunt morbi tristisque senectus
        et labor, et durae rapit inclementia mortis.

Here the central themes of the Book are announced in their near relationship to each other: *death* goes ever close on the heels of *love*. The best days—the days of *amor*—are ever threatened by the inevitable symptoms of mortality. The transition here from the specific *mares* and *pecuaria* (64) to the generic *miseris mortalibus* (66) must not be lost: it is the first indication that Virgil is concerned with much more than cattle or horses and that when he talks of animals, he is concerned with a mortal condition; men too have to endure disease, old age, trouble and the unkindness of harsh death.

The ensuing description of the sire-horse (72–94) again emphasizes bigness (87: duplex agitur per lumbos spina, cavat-que/tellurem, &c.) and spirit (altius ingreditur). Virgil obviously wants to create an impression of gross power: animal love is *not* a gentle thing. But the most striking feature, perhaps, of his picture of these spirited *mothers* and *sires* is the empathetic character of it: empathy, as we have seen, comes into his account of the earth (in I) and the vine (in II) and especially the birds who foretell the weather, but here the animal's point of view is central and really displaces that of the farmer himself. Consider the lines:

75　Continuo pecoris generosi pullus in arvis
altius ingreditur et mollia crura reponit;
primus et ire viam et fluvios temptare minantis
audet et ignoto sese committere ponti
nec vanos horret strepitus. Illi ardua cervix
argutumque caput, brevis alvos obessaque terga,
luxuriatque toris animosum pectus.

The simile of the equine Saturn is the final evidence of the empathy at work here:

92　talis et ipse iubam cervice effundit equina
coniugis adventu pernix Saturnus et altum
Pelion *hinnitu* fugiens *implevit acuto.*

The gods can take equine form because in fact the horse is, so to speak, human already. He is sufficiently close to man so that man's emotions (or an anthropomorphic god's emotions) can be read into his. On the other hand he is sufficiently far from man so that he can be treated as the animal that he is. The callous attitude of the breeder toward the least indication of senility is stressed:

95　Hunc quoque, ubi aut morbo gravis aut iam segnior annis
deficit, abde domo *nec turpi ignosce senectae.*

The absence of pity for age—the calculating and brutal practicality here—is all the more disturbing because of the empathy so recently shown. Virgil thus establishes the exact note he wants for this part of his poem: the pathos of animality, the incongruity between the *human* aspirations and emotions and the sheerly *animal* facts of senility and death. As we go on in the poem, we shall see that this is not just an expression of sympathy for dumb animals facing a harsh natural law (which the breeder must heed) but a much more generalized recognition of the fate of all that is animal and mortal: to men, too, love and death come in much the same sequence and poignance.

The feeling here is harsh and almost crudely brutal but Virgil
so intends it; this book is not meant to be pleasant, light or easy.
The descriptions of the race-horse (103–12) combine the
human and the animal:

103   Nonne vides, cum praecipiti certamine campum
           corripuere ruuntque effusi carcere currus,
           cum spes arrectae iuvenum exsultantiaque haurit
           corda pavor pulsans? Illi instant verbere torto
           et proni dant lora; volat vi fervidus axis;
           iamque humiles iamque elati sublime videntur
           aëra pervacuum ferri atque adsurgere in auras;
           nec mora nec requies; at fulvae nimbus harenae
           tollitur, umescunt spumis flatuque sequentum:
           tantus amor laudum, tantaest victoria curae.

Here Virgil is primarily concerned with the selection of a good
sire: the breeder must emphasize above all spirit and youth
(animus aevumque). So the description really has as its raison
d'être the racehorse himself, not the charioteer. Yet though
corripuere and *ruunt effusi* seem to refer to the *horses*, lines 105–9
plainly refer to the drivers whose hopes are raised, whose
pulsing emotions drain their exultant hearts, who bend low,
loose the reins and ply the whip, who go up and down with the
bouncing chariot as it flies along. Such is their zeal for glory,
their intentness on victory! Yet, clearly the general feeling-
tone of the passage includes *both* horse *and* man: the breeder
must choose a horse *iuvenem, calidum animis et cursibus acrem* (118–
9) and pay no attention to his pedigree if these qualities are
lacking. The fact is that human and animal emotions here
almost merge: the horses, as it were, share and exhibit the
spirit of their drivers and thus qualify in spirit and keenness for
selection as proper sires. Again the line between man and animal
is very thin.

The empathy of Virgil comes out quite strongly in the next
part (138–208: Care and Training). The trainer encourages
and corrects his charges like a teacher:

164   iam vitulos *hortare* viamque insiste domandi,
           dum *faciles animi iuvenum*, dum mobilis aetas.

185   tum magis atque magis *blandis gaudere* magistri
           laudibus et plausae *sonitum* cervicis *amare*.

The problem of breaking in a horse is chiefly one of controlling his spirits: ante domandum *ingentis tollent animos*. At every point we see things from the animal's viewpoint, as in the account of the recently weaned foal:

187   Atque haec iam primo depulsus ab ubere matris
             audeat inque vicem det mollibus ora capistris
             invalidus etiamque *tremens*, etiam, *inscius aevi*.

The subjunctives: *audeat* (188), *incipiat* (191), *vocet* (194), *ponat* (195) have the foal and then the three-year old as subjects; it is to him that the long simile of lines 196–200 applies.

In the next part (Ac 209–83) the personification of the animal reaches its climax and leads to the digression on *Amor* that properly begins at line 242: *omne adeo genus*, &c. The *ostensible* reason for the whole section is the strengthening effect of love on the steer or stallion: no industry of man can stimulate their strength like the power of Venus (209–10). But this is clearly but an excuse: Virgil's primary concern here is not with the training or strengthening process but with love itself. He had already (Aa) introduced the topic (amor) as a necessary element in mating but not as a primary emotion of the animal itself. The training section (b), however, prepares us for a closer and more empathetic consideration of *amor* since it concentrates our attention on the animal as a creature in its own right and with its own feelings. We are thus ready to devote our full attention to what is, actually, the central subject of this half of the Book.

The picture of the cow enticing and exciting the bulls:

215   Carpit enim viris paulatim *urit*que videndo
             femina *nec* nemorum *patitur meminisse* neque herbae,
             dulcibus illa quidem *inlecebris*, et saepe *superbos*
             cornibus inter se *subigit* decernere *amantis*.

at once raises the level of empathetic intensity: the emotion is stronger and the personification more pronounced. This is again heightened by the portrait of the defeated bull (victus abit ... exulat ... multa gemens ignominiam ... tum quos amisit inultus amores) who overcomes his shame by exile, preparation and a victorious return. The simile of the wave whitening to break (237–41) clinches and concludes the impressive episode.

Virgil has prepared the way for his peroration which, like his other perorations (e.g. at the end of I and II), raises the subject from the specific agricultural to a general and philosophic level. What now concerns him is love in general:

242   Omne adeo genus in terris *hominum*que ferarumque
         et genus aequoreum, pecudes pictaeque volucres
         in furias ignemque ruunt: *amor omnibus idem.*

The emotion of men, beasts, fish, cattle, birds is one and the same: *amor*. And it is in this broad and animal context (he hastily mentions the love of boars, tigers, the *Sabellicus sus* along, again, with that of horses) that he finally includes the *human amor*:

258   Quid iuvenis, magnum cui versat in ossibus ignem
         durus amor? nempe abruptis turbata procellis
         nocte natat caeca serus freta; quem super ingens
         porta tonat caeli et scopulis inlisa reclamant
         aequora; nec miseri possunt revocare parentes
         nec moritura super crudeli funere virgo.

He does not name Leander and Hero because he clearly wants to preserve the animal and anonymous context of *amor* as here described. *Amor* is, in this view, a terrible *furor* by which man himself is assimilated to the animal. Thus Virgil immediately follows the mention of Hero and Leander by a reference to lynxes, wolves, dogs, stags. Then the line:

266   Scilicet ante omnis furor est insignis equarum

not merely reintroduces (in conclusion) the equine theme but reiterates the theme of love's animal intensity: its seal and emblem is the terrible *hippomanes*, at once the cause (love-madness) and the product (the actual *virus* or secretion) of amatory fury.

This whole section or half (A) of the Book in this way preserves a curious ambivalence between the animal and the human, nature and man. The point of view of the first two books (nature as man's opponent *or* friend) is seemingly reversed: we now descend, as it were, to the animal and natural level and possess the animal consciousness by a kind of empathy. The animal is partially humanized and the human is partially *animalized*. For while the cattle and horses are seen from within as conscious, feeling beings, they remain the animals that they

are: Virgil looks at them with the eye of the poet and philosopher. Concurrently, our feeling for nature changes: it is no
longer the *object* which confronts man—whether in hostile or
friendly guise—but the force which moves him also and which,
in an important sense, he *is*. This accounts for the striking
amorality of the whole section: love and death are seen, so to
speak, as brute facts; death is at first only casually referred to
(being reserved for the next section) but love emerges in its full
animal, sexual power ruling both beasts and men and over-
coming in its violence all rational moderation. This, to be sure,
is due in part to the limited scope of the section (cattle and
horses, not men, are the theme) but the cattle and horses are,
surely, in part also, symbols of mankind or rather have something which they *share* with mankind. There is more to man—
Virgil here as in I and II takes one aspect at a time—but there
is certainly *this*. The problem, of course, is to escape, to tame
these crude natural passions: this amoralism is indeed less (in
some respects: more) than human. But it is a fact to be encountered and recognized. The mood of this section is not dark but
it may certainly be called grimly realistic; the lightness and
hilarity of II have definitely receded.

Virgil's hesitation at introducing the sheep and goats—his
apparent concern at the insignificance of the topic, *angustae
res*—undoubtedly conceals a warning to the reader. There is a
special significance in the size of these animals, a special difference
between them and the cattle and horses just discussed. And
herein, indeed, Virgil hints a paradox: despite the small size
of his subject he is singularly inspired and speaks his inspiration
in good Lucretian language; his mouth must now utter a
grander note:

294   Nunc, veneranda Pales, magno nunc ore sonandum.

We can, I think, say at this point that *despite* (and in a certain
sense *because* of) his topic, his theme is the greater and the more
sober.

The first hint of what he means comes at the start of his
description of the sheep: it is important, he says, to give them
a good, soft bed of straw and to cover the ground well

glacies ne frigida laedat
molle pecus scabiemque ferat turpisque podagras.

The sheep are sensitive creatures who have to be protected against the *cold*: otherwise they will suffer, catch disease, *die*. Ergo omni studio glaciem ventosque nivalis ... avertes (319–20). The connection between these animals and death, the theme of mortality, has been suggested but as yet faintly.

We note in this passage (298–321) a quite different way of treating the animal from that of the first section (A): there is no empathy—no sense of the sheep and goat as consciousnesses —but only a sense of them as objects of human care or *passive victims* of neglect. Above all, there is no reference at all to mating and breeding. The account of the spring pasturage (322–38) mainly deals with their fodder (the nice, green grass), the abundance of water, the presence of ample shade. Everything it would seem is in contrast to the cattle and horses of the last part. There Virgil wanted amorous beings, beings of passion, individuated and quasi-human. Here a collective anonymity and impersonality will suffice: in size, in featurelessness, in *passivity* they are fitted to suffer and to die.

After the brief section on their feeding in winter, spring and summer (295–338), he turns aside from sheep and goats *as such* to the Libyan and Scythian shepherds (339–83). Certainly the sheep and goats play here a very minor role: they seem in fact but an excuse to introduce vivid pictures of the desert nomads and the cave-dwellers of the far North. The most obvious reason for these pictures is the incentive they offer the Italian shepherds and goatherds: why need I mention the Libyans and Scythians? (Quid tibi pastores Libyae, &c., l. 339) asks Virgil in effect; the true shepherd should already know that his job is one well worth even the most extraordinary difficulties. But what Virgil is really doing is to press a rather tenuous connection of topics in order to secure the feeling-tones, the succession of moods and colours that he wants. After having introduced —in a quite minor way—the care of sheep and goats in the winter (the hint of danger, of death is here very mild) he immediately proceeds to the happy, joyful spring scene (the only really cheerful passage of the book): this is, so to speak, the high point, the bright extreme from which he descends to the utter darkness of the Plague at the close of the Book. His next topic—the Desert nomads—is certainly a contrast to the lush Italian spring but it is not in itself particularly unpleasant. It is only with the

N

chill Scythian winter that the note of death (always the motif of
coldness is associated with that of death) and hopeless terror is
really sounded.

We see the animals huddled together in the snow bank
unable to resist their own butchery:

367   Interea toto non setius aëre ninguit:
        intereunt pecudes, stant circumfusa pruinis
        corpora magna boum confertoque agmine cervi
        torpent mole nova et summis vix cornibus exstant.
        Hos non immissis canibus, non cassibus ullis
        puniceaeve agitant pavidos formidine pinnae,
        sed frustra oppositum trudentis pectore montem
        comminus obtruncant ferro graviterque rudentis
375   caedunt et magno laeti clamore reportant.

The contrast between the plight of the animals—*graviter
rudentis*—and the happy killers (laeti . . . reportant) reflects
again that motif of human callousness (man's casual acceptance
of the conditions of nature) which we saw above in lines 95–96,
and the whole passage, of course, reinforces the motif of *coldness/
death* already sounded in lines 298–9, 318 f. Virgil's return to the
empathy of the first part is marked at this point by his shift
from sheep and goats to cattle and deer: intereunt pecudes,
stant circumfusa pruinis/*corpora magna boum* confertoque
agmine *cervi*.

He is depicting the ferocity and pain which lie in nature
itself and the concomitant callousness of man, his willing
assistance of nature in the destruction of helpless beasts whose
suffering he can descry and feel. The Scythian, who spends his
time underground drinking his strange beverages, is the
extreme point in human endurance and indifference. He lives
in a world where all is given over to the coldness of death but he
can find security, even pleasure, deep beneath the icy surface:

376   Ipsi in defossis specibus secura sub alta
        otia agunt terra.

Man is more than an animal since he can transcend and remake
his environment. But he is also the *creature* of his environment:

381   Talis Hyperboreo septem subiecta trioni
        gens *effrena* virum Riphaeo tunditur euro
        et pecudum fulvis velatur corpora saetis,

Life in the north is so harsh that all emotional rapport between man and beast has been broken down: only a fierce and un-cultured people—a people without true humanity—can endure such a climate. The smiling nature of spring-time Italy (so wonderfully depicted in Book II and just above: 322–38) has turned its face from us and the nature we now see is *cold*, harsh and unfeeling. Even this, however, is but the prelude to something much worse.

In the next part (C: 384–469) Virgil prepares us for the finale (the overwhelming presence of death) by describing the dangers which ever beset the flocks. Thistles, briars harm the sheep's coat (384 f.); robbers threaten the folds (406 f.); snakes can lurk there (415 f.); diseases are the worst menace (440 f.). Ostensibly he is concerned with a quite prosaic history of mishaps and remedies: actually he is skilfully building to a climax. The motif of the *passive victim* so slightly suggested at the beginning of this section (295 f.) is now carefully elaborated. The picture of the *lurking snake* of Calabria (426 f.) crystallizes the note of fear and danger and prepares us for the more ominous surprises of disease: dira per incautum *serpunt* contagia volgus (469).

The final description of the plague of Noricum (470–566) gives climactic emphasis to the terror of death and the cruelty of nature. There is no theodicy here: the ox dies at the altar; the farmer's primitive innocence of life avails him nothing. In fact the Golden Age returns in horrible travesty as the wolf forsakes the sheepfolds and the dying deer wander among the hounds. It is not love nor work but death which now conquers all things.

The empathy of Virgil—his feeling with and for the animals —once more fully emerges. And we note, along with this, that the animals emphasized are no longer sheep or goats but cattle and horses (486 f., 499 f., 515 f.). The poor beasts are filled with the sadness, incongruity and pain of death:

498   Labitur *infelix studiorum atque immemor herbae*
           victor equos
517   It *tristis* arator
           maerentem abiungens *fraterna morte* iuvencum.

So the motif of the *passive victim* (heretofore symbolized by the reduced size, passivity and collectivism of sheep and goats, except indeed in the one 'prophetic' passage about the beasts of Scythia) is now heightened to encompass the more sentient, conscious and individualized animals and finally even man himself.

For man now feels at one with the animals; he too is the victim of a quite unjustifiable fate:

525 Quid labor aut benefacta iuvant? quid vomere terras
   invertisse gravis? Atqui non Massica Bacchi
   munera, non illis epulae nocuere repostae;
   frondibus et victu pascuntur simplicis herbae,
   pocula sunt fontes liquidi atque exercita cursu
   flumina, nec somnos abrumpit cura salubris.

The echo of the happy farmer of the close of Book II (458 f., 503 f.) rings here in grim mockery: what matter innocence and the simple life, rustic freedom from corrupt civilization, if this is the reward and the end? The idyllic picture of Daphnis' restoration of the Golden Age:

Ec. 5. 60 nec lupus insidias pecori, nec retia cervis
   ulla dolum meditantur: *amat bonus otia Daphnis*

is horribly realized:

537 Non lupus insidias explorat ovilia circum
   nec gregibus nocturnus obambulat: *acrior illum*
   cura domat.

Virgil could not have made his point more clearly than by reintroducing just here the Saturnian theme. The reality of death is without pity or justice. It is the amoral triumph of *pallida Tisiphone* that Virgil celebrates and man is also involved in it. The carcasses of the stricken animals are contaminated: any attempt to use them—e.g. to wear their wool—will *bring on man himself* the terrible pustules and sweat of the disease; its *sacer ignis* will eat his pest-ridden body.

The contrast with Book II could not be plainer. Against the picture of the happy co-operation of nature with man is now set the picture of brutal love and brutal death, nature in all its amoral violence and destructiveness. Man is no longer the hard exploiter (as in Book I) or (as in II) the joyful companion of a fruitful and just earth (justissima tellus) but rather is himself one with the animals in his ungovernable passions and his miserable end. The huge cattle and horses, the diminutive sheep and goats illustrate the power of love and the powerlessness of life as both confront their moments of passion and of death. But though the identity of man and animal is suggested and on occasion explicitly declared, the difference is also insisted upon. Man is not simply a beast and indeed his only hope of transcending the grim amorousness and morbidity which dominate this book is to possess a morality which raw nature (both in himself and in his environment) does not reveal.

IV. Virgil now turns from the *corpora magna boum* and the passive sheep and goats to the lively, buoyant and aerial bees. The heaviness and gloom of III is at once lifted: all is now light and gay. In the proem (1–7) the *dual* aspect of the subject is emphasized: it is light (*levium rerum*) and slender (tenuis) as are the bees themselves but it is also concerned with high matters of politics and social life:

4   magnanimosque duces totiusque ordine gentis
          mores et studia et populos et proelia dicam.

And it is this very duality that determines the peculiar tone and mood of the Book (rather the first half of the Book).

The bees are images and symbols of men or, more exactly, their society is, in important respects, a simulacrum of human society,[1] but they are not really taken with complete seriousness: they are also light, thin, airy beings quite at the mercy of the smallest human or natural disturbance. Furthermore they are by their very nature exempt from the major animal passions: they know not love, they have no sense of individuality, they live by and for the group to whose preservation they constantly sacrifice their own lives. They are in one sense the most; in another sense, the least human of Virgil's animals. Hence the atmosphere of delightful parody which pervades the first section of this part of the book (8–115). Virgil is, to be sure, serious in his appreciation of the importance and beneficence

---

[1] On the bees as a symbol for the human state or society, cf. Hellfried Dahlmann, 'Der Bienenstaat in Vergils Georgika' (*Akad. der Wiss. Mainz, Abhand. Geistes und Sozialwiss. Klasse* (1954), 10). Dahlmann well brings out the parallels between the praise of the farmer in Book 2 (458 f.) and the bees. The bees thus correspond to the human or social ideal. This is far more significant than their topical, political meaning as the bees of Actium (cf. L. Herrmann, *Revue des Études Anciennes* 33 (1931), pp. 219–24 and Perret, pp. 83–85).

of such a purely social or collective existence but he is serious
also in his appreciation of its limitations. There is always a
sense of something lacking, of the *more to be said* in his description of the bees and it is this, in fact, which his insistence on the
paradox of their insect polity (this strange republic of insignificant bees) brings out. The hive is and is not a type of the
human state. Likewise its resurrection is and is not a symbol of
human resurrection.

The atmosphere and tone at once suggest that of Book II:
here man and nature are once more happily co-operating; the
bees fit and require a happy, bright landscape of verdure,
flowers and pleasant waters:

18   At liquidi fontes et stagna virentia musco
             adsint et tenuis fugiens per gramina rivos
30   Haec circum casiae virides et olentia late
             serpulla et graviter spirantis copia thymbrae
             floreat, inriguumque bibant violaria fontem.

The first section (8–115) of the *Bees* describes the location
(statio) of the hive, the process of swarming, and the selection
and care of the king: in short the *establishment* of the hive. Then
after the digression on the 'Old Man of Tarentum' (116–48)
comes the central panel of the *Bees*, the account of their
character as social insects (149–227). This is followed by a third
and final section on the care of the bees (228–280) which, like
the corresponding section on the sheep and goats in III (384–
469) concludes the *Bees* and prepares us for the long 'digression'
which follows.

In the first section (8–115) man is firmly in control: he chooses
the location (statio) of the hive and prepares the hive itself; he
eliminates the inferior king or clips the king's wings; he keeps
the bees at home by making the hive's environment attractive.
The bees are revealed in both their peaceful and bellicose
aspects: we see them as they

55   nescio qua dulcedine laetae
              progeniem nidosque fovent

and as they

73   trepidae inter se coeunt pinnisque coruscant
              spiculaque exacuunt rostris.

But man can manage both their harmonious and their warlike phases. The contrast between the fierce battle:

82   Ipsi per medias acies insignibus alis
     ingentis animos angusto in pectore versant
     usque adeo obnixi non cedere

and man's calming of it by a pinch of dust (pulveris exigui iactu, 87) underlines the incongruity between the ambition and the impotence of these tiny creatures. Man by killing the king, by pulling off its wings, can get what he wants from the whole hive. The contrast between the two kings in lines 91 f.—one *insignis et . . . clarus*; the other uncouth in his sloth (desidia) and trailing his broad belly—may suggest Actium, the contest of Octavian and Antony, while the insistence on the resemblance of the swarm to its king may refer to the effect of different leaderships on the Roman people, but we must not overrate the symbolism here. What is important is the tone of parody, the sense of disproportion between the ambitious pretence and the ludicrous reality. But there is more than this: there is also a sense of the futility and triviality of all this warring and commotion—

105   instabilis animos ludo prohibebis inani.
     Nec magnus prohibere labor.

We can sympathize with the suffering bull or horse, even with the dying sheep, but heroism in the bee is somewhat absurd. There is a hollowness, an absence of solid reality in the descriptions here that warn us against taking the bee symbols too seriously. Man, Virgil seems to be saying, is like this but not when he is really human, really aware of himself. For he can see through the pantomime: the bees can not.

The digression on gardens (116–48) and in particular on the Old Man of Tarentum (125–48) has several puzzling aspects. Was it that Virgil wanted to get in a brief section on gardens but did not dare to develop the theme at any length? Precisely what did he intend by his loving, almost idyllic description? It reads in its really personal warmth almost as if Virgil himself had seen and admired the vegetables and hyacinths which grew so lushly in such unfavourable soil! Once, however, we realize the mood of the passage, we can see its meaning in its context. Virgil surely has no *agricultural* point to make: he is not at all concerned with gardens as such.[1] Rather he wants to mark the break between the introductory section on the *Establishment of the Hive* (8–115) and the central 'panel' (149–227) on the *Nature or Character of the Bees*; also to emphasize once more the theme of man's happy co-operation with his natural environment, wherein, as we have seen, Book IV recalls II. The bees flourish on flowers and man can only keep the bees at home by planting flowers near them. Hence flowers and gardens and hence, naturally enough, that ideal garden-apiary he once saw near Tarentum. Poetically Virgil's problem here was to prolong, to intensify, to give climax to the joyful mood of the whole section, to establish once more the combination of flowers, bees and man—the theme of nature at one with man in joyous reciprocity—in its full, colourful immediacy. The fact that the old man has made his wonderful garden out of abandoned land (pauca relicti/iugera ruris) no good for cereals, pasturage or vineyard, is of course a tribute to that *labor* which plays such a role in I and II. But his lot is not harsh; he is indeed as happy as a king: *regum aequabat opes animis*.

Virgil has deliberately framed this 'digression' as a self-avowed *praeteritio*: an *I would tell, had I but time* followed by the tale itself. He begins (116):

> Atque equidem, extremo ni iam sub fine laborum
> Vela traham et terris festinem advertere proram, &c.

and closes:

> 147   Verum haec ipse equidem spatiis excclusus iniquis
> praetereo atque aliis post me memoranda relinquo.

This is, of course, rhetorical pretence. Virgil had no intention of devoting more space to gardens but he was greatly concerned to emphasize and underscore the importance of the topic he was about to treat. The digression so carefully put in the form of a *praeteritio* is designed to provide the requisite contrast and background for his central 'panel'. It points up the happy 'civilized nature' (most aptly symbolized by the garden) of the

---

[1] Speculation on the identity of the Old Man of Tarentum (cf. Wilkinson, *Greece and Rome*, 19 (1950), p. 22; P. Wuilleumier, *REL*, 8 (1930), pp. 325–40; and A. M. Guillemin, *Virgile* (1951), pp. 151–2) seems to me quite superfluous. Virgil's main point is to suggest the mood of Book 2 (esp. ll. 513–22), a situation where there is both human *labor* and natural exuberance (nec requies quin aut pomis exuberet annus, &c.).

first section precisely in order to bring out the quite different tonality of the section beginning at line 149.

The opening lines strike the new note:

149   Nunc age, naturas apibus quas Iuppiter ipse
         addidit, expediam, pro qua mercede canoros
         Curetum sonitus crepitantiaque aera secutae
         Dictaeo caeli regem pavere sub antro.

We now turn from the bee-keeper to the bee: we now see things from the bee's point of view. But, more important, we see the bee's nature or character as a divine gift and the bee himself as part of a divine, immortal spirit. The tone of parody is now gone: this account of the divine nature of the bee sounds almost like revelation, though revelation in a rather minor key. The essence of this divinity of the bee is what we might call communal altruism expressed in ceaseless work and self-ignoring loyalty to the whole hive, to the king:

153   Solae communis natos, consortia tecta
         urbis habent, magnis agitant sub legibus aevom
         et patriam solae et certos novere penatis.

They are the only beings who hold everything in common and devote everything to their country and their gods.

Two aspects of this communal altruism are particularly stressed: work and self sacrifice. The detailed description of the bees' co-operative division of labour—its intricacy, its precision —leads to the key line:

184   Omnibus una quies operum, *labor omnibus unus*

This refers not merely to their simultaneous activity and repose (mane ruunt portis ... post ... siletur) but to the common mainspring of their life, their unanimous dedication to toil. We think at once of the key lines of III:

242   Omne adeo genus in terris hominumque ferarumque
         et genus aequoreum, pecudes pictaeque volucres
         in furias ignemque ruunt: *amor omnibus idem.*

Here indeed lies the difference: the bees can concentrate all their energy on communal work because they have no disturbing passions; they have no love, no offspring produced by sexual congress and parturition. Nothing matters but their hive and their king.

In lines 197–227 Virgil turns from the theme of *labor* to the theme of self-sacrifice. He stresses the absence of sex (198–202): he represents the bees as picking their future citizens and kings from the leaves. So there is nothing in themselves to compete with their communal devotion: they will work till they die under the burden (animum sub fasce dedere). Likewise, death in defence of their king is sweet to them: pulchram . . . petunt per vulnera mortem. This is the proof of their divinity and immortality: they possess a share of the divine spirit (deum . . . ire per omnia) and with other sentient beings return to the source of life. They cannot die (nec morti esse locum) but fly yet alive to the stars, to the sky.

It seems clear that Virgil has here expressed a civic ideal to be set against the disruptive passion of *amor* in the first part of III and a theological ideal to be set against the death-dealing nature of the second part of III. *Labor omnibus unus* is the answer to *amor omnibus idem* and (*non*) *morti esse locum*, the divine immortal spirit (esse apibus partem divinae mentis et haustus aetherios), to the *sacer ignis* of the plague. Also the divine polity of the bees symbolizes the kind of *labor* and *fides* which can cure the divided and corrupt republic of the close of Book I and restore the golden-age co-operation of man and nature in Book II. But we must not make too much of this one section: it was preceded by a much less serious, almost satirical, description of the bees—such insignificant creatures with such great ambitions —and is followed by a further section in which the bees are subjected to disease and even annihilation which no desire of theirs to immortalize the species (at genus immortale manet, 208) can quite prevent. The revelation of the problem of death lies at a deeper level than that of the stoic pantheism set forth in lines 219–27. The communal passionless altruism of the bee symbolizes but one side of even an ideal humanity: man, both for good and for bad, transcends the animal.

The next section on the *Care of the Bees* (228–280) descends to the practical, agricultural level characteristic of all passages in the *Georgics* which immediately follow passages of relative sublimity and poetic exaltation. But the language gradually rises in tone and significance: the brief account of taking the honey is followed (note here the corresponding section of III on the care of the sheep and goats, III, 384–469), by a description of the diseases and pests which beset the hive (239 f.). The way is thus prepared for the ultimate calamity (we note again the parallelism of III where also the account of pests and diseases leads to the ultimate calamity of the Plague):

281   *Sed si quem proles subito defecerit omnis*

Here then is the cue for Aristaeus and his story: omnem/expediam repetens ab origine famam.

Virgil, however, does not immediately begin the tale promised in lines 285–6 but recounts first the *bougonia* (the miraculous rebirth of the swarm from the rotting carcass of a calf) as it was experienced and practised in Egypt. It seems clear that lines 281–314 form a transition between the *Bees* and the concluding Aristaeus episode (315 f.) though that is provided with its own invocation and introduction. Later we shall consider these lines (281–314) for their bearing on the much-mooted question of the supposed 'revision' of the poem after Gallus' death.[1] Now our only concern is to see them in the context of the whole poem as its stands. Why (aside from the possible exigencies of revision) does Virgil put the *bougonia* here, anticipating the dénouement of the Aristaeus story and thus making lines 548–58 (the actual *bougonia* of the story) both repetitious and anticlimactic?

The answer, it seems to me, is clear enough (again if we do not try to look beyond the actual text): Virgil's concern in the Aristaeus story is not so much with the *bougonia* itself (that is now taken for granted) as with its *raison d'être*, the reason why Aristaeus, in the first place, required divine aid in discovering it. In other words, the Aristaeus story contributes to the poem a quite new element which is only formally, or so to speak by courtesy, related to the bees. This is also suggested in the unprecedented special invocation that opens the story (315):

> Quis deus hanc, Musae, quis nobis extudit artem?
> *unde nova ingressus* hominum experientia cepit?

Virgil, in other words, wants to mark off the *story* (and the explanation of the *bougonia*'s origin which it provides) from the *bougonia* itself as clearly as possible. Later, he declares in line 285, he will tell the whole story from the *beginning* (i.e. as he does from l. 315 on):

[1] See Appendix 7.

285   Altius omnem
           expediam prima repetens *ab origine* famam.

Now (i.e. at l. 285 and up to 314) all he wants to deal with is the
bougonia itself.

This is a most significant clue, I think, to the meaning of the
whole poem.[1] The *bougonia* in one sense completes the *Georgics*:
the resurrection of the bees from the carcass of the bull-calf
(vitulus) is the obvious answer to the Plague of III: death has
now been overcome by renewed life; the bees emerge from a
putrefying corpse like one of the corpses described at the end of
III. The symbolic difference already made clear (ll. 149–227)
between the immortal, passionless and selfless community of
the bees and the passion-ridden mortality of other animals is now
symbolized again in the *bougonia*. (Here again we see how
devoted work—work taking the place of other passions—and
complete allegiance to the community can triumph over the
corruption, strife and anarchy of self-seeking, individualistic
passion.) Here nature is no longer the harsh task-master (as in
I) or an amoral fate (as in III) but (as in II) the wonderful
friend. It is just at the approach of spring and its new warmth
that the *bougonia* takes place:

305   Hoc geritur zephyris primum impellentibus undas,
           ante novis rubeant quam prata coloribus, ante
           garrula quam tignis nidum suspendat hirundo.
           Interea teneris tepefactus in ossibus umor
           aestuat, et visenda modis animalia miris.

In this mood of soft spring resurrection, death and all the
bitterness of work, all the disruptive and destructive aspects of
passion disappear: the co-operation of man with nature, or,
more exactly, of all parts of nature with each other, seems finally
established.

But it is clear also how many problems have been passed over
and neglected! What is absent from these lines (281–314) is any
sense of evil and of the real tragedy of life. We cannot simply
say that the 'ideal' polity of the bees is the natural corrective of
passion and mortality and hence the natural principle of
resurrection. We cannot see in their sexless, passionless *labor*,

---

[1] But of course not a 'clue' that *necessitates* the double *bougonia*. Virgil could have
made his point *without* the repetition for whose origin we must seek elsewhere (i.e.
in the circumstances of the book's composition). See the discussion in Appendix 7.

their complete rejection of the individual and his rights, a 'remedy' to all the ills described in III, the kind of society which can achieve the joyful co-operation with nature described in II. The reconciliation of passion and work, the individual and the state, life and death requires *moral* understanding and a sense of tragedy—*humanitas* as, in short, Virgil conceived *humanitas*. Resurrection also requires death as its counterpart and the relation of the two must be at bottom a *moral* relation. Without some such conception of things, the great 'digressions' at the end of Books I and II, the profound feeling for the force of passion and death in III, are only trivialized. This is why the *Georgics* cannot indeed end with the *bougonia* or with resurrection as a kind of unmotivated, natural fact. We cannot understand the poem finally until we have understood its actual conclusion, its conception of the moral *cause* and *origin* of resurrection.

Here then we come to the *crux* of Virgil's agricultural symbolism. The *Georgics*, as we have seen, fall into two parts, the *first* (Books I and II) being concerned with *man* as he encounters inanimate nature (the soil, the sky and its weather, vineyards and trees); and the second (Books III and IV) with sentient animals seen in large part from within as creatures with their own passions and feelings, the proper subjects of admiration and pity. But this dual division is cross-cut by another dual division: the correspondence in mood and feeling between Books I and III and between Books II and IV. In I and III we see the dark side of man and nature: on the one hand, the harsh struggle of man with nature and the cosmic sympathy of the two disarranged and troubled by man's inability to control himself; on the other hand we see the tragic forces at work within nature itself, blind passion and overwhelming death. Here the animals —both the larger cattle and horses and the smaller sheep and goats—stand, *in part*, as symbols of human characteristics, of human experiences. More exactly: man is here and for this limited purpose the kin of the animal. In II and IV the emphasis is reversed: man finds nature extremely co-operative and sees in it once more a paradise, threatened by the false ambitions of civilization to be sure, but still possible and actual and given even a 'local habitation and a name' in rural Italy. Similarly, we see in the bees the kind of society—passionless, selfless, laborious, happy—which is the co-operative ideal: given a single, wise monarch all will be for the best. Again the bees 'stand for' a social, human ideal but they in no sense lose their insect natures. Hence the mythical transformation of dead cattle into live bees can 'stand for' a transformation of human characteristics and attitudes: the realistic, acquisitive *labor* of I becomes, so to speak, the ideal, co-operative *labor* of II just as the passionate and tragic victims of III become the harmonious workers of IV. Life emerges from death: in political terms, the Augustan restoration from the anarchy of civil war; in symbolic terms, the Golden Age from the Age of Iron.[1]

This recapitulation of the main symbolic structure of the poem 'shows up' the difficulty clearly enough. Man and the animal cannot be simply equated in this way. Had Virgil written only an allegory, with animals representing human traits and man himself omitted, then the scheme might be granted logical or, better, aesthetic coherence. But man remains in the picture and the difference between man and animal is maintained: hence we cannot treat man just as an animal and we cannot simply correlate the animal symbols with human reality. This does not mean that Virgil did not employ such a symbolism as just described—the correspondences and correlations are too frequent and too pointed to make this really doubtful—but it does mean that it cannot be pushed too far. There comes a point where the symbolism does not carry its weight, where man has to re-emerge from the symbols and, so to speak, correct or illuminate them by personal intervention. This, as I see it, is precisely the function of the Aristaeus story.

II

It is essential first to analyse carefully the structure of the *Aristaeus*. The following *schema* will make this clear:

1. (ll. 315–16 = 2 lines): Introductory link with the preceding account of bee-keeping.

---

[1] Cf. the analysis of J. Bayet, 'Les Premières Géorgiques de Virgile' (*Revue de Philologie*, 56 (1930), pp. 246–7). His contrast of Books 3 and 4 ('le thème de la chasteté et de l'immortalité opposé à celui de l'amour et de la mort') seems to me very apt but I cannot agree with his theory of a wide separation (in *both* style and time) between Books 1–2 and Books 3–4. The differences here are, as I see it, *part of a total plan* which this whole chapter has been designed to adumbrate.

Quis deus hanc, Musae, quis nobis extudit artem?
unde nova ingressus hominum experientia cepit?

2. (ll. 317–32 = 16 lines): The wretched plight of Aristaeus: his *plaint* to his mother Cyrene (321–32).

3. (ll. 333–60 *inferret* = 27⅔ lines): Cyrene at the bottom of the stream Peneus hears Aristaeus and tells her attendant nymphs to lead him down to her. (Recital of the nymphs by name and their occupations.) The passage is clearly demarcated at the beginning by the *At mater* which starts line 333 and at the end by the *At illum* (at the start of the next section) which follows the sentence ending with *qua iuvenis gressus inferret* in line 360.

4. (ll. 360 [end]–386 = 26⅓ lines): Aristaeus' descent to his mother: his amazement at the scene he discovers. Aristaeus' reception by his mother and her nymphs. The passage is punctuated by *Postquam* (start of l. 374), though there is no reason for making lines 374–86 (= 13 lines) a separate part.

5. (ll. 387–414 = 28 lines): Cyrene's speech describing Proteus and the way to make him communicate the answer to Aristaeus' difficulty.

6. (ll. 415–18 *vigor* = 3⅔ lines): Cyrene annoints Aristaeus with ambrosia thus giving him beauty and vigour.

7. (ll. 418 [end]–424 = 6⅓ lines): The cave of Proteus described: Cyrene hides Aristaeus in it. The passage is demarcated by the abrupt transition of line 418: *Est specus ingens* with the initial *est* indicating an *ekphrasis*.

8. (ll. 425–52 = 28 lines): Proteus comes to the cave. Aristaeus attacks him as directed by Cyrene. Proteus finally submits and prophesies. The passage is demarcated at the beginning by the temporal word: *Iam* (start of l. 425) and the shift of tense from *resistit* (last word of 424) to *ardebat* (426).

9. (ll. 453–527 = 75 lines): Proteus tells the story of Orpheus and Eurydice.

10. (ll. 528–47 = 20 lines): Cyrene interprets Proteus' story and tells Aristaeus how to act.

11. (ll. 548–58 = 11 lines): Conclusion: Aristaeus follows Cyrene's directions: the bees emerge from the carcasses

of the slaughtered cattle. Introduced and demarcated by the typically epic: *haud mora.*

If we think only of the *major* divisions here, we have:

1. Aristaeus and his complaint (317–32 = 16 lines).
2. Cyrene and her nymphs (333–60 = 27⅔ lines).
3. Aristaeus joins Cyrene (360–86 = 26⅓ lines).
4. Cyrene's speech of advice to Aristaeus (387–414 = 28 lines).
5. Interlude: Aristaeus, the cave (415–24 = 10 lines).
6. Aristaeus and Proteus in the cave (425–52 = 28 lines).
7. Orpheus (453–527 = 75 lines).
8. The Interpretation and Enactment of Proteus' message (528–58 = 31 lines).

Thus the balance of 2 and 3 and of 4 and 6 is obvious. Omitting the obviously introductory first part, we can easily see the basic system of balance:

I: Getting the oracle (parts 2–6 = 120 lines).

II: The Oracle, its interpretation and enactment (parts 7–8 = 106 lines).

It is quite clear that the centre of attention is the oracle or, in other words, the Orpheus story. The elaborately stylized meeting of Aristaeus and Cyrene (parts 2 and 3) provides the setting of Cyrene's speech of advice (4). This in its turn motivates the precisely balancing section on the enactment of her advice (6). Everything thus leads directly to the *oracle*. But this, when it comes, is surprising: Proteus does not, as we might prosaically expect, tell Aristaeus what to do but merely the reason for his misfortunes. Secondly he does this in the first four lines (Non te nullius exercent numinis irae; Tibi has . . . Orpheus . . . poenas . . . suscitat) and might, so far as Aristaeus' interests are concerned, have spared the other seventy-one lines of his speech. This enigmatic 'answer' in fact required Cyrene to reappear, interpret Proteus' tale (or at least the first four lines of it) for her son's benefit, and thus produce a happy ending: it again accentuates the centrality of the Oracle and provides a conclusion for the Aristaeus-Cyrene story. Thus, though everything is designed to emphasize the oracle or

Proteus' speech, the oracle itself is paradoxically independent of the rest.[1]

The explanation of course is obvious. This is another frame 'epic' like the *Peleus and Thetis*. The frame does, to be sure, relate the whole to the subject of bee-keeping, but its dimensions and details go far, far beyond anything that the bees *per se* could require. Rather, like the *Peleus and Thetis* story in relation to the *Ariadne*, the frame's primary function is to set off the central panel or picture, the Orpheus-Eurydice narrative. Here, however, unlike Catullus, Virgil rather drastically changes the quantitative proportions of the frame and picture. Thus:

In Catullus 64: *Ariadne* = 213 lines.
Peleus and Thetis = 194 lines.
In Virgil: *Orpheus-Eurydice* = 75 lines.
Aristaeus = 171 lines.

But the reason for the difference is, in the light of the analysis above, quite evident. Virgil does not care to emphasize the picture by its mere size or extent since this would involve expanding what he is above all concerned to compress or concentrate (as we shall see). Rather he gives it emphasis by the far more artistic device of putting it in a plot which revolves around it and makes it its climax. But he did much more than this: he also constructed the frame (i.e. the Aristaeus-Cyrene story) so that its style and subject matter would form a decorative contrast to the style and subject-matter of the picture proper (i.e. the *Orpheus*). This itself required diffuseness in the frame to offset the concentration in the picture.

The first characteristic of the 'frame' to strike us is its obviously epic style. This is apparent first of all in its *narrative symmetry*: each section roughly balances the other; the speeches balance and are balanced by the narrative proper. Thus part 2 (the description of Cyrene and her nymphs) is balanced by the reception of Aristaeus (3). Cyrene's speech of advice (4) is exactly the same length as Aristaeus' enactment of it (6). Though we can divide the whole *Aristaeus* into separate parts,

[1] Roughly speaking this scheme of the *Aristaeus* corresponds to those of E. Norden ('Orpheus und Eurydice', *Sitzungsberichte Preuss. Akad. Phil. Hist. Klasse* (1934), pp. 626 f.) and E. de Saint-Denis (*Virgil, Géorgiques*, Budé ed. 1956). It was, however, made quite independently of them.

o

there is no elliptical hiatus between them: thus though line 333 involves a definite transition (from Aristaeus to Cyrene and from the land to the depth of the stream) its relation to what goes before is absolutely clear: at mater sonitum thalamo sub fluminis alti/sensit. So with the transition back to Aristaeus: at/illum curvata in montis faciem curcumstetit unda. The abrupt *Est specus ingens*, &c., of line 418 does not surprise the reader as he has already been prepared for it by Cyrene's speech.

The main features of the *Aristaeus* (as distinguished from the *Orpheus*) arc all characteristically epic: the long elaborate speeches (parts 2, 5, 10), the *ekphraseis* of the under-water court (3) and of the cave (7), the epithets (Pastor Aristaeus, Peneia Tempe, Thymbraeus Apollo, Asia Deiopea, mare purporeum, Panchaeis ignibus, ardentem Vestam, grandaevos Nereus, &c.) are the most obvious earmarks. The diction, periodization, metre are almost clamorously epical. Thus the lines:

```
363   Iamque domum mirans   genetricis et umida regna
      speluncisque lacus clausos   lucosque sonantis
      ibat et   ingenti motu stupefactus aquarum
      omnia   sub magna labentia flumina terra
      spectabat   diversa locis,   Phasimque Lycumque
      et caput,   unde altus primum se erumpit Enipeus,
369   unde pater Tiberinus,   et unde Aniena fluenta.
```

Note here the cola (spaced), the lengthening of the sentence by participles (mirans, stupefactus), the solemn anaphora (repetition of *que*, *unde*), the postponement of the intransitive verb *ibat*, the piling up of proper names, the epithet *pater*, the effect of climax produced by the second and third cola from the end and the closing cadence of the last colon. The caesurae and diaereses (marked) emphasize the artful construction of the cola (two each in ll. 363–4, two long cola after diaereses in ll. 365–6, then four short cola in ll. 367–8 followed by the long impressive second colon of l. 368 and the closing diminuendo cola of l. 369). The alliteration (*s* in l. 364, *l* in l. 366), the use of spondees in line 368 leading up to the *erumpit Enipeus*, the heavy pauses and spondees of line 365 before *stupefactus*—all magnify the solemnity of this picture of Aristaeus among the roaring waters.

This is epic but it is much closer to Homeric epic than the *Aeneid*. First the relative *objectivity* of the style is impressive. No character is addressed by the narrator and in general the *sympathetic-empathetic manner of narration is all but totally absent*: what is described (especially in the narrative parts 3, 4, 8) is either a *mise en scène* or purely physical action (as, e.g. the conflict of Proteus and Aristaeus in part 8). Typical of the *mise en scène* is the following description of the nymphs:

345   Inter quas curam Clymene narrabat *inanem*
        Volcani Martisque dolos et *dulcia* furta
        aque Chao *densos* divom numerabat amores.
        Carmine quo captae fusis dum *mollia* pensa
        devolvont, iterum *maternas* impulit auris
        luctus Aristaei, *vitreisque* sedilibus omnes
        obstipuere; sed ante alias Arethusa sorores
        prospiciens summa *flavom* caput extulit unda.

The adjectives underlined have little if any empathetic content. The nymphs, the story Clymene tells, the spinning, the action of Arethusa are not seen from the inside at all: they are facts, sights, objective and decorative. The idea of listing the names of the nymphs (given in ll. 336–45) and the *situation* (the nymphs and a mother-goddess hearing from afar the complaints of a son) come straight from the *Iliad* (18. 35 f.). Compare

    ... · ἄκουσε δὲ πότνια μήτηρ
    ἡμένη ἐν βένθεσσιν ἁλὸς παρὰ πατρὶ γέροντι,
    κώκυσέν τ' ἄρ' ἔπειτα· θεαὶ δέ μιν ἀμφαγέροντο,
    πᾶσαι ὅσαι κατὰ βένθος ἁλὸς Νηρηΐδες ἦσαν.
    ἔνθ' ἄρ' ἔην Γλαύκη τε Θάλειά τε Κυμοδίκη τε.
    Νησαίη Σπειώ τε Θόη θ' Ἁλίη τε βοῶπις, κτλ.

with

333   At mater sonitum thalamo sub fluminis alti
        sensit. Eam cirum Milesia vellera nymphae
        carpebant hyali saturo fucata colore,
        Drumoque Xanthoque Ligeaque Phyllodoceque, &c.

The two lists of names, to be sure, differ and Virgil's picture is calmer than Homer's. It is not for some time (at second hearing: *iterum*, l. 349) that the nymphs are really roused by Aristaeus' complaints. This gives Virgil a chance to show them in a scene of idyllic peace in the quiet depth of the stream, spinning and listening to Clymene retelling the story of Vulcan and Mars (*Odyssey* 8. 266 f.).

The fourth part (Aristaeus' descent and reception at the bottom of the stream) is equally Homeric and indeed contains reminiscences of *Iliad* 24 (Iris' descent to Thetis in the ocean and reascent), *Odyssey* 11 (243), *Iliad* 16 (391). We can compare

Il. 16. 391   ἐς δ' ἅλα πορφυρέην μεγάλα στενάχουσι ῥέουσαι

with

373   in mare purpureum violentior effluit amnis

and

Il. 14. 201   Ὠκεανόν τε, θεῶν γένεσιν, καὶ μητέρα Τηθύν.
14. 246   Ὠκεανοῦ, ὅς περ γένεσις πάντεσσι τέτυκται·

with

382   Oceanumque patrem rerum nymphasque sorores.

The major indebtedness of Virgil to Homer at this point is to the Proteus story of Menelaus (*Odyssey* 4. 351 f.). Here we have Proteus coming to his cave at noon with his seals, counting them and going to sleep (400, 403, 450–1, 453), the attack upon him by Menelaus and his three companions (454), his metamorphoses into a lion, serpent, leopard (456–8: in Eidothea's account also into other shapes including fire, 417–18), his return to his old shape (460), his feigned ignorance of Menelaus' request (462–3) despite Menelaus' conviction that he really knows without needing to be told (465). Finally he reveals that Menelaus has offended the gods by not sacrificing to them, and tells him also the fate of his fellow Greeks (Ajax, Agamemnon, Odysseus). The correspondence is at times verbal:

Od. 4. 465   οἶσθα, γέρον· τί με ταῦτα παρατροπέων ἐρεείνεις;
Vir. 447   "Scis, Proteu, scis ipse; neque est te fallere quicquam;
Od. 4. 417   πάντα δὲ γινόμενος πειρήσεται, ὅσσ' ἐπὶ γαῖαν
Vir. 441   omnia transformat sese in miracula rerum.

Cyrene's description of Proteus:

> novit namque omnia vates,
> quae sint, quae fuerint, quae mox ventura trahantur;

is from *Iliad* 1. 70 (of Calchas):

> ὅς ᾔδη τά τ' ἐόντα τά τ' ἐσσόμενα πρό τ' ἐόντα,

There are, however, many departures of Virgil from Homer, and especially in the Proteus story. The cave is described at some length in Virgil: it is merely mentioned in Homer. Virgil emphasizes (as Homer does not) the heat of noon and its effect. In Virgil Aristaeus attacks Proteus alone after being given divine vigour by his mother's ambrosia; in Homer Menelaus has three companions and the ambrosia is given them by Eidothea to conceal the smell of the seal hides. The business of the seals is played down in Virgil and the concealment under the hides is omitted.

In general the Homeric atmosphere is maintained in the *Aristaeus* as it is in no other portion of Virgil's poetry. But Virgil achieves an idyllic, quiet and picturesque effect which we do not find in Homer's accounts of Thetis hearing the groans of Achilles or of Menelaus' attack on Proteus. The lightness and rapidity of Homer is largely but not entirely lost. Obviously, Virgil is trying to select an exotic, a hardly human portion of Homer and to heighten its exotic character while preserving a due decorum (hence the omission of the seal-skins, their smell, &c.). The pathetic and emotional element is deliberately played down. Even the quite physical and wholly unemotional action of Aristeaus' attack on Proteus is much reduced in intensity of effect by being anticipated in Cyrene's explicit directions. In short the *Aristaeus* is almost utterly devoid of Virgil's characteristic *ethos*, that concentrated inner drama and that pathetic style in which we always seem to hear 'the still sad music of humanity'. It contrasts not only with the *Aeneid*, but with the rest of the *Georgics* and with most of the *Bucolics* (cf. e.g. *Eclogues* 1, 2, 4, 5, 6, 8, 9, 10).

All this changes in the *Orpheus*. The contrast of styles between the *Orpheus* (i.e. part 9 of the schema on p. 191) and the *Aristaeus* (i.e. the rest of the whole episode: all the parts of the schema on p. 191 *with the exception of part 9*) is very striking and is certainly quite deliberate.

We can analyse the *Orpheus* as follows:

I. (ll. 453–9 = 7 lines): Introduction: Aristaeus is not the object of some divine hatred: he is rather punished for his own crimes by Orpheus, inconsolable at the loss of his wife Eurydice; *she* in fleeing from Aristaeus did not see the large snake lurking in the grass

II. (ll. 460–3 = 4 lines): Eurydice is mourned by the chorus of Dryads and by the entire countryside. Between line 459 and line 460, the death of Eurydice (indicated by the *moritura* of l. 458) is elliptically understood. Line 460 (At chorus aequalis, &c.) thus represents a transition in time; the *At* indicates the shift of time and of subject.

III. (ll. 464–6 = 3 lines): Orpheus (*ipse*, start of l. 464) ceaselessly mourns for Eurydice.

IV. (ll. 467–70 = 4 lines): He even goes to Hades and approaches its *implacable* ruler. The transition from his mourning to his Hades-Journey is indicated by the *etiam* of line 467: Taenarias *etiam* fauces, alta ostia Ditis.

V. (ll. 471–84 = 14 lines): The effect of Orpheus' singing on the dead, the Eumenides, Cerberus, Ixion. There is no transition from Orpheus' descent to Hades (IV) to this part (V) save the *At* of line 471:

At cantu commotae Erebi de sedibus imis

Line 481 (Quin ipsae stupuere domus atque intima Leti) introduces a more or less distinct subsection, that of the monsters of *intima Tartara*: Eumenides, Cerberus, Ixion, as distinct from the mass of the dead (ll. 471–80).

VI. (ll. 485–506 = 22 lines): The return of Orpheus and Eurydice; Orpheus' fatal look; the second parting with Eurydice. The transition from Part V (the song) is indicated by the *iam* of line 485 (Iamque pedem referens casus evaserat omnis) and the pluperfect, *evaserat*. Thus the yielding of Dis and Proserpina, their terms, &c., are omitted save for the later parenthetical reference of line 487 (namque hanc dederat Proserpina legem).

VII. (ll. 507–15 = 9 lines): His grief at the second separation. This is intimately related to the preceding:

506–7   Illa quidem Stygia nabat iam frigida cumba
         Septem illum totos perhibent ex ordine menses

Note the *perhibent* and indirect discourse which indicates a shift from the direct reporting of the preceding section to the indirect or second-hand reporting of this section.

VIII. (ll. 516–27 = 12 lines): Orpheus refuses all further love and marriage and remains alone in the cold North mourning Eurydice and his lost opportunity (inrita Ditis dona). The women in their anger at his contempt for them tear him in pieces and his head floats down the Hebrus while his tongue still calls out the name of Eurydice.

This division, which is not based on any arbitrary theory of symmetrical arrangement but follows Virgil's own transitions, indicates the general movement of the poem. In schematic form we have:

1: The death of Eurydice: (ll. 453–9) 7 lines.
2: Mourning for Eurydice's *original* death and separation from Orpheus (Parts II and III, ll. 460–6) 7 lines.
3: The *inhumanity* of Hades (Part IV, ll. 467–70) 4 lines.
4: The Triumph of human song (Part V, ll. 471–84) 14 lines.
5: The *second* separation of Eurydice from Orpheus (Part VI, ll. 485–507) 22 lines.
6: The *second* mourning for Eurydice (Part VII, ll. 507–15) 9 lines.
7: Conclusion: The death of Orpheus (ll. 516–27) 12 lines.

It is thus quite clear that 2 and 6 (the two mourning passages) correspond as do 1 and 7 (the two deaths). But the pathos and meaning of the corresponding passages is wholly different: 1 and 2 describe human death and mourning in their normal meaning. What gives an utterly new significance to the later mourning and death (6 and 7) is the fact that the grief and contempt for life (which produced Orpheus' death) is caused by his own folly. The singer who could by his song vanquish even the implacable hearts of Dis and Proserpina and recover his love, has lost all by his own delirium or *furor*. There is no second chance. Fate remains finally inevitable because man cannot finally control his passion. All that is left is a grief which passes into insensibility and death. It is thus quite plain that 5 above (Part VI in the full schema) constitutes the climax and turning point of the poem.

This great poem presents two major aspects: the aspect in which it is properly speaking a neoteric 'little epic' or 'elegiac-type' narrative; and the aspect in which it, far more than the song of Damon or of Corydon or the brief account of Pasiphae, represents a new (non-neoteric and non-elegiac) type of narrative.

1. It is 'neoteric' or 'elegiac' both in its obvious asymmetry and ellipsis and in its obvious subjectivity of style. Our analysis has made clear the evident elipses: the *actual* death of Eurydice is omitted (all we see is the girl running toward the hidden snake); the transition from Orpheus' entrance into Hades to his song is left out; the story of how Dis and Proserpina relented and granted Eurydice's conditional return is not told (only alluded to in a passing phrase); the transition from the second parting to Orpheus' seven months of mourning beside the river Strymon is barely indicated; the motivation of the Ciconian women who killed and mutilated him is just touched upon (no more). It is in fact doubtful whether anyone who did not already know the story could follow Virgil's narrative with perfect intelligence. It is thus assumed for the first thirty-four lines that the reader knows who Eurydice is, for she is merely referred to as Orpheus' *coniunx*. Furthermore, the asymmetry of the narrative is evident: the second separation (Part V) is both longer and far more emphatic than any other part. The second mourning (Part VII) is three times the length of Orpheus' first mourning (Part III) and longer than Parts II (the Mourning of the Dryads and countryside) and III put together. This is not the style of epic as we can see most easily by comparing the structure of the *Orpheus* with that of the *Aristaeus* discussed above.

More important: the style of the *Orpheus* is utterly subjective in contrast to the objectivity of Homeric epic or the *Aristaeus*. Nor is this due simply to the fact that it is part of Proteus' speech to Aristaeus. The *te* of line 457:

> Illa quidem, dum *te* fugeret per flumina praeceps

is addressed to Aristaeus but after this Aristaeus drops out of the picture. In lines 465–6:

> *te*, dulcis coniunx, *te* solo in litore secum,
> *te*, veniente die, *te* decedente canebat

Eurydice is directly addressed by the narrator as is Ariadne by Catullus, Scylla by the author of the *Ciris*, Io by Calvus. Actually these lines imply not *merely* an appeal to Eurydice by the narrator but an empathetic identification of the narrator with Orpheus so that the lines tremble so to speak on the verge of direct quotation—Orpheus himself calling to Eurydice.

But the empathy and sympathy is far more subtle and pervasive than can be expressed by actual invocation of Eurydice or Orpheus. Consider such lines as

470	nesciaque *humanis precibus mansuescere* corda
488	cum subita *incautum* dementia cepit amantem
489	*ignoscenda* quidem, scirent si ignoscere manes
501	prensantem *nequiquam* umbras et *multa volentem dicere* praeterea
504	*Quid faceret? quo se rapta bis coniuge ferret?*
512	amissos queritur fetus, quos *durus* arator
527	a! *miseram* Eurydicen anima fugiente vocabat

I have underlined here the most obviously empathetic-sympathetic words: the narrator, full of sympathy for Orpheus, sees the *inexorable* hearts of the rulers of Hades, trembles at the *incautious* lover, feels how *pardonable* his error was, feels his *vain desire* to say more, shares his dilemma after Eurydice's second parting, pities the nightingale whose nest the *hard-hearted* ploughman has robbed and of course mourns for *poor* Eurydice.

2. Thus of the divergence of this style from that of the *Aristaeus* or of objective 'Homeric' epic style in general, there cannot be the least doubt. But this approach hardly does justice to the unique character of the *Orpheus*. It is quite unlike the *Ariadne* episode of the *Peleus and Thetis* or the story of Scylla in the *Ciris* or, presumably, Calvus' *Io* or Cinna's *Zmyrna*. It is much more like Virgil's bucolic narrative in the eighth eclogue (Damon Song). But is it a far more developed and intense instance of the narrative style or approach we studied there. Here, as there, the static 'moment' of former neoteric narrative is assimilated to a dramatic whole and put in a biographical-temporal framework, but this, in comparison, is a major work despite its brevity. What Virgil is here trying to achieve is a sense of the tragedy of human passion. Orpheus in this poem confronts the huge inhumanity of death but this in itself is not the point of his tragedy. Orpheus can actually conquer death by his poetic genius, by a song. Yet he cannot conquer his own impulses which destroy him in the very moment of triumph. And this is the real reason why death conquers him at last.

The poem is intensely dramatic. The ellipses do not asymmetrically curtail the *narrative Virgil is concerned with* but they do concentrate it with great effect. We proceed at once from

the fatal snake to the mourning Dryads and mountains and
rivers (Part II) and finally to Orpheus himself *solo in litore secum.*
The grand landscape of lines 462–3:

> altaque Pangaea et Rhesi Mavortia tellus
> atque Getae atque Hebrus et Actias Orithyia

fades away and we see the lover alone in his grief. The contrast
of the universal grief with *his* grief is very effective: his loneliness, his pathos is enormously heightened. Then we proceed
immediately with him to the gates of Hell (Taenarias fauces):
there is no need to underline his resolve or its reason. The next
four lines (467–70):

> Taenarias etiam fauces, alta ostia Ditis
> et caligantem nigra formidine lucum
> ingressus manisque adiit regemque tremendum
> nesciaque humanis precibus mansuescere corda.

produce at once and with marvellous compression the effect of
terrible and inhuman power—dark, tremendous and merciless:
the odds against which Orpheus alone is to try the charm of his
song.

The next part (V) opens with the striking:

> At cantu commotae Erebi de sedibus imis

The *at* sets Orpheus' song against the whole weight of the four
preceding lines: the might of hell itself. The slow beginning
(spondees), the synaloepha in the third (dactylic) foot, the final
long *i* sounds produce a magical effect: we see all the denizens
of hell, slowly, starting from the very bottom, begin to move in
dance as Orpheus plays: then comes the magical

> umbrae ibant tenues

where the imperfect *ibant* has certainly an inchoative sense
(began to move). Ghostly indeed is the rhythm of these words
(*umbrae ibant* is surely one of the most effective synaloephae in
Virgil). Who moves in this dance? All the shades, thick thronging as the birds that come in spring, for the dead are many:

> si lunga tratta
> di gente ch' io non avessi creduto
> che morte tanta n'avesse disfatta. (*Inf.* III. 55–57)

The shades are filmy stuff (tenues, simulacra) and, above all
pathetic: boys, unmarried girls, youths laid on the pyres before

their parents' eyes. Thus the *insubstantiality, universality,* and *pathos* of *death* are accented in these lines (471–80). And how unlovely the home of the dead! All are now bound forever by the sluggish marsh of Cocytus and the meandering Styx. Yet the power of song can move even these to dance. Why even (Quin) the monsters of Tartarus, the Eumenides and Cerberus dance and Ixion stays his wheel!

All this part (V) is seen *from the point of view of Hades,* the dead, the Eumenides, Ixion. We *see* Orpheus' song taking gradually, slowly its hold on the most recalcitrant audience imaginable: the tremendous incongruity between song and this grim environment is miraculously resolved.

Now, in Part VI, the great feat has been accomplished. Now Orpheus *had* overcome every impediment and *was on his way* with Eurydice to the upper air:

485   Iamque pedem referens casus evaserat omnis
          redditaque Eurydice superas veniebat ad auras

These lines not merely cover the ratification of Orpheus' musical achievement: they indicate by their dactylic rhythm his and Eurydice's triumphal advance toward the world of life. Then suddenly everything is changed:

488   cum subita incautum dementia cepit amantem,
          ignoscenda quidem, scirent si ignoscere manes:
490   restitit Eurydicenque suam iam luce sub ipsa
          immemor, heu, victusque animi respexit. Ibi omnis
          effusus labor atque immitis rupta tyranni
493   foedera, terque fragor stagnist auditus Averni

These lines marvellously render the sudden shift from the triumph of Orpheus' and Eurydice's upward march to the fatal moment which immediately destroys all the fruits of his victory. It is not merely that Orpheus is seized by the mad desire to look back but that, in consequence, the grim powers of hell reassert once and for all their authority.

Line 488 with its emphasis of *incautum* (spondaic and preceded by a synaloepha that miraculously suggests the speed, the breathless, almost unpronounceable haste of Orpheus' fatal error); the spondaic pathos of line 489 (with its harsh *sc*'s and its doleful long *i*'s); the emphasis of *restitit* and *iam* in line 490; the terribly swift transition from *respexit* to the next sentence;

ibi omnis in line 491 (making the new sentence begin from a weak caesura); the effect of *labor*'s gains leaking suddenly away in the *effusus labor* of 492; and the thrice re-echoed signal of Orpheus' doom in line 493 (with its triple cola), all give full metrical and onomatopoeic significance to the *suddenness* of the change and its grim finality.

Then abruptly without introduction come the five lines of Eurydice's last words to Orpheus (494–8):

> Illa 'Quis et me' inquit 'Miseram et te perdidit, Orpheu,
> quis tantus furor? en iterum crudelia retro
> fata vocant conditque natantia lumina somnus.
> Iamque vale; feror ingenti circumdata nocte
> invalidasque tibi tendens, heu non tua, palmas'.

What impresses here is the dramatic quality of this speech. It is no lament, no monologue, no recital of woes, no expansion of a static pathetic situation (as the speeches in the *Ariadne* and *Ciris*) but, like the words of Pasiphaë in *Eclogue* 6, part of the action itself. The swiftness of Eurydice's words in line 494 (emphasized by the synaloephae *me inquit, miseram et*: note also the beginning of the quotation after a weak caesura) is due not only to her surprise but to *her sense of the shortness of time allotted her*. After the *quis tantus furor* of line 495 we sense the death-drowsiness coming once again upon her, her eyes swim, the huge night surrounds her as she extends her hands to Orpheus—she is, alas, no more his own! He strives but cannot grasp her now unsubstantial shade: she leaves him with so much more to say!

Now a by swift elliptical transition (l. 502) we see Charon refusing him further passage; we feel his dilemma (504–6):

> Quid *faceret?* quo se rapta bis coniuge *ferret?*
> quo fletu manis, quae numina voce moveret?
> Illa quidem Stygia *nabat* iam frigida cumba.

All is vain: she *was already*, with the chill of death upon her, *crossing* the Styx in the fatal boat. The *nabat* here with its sense of finality (while Orpheus debated what to do—quid faceret—she was already on her way, *nabat*, indicative factual imperfect) corresponds to the triumphant *veniebat* of line 486. All is now lost. Here the shift from direct to indirect discourse (507):

> Septem *illum* totos *perhibent* ex ordine menses
> flesse, &c.

tells the story. Orpheus' drama has been played out: the rest is epilogue and undramatic grief which is most appropriately told at second remove, indirectly, without dramatic emphasis.

VII. Orpheus can now only mourn the past. His song can still calm tigers and move oak trees (l. 510) but it cannot serve his heart's desire: he is like the nightingale mourning the fledglings that the cruel ploughman has taken from its nest; he can sing only from grief, only in lament for the past. Otherwise song has no meaning for him. Thus the end is foredoomed. His utter indifference to love and marriage (l. 516) directly provokes the Ciconian women but this is only because he no longer cares to live. The final scene of his head being borne down the river still calling on Eurydice may strike us as macabre or artificial: it at least indicates the obsession which has destroyed Orpheus' interest in life.

This is, in its own way, continuous narrative. Indeed, the narrative is only speeded, not cut off by the ellipses. For Virgil is not here trying to *reduce* the narrative to a simple static situation (as both Hellenistic and Neoteric poetry did) but to *concentrate* it and give it precisely the emphasis he wants. Eurydice running toward the snake—Orpheus mourning her against the mighty backdrop of mourning nature—his entrance into Hades—Hades moved by his song—his fatal *furor* and Eurydice's departure—his song turned to unappeasable grief—his death—each of these are links in a single narrative but its unity is not the factual story of what happened so much as the emotional effect of what happened as reflected in Orpheus and Eurydice and as both of these are reflected in the narrator. In other words, this is subjective drama: what moves it or makes it dramatic are the things in the soul's depths, love, the power of song, blind impulse, as these assert themselves against the huge and implacable powers of Hades and Death. Orpheus' love, his power of song and his *furor* (or fatal inability to control his love) are not isolated in static vignettes but are dramatically set against each other in temporal succession: his love motivates the song which moves Hell; then his *furor* makes tragedy out of both his love and his power of song.

This dramatic-temporal movement is also clear from a consideration of the *times* and *tenses* indicated at each step or section of the narrative:

1. Illa quidem *dum te fugeret* per flumina praeceps
   ... hydrum ... non ... vidit *moritura* puella
   servantem ripas.
2. *At* chorus Dryadem *implerunt* montis
3. *Ipse* ... solo in litore secum ... *canebat*
4. Taenarias fauces *ingressus* manis *adiit*.
5. *At* cantu commotae umbrae *ibant*
   Quin ipsae *stupuere* domus
6. *Iamque* pedem *referens evaserat*
   Eurydice *veniebat* ad auras
   cum subita ... dementia *cepit* amantem
   restitit Eurydicenque *respexit*
   Ibi omnis *effusus* labor
   Illa *inquit*
   nequiquam praeterea *vidit*; nec portitor Orci
   amplius *passus* transire paludem
   Quid *faceret*
   Illa Stygia *nabat* cumba.
7. Illum perhibent septem totos menses *flesse* et *evolvisse*
8. Nulla Venus ... animum *flexere*
   spretae matres *discerptum* invenem *sparsere*
   Tum caput *revolsum cum* Hebrus *volveret*
   a! miseram Eurydicen *vocabat*
   Eurydicen *referebant* ripae.

If we consider the tenses here carefully, it is apparent that the central point of view is not so much that of Orpheus (still less Eurydice) as that of the narrator. It is he who directs our vision and turns it from the fleeing Eurydice to the mourning Dryads, then to Orpheus singing alone and then to the terrible spectacle of the underworld. In Part 1 the blend of past, present and future (moritura ... vidit ... servantem) represents three view-points: the narrator speaking of a past event (vidit); the narrator *anticipating* the event (moritura); and the present of the girl's actual experience as she approaches the *waiting* snake. In 2 the mourning of the Dryads, &c., is depicted again in the simple narrative past (perfect) but in 3 the imperfect *canebat* forces attention on Orpheus—we see him singing; then the perfects of Part 4 (*ingressus ... adiit*) break the relatively immobile or habitual imperfect of Part 3 (canebat). The inchoative imperfect of *ibant* (472) again takes us from the narrative past to the actual drama. The perfect of line 481 (stupuere) indicates not a return to the narrative past but the character of the monsters' response to Orpheus' song (in contrast to the dance of the shades).

In Part 6 the tenses are related to the climactic drama of the second separation. We see first the pair approaching the upper world (veniebat ad auras): all Orpheus' misfortunes are now *past* (casus *evaserat* omnis). But this happy condition is abruptly broken (*cepit, restitit*). Time now shrinks to the momentary present of Eurydice's few tragic words (*inquit*—present). Then all, at once, is over and past (*dixit*—perfect). She flees (fugit) and while Orpheus wondered what to do (Quid faceret?) the bark was *already taking her back* (nabat iam) to Hades.

Thereafter (Part 7) the story is essentially told. We hear from other sources how he mourned her final loss. We revert to the direct narrative past, only to recount his later apathy and tragic death but there is a last glimpse of enacted drama when we see his head crying Eurydice's name as it is borne down the stream.

All this is seen through the narrator's emotions. At each point he sympathizes with the emotion of the moment. We see his initial sympathy with Orpheus and Eurydice:

455   hautquaquam ob meritum poenas,

his sense of the poor girl and the dreadful snake:

458   *immanem* ante pedes hydrum *moritura* puella

His concern for the bereft Orpheus leads him to address Eurydice directly (See how he wept for you!):

465   te, dulcis coniunx . . . canebat.

Then we share his sense of the pathos of death as he views the macabre dance:

476   pueri innuptaeque puellae

The moment of Orpheus' disastrous backward glance moves him most of all. Madness indeed but

489   ignoscenda quidem, scirent si ignoscere manes.

Poor Orpheus! *Immemor, heu, victusque animi*. In the tension of his emotion the narrator completely identifies Orpheus' dilemma with himself:

504   Quid faceret? quo se rapta bis coniuge ferret?

The *quid faceret* and *quo . . . ferret* are more than an elliptical
reproduction of Orpheus' thoughts: they are also the narrator's
own thoughts. Here empathy and sympathy completely con-
verge. The great simile of lines 511–15 symbolizes the tragedy:
it is subjective interpretation, empathy, sympathy together. The
final sequence of the three Eurydices (525, 526, 527) is at once
narrative and heartfelt grief (a! miseram Eurydicen).

As a whole, the *Orpheus* is the first great example of a new
style.[1] The diffuse, pictorial and unemotional *Aristaeus* sets off
its concentrated brilliance—its intense, packed drama of
human emotion felt and described from within. This is no
static situation which could be depicted on a tapestry or made
the subject of a monologue or deliberative dialogue like that of
the *Ciris*. It is brief not because it deals with a single emotional
'moment' but because it eliminates every undramatic inessential.
Unlike Hellenistic and neoteric narrative, it suggests rather than
expatiates.

The stylistic differences between the *Aristaeus* and *Orpheus*
sections of the poem (or episodes) reflect also a difference in
content and meaning. Just as in the *Peleus-Thetis* of Catullus
(64), the two themes are reversed images of each other: the
successful resurrection of the *Aristaeus* is counter-mirrored by
the unsuccessful resurrection of the *Orpheus*. In this Virgil
conforms to the technique of Catullus [2] (cf. above pp. 27–29).
But the contrast of the two themes in Virgil is much more
pronounced. Furthermore the much greater heightening and
emphasis of the central panel (the *Orpheus*) corresponds to the
much greater weight of meaning laid on it. Here also the
dramatic origin of the Orpheus theme—its emergence from the
inner drama of the *Aristaeus*—gives it a force and significance
which the purely pictorial origin of the Ariadne theme in
Catullus could not permit.

Eduard Norden's careful analysis of the evidence seems to
show, with very great cogency, the originality of Virgil's use of
his sources in this whole episode.[3] No one before Virgil had

---

[1] This style is clearly closer to the *Aeneid* (e.g. *Aeneid* 4) than to either the *Aristaeus*
or neoteric poetry in general. But it is not yet true *epic*; for its difference from the
Aeneid, see Appendix 7.

[2] F. Klingner ('Catulls Peleus Epos', *Sitzungsberichte Bayer. Akad. Phil. Hist.
Klasse* (1956), 6, pp. 74–75) was aware of the parallel between Catullus (64) and
Virgil here but did not develop it.   [3] Op. cit. on p. 193, n. 1.

joined the story of Aristaeus—the mythical *theios-aner* and inventor of bee culture—to the *bougonia*. No one, either, had coupled the Aristaeus theme to the Proteus theme, or above all, had coupled the Aristaeus with the Orpheus story. That Eurydice encountered the fatal snake in fleeing from *Aristaeus*, seems a clearly Virgilian invention. Our task now is to see precisely what Virgil intended by these innovations.

Those who have tried to find inconsistencies and contradictions in the Episode,[1] with an eye, of course, for traces of the 'revision' mentioned in Servius, have all pointed to the quite obvious fact that Aristaeus' mother, Cyrene, did not really need the 'oracle' of Proteus in order to tell her son what to do about his bees. Not only does Proteus fail to give the information anticipated in Cyrene's instructions to her son:

396   Hic tibi, nate, prius vinclis capiendus ut omnem
         expediat morbi causam *eventusque secundet.*
         Nam sine vi non ulla dabit *praecepta,*

but Cyrene herself seems to know about it already, since when she reappears after Proteus' departure she says:

531   Nate, licet tristis animo deponere curas.
         Haec omnis morbi causa, hinc miserabile *nymphae,*
         cum quibus illa choros lucis agitabat in altis,
         exitium misere apibus.

Proteus had not mentioned the *nymphs* but only Orpheus: *tibi has . . . Orpheus poenas suscitat.* Nor had he given any *praecepta*: these Cyrene adds on her own authority.

Such 'inconsistencies', however, have little aesthetic or poetical significance. As Norden has well shown, it was essential to Virgil's purpose that Cyrene should play a role at the end of the episode which would balance and give sequence to her role at its beginning. Otherwise indeed, the introductory portion (the underwater palace, the descent of Aristaeus, &c.) would be absurdly otiose. Nor is it really necessary to assume that the whole Proteus business is superfluous even on the most literal level: Cyrene could quite well deduce the consequences of Orpheus' and Eurydice's companions' anger once she knew the nature of their animus against Aristaeus. But Virgil is not really concerned with such details. The fact that Cyrene was

---

[1] See Appendix 7.

P

either already informed or remarkably skilled in interpreting
a rather cryptic hint does not really trouble us as we actually
read the narrative. We should surely have been much more
troubled had Cyrene never returned to complete the episode
for in that case our sense of aesthetic balance and harmony
would have been sadly assailed.

But what stands out from this analysis of the 'inconsistencies'
is the crucial significance of Proteus. Obviously by putting the
Orpheus story in his mouth, Virgil gives it a dramatic setting
such as it could not possibly have had if left to Cyrene alone.
More than that, its attribution to Proteus calls attention to its
significance for the structure of the whole episode and indeed
the *Georgics* as a whole. Proteus is the seer who knows all the
past, present and future:

392   novit namque omnia vates,
393   quae sint, quae fuerint, quae mox ventura trahantur.

He is the man who can reveal the mystery, discern the meaning of
things. But this mystery, it is clear, is not just the *bougonia*;
Virgil, as we have seen, has already de-emphasized and in
effect discounted the bougonia by giving a full description of it
before introducing the Aristaeus story. Thus what he is surely
concerned with here is not the remedy (this is now known:
Cyrene can quite competently repeat it to Aristaeus) but the
original cause of the disaster. The first lines of the *Orpheus* alone
make this plain:

453   *Non* te *nullius* exercent *numinis irae*;
        magna luis *commissa*. Tibi has miserabilis Orpheus
        hautquaquam ob meritum poenas, ni fata resistant
        suscitat et rapta graviter pro coniuge saevit.
        Illa quidem, dum *te* fugeret per flumina praeceps, &c.

The problem at this point is truly a moral one: to bring home
to Aristaeus the nature and gravity of his crime, to make him
realize the intensity and poignance of the suffering his cruel
passion has caused. Only when this guilty 'secret' has been
exposed and atoned for can the resurrection he desires be
accomplished. All the rest—the practical details of the sacrificial
atonement, &c.—can be left to Cyrene; they would not fit at
all the oracular and high-poetic role here attributed to Proteus.

Actually, however, Aristaeus remains a shadowy and un-substantial figure. The world he moves in is magical, mysterious and unreal. The waters into which he descends are remote indeed from the agricultural landscape with which we have so far been concerned and they are even very strange to him: domum mirans genetricis et umida regna. The ambrosia with which he is anointed, above all the shapes which Proteus assumes, lack the 'taken for granted' or realistic tone of their Homeric original: they are presented rather as the miracles that they are—*miracula rerum* (441). There can be no doubt that Virgil creates this magical watery world as a deliberate contrast to earthly reality. We go to it, as Aristaeus goes to it, to find the secret that cannot be found on earth itself. Thus he must *descend* into the very depths of the waters, anoint himself with the unearthly ambrosia and master the daimon of meta-morphoses before he can receive the pass-word, the necessary explanation. It is all a fairy story in which, however, the mean-ing of workaday existence is to be learned. We can I think see also a certain significance in the very insubstantiality of Proteus: he is a god with a human shape but he can also put on all other shapes:

441   omnia transformat sese in miracula rerum
         ignemque horribilemque feram fluviumque liquentem.
407   Fiet enim subito sus horridus atraque tigris
         squamosusque draco et fulva cervice leaena.

But when caught and held, he will resume his true (human) shape and tell the truth that no other can tell. Is not Virgil hinting here at the reality which lies hidden in symbols: is he not in effect saying that the time has come to discard the animal shapes and symbols and to reveal man to himself as man really is?

In any event, the Aristaeus part of the episode remains a fairy story: we cannot quite take his atonement seriously; the sacrifice to the nymphs seems hardly sufficient and there is no real evidence of contrition in Aristaeus himself. But it is not the *Aristaeus*, it is the *Orpheus* which is the key to the mystery. Proteus tells not merely the tale of Aristaeus' crime but the tale of Orpheus' own error. Thus the *Orpheus* is clearly intended as more than a revelation of Aristaeus' past: it stands also in its own right as a story of resurrection—though of tragically flawed resurrection—corresponding to and mirroring the successful resurrection of the Bees. Here, but in reverse, we can see the same problem all over again. But here we are no longer in a world of pure fairy-tale: there are to be sure mysterious and wonderful things in it (supernatural power of song, descent to the underworld, fabulous monsters and the softening of inexorable hearts) but in it also and much more significant are fierce passions and genuine tragedy. At bottom the essential drama of the *Orpheus* is a very human one which its unearthly surroundings only accent by contrast. What, then, does such a drama reveal? What *is* the secret of Proteus?

As we have seen in our analysis of the narrative, the climax of the story is not the triumph of Orpheus, the singer and lover, over the inexorable powers of Hell (nescia . . . humanis precibus mansuescere corda) but the moment of madness (subita . . . dementia) in which he undid all that he had achieved and lost forever the chance of bringing back Eurydice to life. The reproach of Eurydice: *quis tantus furor?* expresses, through the lips of his most sympathetic possible critic, the judgement which must be passed on his mad act. We can justifiably generalize the event by saying that humanity is at once capable of an art which can move the immovable and of a passion which can lose all that its art has gained. The fact that this is described with Virgilian *humanitas*, that the pardonable character of the action is stressed—ignoscenda quidem scirent si ignoscere manes—in no sense eliminates its folly and its tragedy. Love and death are linked here as closely as in Book III. The recklessness of Orpheus is almost that of Leander, as are its consequences:

III. 262   nec miseri possunt revocare parentes
                  nec moritura super crudeli funere virgo.

So we see that despite the nobility and humanity of Orpheus' attempt to win the victory over death, he lacks the strength of character, the control of passion which are the indispensable conditions of victory. The problem of resurrection is at bottom a moral problem. We must not be deceived by Virgil's evident sympathy: here, as in the *Aeneid*, his *humanitas* never conceals, even while it pities, the consequences of moral weakness.

We thus reach quite a new perspective from which to interpret the four books of the *Georgics*. The antitheses between man and nature in Book I; between the *amor* symbolized by the large animals, and the *labor* symbolized by the bees of Books III and IV; between the hostile nature of Book I and the co-operative nature of Book II; between the iron age and the age of gold; between, even, death and life, are each and all resolved when man, exercising his full moral powers of control, work, self-sacrifice and devotion to his *patria*, finds himself supported by the *logos* and indwelling spirit of the whole cosmos. Mishap, failure, human error, occasional loss of control, are ever present and are not necessarily final or irreversible: atonement and a second chance, restoration and rebirth are also part of the divine scheme. Cosmic sympathy is real: even the powers of hell can be moved and bent. But here again the rule of the cosmos combines mercy with stern justice: Orpheus got a reprieve but only under new conditions which he could not keep. Aristaeus, it is to be presumed, was induced to heed the lesson and learn the folly of his passion in perceiving its tragic, human consequences. The problem of the cosmos or of nature thus attains at last, or rather reveals at the core, a *human* dimension. Man is, so to speak, at the centre of a vast network of cosmic sympathy and moral law. There is both *iustitia* and *humanitas* at the heart of things.

This conception is given of course an Augustan colouring. The appeal to the *Indigites* in I:

> 500   hunc saltem everso iuvenem succurrere saeclo
> ne prohibete! satis iam pridem sanguine nostro
> Laomedonteae luimus periuria Troiae

is seemingly reflected in the atonement and restoration of Aristaeus to whom Cyrene gives the word:

> 534   Tu munera supplex
> tende petens pacem et facilis venerare napaeas;
> namque dabunt veniam votis irasque remittent.

It is quite unnecessary and somewhat inept to identify Aristaeus with Augustus (are we to attribute similar *magna commissa* to the latter?) but certainly Aristaeus stands in some way for the sinful self-destruction, atonement and revival of the Roman people.

More important than this, however, is the moral implied by the Orpheus story: the law of self-control which even the most sympathetic *amor* and the most resplendent *art* must observe. For the *Orpheus* not merely inversely mirrors the *Aristaeus* (as the *Ariadne* inversely mirrors the *Peleus and Thetis*) but completes it. The error or crime of Aristaeus is not identical with that of Orpheus but the moral atmospheres of the two errors merge and supplement each other. More exactly: we do not quite realize the crime of Aristaeus—it is so hastily and elliptically told, so small a part of either story—but we do see its consequences and above all what the consequences of *another* passional error can be. What stands out and is meant to stand out is the central Orpheus panel, where the elliptical, concentrated, emotional style and above all, for once, a penetrating vignette of human feeling, come at exactly the point where we are led to expect revelation. The human meaning, the human price of passion, atonement and resurrection emerge in a blaze of light at the decisive, last instant.

CHAPTER VI

THE ODYSSEAN *AENEID*

T HE *Aeneid* seems at first sight something radically different from either the *Eclogues* or the *Georgics*. We can understand why the 'young Virgil,' the Virgil of 42 B.C., should have turned from his projected *res romanae* to the 'soft and pleasing' verse of the eclogues. He was both too immature and too aware of Homer's unapproachable excellence to undertake such a task at the time. But the *Georgics*, the work of the next ten years, seems a most extraordinary approach to epic. Virgil did not, as we might have thought, prepare for the *Aeneid* by extensive experiments in narrative verse: he came to it, instead, by the quite non-narrative route of didactic. How are we to explain such a seemingly paradoxical development?

But this apparent paradox is really the clue to the whole problem of the *Aeneid*. We have seen in chapter iii (*The Subjective Style*) that the Dido episode of Books I and 4 was a fusion of three elements: the psychologically continuous narrative; the essential symbol-complex of *fatum—furor—pietas*; and the Homeric motifs. The Damon song of the eighth eclogue and, much more significantly, the Orpheus episode of the Fourth *Georgic*, illustrate Virgil's concern with psychological continuity in narrative. But the scale of these narratives is small;[1] he had certainly not yet tried to use this kind of narrative as the major vehicle of his ideas. Nor had he shown any interest at all (save for the description of Proteus in the Aristaeus episode) in Homeric motifs. What did directly concern him, however, was the elaboration of his Augustan symbols. This is in fact the bridge that connects the *Georgics* with the *Aeneid* and, indeed, the *Eclogues* with both. It is only when we take this first and try to see its significance for Virgil and for his whole conception of Roman Epic, that we begin to understand the genesis and actual structure of the *Aeneid*.

In both the *Eclogue Book* and the *Georgics* an evil or corrupt past dominated by destructive passion is opposed to a new hope

---

[1] With the scale goes also, of course, a considerable difference of style. The *Aeneid* is *epic* as *Bucolics* and *Georgics* are not. On this see Appendix 7.

embodied in a saviour (Caesar-Octavian) who represents the principle of resurrection and rebirth. In each work the resurrection motif comes at the central or decisive point: at 5, the middle piece of the ten eclogues, or at the *Aristaeus* or second part of *Georgics* IV where the antitheses set up between Books I–III and II–IV (first half) are finally resolved. We can represent the ideological scheme of both works somewhat as follows:

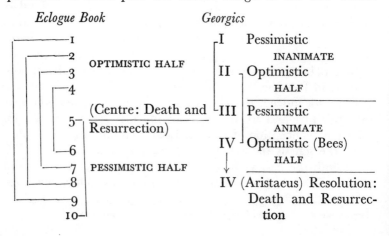

| MAN | SOCIETY |

The passionate man characterized by *indignus amor*, *furor* and death: *Eclogues* 6, 8, 10; *Georgics* III

The anarchic society (*furor* on a social scale) *Georgics* I (esp. conclusion); *Eclogues* 6, 9

Caesar-Octavian
Eclogue 5, *Georgics* IV: 281–558
Resurrection
Salvation

The pious or rational man (passion controlled) *Eclogues* 2, 4; *Georgics* II (the happy swain)

The peaceful, well-ordered society (Saturnia regna) *Eclogues* 1, 4; *Georgics* II, IV (first part)

This is of course a schematic reduction of a very complex poetic reality and is certainly not to be applied with procrustean literalism. But it is hard to avoid the conviction that it reproduces in some part the actual design of the two works.

Eclogue Book   *Georgics*

1
2   OPTIMISTIC HALF
3
4

5   (Centre: Death and Resurrection)

6
7   PESSIMISTIC HALF
8
9
10

I   Pessimistic
     INANIMATE
II   Optimistic
     HALF

III   Pessimistic
     ANIMATE
IV   Optimistic (Bees)
     HALF

IV (Aristaeus) Resolution: Death and Resurrection

What is important in the scheme is Virgil's central emphasis of the death-resurrection motif. Both the *Eclogues* and the *Georgics* fall into antithetic halves that are united or reconciled by the use of this motif. It is profitable here to inspect the arrangements of these poems once more.[1]

Now the scheme of the *Aeneid* certainly corresponds very closely to the scheme of both works, combining as it were the arrangements of each. It falls, as everyone is aware, into two sets of six books (1–6, 7–12) corresponding loosely to the *Odyssey* (where Books 1–12 describe Odysseus' actual *nostos* or return to Ithaca and 13–24 describe his actions in Ithaca). This is clearly indicated for example, in the very structure of Book 7 with its new appeal to the Muse and its partial recapitulation of the movement of Book 1 (re-entry of Juno as the major disturbing element). But this 6–6 arrangement of books is paralleled by another which is quite analogous to that of the *Eclogues*:[2]

1		Juno: storm: peace
2		Defeat of the Trojans (Aeneas)
3		Interim of wandering (uncertainty of Aeneas)
4	Odyssean,	Tragedy of Dido
5	PREPARATORY	Interlude of Games: Nisus, &c.
6	HALF	The Future: Show of Heroes
7	Iliadic	Peace: Juno: war
8	FULFILMENT	The Future: shield
9	HALF	Interlude of *Aristeiai*: Nisus, &c.
10		Tragedy of Pallas
11		Interim of movement (uncertainty of Turnus)
12		Victory of the Trojans (Aeneas)

It is not necessary to exaggerate the correspondences between the books in order to see that this scheme must have been, to some degree at least, actually present to Virgil's mind. The deliberate parallelism between 1 and 7, 4 and 10, 5 and 9, 6 and 8 is quite unmistakable: thus 7 reproduces, inversely, the order of 1; 4 and 10 contain the two major tragedies of the poem (Dido, Pallas); 5 and 9 reveal a whole series of correspondences

[1] See p. 129 and p. 216 opposite.   [2] See Appendix 9 and p. 418 below.

(interventions of Juno via Iris, an attempted ship-burning prevented by a miracle, an episode involving Nisus and Eurya-lus, an Ascanius episode, &c.); 6 and 8 each culminate in a major revelation of the Roman future.[1] The important thing, however, is not so much the arrangement in itself as the fact that it reveals the centrality of Book 7 and its direct relation to the corresponding 6 and 8. Book 7, of course, brings Aeneas to Italy and, with Allecto, inaugurates the Latin War. It is the war for which Aeneas has been prepared in 6 and which he actively accepts as his predestined duty in 8. In 6 he merely *sees* the future of Rome; in 8 he takes the future (depicted on the shield) upon his own shoulders into the Latin War. Thus though 7 is in this sense the centre of the poem (that to which everything leads, from which everything follows), 6 is the culmination of Aeneas' preparation *for* the War, inaugurated in 7, and met by Aeneas' arms in 8. It is surely no coincidence, therefore, that it, like the correspondingly pivotal portions of the *Eclogues* and *Georgics* (i.e. *Eclogue* 5 and the *Aristaeus*), is a kind of death and resurrection, a journey to and from the Underworld.

Seen in this way, the ideological similarity of the three works becomes relatively clear. The sixth book of the *Aeneid* is the turning point, the death and resurrection piece, that converts the defeat, passion, and uncertainty of Books 1–5 into the victorious and unshaken valour of Books 8–12. In 4 Aeneas barely escapes from *indignus amor* (his own and Dido's); in 10 he wins a great victory mainly through the effect upon his spirit of his *worthy* affection for the dead and defeated Pallas. In 2 he is prostrated by the fall of Troy and loss of Creusa; in 12 he finally wins a new kingdom and wife. In 1–5 he falters and has to be prodded by Jupiter and Anchises; in 8–12 he never loses his courage or his resolution. In short, the *Aeneid* is, like the *Eclogues* and *Georgics*, the story of death and rebirth by which unworthy love and destructive *furor* are overcome by the moral activity of a divinized and resurrected hero.

The difference between the *Aeneid* and the other two works is that the former is a narrative of human actions whereas the *Eclogues* and *Georgics* are not narratives in this sense at all. The death and rebirth motif in *Eclogue* 5 or in the *Aristaeus* is

---

[1] See pp. 273, 331 below.

isolated; the influence of the saving hero or god is vague and mysterious. The pastoral and agricultural symbolism of the earlier poems could not, in the nature of the case, be given a fully human meaning. The bees in one sense stand for the unified, disciplined state and the *Aristaeus* for its rebirth from death and destructive passion. But Virgil could not invest Aristaeus with great human significance—he is an utterly remote and legendary figure—and the image of defeated resurrection in the *Orpheus* only negatively suggests [1] the qualities required for a successful resurrection. Yet once Virgil had seen that his projected epic would require a hero who would at some point in the work reveal the characteristics of Augustus or, more accurately, those of the Roman-Augustan ideal, he was forced to relate this hero to all the negative and positive elements of his ideology. Virgil's essential insight, out of which seemingly the whole *Aeneid* grew, was the perception that this hero would have to struggle not only against external *furor* and passion but against the same elements within himself and that he could become the Roman-Augustan ideal only by rising above his original nature to a wholly new and quasi-divine kind of heroism. The death-resurrection motif could then be given a very concrete and very human form and become the central or crucial element in a psychologically continuous narrative of heroic motivation.

The conception of a 'reborn' hero, of the man who by great endurance and action raises himself to divine status, was of course a commonplace of Virgil's era: Caesar and Octavian himself had become divine or semi-divine in virtue of their immense achievements and thus could claim kinship with other *theoi-andres* or divine-men of Roman history, like Hercules, Aeneas and Romulus. No one, however, before Virgil had looked at this kind of man psychologically and seen him as essentially the product of inner struggle and spiritual rebirth. Here Virgil not only combined elements of Stoic psychology with contemporary religion (especially the idea of the divine-man) but also brought to them the subjective style of narration whose inchoate and eliptical origins we have descried in the Damon Song and the *Orpheus*.

---

[1] But it *does* suggest. Orpheus' *catabasis* is the precursor of that of Aeneas. Cf. Appendixes 7 and 9.

Thus Virgil certainly humanized or gave psychological reality to the rather formal and austere image of the *theios aner*.[1] But he did not thereby deprive it of cosmic significance. In one sense Aeneas is quite different from Daphnis or Aristaeus. The Daphnis of *Eclogue* 5 is, like Caesar, deified only *after* death: there is no notion of deification during his lifetime, no conception of a *living* hero's return from the underworld. The transition from a real man to a real god is conceived as a religious or cosmic transformation, rather than the direct result of human *pietas*. The death and resurrection of Aristaeus' bees is also a cosmic symbol, a symbol of nature reflecting and co-operating with human vice and virtue. But though Aeneas is a human figure as these others are not, he is also subject to a cosmic force, to *fatum*, to Rome's ecumenical destiny. The *Aeneid* in fact is the story of the interplay between the cosmic power of fate and human response to it. Rome, we can have no doubt, was in Virgil's eyes really fated to rule the world. But this fate was not designed to operate without regard to human attitudes. There could have been no Rome, as Virgil conceived it, without men like Aeneas, men of supreme *pietas*. In other words *fatum* and *pietas* as well as *fatum* and *violentia* or *furor* (the human opposites of *pietas*) are interdependent. The cosmos (fate) mirrors man as much as man mirrors the cosmos. But this idea, as we have seen, is also a *leitmotif* of the *Georgics*: the degeneration of the soil and of nature in Book I, with the consequent *labor improbus* it imposes on the farmer, is finally associated with man's own anarchy and wickedness; the farmer can have *secura quies*, can be truly happy but only *sua si bona norint*; only then will nature co-operate with him freely and fully. Resurrection is thus possible but has definite moral prerequisites. This we see not only

---

[1] The conception of the θεῖος ἀνήρ, the attainment of divinity by noble deeds of philanthropy or humanity, was almost a commonplace of the Augustan age. *Herculis ritu* Augustus sought the laurel of victory (Horace *Carm.* III. 14). *Hac arte* (i.e. the service of the state by resistance to tyranny and sedition) Pollux and Hercules attained the stars among which Augustus reclines and drinks the divine nectar (*Carm.* III. 3. 9). But this divine man is also, to some degree at least, a Stoic stage: *iustum et tenacem propositi virum.* Cf. my note on p. 335. It is also no accident that Aeneas, like the Heracles of Euripides, is met by the most infernal of all Juno-Hera's agents (Lyssa, Allecto) just after the accomplishment of the *descensus-ascensus Averni.* The θεῖος ἀνήρ is finally tested by counter-fate itself at the height of his career, but note the *difference* between Euripides and Virgil. See p. 286 below. Aeneas' *catabasis* is not a mere exploit (like that of Heracles) but is itself the ordeal that finally makes him a true θεῖος ἀνήρ. He is therefore personally invulnerable to Allecto.

in the *Orpheus* but also in the designed antithesis of *Georgics* I
and II and of III and IV. All the heavens declare the assassination of Caesar but the heavens also declare his resurrection and
co-operate with his divine son's salutary rule. *Pietas* and *furor*
work hand in hand with *fatum*.[1]

We see then that the combination of a symbolic system
(essentially the *fatum-furor-pietas* complex) with a human,
psychologically continuous, narrative was, as it were, potential
in the *Georgics* and even to some extent in the *Eclogues*. Yet the
narrative element in these two works is only embryonic at best
for their symbolism is largely devoid of human content. What
was lacking was quite simply Homer—the narrative content,
scope, and elevation of epic. We do not, indeed, need to dwell
on the crucial importance of this lacuna: the gap between
pastoral or didactic and epic is too great and too obvious to be
minimized. Yet an approach to the *Aeneid* from the *Eclogues* and
Georgics, rather than from Homer or other epic 'models', calls
attention to a fact that has not yet been adequately recognized.
Scholars like Heinze have performed a most fruitful task by
comparing the *Iliad* or *Odyssey* with the *Aeneid* and noting the
differences. But this kind of study has had the disadvantage of
concentrating attention on what Virgil did to Homer rather
than on the much more important matter of what Homer did
to Virgil. To state the point rather less paradoxically: Virgil did
not 'start' with Homer but with his own Augustan 'symbol-
complex' and his own subjective style. He did not so much
'copy' Homer as fit Homeric motifs into a radically un-Homeric
scheme that he had elaborated without reference to either
Homer or the epic genre or indeed any sort of narrative plot
or story. Homer really came last in the genesis of the *Aeneid*:
he was as it were the necessary model, the high classical model
advocated by Horace, but he was a model only in the sense that
he was made to fit a pre-existent structure. What he did to
Virgil—how Virgil's central design, in other words, was
affected by Homeric motifs—is the important question. Homer
contributed nothing to the design itself.

It is here, finally, that we reach the true explanation of
Virgil's 'success' in epic. He could write a great 'Homeric' epic;
he could, as the Antimachi and Choerili could not, assimilate

---

[1] See above p. 160 f. and p. 189 f.

an outmoded form and content to a contemporary subject; he could thus Augustanize Homer and revive heroic myth in truly successful poetry, because he consistently adapted Homer to a thoroughly un-Homeric ideology, always converting the objective narrative of *Iliad* and *Odyssey* to one that was both subjective and symbolic. We have already given an illustration of Virgil's procedure in our analysis above of the Dido episode. But Virgil's real artistry is only revealed in the *Aeneid* as a whole, in its essential architecture and plan.

Essentially the real 'plot' of the *Aeneid* is that of the formation and victory of the *Augustan* hero. Virgil selected Aeneas as his hero because he happened to be the one *theios-aner* (the man who achieved divine status) of Roman tradition who actually belonged to the Homeric saga itself. Hercules was only incidentally connected with Rome; Romulus was already 'historical' and thus alien to the epic-heroic milieu. But Aeneas, of course, is meant to be the prototype as well as the mythical ancestor of Augustus. In the narrative he belongs to his own epic age; Virgil avoided, at all costs, the direct intrusion of contemporary events or persons, of history, into the realm of myth or legend. This would have been fatal to both his symbolic style and his 'prophetic' approach to his own times. Yet the distinction between Aeneas and any genuinely Homeric hero is quite fundamental. His ethos is utterly different from that of Achilles, Hector or Odysseus. Aeneas' goal and object in life is not merely in the near but in the remote future, in Augustan Rome itself. Thus all the intelligible goals of Homeric epic or Greek tragedy, indeed of all Greek literature, are not available to him. His fate is to sacrifice every present enjoyment or satisfaction to an end he cannot hope to witness himself. He bears on his shoulders the *famam* . . . *et fata nepotum*, not unwittingly as an ordinary ancestor, but quite consciously as the avowed servant of a future which has been finally revealed to him. He is thus the great exhibit of *pietas* or of the willing service of destiny. This is emphatically not a Homeric but a Stoic and, above all, a Roman-Augustan attitude. Augustus, himself, was the avowed founder of the future. The profound difference between such consciousness of and devotion to an historical role and the simple wrath of Achilles, patriotism of Hector or nostalgia of Odysseus hardly needs to be emphasized further.

The *pius Aeneas* is thus the ideal man or hero of Virgil's Augustan ideology. But Virgil could not have shown him to be such had he presented him to us ready formed and complete. His *pietas* had to be an achievement or it would not have been truly *pietas*: hence Virgil's epic had to deal with his hero's formation, his attainment of *pietas*, as well as with his mature performance. The battle between *pietas* and *furor*, between pious acceptance, impious rebellion against fate, had to be fought out inside the hero as well as between the hero and his impious opponents. Thus the pivotal 'rebirth' had to come in the middle of the epic and mark the difference between the hero's preparation for victory and the actual winning of it. This, as we have already seen, dictated in effect the plan of the whole poem: six books depicting the inner struggle for *pietas*; six books depicting the triumph of *pietas* over the *impii*. This is, of course, a rather rough and ready summation of complex material but it brings out the essential division of the whole poem, a subjective, internal or psychological section (Books 1–6) followed by a relatively objective, external and military section (Books 7–12). There are, in other words, three levels of conflict in the epic:

    (1) That between Fate (Jupiter) and Counter-Fate (Juno)
    (2) That between Aeneas and his own passions
and (3) That between Aeneas and the *impii*

and, though all these levels extend through the entire *Aeneid*, the *second* is emphasized in Books 1–6 and the *third* in Books 7–12.

The design of each of the two sets of six books had thus to be quite different. The first (Books 1–6, the Odyssean *Aeneid*) needed to be subjective in the sense that the essential narrative was psychological and thus dominated the outer events or even reduced them to the status of symbols of the inner events. The second (Books 7–12, the Iliadic *Aeneid*), on the contrary, quite lacked any such subjective-symbolic basis since the action was no longer psychological or mostly so, but overt and visible, and, in large part, could be described directly without further ado. Virgil's problem was to adapt his Homeric motifs to these two distinct sections. His choice of the *Odyssey* for the first part, the *Iliad* for the second, seems almost obvious, once the problem is stated in these terms. The *Odyssey* or at least its first 12 books is essentially an epic of one man's voyage through very strange and exotic territory as he strives, against both divine and human opposition, to reach his home. This clearly fitted both the external (voyage from Troy to Italy) and the internal (progress from incomplete to complete *pietas*) movement of the first six books. On the other hand, the martial *Iliad*, with its multiple cast of characters, its constant warfare and its far less 'romantic' plot, was understandingly better adapted to the last six books.

Thus, what we shall now call the Odyssean *Aeneid* (Books 1–6) is concerned mainly with the first two levels indicated above, the level of fate and counter-fate and the level of internal or psychological action. There is, in other words, the *subjective* or *empathetic narrative* (basically centred in the psyche of Aeneas though the 'empathetic centre' shifts to Dido at the close of Book 1 and stays with her through most of Book 4) *and* an accompanying set of symbols which represent the action of fate and counter-fate and also relate this to the central empathetic narrative. Here Virgil drew on two more or less distinct strands of the objectively continuous Odyssean narrative: the main story of Odysseus (his *nostos*, detention by Calypso, reception by Alcinous, recital of his past adventures) and, on the other hand, the divine machinery and supernatural side of the *Odyssey* (the preliminary council of the gods, the opposition of Poseidon and assistance of Athene, monsters like the Cyclopes, the land of the dead). Virgil adapted the first strand to the main psychological narrative of the *Aeneid*; the second to the cosmic symbolism of the poem, to the action of fate and counter-fate in all its bearings. But, as we have already clearly seen in our analysis of the Dido episode in chapter iii, the two levels—the psychologically continuous narrative, the cosmic symbolism— are correlated with each other. It is, in fact, the interplay of the two that constitutes the very heart of the epic.

In order to use the *Odyssey* for his subjective narrative, for the story of his hero's conversion to complete *pietas*, for what, as we have seen, was in part at least, a narrative version of the *Georgics* and *Eclogues*, Virgil had to alter the whole arrangement and tonality of his Homeric model. The *nostos* of the *Odyssey*, which is really the immemorial story of a man's homecoming, was thus converted into what was almost its opposite, a man's progress from his home, from the emotional centre of his whole affective life, toward a new, unknown and even dreaded goal. The voyage to Latium was, as it were, the test and symbol of the hero's willingness to give up the past for the future, to submit and piously submit to fate. This is why the story of his departure from home, from Troy, of the initial and primary cause of his 'inverted nostos', absolutely had to be introduced even though it (i.e. Book 2) had no Odyssean or Iliadic precedent.[1] Again the sequence of events in the *Odyssey* (Calypso—the storm—Alcinous—the recital of the past) had to be reversed and transposed and given new emphasis: the encounter with the detaining woman had to become (as it was not in Homer) the centre of the narrative; the storm had thus to precede this and the hero's adventures to be told to the woman, not to a comparative stranger like Alcinous. In this way, as we shall see, the hero's past, present, and future were linked to the most important spiritual hazard he had to run and the quite physical action of the *Odyssey* was given a new psychological meaning. Finally, the *nekuia*—the hero's encounter with the dead—was not only given a quite different position in the plot (at the very end of the *errores* or wanderings, whereas, in the *Odyssey*, it is followed by a whole book of subsequent wanderings and is actually part of Odysseus' long recital to Alcinous, not a decisive event of the main narrative) but was changed to a real *catabasis* or descent of the hero into the Underworld rather than remaining, as in Homer, a mere coming of the ghosts to a hero who statically abides their approach. The changes, in fact, are so drastic that the question arises why Virgil cared to preserve the Homeric motifs at all: it would seemingly have been less trouble to abandon them altogether. In fact, however, they play a most important role, as we shall see: Virgil gained from Homer much more than the cachet of a revered name. But, the important thing to notice here is the extent to which Homer yielded to the exacting demands of Virgil's Augustan plot and subjective style of narrative.

The transformation of Homer's gods and monsters—of the supernatural and miraculous elements of the *Odyssey*—is fully as radical. It has been generally realized that Virgil's Jupiter is primarily the image of a fate, *fatum*, that is conceived in a

---

[1] This point, curiously enough, has seldom been clearly seen or made by critics. Cf. the discussion of Book 2 in Heinze, chap. i *passim.*

Q

fundamentally Stoic way.[1] But the relation of Jupiter to the lesser gods and goddesses (especially Juno and Venus) and the intricate means by which the two levels of deity are made known to the hero and to the other human characters of the story, have as yet been left in a good deal of obscurity. It was, we may say. essential to Virgil's purpose that Jupiter's or Fate's will should be revealed to Aeneas according to a scale of increasing clarity, a scale going all the way from the obscurity of Book 3 (the *errores*) to the final enlightenment of Book 6. It was also essential to his purpose that Aeneas should be opposed by Juno (or 'counter-fate') and aided by Venus in such a way as not to make otiose the more direct actions of Jupiter or the free response to them of Aeneas himself. These two factors are the very conditions of Aeneas' freedom or of his *pietas* defined as a human achievement for which he himself is made responsible. For unlike the much simpler divine machinery of Homer, which is actually a quite integral part of the narrative, Virgil's is in one sense curiously detached from the human action or parallels it with the very minimum of overt intervention. We can really limit Jupiter's overt interferences in the Odyssean *Aeneid* to three: the oracles at the end of Book 2, the mission of Mercury in Book 4, and the mission of Anchises in Book 5. And even these do not simply supersede the human will of Aeneas: his conscience was already active in each of these three cases as we shall see. Certainly neither Juno's opposition nor Venus' aid are decisive. Most often they simply cancel each other out.

But it would be just as great an error in the opposite direction to regard the gods as mere 'reflections' or projections of Aeneas' *psyche*. Virgil really believed in a cosmic fate and a cosmic counter-fate (*ratio* and *furor* on a heavenly scale) and in Rome as much more than a human achievement. But man was, in his eyes, a creature whose free response to fate or counter-fate was the indispensable means through which both had to work. The ensuing correlation of divine and human affairs is thus

---

[1] But we must not exaggerate the Stoicism. The full identification of Jupiter-fatum with Rome is not *per se* a Stoic invention. Cf. Heinze, pp. 293–9. I would add to Heinze, however, that Virgil's failure wholly to assimilate Jupiter to εἱμαρμένη plus πρόνοια is not simply the necessity of his Homeric plot: it is also his sense of the complexity of fate, its emergence as the final result of all that both the sub-fates and human beings can do. In the last analysis, the *Aeneid* is anything but simply Stoic.

intricate as well as necessary; freedom is not an alternative to predestination but an essential component of it. Or put in the terms of the *Aeneid* itself: both men and gods can accept fate with piety; both men and gods can reject fate with *furor*; and fate itself is the predestined product of their interpenetrating acceptances and rejections. It is just this tangled parallelism, but parallelism without identity, of human and divine action that permits Virgil to build an intricate structure of motifs between them. The Storms in Books 1 and 4, Fama and Allecto, Polydorus, the Harpies, &c. are all intermediary motifs in this sense: they connect gods and men—the cosmic and human— in a real blending of inner psychology and outer demonism. Dreams, oracles, portents, prophecies are used in a similar way. So too are physical or natural phenomena. Light and darkness, night and day, colours, sounds, motions, all images of nature in short, are put on a scale of being that insensibly passes from the human or psychological to the superhuman or cosmic. The line between the innermost feelings of men and the outermost activities of nature or the gods is never fixed, but always open to penetration from both sides. In short, though we may say that, on the whole, the divine action of the *Aeneid* is much more symbolic than overt, we must also say that the symbols possess a truly cosmic dimension and far exceed a purely human frame of reference.

The correlation of the two main strands of the *Aeneid*—the subjective, empathetic narrative and the cosmic symbolism: the *human* and *divine* elements of the poem—is made clear at the outset in a 304–line introduction which not only begins the action and puts us at once *in medias res* (as Horace advised) but also performs the proleptic function of revealing both the psychological and cosmic elements of the entire epic. The careful design of these 304 lines is quite clear and can be indicated diagrammatically as on page 228.

The symmetry of the section is unmistakable. The two central balancing parts (*Storm* and *Calm*) are set between the two outer balancing parts (Juno, Venus) and the final Jupiter prophecy resumes, at greater length and with impressive finality, the theme of the seven line proem (virum cano qui fato profugus . . . multa . . . passum . . . dum conderet urbem . . . unde . . . altae moenia Romae). We see the scheme of fate, the opposition of

1. Initial statement of the poem's main
   theme (1–7) = 7 lines
2. *Juno*'s wrath (8–33) = 26 lines
3. The *Storm* (34–123) = 90 lines
   (*a*) Inception and Outbreak (34–91) = 58 lines
   (*b*) Aeneas' reaction to it (92–101) = 10 lines
   (*c*) Effect of the storm (102–23) = 22 lines
4. *Calm* after the storm (124–222) = 99 lines
   (*a*) Neptune calms the storm (124–56) = 33 lines
   (*b*) Aeneas' reaction to the calm (157–207) = 51 lines
   His words to his men (198–207) = 10 lines
   (*c*) Mingled recovery and grief of the Trojans
   (208–22) = 15 lines
5. *Venus*' Perturbation (223–53) = 31 lines
6. Jupiter's Prophecy (254–96) = 43 lines
7. Coda: Mercury sent by Jupiter to prepare a favourable reception in Carthage for Aeneas
   (297–304) = 8 lines

Juno, the protecting aid of Venus and, in the middle, the storm-
tossed Aeneas who is yet assured of calm at the end. We see also
the historical factors: Carthage, the favourite of Juno; Rome,
the darling of Venus; and the predestined victory of the one
over the other. But the essential idea of this section is the contrast of *furor* and *pietas* with which the parallel contrast of fate
(Jupiter) and counter-fate (Juno) is fully correlated. For the
several antitheses here at work:

Jupiter (fate)   vs. the sub-fates (Juno, Venus)
Rome (Venus)   vs. Carthage (Juno)
Calm (Neptune)   vs. Storm (Aeolus)

are unified by the concept of *furor-pietas*, the two opposed
psychological forces which are, so to speak, fate's real *modus
operandi*. The *pietas* and the *furor* with which fate is met represent
the major moral—hence psychological—elements by which the
operation of fate is finally justified and made to prevail in a
fundamentally moral universe.

Even in the seven line proem the *Ira Iunonis* is mentioned
as the prime cause of Aeneas' sufferings. The question of psychological motivation—*why* the goddess should have pursued

so conspicuously pious a hero (insignem pietate virum) with such implacable hate—is thus immediately introduced. The real answer is made clear in the very way a direct or immediate answer is deferred. To the question: *Tantaene animis caelestibus irae?* (i. 11) Virgil begins:

Urbs antiqua fuit . . . Karthago.

The apparent digression (the deferring of a direct answer by the descriptive *Urbs antiqua fuit*, &c.) only makes the final answer so much the more emphatic.[1] The root of Juno's animosity is her thwarted love for Carthage. We are not at once shown *why* this love deserved to be thwarted or why Juno's desire was morally wrong (the whole Dido episode is the real answer: Dido and symbolically Carthage and Juno chose the way of *furor* rather than *pietas*) but we do see the vindictive and hence immoral character of her perverted passion. The mythological causes (Helen, the judgement of Paris, &c.) that Virgil also gives for Juno's resentment, do not so much weaken her primary motivation (her thwarted love for Carthage) as further illustrate her jealous and furious character. She is at once *wrong* (in a moral sense) and *irrational*, for she knows that she cannot prevail in the end. Neither Virgil nor we can dissociate these two elements of her *furor*. Furthermore, the *furor* that she unleases in the storm is, in itself, clearly wrong, a perversion and confusion of the normal, moral order of nature. Aeolus is cozened and bribed to disobey his superior, Neptune, and Neptune (ll. 132–41) is rightly indignant at the unnecessary and immoral havoc he causes. That the issue is really one between *pietas* and *furor* is revealed in one of the greatest of Virgil's similes [2] when he compares Neptune calming the storm to a grave statesman calming a civic riot (seditio):

148   ac veluti magno in populo cum saepe coorta est
           seditio saevitque animis ignobile volgus;
           iamque faces et saxa volant, furor arma ministrat;
           tum pietate gravem ac meritis si forte virum quem
           conspexere, silent arrectisque auribus adstant;

[1] Cf. here F. Klingner's fine essay, 'Das Erste Hirtengedicht Virgils' (*Hermes*, 62 (1927), pp. 129–53: this is rather poorly abbreviated in his *Römische Geisteswelt*, 3rd edn. (1957), pp. 294–308). Klingner's remarks on l. 20 of *Eclogue* 1 (Urbem quam dicunt Romam, &c.) apply to ll. 12–13 here.

[2] On this cf. Pöschl's fine discussion (pp. 23 f. and esp. 34 f.) and the admirable analysis of the simile by Constans, pp. 50 f.

ille regit dictis animos et pectora mulcet:
154   sic cunctus pelagi cecidit fragor.

Obviously a Roman is suggested though we need not try to label him with a specific name: the contrast between the *vir pietate gravis ac meritis* and the *ignobile volgus* armed by *furor* reveals at a stroke the human meaning of the storm and thus makes quite clear its essential symbolism. The shock effect of the simile comes from its *inversion* of a quite commonplace comparison. The likening of an agitated assembly or mob to an agitated sea or to stormy waves was familiar enough: Homer so described the assembly called by Agamemnon in *Iliad* 2 (144 f.) and Cicero in his *Pro Milone* (2) talked of the 'tempests and storms of Assemblies'. But only Virgil *reversed* the simile and compared the storm to a human, political reality. Thus he laid the ground-work for his overtly historical use of the *furor-pietas* theme at the end of the Jupiter prophecy: after the deification of Julius, the gates of the Janus temple will be closed; peace and Roman *pietas* (Fides, Vesta, &c.) will prevail and

294   *Furor impius intus*
saeva sedens super arma et centum *vinctus* aenis
post tergum nodis fremet horridus ore cruento.

The victory of *pietas* over *furor* is here finally and definitively related to the moral superiority of Rome to the *impii* and *furiosi*. Fate is on the side of the pious but it would not have been on their side had they not been pious.[1]

But the moral contrast is not simply external, between the pious on the one hand and the impious on the other. *Furor* and *pietas* also lurk within one and the same breast and the problem is quite as much to achieve the *internal* victory of *pietas* over the emotions and motivations that weaken or oppose it. The symbolic contrast of *storm* and *calm* is centred, as it were, on a psychological contrast between two moods of Aeneas. His initial outburst and perplexity occupies the exact centre of the *Storm* section (3b in the scheme above) while his subsequent recovery of fortitude and *pietas* occupies the centre of the *Calm* section (4b). His words at 94–101 in Book 1 (the first he utters in the whole epic) are, of course, an echo of Odysseus' words in *Odyssey* 5 (299–312), as he too encounters a storm sent by a divine enemy (Poseidon):

[1] See p. 328 for a discussion of the *recall* of this passage in Book 7.

299 Ah me, wretch that I am, what finally now will happen?
300 I am afraid that the goddess spoke the whole truth
When she said that in ocean before reaching my home-land
I should get plenty of trouble: all this now is fulfilled.
Such the clouds with which Zeus girdles broad heaven
    above me.
And he has roused up the deep and on drive the blasts now
305 Of all winds upon me: now my destruction is sure!
Thrice happy the Danaans, four times so, those who then died
In broad Troy, giving the Atridae good service!
Would that I too had then died and gotten my doom
On that day when all Trojans hurled down upon me
310 Brazen spears as they fought round the dead Achilles.
Then I would have had burial and glory from the Achaians;
Now I am fated to die by a death that is loathsome.

But Virgil omits the preamble on the storm (*Odyssey*, 299–305)
and only uses the personal complaint in lines 306–12 of Homer:

92   Extemplo Aeneae solvuntur frigore membra;
        ingemit, et duplices tendens ad sidera palmas
        talia voce refert: 'O terque quaterque beati,
        quis ante ora patrum Troiae sub moenibus altis
        contigit oppetere! o Danaum fortissime gentis
        Tydide, mene Iliacis occumbere campis
        non potuisse tuaque animam hanc effundere dextra,
        saevus ubi Aeacidae telo iacet Hector, ubi ingens
        Sarpedon, ubi tot Simois correpta sub undis
        scuta virum galeasque et fortia corpora volvit?'

It is evident that Virgil is concerned only with the general
psychic mood of Aeneas at this juncture, that he wants to show
us his hero's feelings (in a generalized way) at the very start
of the epic. And this also explains the vast difference between
words that are superficially so similar. Odysseus prefers a
glorious death and *burial* at Troy to an ignominious drowning.
Aeneas prefers a death *ante ora patrum*, a death that would not
separate him from his old companions and homeland, to his
present situation of homeless exile. *He does not mention the danger
of drowning or the lack of a proper burial.* It is not really the physical
calamity that oppresses him but his total situation as the
survivor of Troy. The storm is simply the occasion, the 'trigger',
not the primary cause of his feeling. Here we see, in short, the

hero in despair, seizing the unfavourable circumstance of the moment to reveal his fundamental nostalgia. The very fact that his is no true homecoming or *nostos*, like that of Odysseus, but rather a radical repudiation of his Trojan home, gives the Odyssean reminiscence a peculiar poignancy. The real tragedy is that he is not and cannot be an Odysseus. He can never go home.

But this feeling is doubly wrong in that it is both a yielding to *furor* (an acceptance of the storm as confirmatory 'proof' of his own inner rejection of his goal) and a distrust of that *fatum*, that mission, that he really knows to be divinely guaranteed. Yet this is only one side of his character. With the calm, *pietas* returns. Now (198–209) he reverses his mood and himself encourages the others:

198   'O socii (neque enim ignari sumus ante malorum),
           o passi graviora, dabit deus his quoque finem.
           Vos et Scyllaeam rabiem penitusque sonantes
           accestis scopulos, vos et Cyclopea saxa
           experti: revocate animos, maestumque timorem
           mittite; forsan et haec olim meminisse iuvabit.
           Per varios casus, per tot discrimina rerum
           tendimus in Latium, sedes ubi fata quietas
           ostendunt; illic fas regna resurgere Troiae.
           Durate, et vosmet rebus servate secundis.'
                Talia voce refert, curisque ingentibus aeger
           spem vultu simulat, premit altum corde dolorem.

Now he pictures himself in his new home looking back at the perils of the past (forsan et haec). Now he accepts and insists upon his mission and fate; now he greets danger as a challenge, rather than a cause of despair. It is clear that we cannot take this reversal simply as a reaction to the calm and its visible consequences. Rather Virgil has shown us proleptically the truly pious hero that Aeneas will become when he finally conquers the despair, the submission to *furor*, so evident in his reaction to the storm. This whole passage (1–304), in short, is only an *introduction* to the epic, an introduction in which both sides of Aeneas—his weakness and his strength, his submission to *furor* and his courageous exemplification of *pietas*—are revealed. We see the problem, the failure of character that must be made good, and look ahead to its answer, the final acquisition of a steadfast *pietas*. To the antitheses of Juno and Venus, storm and calm, sedition and civic peace, counter-fate and fate, in short *outer furor* and *outer pietas*, we must now add the inner antithesis of feelings within Aeneas. But we cannot expect their resolution until the whole epic has reached its climax.

Thus lines 1–304 have given us a 'pre-view' of the entire narrative to come. The opposition between Juno and Venus, Carthage (Dido) and Rome (Aeneas), Aeolus (storm) and Neptune (calm), civic violence (seditio) and civic *pietas* all in a sense depend on the 'reactions' of Aeneas to his situation and his fate. The correlation of all the elements is quite clear: the central contrast is between *furor* (inner and outer, cosmic and human, civic and personal) and *fatum-pietas*. It is essential that all the contrasted factors below fate should in some sense react to fate but that fate should be above them all. Jupiter unrolls for Venus the *fatorum arcana* but he does not tell Venus his specific *modus operandi*: nor is she directly charged (as is Mercury, ll. 297–304) with the implementation of Jupiter's or Fate's decree.[1] She, as well as Juno, represents a level below fate and they, indeed, enact fate in a manner that often contradicts their intentions (as we shall see). Finally, Aeneas himself is aware of fate to a much lesser degree than any of his divine advisors. The corollary of that freedom, without which *pietas* would be an empty name, is a limitation of knowledge that leaves the future open to moral choices. Yet one thread runs through the whole complex of forces engaged: *pietas-furor*, the antithetical dyad of moral ideas or feelings related to *fatum* as to the factor which will ultimately use them both to its own moral ends.

It is thus clear that lines 1–304 are meant to stand apart as introduction and, indeed, as a proleptic, prophetic introduction to the whole work. This is also evident from the fact that the analogous Allecto episode of Book 7 chiasmically reverses the order here (in Book 1) and puts the *peaceful* landing and the

---

[1] Cf. Wolf H. Friedrich, 'Exkurse zur Aeneis' (*Philologus*, 94 (1940), pp. 164 f.) who thinks ll. 223-304 are an early bit of *tibicines* (props) that Virgil intended to 'replace' by the Anchises speech of 6. This is why the aid of Venus is 'doubled' by that of Mercury (297-304). Friedrich's essential error, in my view, is his failure to distinguish the roles of Jupiter (and his direct agent, Mercury) from that of a 'sub-fate' such as Venus. It should also be noted that Athene in the *Odyssey* (1) 'doubles' Hermes' later role (beginning of Book 5) of implementing Zeus' decision as to Odysseus' return. Most important of all: Virgil 'reverses' the Jupiter prophecy (the closing of the gates of War) in the designedly analogous section of Book 7 (cf. p. 328 below). Thus Juno (not Allecto) *opens* the gates *there*.

Latin-Trojan *entente before* the violence of Juno and her minion. The reason is, of course, that once the *entente* (foedus) is broken and the Latin War declared, the violence cannot stop until the death of Turnus at the end of the whole epic. In other words, Allecto sets the whole tone of *Aeneid* 7–12 while Aeolus (her analogue in 1) introduces only a momentary disturbance, which is quickly calmed and followed by a peaceful association between the native (Tyrian) and the foreign (Trojan) peoples. The 'storm' is, thus, set off from the ensuing narrative as the 'war' of Book 7 is not.[1] But this is not simply to mark the introduction to Book 1 as a separate, proleptic unit. It also indicates that the action of the Odyssean *Aeneid* is very different from that of its *Iliadic* successor. The storm is only a symbol of another storm to come but this later storm is not primarily physical but psychological and the 'calm' itself is, therefore, deceptive. It is not until the symbolic storm of Juno (the storm that sends Dido and Aeneas to the cave) that we perceive the true meaning of the first.

When we first meet Aeneas, we do not in fact know his real situation—his true relation to Troy, the extent to which he has been isolated by the death of Anchises—and hence cannot truly gauge his psychic vulnerability to the kind of danger that awaits him at Carthage. But this is an ignorance that he shares with the reader for he himself does not realize his own situation. Thus the rest of Book 1 (305–756) is ironic and deceptive: Aeneas sees only his escape from the storm, the restoration of his ships and his men, his favourable and flattering reception by Dido, and does not realize that all this is but the prelude and, indeed, the partial cause of a much more dangerous, if much more subtle, threat to his *pietas* and his whole mission. This ignorance is also reflected in the actions of Venus and Juno: Juno's jealous love for Carthage had resulted, in fact, in the storm that drove Aeneas to Africa and results later in the storm that drives Aeneas and Dido to the cave; Venus' blind affection for Aeneas causes the passion in Dido that could have had such ruinous consequences for him. In short, the narrative that begins at line 305 of the first *Aeneid* is a veritable study in the ominous ambiguity of human and divine action. The physical calm after the storm in effect provides the setting of the

---

[1] See p. 328 below.

psychological tragedy that the storm itself has already symbolized. We pass with line 305 from the prophetic certainty of
Jupiter to the ironic ignorance of all the lesser powers and of
man most of all. But such an ignorance is the essential prerequisite of the kind of moral freedom that Virgil was here
concerned with.

The rest of Book I (after 305) is, as we have already partially
seen, arranged in a kind of crescendo that starts from Aeneas'
meeting with Venus and reaches its climax in the encounter
with Dido. There are here three ironically ambiguous episodes:

1. The meeting with Venus (305–417).
2. Aeneas in the City (418–93).
3. The encounter with Dido (494–722).

We have already discussed (chap. iii) the role of the first two
episodes as dramatic preparation for the third. We must here,
however, consider more particularly their ironic content and
tone.

The encounter with Venus (305–417) is distinguished by the
way in which Virgil uses Homeric motifs to bring out a series
of ironical contrasts. We turn directly from Jupiter's prophecy
and Mercury's assuaging mission—from fate and its operations
—to Aeneas in one of his most pious moods:

305   At pius Aeneas per noctem plurima volvens.

He goes out to reconnoitre (careful leader that he now is) with
the faithful Achates by his side. He meets Venus in the disguise
of an extremely becoming huntress just as he was shortly to
meet Dido, Dido so appropriately likened to the huntress
Diana in imitation of the simile devoted by Homer to Nausikaa.
Their initial parley recalls, quite deliberately, the conversation
of Odysseus and Nausikaa in the *Odyssey* (6. 149 f.) or of
Aphrodite and Anchises in the Homeric Aphrodite Hymn and
strikes at once a lighter, faintly sensuous note.[1] Venus then tells
her son the tragic history of Dido. The ambiguity here, the play
of light and dark, the setting of the tragedy in the shining

---

[1] Sainte-Beuve, *Étude sur Virgile* (1857), pp. 274 f. makes a fine comparison of
Virgil here with the Aphrodite hymn. Only Sainte-Beuve seems to have grasped
Virgil's mixture of sensual and maternal elements in this scene, and to have realized how Virgil 'tout en se ressouvenant de cette amoureuse et voluptueuse rencontre
avec Anchise, en la sousentendant pour ainsi dire . . . a pris plaisir à la transformer
en une scène tendrement maternelle avec le fils'.

Homeric frame—Venus telling Aeneas of Dido, Venus describing Dido's own *pietas* and purpose to her pious son!—are both subtly and finely conceived. Then in response to Venus' inquiry (for in good Homeric fashion she still pretends to be the ignorant huntress) Aeneas tells her who is:

378   sum pius Aeneas.

The irony here has seldom been noticed by commentators. Virgil is not, of course, mocking Aeneas' piety: it is the situation itself which is ironical. Aeneas does not know that he is talking to Venus and Venus is not at this juncture—she is already plotting against Dido, already preparing the amorous trap— concerned with his piety. She is, furthermore, thoroughly amoral and short-sighted in her designs, completely unaware of the strain she is about to put on her son's *pietas*. Her final reversion to herself *in propria persona*, the lovely goddess who once bent over the couch of Anchises,[1] is just sufficiently sensuous to connote what cannot be overtly mentioned without spoiling the precarious dignity of the scene. The mist in which she invests Aeneas is the last touch: here again we think of Odysseus and Nausikaa, of Jason on his way to the palace of Aeetes and Medea. But Aeneas, finally, senses the ambiguity, the trickery, perhaps even something of the amorality:

407   quid natum totiens, crudelis tu quoque, falsis
          ludis imaginibus?

But the primary irony of the episode is of course the contrast between the Homeric vision of Venus and the story of Dido that she retells. For the story reveals Dido as at once Aeneas' *alter ego*—one who also has foiled the crime of the past by founding a city of the future, one who likewise has an object of *pietas* (in the dead Sychaeus and in her own mission of empire) —and a tragic figure whose love has been foully betrayed by the *furor* of her own kinsman. We see in a stroke the passion, the energy, the tragedy of this remarkable woman and we are prepared for the tragedy to come. When we hear how Sychaeus haunted her dreams (in somnis inhumati venit imago coniugis) and drove her to action, we are alerted for his later reappearance: hinc exaudiri voces et verba vocantis visa viri (4. 460 f.). Aeneas is no Pygmalion: it is only symbolically a second murder

---

[1] Cf. *Hymn to Aphrodite*, 174 f.

that Sychaeus comes back in Book 4 to denounce. But both the similarities of character and situation that made for love between the two founders of empire and the obligations that denied the love and turned it to tragedy, have been now delineated. Yet the meaning of this is quite hidden from Aeneas (even though he senses something of Venus' trickery): all, on the contrary, seems thoroughly auspicious from Venus' ambrosial locks and divine step to the evidently favourable omen of the swans. The whole scene is ironical and ambiguous even to its smallest detail.

Thus abruptly have we descended from the level of fate [1] (the Jupiter prophecy) to the level at which the subfatal forces can visibly 'intervene' in human affairs. Venus is here a curious blend of maternal anxiety and erotic impulse: the main point of the episode, however, is that it at once brings the resurgent Aeneas—the hero on the way to recovery and new hope after the disaster of the storm—under the spell of love and Dido, that it determines the point of view he is to take toward the new city and toward Dido herself. Here as in Book 5 (as we shall see) Virgil uses an apparently favourable turn of events, an apparent break in the clouds, to prepare a future disaster. But the underlying reason for the ironical difference between the appearance and the reality is Aeneas' own unsureness, his own inability to preserve his *pietas* under pressure. The brief initial moment of despair (terque quaterque beati, &c.) has not really been replaced by a perdurable *pietas*. This Aeneas does not know nor does Venus. Even the crisis to come, the crisis of Book 4, is, as we shall see, an insufficient test. The whole plan of the Odyssean *Aeneid*, which has been so generally misunderstood, is to reserve for the sixth book, for the symbolic death and resurrection, the full revelation or dissipation of ignorance that alone can produce a final and an unshakable *pietas*.

The second of the three episodes (*Aeneas in the City*, 418–93) shows a very different kind of irony. The shining Homeric frame is gone; the mood abruptly changes to one of bitterness and nostalgia out of which finally hope—ironically deceptive hope—emerges. Isolated, as we have noticed,[2] by the mist,

---

[1] Hans Theodor Plüss (*Vergil und die Epische Kunst* (1884), pp. 49–50) has well seen the distinction between the 'reassurance' as to the true goal of the Jupiter speech and the 'enticement of a false goal' represented by the Venus scene.

[2] See p. 65 f. above.

Aeneas preserves a psychological distance from what he sees which accentuates his consciousness of the distance between his own present plight and his far-away goal. Dido has done what he is as yet far from doing (437: O fortunati quorum iam moenia surgunt!). He, of course, has no sense of what Carthage really represents for himself and for Rome. The parallel between himself and Dido only reveals to him the abyss between intention and fulfilment. His initial nostalgia is enhanced by this glimpse of the long hard way he has to go. Then on the frieze of the Temple of Juno—the irony of the setting is obvious enough—he sees his past, not merely the *Iliacas pugnas* but himself in the company of the other heroes. His rising nostalgia is strikingly confirmed, but he now also feels the first spring of new hope:

450   Hoc primum in luco nova res oblata timorem
           leniit, hic primum Aeneas sperare salutem
           ausus et adflictis melius confidere rebus.

He thus sees in his past, in his *fama* (*feret haec aliquam tibi fama salutem* is his remark to Achates), the earnest of Dido's hospitality. She represents to him now the respect of humanity for noble deeds and its pity for fallen greatness:

461   Sunt *hic etiam* sua praemia laudi;
             sunt lacrimae rerum et mentem mortalia tangunt.

So the respect and pity of Dido for his own past is made a predisposing cause of the *amor* to come. The actual recital of his past in the long narrative of Books 2 and 3 is thus prefigured and with it the whole tragedy of Book 4, as Dido's words

4. 13   Degeneres animos timor arguit. Heu quibus ille
             iactatus fatis! quae bella exhausta canebat!

eventually make plain. The irony of course is that Aeneas can only see *salus*, pity, hospitality, the dissipation of his anxiety, in what is actually his greatest danger. It is his own heart, his own sense of the past and its bitter outcome, his own longing for recognition and safety, in short, his *nostalgia* that really betray him.

We need not linger over the quite overt irony of the third episode (the encounter with Dido, 494–722). When Dido says to him:

628   *Me quoque* per multos *similis fortuna* labores
         iactatam hac demum voluit consistere terra

We see at once in tragic conjunction the two pasts and the two
futures: but their similarity only is apparent to Dido and
Aeneas; Dido's words ironically prefigure her doomed attempt
to overcome the impassible barrier that fate has placed between
Aeneas and herself.

From now on (i.e. from l. 631) everything rushes toward the
tragedy ahead. Aeneas, assured of Dido's hospitality, sends to
the ships for Ascanius, for gifts for Dido and for one particularly
ominous gift, Helen's veil which she brought to Troy

651   Pergama cum peteret inconcessosque hymenaeos.

The pseudo-Ascanius, of course, comes with the veil (the
intervention of Venus now completes her first intervention in
Episode 1, ll. 305–417) and almost at once the note of impending
tragedy is sounded: the Dido who admires the gifts and, most of
all, the false Ascanius, is now *praecipue infelix, pesti devota futurae.*
At last the interim of ironical ambiguity has passed and the
actual tragedy has began.

In one sense, as we have seen, there is a continuous action
which runs from line 631 of Book 1 to the end of Book 4. In the
beginning of 4 we take up Dido almost where we left her in the
banquet hall: infelix Dido . . . longum . . . bibebat amorem
(i. 749). But the inclusion of Aeneas' narrative within the framework of the Dido tragedy is quite essential to the tragedy itself
and to the whole structure of the Odyssean *Aeneid.*[1] So far we
have seen Aeneas only *in mediis rebus*, only at one moment of his
career: we cannot understand the great crisis ahead until we
see how his past has fitted him for it, both what obligations it
imposes and what weaknesses it has revealed. Dido's past, in a
sense, we know (Venus has revealed it); Aeneas' is still most
obscure. But Virgil's purpose (in choosing the context for
Aeneas' narrative) went much further than this. The contrast
of past and present (what Aeneas' *tells* Dido of his past; what
he *is* to her in the present) has a dramatic effect comparable to
that of the Damon song in *Eclogue* 8 but far more ironic. Aeneas'
narrative leads directly to his and Dido's attempt to repudiate

[1] This is a point ignored by most students of Virgil. But, cf. Büchner, 325 and
Perret, 115–16.

their past in a passionate present. The tremendous irony of the situation is that it is just at the time when Dido has begun to forget her own past and drink the 'long draughts of love'—just when Aeneas is most susceptible to her charms and to the feelings of the moment, that she herself asks for his past, for the tale of those obligations and that destiny which are so clearly incompatible with her desires. Indeed the fact that Aeneas himself fails to see or to heed the true lesson of his past, is the surest indication of his own unreadiness for the duty it imposes upon him.

In no other way could Virgil have shown the relation of past, present and future—the conflict of past obligation, present passion, and future destiny—with such poignant clarity. The motif of the regretted past—of the terrible nostalgia involved in a destiny founded on the destruction of the hero's home, on the denial of a return to it—had already been sounded with the initial outcry of despair in the storm and with the tears that greeted the frieze of the Juno Temple. It is, in fact, Dido's amorous curiosity, her respect and pity for the suffering hero, that induces Aeneas to prolong his nostalgic mood in the narrative. But the past *of which he tells* is not the whole past with which he must finally come to terms. The Aeneas that we see in Books 2 and 3 is not the Aeneas that leaves Deiphobus and rejoins Anchises in Book 6. Aeneas' narrative, in short, shows us his inability to grasp the true past, its relation to the future and its ineluctable demand on the present. Dido constitutes his great test precisely because her passion (and his) conflicts with everything he is destined to be. His narrative not only reveals this but reveals also the nostalgia that explains his blindness and his susceptibility.

The setting of the narrative in the torch-lit banquet hall and the darkness of night:

726   dependent lychni laquearibus aureis
            incensi et noctem flammis funalia vincunt.

is, of course, a deliberate adaptation of outer décor to inner mood as well as a preparation for the flame-lit night of Troy's destruction.[1] We have come a long way from the *lux alma* (l. 306) of the early morning in which Aeneas encountered

---

[1] Pöschl is good on this point: cf. pp. 271–2, 250–2.

Venus. The fury and blackness of the lightning-lit storm (eripiunt subito nubes caelumque diemque, 88) had been succeeded by the calm and pleasant daylight: now we revert to troubled darkness and fire once again. This correspondence of cosmic and psychic elements is peculiarly Virgilian.

The second book, with which the narrative begins, is the story of how Aeneas came to leave his Trojan *patria*. It is the story of the destruction of all that had made life meaningful to him and its telling is in itself an ordeal:

3.   Infandum, regina, iubes renovare *dolorem*.

This is the true note of his nostalgia, his sense of a sorrow too deep for utterance, his terrible conciousness of having outlived his world. It is the mood of *terque quaterque beati* once again. Thus the book is not in any sense a *defence* of his withdrawal from Troy. Indeed the very *furor* with which Aeneas had courted death on that frightful night and had repeatedly forgotten even his family in his mad desire for vengeance on the Greeks—in short, his almost Achillean *aidōs*, his *shame* before the defeat and murder of his comrades—is clearly reprehended by his Mother, Venus, and his dead wife, Creusa. When Venus reproves him in the line:

2. 594   Nate quis *indomitas* tantus *dolor* excitat *iras*

and Creusa re-echoes this reproof in the line:

2. 776   Quid tantum *insano* iuvat indulgere *dolori*?

they both condemn his *dolor* as *mad* and *unrestrained*. He had, in fact, acted all through the Book like the Homeric hero who sets his warlike instincts and his thirst for vengeance, the maintenance of his heroic status, before all other interests or claims. And such an Homeric hero he certainly had been. Only the direct intervention of Venus made him return to his family and then only after he had clearly seen the gods themselves engaged in the ruin of Troy.

Aeneas' *dolor* and *furor*, his mad and furious reaction to the catastrophe, are repeatedly emphasized. The vision of Hector (270 f.) and Hector's warning to flee and carry off the *penates* of Troy to new walls overseas, has no effect upon him except indeed to rouse him from sleep and make him see what is happening. Once he sees, his reaction is instinctive and

R

immediate: *arma amens capio*. Not even when he meets Panthus
(318 f.) bringing the city's gods to refuge in his own household,
does he grasp the confirmation of Hector's words that this
implies. He is literally carried away by the *Erinys* of war:

337   in flammas et in arma feror quo *tristis Erinys*
           quo fremitus vocat et sublatus ad aethera clamor.

His whole character is dominated by *furor*, by deliberate
refusal to heed the gods' will to destroy Troy, by deliberate
rejection of *salus*. We learn this from his words to his comrades
in lines 348–54 whose result Virgil summarizes in the single
phrase: sic animis iuvenum *furor* additus (355). He and his
comrades are now likened to hunger-maddened wolves howling
in the darkness: here the Homeric *lions* (to which Odysseus
and Diomedes were compared in the *Doloneia*, *Iliad* 10, 297)
fittingly become *lupi raptores;* what drives these wolves is an
improba rabies (357). But the emotion in Aeneas reaches, perhaps,
its culminating expression in the hidden snake (379 f.) to which
he, by implication, is compared: the Greek Androgeos, surprised by Aeneas, is likened to a man inadvertently treading on a
snake. This prepares us for a new form of Aeneas' rage: on
the advice of Coroebus, he adds *guile* to fury by assuming the
disguise of Greek arms; the treachery of the hidden snake is
thus made conscious policy. But this leads only to a temporary
success and is followed by an 'inverted' or poetic justice:
telis/nostrorum obruimur (410–11).

Aeneas now passes from aggression to retreat. He and his
Trojans are found out and overwhelmed by sheer numbers
(424 f.). He shifts his strategy, enters the palace by a hidden
door and climbs to the roof; but all attempts to dispel Greek
attack (by, for example, hurling down the tower) give the
Trojans no respite. So, for the moment, Aeneas, now balked
and unable to do more, can only *contemplate* events below in the
disroofed palace. It is *now* Pyrrhus, the Greek, who is the snake,
the renascent, vigorous snake come from the winter darkness
of his lair into terrible publicity (arduus ad solem, 475): *he* needs
no diguise *now*. The futility of any attempt to emulate him or the
Greeks, to withstand *furor* with *furor*, treachery with treachery,
is manifest. Finally the palace supports are battered down and
everything stands revealed and defenceless:

483   Apparet domus intus et atria longa patescunt;
         apparent Priami et veterum penetralia regum.

Thus, at the moment of impotence, at the moment when
any emulation of Greek fury by Trojans is seen to be hopeless,
Aeneas witnesses, helplessly alone, the final tragedy of Priam!
For the first time his now thwarted *furor* is arrested by the
thought of his own abandoned family:

560   subiit cari genitoris imago
         ut regem aequaevum crudeli volnere vidi
         vitam exhalantem; subiit deserta Creusa
         et direpta domus et parvi casus Iuli.

The *pietas* here is exclusively familial: there is no vision of a
broader future, no recall of Hector's admonitions. It is now
that Aeneas sees the *lurking* Helen [1] (secreta in sede *latentem*:
the timid snake in its lair) and that his fury flames in a final,
agonized spasm: subit ira (575). All this is required to prepare
and motivate the entrance of Venus. But Venus comes only
to turn his thoughts from mad and impotent vengeance on
Helen to the actual plight of his abandoned family, only to
reinforce an already awakened familial *pietas*. She does this by
finally showing him the gods at work in the destruction of Troy,
by revealing the awesome disparity between their power and
his impotence. He now, at long last, sees that there is but
one course left him, to return and rescue his father, wife
and son.

What does all this show? Not certainly that Aeneas was a
great and good hero who, despite himself, had to yield and
withdraw. This central passage (268–633), is no *apologia* for a
retreat, as has often been thought, but rather a picture of the
old Homeric hero, the man of *dolor* and *furor*, the man of Achillean wrath, that Aeneas once was and could no longer be if he
were to realize the destiny before him. His motivation so far has
been at worst despair, desire for vengeance, reckless fury; at

---

[1] Büchner (331–4) has, it seems to me, correctly argued that ll. 567–88 (preserved by Servius) are Virgilian but *tibicines* (props) that Virgil would have later
replaced since they conflict with the Deiphobus narrative of Book 6. See Appendix
9. In any event, however, Virgil would have introduced Helen. It is quite easy to
see how another version of the Helen scene could have been made consistent with
the Deiphobus story (e.g. she could have been separated from Menelaus and associates, then fearing the last Trojan resisters, have fled for refuge from those she had
just betrayed).

best, Trojan patriotism; and, at the very reluctant last, a glimmer of familial *pietas* that would have been impotent without divine reinforcement. The vision of Hector and its confirmation by Panthus had had no effect upon him: the idea of a new city, a new home for the Trojan *penates*, was utterly beyond the range of his emotions. The intervention of Venus concerned only his return to Anchises, Creusa and Ascanius: it had no direct bearing on his ultimate destiny, supplied no new motivation. The whole picture is quite negative. Certainly Virgil would never have represented Aeneas as weak, cowardly or unmoved by the fate of his companions and his city: he had to be a hero on the old model before he could be one on the new. The important thing, however, is that the old model is defective, that the *dolor* and *furor* of Aeneas' final resistance is not the motivation required for the *pius Aeneas* he is to become, that a radical shift in his whole conception of duty and *pietas* is demanded.[1]

Thus we have so far seen (up to 633) how Aeneas' heroic *furor* was forced to give way to his *familial pietas*. We now see that this too is not enough, that something much more than the *salvation of a family* is now required. The whole action after line 633 (i.e. after his return home, *ubi iam patriae perventum ad limina sedis*, 634) revolves around his father's reluctance to leave. The narrative turns on two crucial points: (1) Anchises' departure from Troy is indispensable to Aeneas' departure (indeed Aeneas deliberately chooses death rather than leave without Anchises, ll. 657 f.); and (2) Anchises will not consent to leave without a clear sign from the gods; he assumes, indeed, that they do not want him to go on living:

641   Me si calicolae voluissent ducere vitam
           has mihi servassent sedes.

Thus in the last analysis the crucial factor is Anchises. Aeneas' *pietas* toward his father goes, so to speak, without saying: for him to leave Anchises to the Greeks, to the fate he had just seen enacted upon Priam, would have been an unthinkable violation

---

[1] This part of the book has been generally misinterpreted. Heinze (pp. 1–81) thinks Virgil chiefly wants to defend his hero against the charge of 'Feigheit oder Schwäche' and that the prospect of a new country and kingdom overseas is a secondary element whose improbability Virgil has only with difficulty concealed.

of familial *pietas*. To be sure Anchises urges him to leave and save Creusa and Ascanius:

638   'vos o quibus integer aevi
          sanguis' ait 'solidaeque suo stant robore vires,
          vos agitate fugam.'

But Aeneas makes short shift of such an exhortation and chides his father for it: tantum . . . nefas patrio excidit ore? Indeed, he could have made no other answer. No token or verbal expostulation could have sufficed under the circumstances. It is quite fruitless to debate what Aeneas should have done if Anchises' mind had not been changed. Under no circumstances could he have commenced his Roman mission with the desertion of his father.

Nor could Anchises have yielded simply to the entreaty of Aeneas. For though, as he saw, there was some reason for the young and strong to escape, some possible future, there was none for him. He was old and useless; he had also experienced the ill will of the gods in the Jovian Thunderbolt that had already shattered his vitality (648–9). Nothing in short marked him out to be the survivor of his *patria*. *Pietas*, indeed, is the duty of sons to parents and parents to sons but, as Cicero observed, it was pre-eminently the duty of citizens to their city: pietas quae cum magna in parentibus et propinquis, tum in patria maxima est (*De Republica* VI. 16). We know too well what Romans thought of the desertion of a *patria* from the famous speech of Camillus in Livy (5. 52). To the Roman mind neither family nor local gods (in short familial *pietas*) could properly exist without a *patria*. There was thus, from Anchises' point of view, nothing to make further life either attractive or honourable. Had, indeed, his refusal to leave actually led to the ruin of Aeneas and Ascanius, his decision might have seemed tragically irrational. But Virgil was here interested only in setting forth the very real conflict between Aeneas' *familial* and Anchises' Trojan-patriotic *pietas*. Anchises, by refusing Aeneas' aid, forced into the open the whole issue of what was to *replace* Trojan *pietas*, on what grounds, for what purpose a family should survive its *patria*.

Thus Anchises sets up a dilemma which only the gods, *in primis* Jupiter, can resolve. The only way to convince Anchises that he was not deserting his *patria* was to enlist his loyalty to a new *patria* or rather to his *patria* reborn. This is what the omens (both the flame on Ascanius' head and the *augurium maximum*, 692 f., that confirms it) accomplish. *Anchises' whole attitude is now transformed:*

> 2. 701 Iam iam nulla morast; sequor et qua ducitis adsum.
> Di patrii, servate domum, servate nepotem;
> vestrum hoc augurium *vestroque in numine Troia est.*
> cedo equidem nec, nate, tibi comes ire recuso.

The key words here: *vestroque in numine Troia est* obviously point not to the old Troy which is finished (fuit Ilium et ingens gloria Teucrorum) but the new Troy which is to be. Anchises' *pietas* is no longer Trojan, but Roman. And so, by inevitable reflex, is that of Aeneas. From now on he looks to Anchises as the father-figure of his new destiny and as the link between his future and his past.[1]

We can now finally grasp the structure of the whole book. The central section (Aeneas' *furor* finally giving way to familial *pietas*, 268–633) is surrounded by two antiphonal sections which describe the Greek plot against Troy (13–267) and the motivation and execution of Aeneas' departure (634–729). Each of these two sections corresponds to the other in great detail:[2] the reason for this is, clearly, that each describes the enactment of the gods' will; in the first, for the destruction of Troy; in the second, for the founding of Rome. The seeds of Rome lie, so to speak, in the ashes of Troy and the fall of Troy is thus surrounded by divine action on both sides. In particular, the Laocoon *prodigium* by which the *doom* of Troy was both prophesied and realized (since it finally induced the Trojans to admit the wooden horse) is countered by an exactly correspond-ing *prodigium* by which the divine *future* of Troy is prophesied and realized (since it induces Anchises and Aeneas to leave). The correspondence of the two *prodigia* is thus basic to the book: the rise of Rome is divinely planned to offset the fall of Troy.

It is particularly instructive to compare the plans of the two sections:

---

[1] This whole episode has been much misunderstood. Thus Heinze (p. 57) speaks of Aeneas' lack of initiative. But, of course, for the reasons indicated, the initiative must belong to Anchises. Cf. also R. B. Lloyd (*TAPA* 88 (1957), pp. 44–55) who rejects other explanations but fails to see the real issue.

[2] This point, so far as I can tell, has not been noticed by the commentators or critics. See p. 248, notes 1, 2.

Laocoon and the Horse:
(13–267).
Invasion of the Greeks.

1. Appearance of the Wooden
Horse. Debate as to its use
(13–39).
2. Laocoon urges its destruction
(40–56).
3. Sinon (57–198): the false
counter-plea.
4. The Snakes (199–233).
5. Admission of Horse and Invasion of the Greeks (234–67).

Detailed Plan of 4 above.
1. Approach of snakes from
Tenedos (199–211).
2. The snakes attack the
children (212–15).
3. Laocoon comes to their aid
(216–19).
4. Death of Laocoon (220–7)
seems to confirm the omen.
5. Interpretation of prodigy as
Laocoon's punishment (228–
33).

Anchises and the Oracles :
(634–729).
Departure of Aeneadae.

1. Aeneas reaches his home (634–
6).
2. Anchises refuses to leave (637–
49).
3. Aeneas and Creusa urge him to
change his mind (650–78).
4. The Omens (679–704) (flame
and comet).
5. Departure of Aeneas,
Anchises and family (705–29).

Detailed Plan of 4 above.
1. Transition to *monstrum*
(679–80).
2. The flame on Ascanius' head
(681–4).
3. His parents rush to his aid
(685–6).
4. *Augurium maximum* confirms
Anchises' interpretation of
flame omen (687–98).
5. Interpretation and acceptance
of the *augurium* by Anchises
(699–704).

Here we have two omens (snakes, flame), both involving
children (the two sons of Laocoon, Ascanius), both exciting the
aid of terrified parents (Laocoon; *nos* = Aeneas, Creusa),
both followed by a confirmatory sign (the destruction of
Laocoon himself, the comet or *augurium maximum*), both affecting
the principal agent of resistance (Laocoon, Anchises), and both
interpreted and enacted. Furthermore each set of omens is
preceded by a case of reluctance and resistance (Laocoon's
resistance to the entry of the Horse, Anchises' refusal to depart)
and, in each case, the interval (part 3 in the scheme) between
the initial resistance and the omens is taken up by attempts to
overcome the resistance (Sinon's clever speeches, the pleas of
Aeneas and Creusa to Anchises).

The parallelism is, moreover, emphasized by the very difference between the two episodes. Bernard Knox [1] has pointed out that the flame which plays around Ascanius' head is described in the serpentine words of the Laocoon passage (*lambere flamma comas et circum tempora pasci* in 682 vis-à-vis *sibila lambebant linguis vibrantibus ora* in 211, *miseros morsu depascitur artus* in 215) but that these words are now put in a beneficent context (*tactuque innoxia mollis . . . flamma*, 683–4) sharply contrasted with their sinister significance before. This is indeed the key to the general difference between the two passages. In the one case, the gods decree doom and catastrophe (indicating in the prodigy the source of the approaching evil, Tenedos whence the Greeks will also come); in the other, salvation and a new future (indicating in the comet of the *augurium* the way of escape, Ida). In the one case, innocent children are horribly destroyed; in the other, an innocent child is harmlessly marked for future glory. In the one, the priest, Laocoon, is the gods' victim (note the crucial simile, 223–4); in the other, the gods' victim (the lightning-struck Anchises) is the true priest whose prayer brings immediate and favourable response.

There has been much debate [2] as to whether the prodigy that destroys Laocoon is a punishment (Strafwunder) or a prophetic omen mistaken for a punishment. The gods, perhaps, do not so much destroy Troy themselves as make the Trojans the instruments of their own destruction when the latter so naturally misinterpret the snake prodigy. But the gods have certainly willed the downfall of Troy (as Aeneas finally sees) and their deception of the Trojans is as deliberate as it is effective. Yet the very ambiguity of the snakes—the lack of clarity as to Laocoon's 'guilt'—is an indication of the more general ambiguity, the deceptive and serpentine ambiguity, in which Troy's fall is involved. Opposed to this is the clear sign of Jupiter, offered in response to Anchises' explicit demand:

---

[1] 'The Serpent and the Flame' (*AJP*, 71 (1950), pp. 379–400). Knox sees the importance of the serpentine imagery but misses the true parallelism between the two sets of *prodigia* (Laocoon, Ascanius-Anchises). So far as I know, this has never been observed before.

[2] Cf. especially Hermann Kleinknecht, 'Laokoon' (*Hermes*, 79 (1944), pp. 66–111). Doubtless Kleinknecht is right but I do not think the tissue is a very important one: whatever the snakes may be (portent or punishment or both), they indicate the hostility of the gods and serve the purpose of Troy's destruction.

693   de caelo lapsa per *umbras*
        Stella facem ducens *multa cum luce* cucurrit.

The sombre gloom is at last illuminated by heavenly light, a
light over Ida that anticipates the later dawn:

801   Iamque iugis summae surgebat Lucifer Idae.

The symbolism of the book so far, is perhaps more effective,
or more integrated and subtle, than that of any other part of the
poem. Virgil's major problem was to indicate the transition
from the darkest evil—destruction, treachery, despair, fury,
violence—to restorative innocence, piety, and hope. Anchises
the weak old man, Jupiter's victim, is the vessel of salvation;
Ascanius, the innocent child, is the instrument of prophecy.
The contrast between their fate and the fate of the other old
man and children—the brutal murder of Priam, the horrible
strangulation of Laocoon's sons—is but an aspect of the deeper
contrast between Troy and Rome, the old and the new. Yet
these are only a small part of the many contrasted motifs in the
book. The serpent with its treachery, its dark lair, its terrible
spring, the night's darkness itself, the devouring fires of burning
Troy, are the unhealthy, deceptive, destructive elements against
which the lambent flame, the glorious comet, the dawn of the
close are finally set. At first nothing is certain. Aeneas himself is
a treacherous snake in the first violent moments of his *furor;*
but he cannot compete with Pyrrhus, the exultant snake of
successful Greek guile and treachery. Here the Laocoon
episode had set the serpentine key for the ambiguous and
treacherous confusion of aims and purposes. Then the appearance of Venus, to save Helen and send Aeneas home, at the
moment of crisis when Aeneas is threatening to cheat the
Greeks of their triumph at the cost of his own life and future,
is a wonderful symbol of the ambiguous forces that work below
the level of fate, yet ultimately make for its victory. There is so
much doubt in all the action. Why are the gods destroying
Troy? All Venus will say is that it is their *inclementia* which is at
work. Troy's fall is, in fact, involved in a confusion of moral
purpose that touches Greek and Trojan alike. But it is out of
this terrible, searing experience that the idea of Rome is conceived. It is not Aeneas' idea, certainly not that of Anchises.

None of the lesser gods have a direct part in it. The act of revealing truth is reserved for Jupiter alone.[1]

But we must not mistake what has happened. Aeneas has not yet exorcized his old nature and his *furor*. The real conversion is not that of Aeneas but that of Anchises.[2] From now on Anchises is the father-figure, the spur and instigator of a most reluctant son. From now on Anchises is the agent of Jupiter and the very embodiment of the new *pietas* of Rome and the future; his presence urges Aeneas forward; his absence spells procrastination and even betrayal. He is in short the great symbol of *conscience* (*pietas* personified) that broods over the whole Odyssean *Aeneid*.

The new relation of Anchises and Aeneas is revealed at once in the concluding section of Book 2 (705 ff.). Aeneas carries Anchises on his shoulders and Anchises holds in his hands the *sacra . . . patriosque penates* of the old Troy and the new Rome. Ascanius holds his father's right hand and runs beside. Creusa only *follows* behind (pone subit coniunx). The symbolism is clear. But Aeneas is far from grasping the meaning of the new *pietas* to which he has been committed. The almost immediate loss of Creusa makes him leave Anchises and Ascanius to the uncertain hands of his *socii* and return in blind grief and fury to the very centre of Troy. Then to him

771   quaerenti et tectis urbis sine fine *furenti*

appears Creusa's shade. Her first words:

776   Quid tantum *insano* iuvat *indulgere dolori* . . .?

mark the extent to which he has not yet mastered his heroic *furor* or *dolor*. We are of course meant to sympathize with the grief of Aeneas—a cold acquiescence in Creusa's loss would have been inhuman—but we are also meant to see that Aeneas' attitude is far from a complete and sufficient *pietas*. But *pietas* in this new sense cannot be *realized* or grasped by Aeneas, in anything like its full reality, without a number of profound

---

[1] On the use of symbols in this book, cf. again Knox's article cited above (a splendid piece of literary criticism) and T. P. Howe, *Classical Journal*, 51 (1956), pp. 55–56, 322–7. It was this aspect of the book that Heinze's 'technical' analysis so largely ignored (cf. again his chap. i).

[2] This is one of the 'key' facts on which the meaning of the whole *Aeneid* (esp. the Odyssean *Aeneid*) depends. But it has seldom or never been clearly explicated. Much of this chapter (as the reader will see) is devoted to its multiple significance.

experiences of which Creusa's death is the first. For her death is now shown to be itself part of the *fatum* to which he must submit: a new bride awaits him in Hesperia after long exile far overseas. *Non haec sine numine divom/eveniunt!* All he can do now is accept Creusa's loss and return to Anchises. The great ordeal—which is to be so terrible a renunciation of his own past and present—has begun. Aeneas is left alone with the aged Anchises, the symbol of duty, and the child Ascanius, the symbol of the future. What this implies in self-control and the conquest of both natural and heroic emotion he can as yet hardly conceive.

The *third* book—like the fifth and the first—shows *light* or relatively light against the *darkness* of 2, 4 and 6. It lacks the poignancy and tension of the Fall of Troy, the tragedy of Dido or the Descent to the Underworld. Even the dangers—the storm, the harpies, Polyphemus, Scylla and Charybdis—do not really engage us as serious threats to Aeneas' mission. There is no sense of constant physical peril such as we find in the *Odyssey*. No book is more Odyssean, yet what gives the tone and sets the mood are precisely its non-Odyssean elements. For its obvious similarity to Odysseus' *nostos* only makes more apparent the fact that it is not a *nostos* at all. Odysseus knows very well where he is going. What detains him is a series of quite tangible accidents. But Aeneas is hampered primarily by his *uncertainty*. He and his companions are

3. 7   incerti quo fata ferant, ubi sistere detur.

Hence the peculiar character and *colour* of the book: it is not tragically dark; no one terrible element, as in each of the even books, dominates it and gives it its tone. Rather it is the absence of the definable and clear, whether light or dark, and the corresponding presence of the indefinite and eerie, the sense of endless quest for an illusive goal in strange country, which constitute the peculiar atmosphere of this book.

This uncertainty, furthermore, is not primarily physical. It is spiritual and moral, and registers in Aeneas as a weariness and soul-sickness which is, in some respects, more unnerving and horrible than the more direct and comprehensible emotions of the even books. We can best comprehend Aeneas here by noting the peculiar mid-point which he occupies between Homer's Odysseus on the one hand and Dante's Ulysses on the other. For while his *attitude* is still that of Odysseus, his *situation* is much closer to the Ulysses of the *Inferno* or of Tennyson. What sustained this Ulysses was an ardent desire for new experience:

xxvi, 112 'O frati' dissi 'che per cento milia
   perigli siete giunti all' occidente
   a questa tanta picciola vigilia
  de 'nostri sensi ch'e del rimanente
   non vogliate negar l'esperienza
   di retro al sol, del mondo sanza gente.
  Considerate la vostra semenza:
   fatti non foste a viver come bruti
   ma per seguir virtute e canoscenza'.

Aeneas wholly lacks such a perspective. The advance into the future—the voyage into the unknown—was seen by him, rather, as a hard obligation of fate, a bitter duty; and the newness and uncertainty of the quest appeared as dreadful rather than romantically attractive. The unknown is an ordeal, not a challenge. Like Odysseus his natural instinct and desire is to return, to go back home, but a true *nostos* is denied him. He is even denied what Andromache and Helenus had found, a small replica of home, a *Troia recidiva: vobis parta quies . . . nos alia ex aliis in fata vocamur.*

On the other hand what he has and what alone preserves him in this realm of ambiguity and doubt is Anchises, the symbol of his conscience, his duty, his *pietas.*

This is therefore the point of view which enables Virgil to convert the most flagrantly mythical material into symbols of the special horror in Aeneas' soul—the horror of the unknown, the strange and the uncertain—and to pit against it the force of the new *pietas* which was born in the embers of Troy. In this sense, Book 3 has claim to be considered one of the greatest triumphs of his art.

The *leitmotif* is always the uncertainty of Aeneas' situation— not merely the uncertainty of his goal in a tangible sense, but the uncertainty of his inverted *nostos*—the fact that he is caught between the past and the future in a present which has no substantiality:

10   patriae lacrimans portusque relinquo
   et campos ubi Troia fuit. Feror exul in altum
   cum sociis natoque, Penatibus et Magnis Dis.

The contrast of *Troia fuit* and *feror exul in altum* is here stark and deliberate. The actual uncertainty is related to the inherent vagueness of the prophecies which guide him. He must find Hesperia and the Lydian Thybris (Creusa's speech, 781–2). But he does not know where this is. The first colonization in Thrace (1–68) is soon seen to be a terrible error; the second (Crete: 69–191) is due to the ambiguity of the oracle (of Delian Apollo): who can their 'ancient mother' be? The vision of the Penates and Anchises' recollection of Cassandra's disregarded prophecy make it clear that Italy must be their goal. But where is Italy? They set out, only to be driven by terrible storms to the shore of the Strophades where they encounter the Harpies. Here Celaeno's prophecy only terrifies and confuses them. At length (3. 294) they reach Epirus and rejoin their old Trojan comrades, Andromache and the seer Helenus. It is Helenus who first tells them how far away Italy really is:

3. 381   Principio Italiam, quam tu iam rere propinquam
          vicinosque, ignare, paras invadere portus
          longa procul longis via dividit invia terris.

So they must leave the *Troia recidiva*, the *felices quibus est fortuna peracta* and venture toward the horrors of Scylla, Charybdis and the Cyclopes. We may call this final period of Aeneas' voyage the *period of desolation*. The initial uncertainty has been dissipated by Helenus' prophecy but a great residuum of doubt, of grief and trouble faintly sketched or deliberately unrevealed, remains. The death of Anchises at the end finally reveals the fatal ambiguity of all prophecy and the true desolation of Aeneas.

The book thus falls into three principal sections:

(1) ll. 1–293: the period of uncertainty.

(2) ll. 294–505: the turning point; the prophecy of Helenus.

(3) ll. 506–715: the period of desolation.

(1) The first section (1–293) shows Aeneas at the maximum of uncertainty, the future as yet opaque and prophecy deliberately ambiguous. Yet Aeneas is not alone: at every turn he has the support of Anchises. His anxiety is not yet that of desolation.

The opening lines indicate these two essential elements of Aeneas' *initial* situation:

3. 5   auguriis agimur divom classemque sub ipsa
Antandro et Phrygiae molimur montibus Idae
incerti quo fata ferant, ubi sistere detur,
contrahimusque viros. Vix prima inceperat aestas
et *pater Anchises dare fatis vela iubebat*:
litora cum patriae lacrimans portusque relinquo
et campos, ubi Troia fuit. Feror exul in altum
cum *sociis natoque, penatibus et Magnis Dis.*

The uncertainty, the exile is balanced by the presence of
Anchises ordering the departure. The contrast of persons—
contrahimus, iubebat, relinquo, feror—symbolizes Aeneas' point of
view: first he uses the general 'we', then he refers to Anchises in
the third person as the one ordering or directing the departure,
then he uses the first person to describe the accomplished action.
Significant here, further, is the *omission* of Anchises from the
final list of Aeneas' company: his comrades, son, the Penates
and Great Gods. The reason is clearly that Anchises is *not* one
of the founding company—he will never reach the Tiber mouth;
he is instead the voice which orders Aeneas on and bids him
give his sails to the fates, but he is subtly dissociated from the
final goal.

Hereafter every successive crisis brings a primary appeal to
Anchises. The Polydorus portent which followed the first
settlement in Thrace is the first instance:

57   Postquam pavor ossa reliquit,
delectos populi ad proceres *primumque parentem*
monstra deum refero et quae sit sententia posco.

It is Anchises, the old friend of Anius (82), who interprets his
prophecy (103–17) and thus brings about the ill-fated settlement in Crete. It is also Anchises whom Aeneas first informs of
his vision of the Penates and who then corrects his erroneous
identification of Crete as the *antiqua mater* by his memory of
Cassandra's unheeded prophecy. It is Anchises who restores
their courage after the Harpies and the ominous words of
Celaeno and orders the departure:

263   Et pater Anchises passis de litore palmis
numina magna vocat meritosque indicit honores:
'Di prohibete minas; di talem avertite casum
et placidi servate pios!' tum litore funem
diripere excussosque iubet laxare rudentis.

Anchises is also the clue to the action of the gods and of the supernatural in this *book* or, better put, *phase* of Aeneas' ordeal. Aeneas at Book 1. 382, in his brief explanation of himself to the disguised Venus, referred to his wanderings as guided by her, *matre dea monstrante viam.* This is clearly inconsistent with the whole plan of Book 3, with the uncertainty caused by ambiguous oracles, false starts and the lack of explicit directives.[1] The very point and mood of the book depend on the absence of clear-cut divine help. Elsewhere in the poem Venus comes to Aeneas only at crucial moments (in 1, 2, 8) when her direct information, warning, or help are essential. But she never intervenes when Anchises is present: Anchises *alone* is sufficient to maintain Aeneas' constancy and *pietas.* Had Venus appeared in this book, the whole force of Anchises' relation to Aeneas would have been lost, and his old association with Venus could hardly have been recalled without a grotesque confusion of motifs and atmospheres. It seems almost self-evident that Virgil when he wrote line 382 did not anticipate the situation of Book 3; but, when he came to write or rewrite [2] the latter, he saw that his scheme necessarily had to exclude Venus.

The 'uncertainty section' of the Book (1–293) itself falls into two parts (after the proem, 1–12):

1. (13–146) the period of False Starts (the mistaken attempts to found the new Troy in Thrace and Crete)

2. (147–293) the search for Italy.

In the first part, the voice of fate is exceedingly ambiguous: only by error can Anchises and Aeneas discover the truth, or, rather, it is only out of their mistakes that their *pietas* emerges and finally compels the Trojan Penates to speak and to reveal their fated home. In the second part, the goal, Italy is known but is invested with a horror and uncertainty that the Helenus prophecy finally dissipates. The mood of each of these two parts is set by a miracle or supernatural wonder that symbolizes the terrible reality of fate, both as something inherent in the very ground and nature of things and as a force used by the demonic powers to instil fear and despair. It is only as Aeneas and

---

[1] This must of course be considered as but part of the whole problem of 'inconsistencies' in the *Aeneid.* See Appendix 9.

[2] Book 3 may well have been started in an earlier (third-personal) form and later revised in a first-personal form (see Appendix 9). But in its present form it seems, clearly, later than 1 (or 7, cf. Appendix 9).

Anchises cling fast to *pietas*, that they are able to distinguish between reality and appearance and at last discover the true meaning of the power that meets them at every turning. Only through their patient endurance of uncertainty is their *pietas* established; only so are they enabled to win a clear revelation.[1] But it is, first and foremost, the *pietas* of Anchises, not Aeneas. The former firmly holds the initiative.

All the four episodes [2] of the section (1–293: the Thracian settlement, the Delos Oracle, the Cretan settlement, the Harpies) are deliberately made parallel to each other and each contains a fourfold sequence: landing, sacrifice, omen or revelation, interpretation of the latter, departure. But the first three are very different from the last. The initial settlement at Thrace reveals (Polydorus incident) an *impietas* in the very soil that drives the Trojans on to the holy soil of pious Delos. But their misinterpretation of the oracle again brings them to the mistaken settlement at Crete. Here also the very soil and climate resist their efforts: but now at last the *Penates* speak and clearly define *Italy* and *Hesperia* as the goal. In the whole sequence, *pietas*, the *pietas* of Anchises and Aeneas, finally wins its reward, for it is only their pious acceptance of each sign that leads them on to knowledge.

The Polydorus episode is a *mirabile monstrum*, an unnatural, incredible event (Aeneas is seized with *frigidus horror* at the bleeding tree; he can hardly believe in what he sees; '*eloquar an sileam?*' he exclaims in recounting it). But the supernatural occurrence reflects an *unnatural* (in the sense of *inhuman*) deed, the impious murder of Polydorus:

56   Quid non mortalia pectora cogis,
          auri sacra fames!

Man's criminal greed and impiety pollute the very soil and vegetation (pollutum hospitium . . . scelerata . . . terra). The

---

[1] The important point is that fate here (in this book) reveals itself through vague *monstra*, oracles, and prophecies (even the Helenus prophecy is deliberately elliptical) precisely because it is meant to be sufficiently ambiguous to test *pietas*. Thus this book is designed to avoid any direct intervention of the *superi*. Juno does not appear and there is no need of Venus' intervention precisely because Anchises is at hand.

[2] Cf. R. B. Lloyd (*AJP* (1957), p. 136) whose analysis of the episodes is useful but whose interpretation is very inadequate. On the whole the best treatment of this phase of the book is that of Friedrich Mehmel, *Virgil und Apollonius Rhodius* (Hamburger Arbeiten zur Altertumswissenschaft I, 1940), esp. pp. 85–98. Note especially his emphasis on the 'changes of mood' (Wechsel von Stimmung) in the book.

dumb voice of nature itself is forced by human violence to speak, as Macbeth once remarked in a famous passage:

> It will have blood; they say blood will have blood;
> Stones have been known to move, and trees to speak;
> Augurs and understood relations, have
> By magot-pies and choughs, and rooks, brought forth
> The secret'st man of blood.

But Aeneas and Anchises piously placate the restless spirit by burial rites and proceed to a soil they *know* is holy:

73   Sacra mari colitur medio gratissima tellus . . .
75   quam *pius* Arquitenens . . . coli dedit

The Delos temple is of ancient sanctity: *saxo structa vetusto*. It is with humility they touch its earth: submissi *petimus terram* (93). The polarism of the two episodes (Thrace, Delos) is apparent, as Walter Jens [1] has shown. Aeneas and Anchises show their own *pietas* by rejecting the polluted and seeking out the holy.

But it is not the ambiguous oracle of Apollo that saves Anchises and Aeneas. A further trial must be undergone. After the ill fated (but much less fearsome) settlement in Crete, they are about to return to Delos for another oracle, when Apollo himself *comes to them* and speaks through the Penates (hic canit et tua nos en *ultro* ad limina mittit). At last *pietas* gains from *fate* the recognition it deserves: and the voices of the polluted earth of Thrace, of the recalcitrant earth of Crete, are finally answered through the voice of those very gods that are fated to find their own holy earth.

But *this* phase of uncertainty (Part 1 of Section 1) is followed by an even worse *monstrum* than that of Polydorus. It is not now a human corruption of nature, a past impiety, that thwarts Aeneas but a much more demonic force, the blind, irrational wrath of the evil gods, the dark powers that hate the light, *pietas* and Fate itself. Aeneas at length begins to see the true horror of his ordeal. The Harpies are not a physical threat, not a tangible danger, but a symbol of the dread which invests the unknown. They dishearten and overwhelm Aeneas by casting a false terror over the future (as he just begins to grasp its reality) and thus express the awesome power of his own fears. But they still retain a superhuman, demonic dimension that

---

[1] 'Der Eingang des dritten Buches der A.' (*Philologus*, 97 (1948), pp. 194-7.)

S

prefigures that of all the powers that try to thwart fate: Erebus Chaos, and Hecate to whom Dido appeals in 4, Allecto in 7, the wrath of Juno herself (flectere si nequeo superos, Acheronta movebo, 7. 312).

Virgil in one sense had a 'model' for the Harpies in Apollonius' *Argonautica* (II. 178–499). But, in Apollonius, the Harpies are merely a physical menace and do not have any psychological significance or atmospheric effect. Their persecution of the aged prophet, Phineus, is stopped by the interposition of the winged heroes, Boreas and Zetes; the pair not only drove the Harpies off but would, in fact, have killed them if Iris had not intervened. Then the relieved Phineus happily prophesies to the Argonauts and tells them of their future dangers and success. Virgil leaves Phineus out of the story (he mentions him only as part of the Harpies' past) and attributes the equivalent of Phineus' prophecy to Helenus later on. Instead, he makes his Harpy episode altogether baleful and maleficent: it is no favourable prognostication he wants here. His Harpies are, furthermore, remote, untouchable beings on whom no human sword or strength can make any impression (sed neque vim plumis ullam nec volnera tergo accipiunt). He accordingly emphasizes simply their uncanny, unearthly frightfulness: tristius haud illis monstrum nec saevior ulla/pestis et ira deum. Their virgin faces, foul bellies, hooked hands and hunger-pale mouths represent the demonization of the human, the mingling of woman and beast in a monstrosity worse than either alone. Virgil thus transmuted the merely marvellous and exotic beast of Apollonius into an evocative symbol of the psychologically strange, unfamiliar and unreal. We need not debate the degree of literalness with which the Harpy is to be taken: it is certainly not an allegory nor even an obtrusively demarcated symbol like Melville's white whale or Ibsen's wild duck. But it is not the simply miraculous creature of Apollonius: it is not something to be pursued and nearly destroyed, but an elusive and foul mouthpiece of all that is fearful, dark and ambiguous in the future.

For the interval between the departure from Crete and the arrival at Actium (just preceding the arrival at Buthrotum where Helenus has his little replica of Troy) was meant to be a period of gloom and despair before the renewal of Trojan associations and the Helenus prophecy. The way for the Harpies is prepared by the storm (192–208) which drives Aeneas off his course.

200   Excutimur cursu et *caecis* erramus in *undis*.

And Aeneas, quite unlike the Argonauts, is both during the storm and in the presence of the Harpies, a wholly passive figure: he is the witness of things that horrify but do not after all inflict positive harm. He is like a man in a rather bad dream and this section of the *Aeneid* is, indeed, dreamlike and invested with all the remoteness, dread and passivity of the dream-state. Thus the appearance of the Harpies and the mood of Aeneas correspond; the outer and inner horrors coincide. Celaeno is the uncanny monster whose prophecy makes articulate the feeling-tone of the moment: the future sensed as something horrendous, the words that Jupiter had uttered to Phoebus Apollo, retold by this *Furiarum maxima*, as if to re-echo the despair in Aeneas' own soul. Only Anchises reacts with strong initiative (263–7).

(2) The second section (294–505) is the turning-point of the book: the long prophecy of Helenus is obviously intended to stay Aeneas until he can receive the more definitely Italian prophecy of the Cumaean sibyl. Thereafter the uncertainty of the first section—*quo fata ferant, ubi sistere detur*—is gone: Aeneas now knows where Italy is and even how he must detour to avoid the Italian Greeks and the straits.

What, however, is ominously lacking from the prophecy is any mention of Anchises' later role. The African adventure and the journey to the underworld are wholly omitted. Helenus bids Aeneas avoid the straits by rounding Sicily. But he clearly *implies* the storm off Africa, for the thing he insists on is the placation of Juno:

3. 438   Iunoni cane vota libens dominamque potentem
             supplicibus supera donis; sic denique victor
             Trinacria finis Italos mittere relicta.

These omissions are followed by the omission of Aeneas' major motivation for the visit to Cumae. Helenus in fact warns Aeneas not to be persuaded to omit the visit (453–6) as if only his comrades' haste and desire to run a straight course would have stood in the way.

Is this to be interpreted as an 'inconsistency' which Virgil would have corrected in the final revision? Wholly aside from the great difficulty of taking 3 apart from 1 (could Virgil possibly have planned the narrative of 2 and 3 without having planned their setting in 1?), the omissions of Helenus are quite explicable in terms of 3 itself.[1] Clearly what Helenus avoids, as Aeneas later complains, is the prediction of Anchises' death. Thus the whole sequence of events which depend on his death (4, as we shall see presently, and 6) is omitted. Helenus, however, does in fact foresee (even though he does not foretell) the death of Anchises, as the abrupt termination of his brief speech (475–81) to Anchises indicates:

3. 480   'Vade' ait, 'o felix nati pietate; quid ultra
              provehor et fando surgentis demoror austros?'

The interpretation of these lines may, at first sight, seem open to doubt, but the sudden stopping of Helenus at this exact point has an ominous suggestiveness which is surely intentional. Anchises can now be *felix* only as the deceased father of a *pious* son. The ostensible excuse for Helenus' abrupt farewell is that further words would delay their voyage and make them miss the favourable winds; but the solemn: *vade, o felix nati pietate* is also meant as a prophetic valedictory.[2]

The Helenus-Andromache episode as a whole is intended to mark the strongest contrast between the two sets of Trojans and between the reactions of Aeneas and Anchises. Not only have Helenus and Andromache founded a new Troy (300 f., 349–55) but they have conceived it in terms of the past—as a memorial so to speak—rather than of the future. Aeneas encounters Andromache at the waters of a second Simois sacrificing to an 'empty' grave of Hector:

302   ante urbem in luco falsi Simoentis ad undam
           libabat cineri Andromache Manisque vocabat
           Hectoreum ad tumulum, viridi quem caespite inanem
           et geminas, causam lacrimis, sacraverat aras.

---

[1] See Appendix 9. The Helenus passage is clearly *meant* to be elliptical and ambiguous. Cf. 377 f.: pauca tibi e multis . . . expediam dictis; prohibent nam cetera Parcae scire Helenum farique vetat Saturnia Iuno. And later (461): haec sunt quae *nostra liceat* te *voce* moneri.

[2] Helenus carefully confines his advice *to Anchises* to the one statement (477–9) that he must leave Italy (Ausoniae tellus) as soon as he has reached it (**hanc** arripe velis. Et tamen hanc pelago *praeterlabere necesse est*).

Helenus' city in Epirus is clearly no new creation like Rome. There is no intentional mixture of the old and the new (Trojan and Latin) but mere reproduction of the old. Aeneas and his *socii* are here the future confronting the past. But the sight of this *Troia recidiva* is supremely affecting and even enviable to the nostalgic Aeneas:

492   Vivite felices, quibus est fortuna peracta
            iam sua; nos alia ex aliis in fata vocamur.
            Vobis parta quies, nullum maris aequor arandum,
            arva neque Ausoniae semper cedentia retro
            quaerenda.

Yet Anchises keeps urging the fleet to prepare for departure:

472   Interea classem velis aptare iubebat
            Anchises, fieret vento mora ne qua ferenti. (cf. 453)

even while (*interea*) Aeneas is receiving Helenus' elaborate presents (463–71) and obviously dreading the voyage ahead.

This contrast between Anchises, alert and forward-looking yet so close to the death which is elusively indicated throughout this scene, and Aeneas, young and vigorous yet overcome with emotion at finding this relic of his past, this replica of the old Troy, prepares us for the next section. The beginning of a new phase of Aeneas' journey is also the beginning of a new and far more anguished experience, the experience of loss and desolation, of life without Anchises. Anchises, the aged, has literally outlived the past and become the agent and emblem of the new, Roman *pietas*; Aeneas, however, so much younger and less mature, has still to overcome the powerful memory of Troy, the sense that it remains his spiritual home, ever pulling against his destined future. We are already beginning to wonder: how can he get along *without* Anchises?

(3) The *third* section (506–715) falls into three parts: the arrival at Italy and the turn toward Sicily (506–69); the episode of the Cyclopes (570–691); the death of Anchises (692–715). Each plays a special role in a really organic whole.

After a short voyage (506–20) Italy is sighted for the first time, obscure and low in the first light of dawn:

3. 521   Iamque rubescebat stellis Aurora fugatis,
           cum procul obscuros collis humilemque videmus
           Italiam.

The symbolism here is too evident to need extensive comment: the inchoative *rubescebat* (the dawn was beginning to redden), the lowness and obscurity, all emphasize the first, faint beginning of the new as well as its ambiguity and distance, the long way which separates their present stage of progress from the final goal. Supremely symbolic and full of hidden pathos is the role of Anchises here:

3. 523   Italiam primus conclamat Achates
Italiam laeto socii clamore salutant.
Tum pater Anchises magnum cratera corona
induit implevitque mero divosque vocavit
stans prima in puppi:
'Di maris et terrae tempestatumque potentes,
ferte viam vento facilem et spirate secundi!'

The energetic and directing initiative of Anchises now seems deliberately magnified. He interprets the meaning of the war-horses (*Bellum, o terra hospita, portas*), he bids them heed the warning of Helenus and avoid Scylla and Charybdis by the circuit of Sicily. Virgil thus enhances his vitality and responsibility as the moment of his death approaches.

The second part of this section (570–691), which separates Anchises' final and dominating *role* (in the discovery and temporary avoidance of Italy) from his death, is the Cyclopean (Achaemenides) episode. Why did Virgil insert this at just this point in the narrative? The facts that they had now reached Cyclopean territory and that the Cyclopes constituted an important incident of the *Odyssey*, are in no sense sufficient answers in themselves.

The Trojans find a harbour safe from the winds but full of the mysterious horror of the great volcano, Aetna:

3. 570   Portus ab accessu ventorum immotus et ingens
ipse, sed horrificis iuxta tonat Aetna ruinis.

They are awed by the terrible sight and sound:

3. 576   erigit eructans liquefactaque saxa sub auras
cum gemitu glomerat fundoque exaestuat imo.

In the night they sense and hear *immania monstra* which they cannot see (*nec quae sonitum det causa videmus*). Stars and sky are hidden in cloud: the *nox intempesta* covers the moon. Then on the ensuing day they encounter the moving and strange sight of the abandoned Achaemenides (*ignoti nova forma viri miserandaque*). What is stressed here is the horror and pathos of Achaemenides' lonely encounter with the *inhuman* and uncanny. He asks not safety or life but the recovery of human experience:

3. 653   satis est gentem effugisse nefandam.
            Vos animam hanc potius quocumque absumite leto.

The sight of Polyphemus enhances this impression. This is another *monstrum*:

            horrendum, informe, ingens.

The other Cyclopes reinforce the horror:

3. 678   Aetnaeos fratres, caelo capita alta ferentis,
            concilium horrendum.

Virgil, unlike Ovid who parodied this episode in his *Metamorphoses*, stresses the awful (*ingens*), the mysterious and *inhuman* quality of the Cyclopes. Achaemenides is the man whose homeward voyage has been tragically transformed; he is deprived of his *nostos* and condemned to a life among monsters whose presence seems to obliterate his very humanity. To him Anchises now offers the kindness of his pious nature:

3. 610   Ipse pater dextram Anchises haut multa moratus
            dat iuveni atque animum praesenti pignore firmat.

Achaemenides—rescued from his terrible isolation—then becomes their guide along the coast of Sicily:

3. 690   Talia monstrabat relegens errata retrorsus
            litora Achaemenides, comes infelicis Ulixi.

The meaning of this remarkable episode, clear as it seems, has apparently escaped the attention of commentators. It can, in fact, be understood only as a symbol of Anchises' death. For his death is the event to which this final section of the book (506–715) has been looking forward:

708   *Hic* pelagi tot tempestatibus actus
        heu genitorem, omnis curae casusque levamen
        amitto Anchisen: *hic me*, pater optime, *fessum
        deseris*, heu tantis nequiquam erepte periclis!
        Nec vates Helenus, cum multa horrenda moneret,
        hos mihi praedixit luctus, non dira Calaeno.

But these words of Aeneas literally recall the former words of Achaemenides:

616   *Hic me,* dum trepidi crudelia limina lincunt,
        immemores socii vasto Cyclopis in antro
        deseruere.

Both Aeneas and Achaemenides had been *deserted* in their hour of need by the one man on whom their safety and hope depended. In Achaemenides, therefore, Virgil, constructed his most poignant image of the thwarted *nostos,* and his most vivid exemplification of the difference, the pathetic contrast between Odysseus and Aeneas. Aeneas, of course, had already lost his home but, at least, under Anchises' guidance and paternal initiative, he had begun the quest of another. Now he was truly left to himself, left alone to confront the horrors of his elusive and terrible journey. What was the presence of Ascanius, the mere boy, or that of his *socii,* of whom in fact we have hardly been aware, in comparison with this loss? Anchises had boldly greeted the abandoned Greek (the treachery of Sinon was not to be repaid in the same coin) only to abandon, so shortly after, his own Aeneas! Now at last the ambiguity of the future—what no prophet could or would foretell—had resolved itself in an outcome exceeding all expectation. Aeneas had indeed been left alone in a world of *monstra.* Anchises, so it seemed, had assumed the initiative only to relinquish it in Aeneas' hour of peril. After the uncertainty, the *horrenda,* came now, worst of all, an utter desolation.[1]

Aeneas' narrative has thus revealed the nature of the man who was exposed to the passion of Dido and of his own heart. Book 4 takes up the action where it was left at the close of Book 1 but the hero's past revealed in Books 2 and 3 is an indispensable clue to the role he plays in 4. We can now look back and appreciate the mood of *terque quaterque beati.* The man who uttered those words had just been deserted by his father and conscience, Anchises. The hero who had been so dominated by fury and uncontrolled *dolor* during the Fall of Troy, and had been at best motivated by *pietas* toward his dying city and his own

[1] Achaemenides, so Heinze thinks (p. 112), is Virgil's own discovery: Dionysius (12. 22) describes a meeting of Aeneas with Odysseus himself. But Heinze, like other critics, fails to deal with the episode's *meaning* though this, surely, is not in the least doubtful.

family, had hardly had time to grasp the full significance of the
signs by which Jupiter had decreed another *pietas*, a wholly new
patria. Anchises alone had been truly converted, alone had
fully identified himself with fate. Compared to him, therefore,
Aeneas played a passive role in Book 3. Anchises' death thus
posed the crucial problem of the succeeding books: could Aeneas
supply the personal initiative, the self-generated *pietas* required
for the accomplishment of his arduous mission? The narrative of Books 2–3 has shown to Dido and to us the nature of his
destiny and the consequent impossibility of his denying it. But it
has also shown the *dolor* and *furor*, the black despair, the absence
of initiative, the dependence on Anchises, that together made
Aeneas so exceedingly vulnerable to all that Dido represented.

Book 4, however, seems, at first, only to carry on the emphasis
on Dido, the empathetic identification with Dido, that had
already been established at the end of Book 1. But the long
narrative had intervened and it is therefore with some sense of
shock that we turn from the Aeneas of Books 2 and 3 to the
Dido of the first line of 4:

> *At* regina gravi iamdudum saucia cura.

Why indeed is the emphasis of 4 so wholly, so almost exclusively
on Dido and *her* tragedy? Why does Aeneas, display such scant
initiative, give so much the impression of a man driven by
forces outside himself? We can make two answers which in a
final analysis amount to the same thing.

1. Dido is obviously an *alter Aeneas*. Like him she had a
mission to found a new city overseas; like him she had a special
pietas toward the dead (Sychaeus is, in effect, Dido's Anchises);
like him she was lonely and vulnerable. She is thus the great
example of *pietas* worsted by the *furor* of passion. She does what
Aeneas finally was saved from; she sacrifices her duty to her love.
But Virgil, by emphasizing her, by making her the empathetic
centre of the book, does not simply provide us with a contrast
to his hero and show us, in effect, the superior morality of
Aeneas. Indeed his concentration on Dido enables him to cover
Aeneas' own emotions with a kind of veil. The hero in his
moment of eclipse, is permitted to take the background and to
reveal his moral failure by passivity and silence rather than by
positive action and speech. This is unquestionably one reason

for Dido's prominence in the book: the faults of the hero are to
some extent covered by the overt violence of the heroine.

2. But there is another and a more fundamental reason for
Dido's prominence and Aeneas' passivity. It is that Aeneas'
absence of initiative in the book is itself a revelation of his
moral failure, of his *culpa*. He is caught and temporarily lost
in the tempestuous passion of Dido and in his own passion for
her; in this sense the book's domination by Dido is a clear index
of Aeneas' weakness. We see the true vulnerability of the man,
the real consequence of the loss of Anchises, his unreadiness
for a destiny that required initiative of the most resolute kind.
In short, the problem posed by Book 4 is precisely Aeneas'
eclipse, his passivity and weakness. Beside the positive violence
of Dido, he retains at least something of his heroic and even of
his pious identity. But, by the same token, he fails to be what he
has to be if he is really to lay claim to either heroism or *pietas*.

We need not repeat the analysis of the book given in chapter
iii above. All that we are concerned with here is the moral
situation of Aeneas. It is clear that Aeneas was overcome by
his passion for Dido and was, temporarily at least, unfaithful
to his mission. He really fell from grace, really ceased to be
pius. The attempt of some commentators and critics to deny
this (especially the reality of his passion for Dido) can hardly be
sustained by the text.[1] He was, as Virgil says he was, *magno . . .
animum labefactus amore* (395). It is only after we see him through
Mercury's eyes:

260   fundantem arces et tecta novantem

and arrayed in the garments Dido had embroidered for him
with her own hand—he was obviously enjoying something like
the status of a Carthaginian consort—that we are given for the
first time in the book an empathetic clue to his own feelings.
They are, clearly, feelings of guilty compulsion:

281   Ardet abire fuga dulcisque relinquere terras,
             attonitus tanto monitu imperioque deorum.
             Heu quid agat? quo nunc reginam ambire furentem
             audeat adfatu? quae prima exordia sumat?

---

[1] Cf. Cartault, p. 299: 'Ce que Virgile a emprunté à l'Odysée, c'est l'insensi-
bilité d'Enée etc.' to which Fiore and others have sufficiently replied. (Cf. the
discussion in Pease, pp. 45–47.) Pöschl thinks Aeneas shows *not* 'Liebesleidenschaft'
but 'Mitgefühl'.

His conscience has obviously been awakened by Mercury's harsh words (pulchram . . . uxorius urbem exstruis? &c.). He knows he must go: like any guilty man he wants to get it over, cut the troublesome emotions, do what he has to do without more words and tears. Finally, however, he does bring himself to speak to Dido: she, of course, will not hear reason; he is again much shaken, but nevertheless leaves her and obeys the gods. Now for the first time in the book he is called *pius* (392). But in what sense is he *pius?* The problem here can be simply stated: are Aeneas' feelings at this point those of a man who has fully recovered his *pietas*, fully mastered his past *culpa*, or are they, on the contrary, the index of an essential weakness that his hasty departure cannot cover or excuse?

This is the real issue of the Dido episode. It is essentially that of the meaning of the fourth book *in relation to the books that precede and follow it.* If we suppose that Aeneas could quickly and completely recover his *pietas* when the divine warning came, then we shall have to take Book 4 as a more or less self contained thing. Aeneas was *pius* before he met Dido (1. 305, 378), *pius* when he left her (4. 392), and what happened in between was a lapse whose effect had no further consequence.[1] Books 5 and 6, in that case, will constitute an essentially independent epilogue to Books 1–4 and our conception of the unity of the Odyssean *Aeneid* will be accordingly determined. We can settle the question only by considering what Aeneas said to Dido and how he acted thereafter.

Aeneas' single speech to Dido (333–61) presents us with one most significant fact. Even before the terrible message of Mercury and Jupiter, he had seen Anchises in his dreams:

351   Me patris Anchisae quotiens umentibus umbris
        nox operit terras, quotiens astra ignea surgunt,
        admonet in somnis et turbida terret imago.

This 'return' of Anchises is our first indication that Aeneas had not recovered from his death at the end of Book 3. He had in effect lost his conscience in losing his father: the recovery of conscience was, therefore, signalled by his father's 'return' to his dreams. Aeneas had simply lacked the strength of *pietas* to

---

[1] Perret (pp. 112 f.) for example takes Books 5–6 as mere *addenda* to 1–4, *addenda* that have no essential relation to what precedes.

stand up to Dido and his own passion: he was still, psychologically speaking, 'dependent' on Anchises. But even the
'return' of Anchises was not enough: the intervention of Jupiter
and Mercury was also required. The essential weakness of
Aeneas in this crisis is thus apparent: he had, at this point, to
be prodded and prodded again to do his duty and recover, in
some sense, his *pietas*. It would I think be most false to the text
to interpret the Mercury episode as a mere 'reflection' of
Aeneas' conscience: Mercury certainly appeals to his conscience and certainly reinforces his dreams, but he is also meant
to bring a genuine shock from the outside. When Aeneas says
to Dido:

358   ipse deum *manifesto in lumine* vidi
            intrantem muros vocemque his auribus hausi.

he is referring to a more than subjective experience. He is a
man who has heard the voice of fate and still trembles.

Furthermore, the moral situation of Aeneas is revealed in
every part of his speech to Dido. He says in effect: 'I cannot
possibly say all that is in me to say. I can never repay you.
I shall never, never forget you. In brief, I can only plead as
excuse (1) that I never undertook or promised marriage with
you; (2) that if I had had my own way (as I indeed have not had)
I would have stopped at Troy and rebuilt it. But Apollo and the
fates send me on to Italy: that is now my only possible *patria*.
If you have your own city, why cannot I have mine? I too have
the right to seek a home beyond the seas. Further, I cannot stay:
my father haunts me in my dreams, my boy Ascanius is being
deprived of his rights; finally Jupiter has warned me by his own
messenger. I saw the god himself in the plain light of day!
I heard his very voice! Don't then detain me longer. It is not
by choice I go to Italy.' There is nothing in this speech that is
not technically correct. But it is delivered to one who has no
use for technicalities. Furthermore, Aeneas has wholly failed
to take any account of Dido's and his own emotions. The
almost legalistic insistence on his non-promise of marriage, the
tacit supposition that she begrudges him a new *patria*, are in
fact the excuses of a man whose conduct is inexcusable except,
perhaps, on a purely emotional level. He should have avoided
excuses and taken his share of the blame. But his very inability

to do this, to acknowledge his own fault (though Mercury had clearly pointed it out to him) is an evident sign of his still-continuing weakness. He could, in his heart of hearts, face neither Dido nor himself.[1]

Nor could his renewed *pietas* (after 392) dispense with further divine warning. On that last night when Dido plots her own destruction and his too, he slumbers on the deck of his ship seemingly quite unaware of all danger, until Mercury rudely reminds him of his situation and his duty:

560   nate dea, potes hoc sub casu ducere sommos
           nec quae te circum stent deinde pericula cernis
           demens. . . .?

The fact, of course, that Aeneas did recover from his passion, did leave Dido, did, finally, stand firm like the oak (despite all his tears):

449   mens immota manet; lacrimae volvontur inanes

is something not to be underrated or forgotten. Aeneas, so similar to Dido, was also very unlike her. Whatever pity Virgil may have had for her (and he had much), he has left us in no doubt as to her *impietas* and *furor*. She had dreamed of Sychaeus (460–1) as Aeneas of Anchises, and with the same bad conscience. She fully recognized her crime:

550   Non licuit thalami expertem sine crimine vitam
           degere more ferae, talis nec tangere curas.
           Non servata fides cineri promissa Sychaeo.[2]

But the real tragedy was, in the last analysis, the turning of love into hatred. Her prayer:

621   Tum vos, o Tyrii, stirpem et genus omne futurum
           exercete odiis cinerique haec mittite nostro
           munera.

is the very triumph of *furor* over *humanitas*, and thus prefigures the later reversal of this triumph by Rome. Like Juno, she

---

[1] Paratore (*Virgilio, Eneide, libro quarto*, 1948) takes the speech as showing the 'superhuman strength' (sforzo sovrumano) of Aeneas! Compare this with the trenchant analysis of Francesco Arnaldi (*Studi Virgiliani*, pp. 85 f.) who says of Aeneas here: 'Accusa perché ha paura di se stesso.'

[2] Cf. on the exegesis of this disputed passage, Pease, *ad loc.* I follow him (and Ogle) in taking it to mean: 'I was not free (as you, my sister, thought) to live like a beast beyond the bonds of matrimony without thereby incurring the stain of moral guilt, etc.'

finally brought on the very result she abhorred. This is why Aeneas is finally and rightly the moral superior of Dido. It does not matter that he had advantages (his sex, the backing of fate, the Gods) that Dido did not have. The fact itself is clear. In a real sense he did recover his *pietas* without losing his *humanitas*. But he had not as yet overcome the weakness that this crisis had tested and shown to be all but disastrous. The reappearance of Anchises and, most of all, the intervention of Jupiter, were signs that he was as yet anything but self-sufficient, anything but ready for the ordeal in Latium.

The fifth and sixth books, from this point of view, must be considered the completion of the fourth. Because Aeneas was not yet prepared for Latium, he had to acquire both new experience and new knowledge. The sixth book is in fact the place where he does acquire these, but the fifth book is the place where we finally see *why* the acquisition was necessary and what its human cost was to be. It is here that Aeneas' weakness is driven home to him, as it was not in the Dido episode, and where the relation of this weakness to the task ahead, the Latin war, is finally made plain. Here the Aeneas who fled from Dido accepts the necessity of the journey to Hades. In this sense the fifth book is a direct continuation of the fourth. In another sense, however, the fifth is the deliberate opposite of the fourth: it is, like 3, an interlude between the intensity of the 'even' books that surround it. It is in some sense the pause that separates the tragedy of 4 from the ordeal of 6. But like 1, which it in many ways resembles, it prepares for calamity by an appearance of calm and of recovery from previous storms. The transition from the pleasant games to the ship-burning is abrupt and startling yet, looking back, we can see how this was really anticipated in the preceding narrative. The book is particularly remarkable for its effective recall of motifs from previous books (especially 2) and for its reference ahead to the following books (especially 9). It is in fact a most subtle and complex composition in which nothing is quite what it appears, at first sight, to be. There is an undertone of calamity in its joy; an undertone of joy in its calamity; and a final synthesis of both at the end.[1]

---

[1] Most commentary on this book is rather unhelpful. Best perhaps are Büchner (316 f., 352-8) and Giusto Monaco (*Il Libro dei Ludi*, 1957). The major mistake (in my view) of most treatments is their failure to see that it is *not* fundamentally a book about *games*. Heinze, I suspect, knew better but was unfortunately prevented from

It is most carefully designed. Indeed, its structure is in large part the key to its meaning:

I. Divine Prelude: Palinurus and the diversion of the voyage from Italy to Sicily (1–34)

II. The Anniversary of Anchises' death (35–603)
  (a) The Ceremony at the grave, the snake (35–103)
  (b) The games: contests (104–544)
    (i) The ship-race (104–285)
    (ii) The foot-race (286–361)
    (iii) The boxing match (362–484)
    (iv) The archery contest (485–544)
  (c) The *Troius lusus* (545–603)

III. The Burning of the Ships (604–778)

IV. Divine Postlude: Death of Palinurus (779–871)

I. The two central episodes (anniversary games, ship-burning) are surrounded by a prelude and postlude in which the gods appear and enact their will through the helmsman, Palinurus. The book is thus begun and closed by divine action: the human events are, as it were, divinely shaped. The first divine episode is in fact the symbolic key to the whole book: the second, as we shall see, provides the transition to Book 6.

The book begins with Aeneas at sea but glancing back toward the flames of Dido's pyre. He as yet only suspects the truth and certainly has no idea of the depth and extent of Dido's tragedy:

5. 4   Quae tantum accenderit ignem
          causa latet; duri magno sed *amore* dolores
          polluto, notumque *furens* quid femina possit,
          triste per augurium Teucrorum pectora ducunt.

But this *triste augurium* is immediately followed by the storm which hits the *Aeneadae* as soon as they reach the high seas. Palinurus sees that the very winds resist the course toward Italy, and that he must put back toward Sicily and the port of Eryx, where the Trojan Acestes lives and Anchises lies buried. He cannot contend with Fortune:

doing full justice to this book simply because he did not (in view of Norden's expected commentary on 6) concern himself particularly with the relation of 5 and 6. Büchner sees the book's relation to 6 but misses that to 4 though this is the whole point of the 'divine prelude' (ll. 1–34). Camps (*CQ* (1954), pp. 214–15 and 1959, pp. 53–56) acutely points out its correspondences with 9 but unfortunately does not deal with their *raison d'être*.

22   Superat quoniam Fortuna, sequamur,
         quoque vocat vertamus iter.

And Aeneas in turn welcomes the chance to return to the *ossa
Anchisae*: the winds demand it; to struggle against them is vain.
Thus the diversion from Italy and the 'return to Anchises' is
both fated and piously accepted. The symbolism here is
unmistakable: Aeneas' escape from Dido is also the renewal of
his bond with Anchises. He is not yet ready for Italy; the gods
therefore send him back to Sicily and Anchises. The consequence of his fall from grace in Book 4 is his return to the
'conscience' and father of Book 3. Yet the true meaning of this
fateful event is hidden from Aeneas: he imagines that his return
is nothing but an act of filial piety toward the dead. He sees
the hand of the gods:

56   Haud equidem sine mente, reor, sine numine divom
         adsumus.

But he sees them as interested solely in the *anniversary* of
Anchises' death.
    II. Thus, the whole anniversary section (35–603) is charac-
terized by a quite easy and relaxed *pietas*. Anchises is viewed
not as a living spirit and conscience but as an ordinary dead
man to be honoured by appropriate ceremony. The intent is
not to raise a ghost but to make it lie easy. In fact, Aeneas
displays some scepticism as to the real value of the rites:

80   salve, sancte parens, iterum salvete, *recepti*
         nequiquam cineres, animaeque umbraeque paternae!

The appearance of the snake at the tomb-ceremony (84 f.),
however, is the first indication that things are not quite what
they seem. For the snake with its glistening sheen (incendebat
fulgor) like that of the rainbow, and its innocent motion:

92   libavitque dapes rursusque *innoxius* imo
         successit tumulo et *depasta* altaria liquit.

clearly recalls the lambent flame that encircled Ascanius at the
close of Book 2:

2. 683   *fundere lumen* apex, tactuque *innoxia* mollis
         lambere flamma comas et circum tempora *pasci*.

We note in both places the light, the innocence in threatening garb, the gentle contact, the fear succeeded by reassurance.[1] The snake is surely Anchises in a typical form of the dead[2]—the uncertainty expressed (incertus geniumne loci famulumne parentis esse putet) is, however, a revelation of the ambiguity in Aeneas' mind—but it is also an Anchises identified with the omen that had led him from Troy to Sicily. For the moment, however, he accepts the role in which Aeneas sees him and remains the benevolent genius of his tomb: he is now very different from the *turbida imago* that had troubled Aeneas' dreams at Carthage. The recall of the omen of 2 seems for the moment to have merely a *recollective* significance.

The anniversary games that follow the ceremony, thus take place in the relaxed and innocent atmosphere of a simply memorial occasion. Their model is, of course, the twenty-third book of the *Iliad* (the games for the dead Patroclus) and they thus constitute the only episode of the Odyssean *Aeneid* that is strictly Iliadic. Why is this? It is at the very least suggestive that this book (5) recalls the later, 9 (an integral part of the Iliadic *Aeneid*), in great detail. There are, in fact, six important parallels between the two books:

1. Both contain an intervention of Juno *via* Iris (in 5 directed to the Trojan women; in 9 to Turnus).
2. Both contain an attempted ship-burning miraculously stopped.
3. Both contain an exploit of Ascanius (*Troius lusus*, killing of Numanus).
4. Both contain a premature attempt of Ascanius to act as an Aeneas-substitute (in 5 with the Trojan women, in 9 as the *patron* of Nisus and Euryalus).
5. Both contain a Euryalus-Nisus episode.
6. Both contain episodes involving Mnestheus (the ship-race, archery contest in 5; defence of the gate against Turnus in 9).

There is thus no doubt that Virgil planned the parallelism of 5 and 9.[3] In particular, the important role of Mnestheus in

---

[1] Knox (*AJP* (1950), pp. 379–400) sees the similarity of the passages but misses the reason for it.　　　　　　　　　　　　　　[2] Cf. Monaco, op. cit. p. 64.
[3] See Appendix 9 and pp. 344 f. below.

T

the ship-race and his somewhat lesser role in the archery
contest prefigure his importance as chief defender of the camp
against the incursion of Turnus (9. 778–814); the episode of
Nisus and Euryalus specifically anticipates their *aristeiai* and
tragedy later on (9. 176–502). The games, in other words, are
as it were 'pre-views' of martial prowess to come and thus
anticipate the impending struggle in Latium. The equestrian
manoeuvres of Ascanius and the other Trojan boys—the *Troius
lusus*—are explicitly referred to as *pugnae simulacra* (585). In
Iliad 23 the various heroes exhibited in games the spirit and skill
they had already shown in the fighting; here we see the situation
reversed, the future heroes of the Latin War exhibiting in
games the qualities they are about to show in war. Thus Virgil
deliberately anticipates the Iliadic future in this otherwise
Odyssean narrative.[1]

But the games also anticipate the future in a much more
direct and literal sense. The first two (the ship-race, the foot-
race) involve Aeneas' Trojans only and, as we have just seen,
look ahead to the martial exploits of the particular heroes
(Mnestheus, Nisus, Euryalus) involved. But the last two contests
(the boxing-match, the archery contest) are centred on the
Sicilians, Entellus and Acestes. Furthermore, the games are
arranged in a kind of emotional crescendo so that the last two
and, particularly, the last of all (the archery contest) constitute
the climax of the series. The ship-race is obviously the most
relaxed and genial of the set: it is full of youthful competition
and (an unusual thing in the *Aeneid*) of broad humour (as in
the description of Monoetes' rough handling by Gyas).[2] The
foot-race is still a contest of youths but is dominated by the
affection of Nisus for Euryalus in a way that cannot but arouse
melancholy thoughts of their tragedy to come. But the boxing-
match wholly rises above the level of juvenile competition and
shows in the humiliation and recovery of the aged Entellus,
in the respect shown for him by Aeneas, and in the divine aura
and past Sicilian glory with which he is invested, a quite new
solemnity and seriousness of purpose. The hand of the gods

---

[1] See Appendix 9, p. 419. Books 5, 6, 7, 8, 9 clearly form *one* group related by the
theme of the Latin War. The crisis (ship-burning) of 5 *relates* the indecision or
weakness of Aeneas (already revealed, of course, in 4) to the impending war. The
question is now: has he the courage and fortitude for the great test ahead?
  Cf. chap. iii, p. 59 above.

seems once more visible, as Aeneas recognizes when he withdraws Dares from the fight:

465   'Infelix, quae tanta animum dementia cepit?
       non viris alias conversaque numina sentis?
       cede deo.'

But the gods—indeed Jupiter himself—are made completely
manifest in the final and culminating archery contest. The
contest in fact is won when Eurytion, the Trojan, shoots the
dove in mid-air (Mnestheus' shot had already released it from
the mast). But Acestes shoots anyway into the clear void as if
only to exhibit his skill and 'sounding bow'. He is, as it were,
singled out as 'hors de combat', above the rest, like Aeneas
whose prominence he has in fact shared from the moment of
Trojan arrival at Sicily. We are thus prepared for the omen that
comes to him, the arrow's metamorphosis into a flaming comet:

525   Namque volans liquidis in nubibus arsit harundo
       signavitque viam flammis tenuisque recessit
       consumpta in ventos: caelo ceu saepe refixa
       transcurrunt crinemque volantia *sidera ducunt.*

There has been a good deal of scholarly debate as to the significance of this omen [1] though its relation to Acestes and to his
future role as founder of Acesta (the colony designed for the
women and those too tired and weak to go on to Latium and
the impending war) seems unmistakable. But it has also a clear
reference to Anchises and distinctly recalls his *augurium maximum*
of Book 2:

2. 693   de caelo lapsa per umbras
       stella facem ducens multa cum luce *cucurrit.*
       Illam, summa super labentem culmina tecti,
       cernimus Idaea claram se condere silva
       signantemque vias.

Thus the arrow-omen corresponds to the brilliant snake as the
augurium maximum of the comet corresponds to the Ascanius
flame in Book 2. Anchises' 'return' is indicated and confirmed
(though Aeneas does not realize it at the moment). All this, of
course, is predicated on the ship-burning, the event which is at

---

[1] Cf. Monaco, op. cit. pp. 107–10. All the exegetes (Plüss, Heyne, Wagner,
Deonna, Piganiol, Longi, &c.) miss the designed parallelism with the comet-omen
of Book 2.

once the *raison d'être* of Acesta and the direct cause of Anchises' reappearance, no longer as a mere dead man but as an active spirit who can revive and fortify his son's *pietas* at the moment of crisis and despair.

So the coming catastrophe is foreshadowed in the very midst of apparent hilarity. The *Troius lusus*—the *sumulacra pugnae* put on by Ascanius and the boys—now marks the interval between the comet-omen and the foreshadowed event, the ship-burning. It would have been most inappropriate for Virgil to have let the one follow directly upon the other. And the Trojan game in itself also looks ahead, but this time to the Augustan future, to its re-establishment under Augustus at the very climax of all Roman history as Virgil conceived it. The contrast, the shock effect, of the ship-burning is thus dramatically enhanced.

III. The crisis comes suddenly:

604 Hinc primum Fortuna fidem mutata novavit
   Dum variis tumulo referunt sollemnia ludis,
   Irim de caelo misit Saturnia Iuno.

The mention of Juno is, of course, the clue to what follows. Here, as at the cave in Book 4 and in the storm of Book 1, she intervenes to divert Aeneas from his goal, and thus to thwart the will of Jupiter and the Fates. On these three acts of Junonian hatred, depends the whole of the Odyssean *Aeneid*. Each is followed by an evident declension or eclipse of the hero's *pietas*: the despair of *terque quaterque beati*, his uxorious passion for Dido, and his even more dangerous forgetfulness of duty here. And these in their turn are followed by counter-interventions of Jupiter: the missions of Mercury in Books 1 and 4 and of Anchises here. But the very fact that in these crises (the first is, as we have seen, proleptic and symbolic, a kind of pre-view of the major crises in 4 and 5) Aeneas needed to be reminded by an emissary of Jupiter is, as we have also seen, a sign of weakness. As the narrative approaches the really great test, the Latin War, the question becomes more and more one of his adequacy to meet it. Juno's supreme act of intervention is manifestly her use of Allecto to provoke the war itself (Book 7). And this is the real test of his *pietas* (and indeed of his other great qualities as well) precisely because his problem here is not to escape or withdraw (as in 2, 4) but to endure, to depend on his own strength and fortitude. At the end of 4 we do not really know whether Aeneas can meet this test even though we strongly suspect that he cannot. We do not therefore know, or at least sufficiently know, whether the ordeal of the sixth book is really necessary. It is the intervention of Juno here, at the end of 5, which gives us the answer.

Juno's minion, Iris, disguised as the aged Beroe, finds the women together (while the men are off at the games) weeping for the lost Anchises and regarding the deep sea before them. Their mood is that of Tennyson's lotus-eaters:

> Hateful is the dark-blue sky
> vaulted o'er the dark-blue sea.
> Death is the end of life; ah, why
> should life all labour be?

5. 615
> Heu tot vada fessis
> et tantum superesse maris, vox omnibus una.
> Urbem orant, taedet pelagi perferre laborem.

And the false Beroe repeats the very theme of the *terque quaterque beati*: O miserae, quas non manus ... Achaica bello traxerit ad letum *patriae sub moenibus!*[1] Wretched *not* to have died at Troy! The women, nevertheless, do not actually set fire to the ships until Iris sheds her disguise and reveals her divine form: tum vero attonitae monstris *actaeque furore* conclamant ... rapiunt ... ignem. So closely do the human and divine *furores* resemble each other yet retain after all their separate identities: the women by themselves were not bold enough to commit so demonic an act.

But the despair which thus manifests itself in overt fury is not confined to the women. Yet it is not so much Ascanius and the other Trojan men; it is Aeneas himself who shares their weakness. The initial reaction of Ascanius, the first to reach the spot, is an almost comical exhibition of precocious *pietas*: quis furor iste novus? he demands and with a cry of 'En, ego vester/Ascanius' dashes his mock-helmet before their feet. He attempts in his immaturity to act like his father but his father belies the imitation. When he comes, he prays to Jupiter *either* to quench the flames *or* to slay him with a thunderbolt. But when Jupiter immediately answers his first wish and sends a

---

[1] Cf. 1. 94 f.: o terque quaterque beati quis *ante ora patrum Troiae sub moenibus altis* contigit oppetere!

downpour sufficient to save the ships, Aeneas quite fails to grasp the significance of the divine action. He sees only the four lost vessels and begins to despair of his whole enterprise:

700   At pater Aeneas *casu concussus acerbo*
nunc huc ingentis, nunc illuc pectore curas
mutabat versans, *Siculisne resideret arvis*
oblitus fatorum, Italasne capesseret oras.

Here it is not Aeneas who encourages his men (as at 1. 198–208); it is one of his men, the hitherto unknown prophet Nautes, who encourages or tries to encourage Aeneas:

709   Nate dea, quo fata trahunt retrahuntque sequamur;
quidquid erit, superanda omnis fortuna ferendo est.

Nautes sees that the loss of the four ships will require a rigorous elimination of the women and the aged, all who are wearied of action, all the weak and timid, *quidquid tecum invalidum metuensque pericli est.* He accordingly predicts the founding of a new city, Acesta, in which Acestes can settle and rule these unreliable Trojans. But even such advice and prophecy does not remove Aeneas' uncertainty:

719   Talibus incensus dictis senioris amici
tum vero in curas animo diducitur omnis.

This then is the crucial moment. Night has now come and Anchises' form (facies) seems suddenly to slide from the heavens and address Aeneas:

724   Nate, mihi vita quondam, dum vita manebat
care magis, nate, Iliacis exercite fatis,
imperio Iovis huc venio, qui classibus ignem
depulit et caelo tandem miseratus ab alto est.

The *augurium maximum* of Book 2 is once more recalled: *caelo facies delapsa parentis* (5. 722) is a phrase reminiscent of the *de caelo lapsa per umbras stella* (2. 693). *There* Anchises was, so to speak, commissioned by Jupiter to go with Aeneas toward the New Troy. *Here* he is commissioned by Jupiter (imperio Iovis) to bring Aeneas back to his duty. In Book 4 he had been only a *turbida imago* preceding and foreshadowing Mercury, the actual messenger of Jupiter. He now plays both roles: both that of the father or father-image and that of Jupiter's direct agent. The reason for his new status is at once revealed. He confirms the advice of Nautes and *now* gives the true reason for the elimination of the weak and the unwilling:

729   lectos iuvenes, fortissima corda,
     defer in Italiam. *Gens dura atque aspera cultu*
     debellanda tibi Latio est.

But *before going on to Latium*, Aeneas must come to Anchises in the underworld:

731   Ditis tamen ante
     infernas accede domos et Averna per alta
     congressus pete, nate, meos.

Why is this? Anchises' only explanation (737) is that Aeneas will then be shown his future race and walls: genus omne tuum et quae dentur moenia.

But we can easily read between the lines (and are surely intended so to read) the true reason for Anchises' strange request. Only the relatively small number of brave and tried fighters are to be taken to Latium: exigui numero sed bello vivida virtus (753); the spiritless and unambitious (animas nil magnae laudis egentes) are to be left behind in the new Acesta. The burning of the ships has revealed the danger and the burden entailed by the presence of the weak and the timid, of all who lacked heart for the great test to come. Yet Jupiter here, as before, has woven catastrophe into the very warp of Fate and made Juno serve the very cause she defies. The loss of the four ships compels the selection and concentration of forces necessary for the rigours ahead. But what applies to Aeneas' whole company, applies *a fortiori* to himself. He who had been so weak in disaster, so forgetful of his destiny (*oblitus fatorum*, a unique phrase applied to Aeneas only in this one instance) was *also* not ready for the Latin War. The women had only expressed the same despair he himself had expressed in the *terque quaterque beati*. *Before* he could go on to Latium, he had to learn a lesson, grasp, as he had not yet grasped, the true nature of his mission and of the *pietas* on which the destiny of the Roman race was to depend. The whole sequence of events in this book—the initial change in the winds that brought Aeneas back to Anchises, the omens (snake, arrow-comet) that heralded both the future role of Acestes and the 'return' of Anchises, the ship-burning which both prepared the Trojans for future war and provided colonists for Acesta—had been divinely shaped: Aeneas, however, had quite failed to understand either the will of Jupiter or his own obligation. But even this weakness is made part of the divine plan: we now see that the return to Anchises in the underworld is to be the decisive event that will prepare Aeneas for Juno's greatest effort and his own greatest test.

The fact is that up to this point Aeneas had failed at every great crisis. He had of course been rescued each time by Jupiter but such rescues were after all the index of weakness, not strength. He had not stood on his own feet: the loss of Anchises had in fact meant disaster, for Aeneas had not as yet found any equivalent of Anchises within himself. Now on the eve of the supreme crisis (Allecto), he needed to be reborn, remade, enabled to exercise *pietas* not as something enforced from without but as something renewed from within. This is the most fundamental meaning of Anchises' demand for their reunion in the underworld.

We must not, however, misinterpret the meaning of such 'failure'. It would indeed be a fatal error to suppose that Aeneas had not ever been a true hero or truly *pius* before the *catabasis* of 6. The point is that he is fated to become something wholly extraordinary in the way of heroism and *pietas*. His failures have been those of a brave and pious man who had not yet, however, reached the new heights required for his task in Latium; he had not yet, in fact, shown the quality of a true *theios-aner*. The man who fought so bravely at Troy, endured such hardship to save his father, son and *socii*, and, above all, did comply with Fate each time its voice spoke really clear, was in Virgil's eyes both brave and *pius*. But he had not yet reached the perfection of *pietas* that a 'divine-man' should possess.

IV. The book closes (779–871) with a postlude in which the gods, as in the prelude (1–34), show their hand in shaping the destiny of Aeneas and the Trojans. The two sections (I and IV, see plan, p. 271) obviously correspond. In the first Palinurus heeds the divine will expressed by the *wind-storm* and urges the return to Sicily; in the second Palinurus is made the victim that Neptune demands for his *calming of the waters* during the Trojan voyage to Italy:

815   unum pro multis dabitur caput.

Palinurus is the sacrifice that ensures Aeneas' safe arrival at the gate of Avernus: tutus . . . portus accedet Averni (813). Aeneas' underworld journey is thus preluded by a living offering—a death for the life (his own) that Aeneas will bring back from death.[1] In another sense, Palinurus' death is the sign that Aeneas' long voyage has reached its close: the faithful helmsman is no longer needed; Neptune can now claim him for himself. And Neptune is, of course, re-enacting his role of calmer of the sea that we last witnessed in Book 1. Venus and Neptune come, as it were, once more to undo the work of Juno: their task, however, is in no sense the equivalent of Jupiter's; Aeneas has already been rescued from the real crisis of the book. This, so to speak, is but a rounding out of the process that began with the sea-storm. (The reference back is to both the storm of Book 1 and the wind-storm of the prologue just above.) And, in a more general sense, Palinurus himself is the sacrifice for all the Trojans; he is the *one* who dies for the *many*. This is the law of patriotic devotion which we shall see at work throughout the Iliadic books to come. Finally, the mood of this episode—at once dark, quiet and mysterious, full as it were of the drowsiness of death—prepares us for the *nekuia* to come.

The hero's descent to the underworld of the dead had thus been ordered: the ordeal itself remained. He must not only go down: he must also reascend. He must undergo the death out of which alone rebirth could come. Virgil's problem in the sixth book was to express the theme of death and resurrection—the unifying theme of both *Eclogues* and *Georgics*—in terms appropriate to his hero's mood and situation. Mythology and philosophical doctrine had to be transmuted into an intelligible human experience. This required the most careful and elaborate manipulation of symbols. Both the details and the general architecture of this remarkable book are meticulously designed. We must *first* note the essential plan:

---

[1] Palinurus, however, is *not* an offering in the same sense as Misenus in Book 6. Palinurus is the one who dies for the many (pro multis)—for the success of the whole enterprise (including Aeneas). Misenus is the type of the *profane*, of the pollution incurred by ordinary (non-sacrificial) death and thus of the purification by which Aeneas escapes the lot of the *profani* and becomes able to return. He is, in other words, a sacrifice (the parallel and prelude of the proper *piacula*—black cattle) to Hecate and the underworld deities (see p. 288 below); Palinurus is a sacrifice to the *superi* (Neptune in particular) and thus the pledge of their aid.

I. Preparation (1–263)
II. The descent: the Mythological Hades (264–547)
    (*a*) Entrance, the *Vestibulum* (264–94)
    (*b*) The hither side of the Styx (295–383)
       (i) The *insepulti* (295–336)
       (ii) Palinurus (337–83)
    (*c*) Crossing the Styx (384–416)
    (*d*) Between the Styx and the fork in the road (417–547)
       (i) Preliminary view (417–49)
       (ii) Dido (450–76)
       (iii) *Arva ultima:* Deiphobus (477–547)
III. The Left-hand Road: description of Tartarus (548–627)
IV. The Right-hand Road to Elysium (628–78)
    (*a*) *Moenia Ditis:* deposition of Golden Branch (628–36)
    (*b*) Elysium (637–78)
V. The Philosophical Hades: the Valley of Lethe and the souls of future Romans (679–892)
    (*a*) The meeting of Aeneas and Anchises (679–702)
    (*b*) The theory of reincarnation (703–51)
    (*c*) The show of the Heroes (752–892)
VI. The reascent: the two gates (893–901)

I. *The Preparation* (1–263)

The subject of this section, which in itself is a veritable chef d'oeuvre, is the hero's preparation for the descent or *catabasis* into the underworld. It ends with his actual entrance of the cave that leads into the *vestibulum* of Hades. The Sibyl precedes; Aeneas boldly follows after:

262   furens antro se immisit aperto;
         ille ducem haud timidis vadentem passibus aequat.

The elaborate preparation for this bold departure was of course designed to ensure the hero's return or, to use a stronger word, resurrection. To go down to Hades was easy; the coming back was the difficulty. In other words: death had to be countered by a principle of life or rebirth. These are, therefore, the two main motifs of this section—ordinary or profane mortality and extraordinary immortality. For the hero's 'immortality', in this sense, is represented as a quite special thing; he is one with the very few—Hercules, Orpheus, Pollux, Theseus—who have gone down and come back. And he is unlike even these in that he alone carries the sign of Fate itself (*fatalis virga*; cf. the Sibyl's colloquy with Charon, 399 f.). But the *catabasis* is none the less a terrible ordeal (insanus labor), the most terrible indeed of the whole Odyssean *Aeneid*, and could not have been undertaken without the active desire of Aeneas himself. Rightly does the Sibyl refer to his great *amor* and *cupido* (Si tantus amor . . . tanta cupido bis Stygios innare lacus, &c.) and point him out to Charon as an astounding *pietatis imago*. But even so Aeneas was not yet perfect in *pietas*: the note of *destiny* and of its inexorable schedule had to be sounded many times before he would heed and wholeheartedly obey. The Sibyl is here the very incarnation of Fate, the interim conscience who supports and guides the hero in the last stages of his 'return' to the father who is also now a fate-figure, wholly identified with the destiny of Rome.

The 'preparation' section thus introduces all these motifs— fate, death, rebirth, the ordeal, the *pietas*, the schedule of destiny, the interim conscience—and binds them together in a wonderful crescendo that rises from the landing to the *catabasis* itself. Most scholars [1] and critics, have, unfortunately, directed their attention to the single, apparently disparate strands out of which the section is composed, such as the 'golden bough' and the Misenus story; the Sibyl's mingled roles of *priestess* of Apollo, *vates* or seer, and *catabasis* guide. Then there is the apparent indifference of Aeneas to the 'prophecy' which he has ostensibly come to hear; the seeming irrelevance of the door-reliefs at the very start of the book. Once however, we grasp the structure and movement of this section, its dramatic whole-ness, its essential meaning as one tremendous *preparation*, we can easily see the artistic necessity for all the seeming disparities. It is a continuity composed of five rather distinct parts:

1. (1–13) Landing.
2. (14–41) The temple-doors.
3. (42–97) The prophecy.
4. (98–155) The conditions to be met.
5. (156–263) The conditions fulfilled.

The landing (1) at once separates the hero from all the rest: they are rejoiced to be finally in Hesperia

---

[1] Cf. for example, Norden's commentary on all these points.

5   iuvenum manus emicat ardens
       litus in Hesperium

but Aeneas is only conscious of his ordeal:

9–11   *at* pius Aeneas arces quibus Apollo praesidet . . .
       Sibyllae antrum immane petit.

So—the cardinal distinction between the holy man of destiny
and the *profani* is first adumbrated.

But Aeneas is detained by the wonderfully sculptured doors
of the temple of Apollo (2). Here, voluminous and learned
commentary has greatly obscured a most significant episode.
What Aeneas sees is the work of Daedalus, done just after his
escape from Minos and Crete. The subject is appropriately the
minotaur and labyrinth: on one side, the crime of the Athen-
ians and its punishment, the yearly sacrifice of their youth to
the Minotaur; on the other, the Minotaur story itself—the
atrocious *amor* of Pasiphaë, the terrible, tangible evidence of her
love, the labyrinth in which it was concealed, and finally the
pity for the love which made Daedalus present Pasiphaë with
the thread that could lead her to her dreadful offspring.[1] The
work is full of sentiment and passion even though Daedalus'
paternal heart did not permit him to finish a representation
of the ill-fated Icarus.

It seems plain that the labyrinth in some sense symbolizes
the underworld, the Kingdom of the Dead,[2] and the terrible
and guilty secrets hidden within it. But it symbolizes also,
just like the 'mythological' part of Hades itself (as we shall see),
the labyrinthine past and its hidden contents. Aeneas here, as
in the closely analogous scene of Book 1, gazes at his own past,
though this time at his past symbolically disguised. He sees the
Veneris monumenta nefandae; he sees love possessed of a talisman
that can lead it to its dreadful hidden result; he sees, in other

---

[1] The commentators seem agreed that the *regina* of l. 28 is Ariadne but *regina*
applies much more naturally to Pasiphaë and the whole passage refers to her. It is
but human that she should want to see her terrible child (Veneris monumenta
nefandae) and that Daedalus should pity the poor mother.

[2] On this cf. P. J. Enk, 'De Labyrinthi imagine in Foribus Templi Cumani
inscripta' (*Mnemosyne*, 1958, pp. 322–30). He refers to a quotation of Varro in
Pliny's *Natural History* (XXXVI. 91) about a labyrinth built into the tomb of the
Etruscan Porsina. Here also the rare word *inextricabilis* occurs. The labyrinth thus
suggests death, the underworld from which it is difficult to get out without a
thread or talisman (Varro, as quoted by Pliny, says: quo si quis introierit *sine
glomere lini* exitum invenire nequeat).

words, the mingled horror and pity, the nostalgia and pain of passion brooding over its guilty secret. For here, unlike the scene at the Juno temple of Book 1, he sees and pities not his heroic but his erotic past. He knows in his heart of hearts that he is no Orpheus; his talisman is to be the emblem of fate, not love; his object of quest is not Dido, but Anchises. He is however fascinated and forgetful of the time—quin protinus omnia perlegerent oculis—and has to be warned by the Sibyl:

37   non *hoc ista* sibi *tempus spectacula* poscit.

Thus is he for the first time apprised of the *schedule of destiny* and of its inexorable demands: the contrast between *ista spectacula* and *hoc tempus* is indeed the contrast between past and present, love and duty, empty recollection and the insistent urgency of fate. The Sibyl has from the start assumed the role of a reminding conscience.

Now comes the prophecy proper (3), for which in one sense he is prepared. But his real object, of course, is to go down to Hades and rejoin Anchises. He has no more need of violent and ambiguous vaticinations: he is now at last in Italy and has resigned himself to the necessity of the war in Latium. It is indeed not prophecy as such, but the sheer presence of the God, of Apollo, and of Apollo as the mouthpiece, the ratifier of Fate, with whom Aeneas is here concerned. Before he can accost the Sibyl *in propria persona*, as his future guide to the underworld, he must treat with her as the mere instrument of the god. 'Poscere fata tempus' ait: 'deus ecce deus': she is literally filled with the divine *afflatus*: maiorque videri nec mortale sonans, adflata est numine quando iam propiore deo. Aeneas is stricken dumb at the presence and has to be aroused to the etiquette demanded: 'cessas in vota precesque, Tros' ait 'Aenea? cessas?' But what he prays for is *not* prophetic information but the *assent* of the divine will: da—non indebita posco regna meis fatis— *Latio considere Teucros.*[1] The god's answer, spoken *through* the Sibyl (fera corda domans) and re-echoed from the hundred doors of the huge cavern, is an exceedingly bleak and ambiguous

---

[1] In other words: 'Grant me the fulfilment of my destiny.' Aeneas does *not* therefore say: 'Tell me what my destiny is.' He is at no point in this episode interested in further prophecy. This has not been clearly understood (cf. Büchner, Servius, Norden ad loc.) because the unity of the whole section has not been clearly understood.

testimony (horrendas . . . ambages) almost recalling that of Calaeno herself: in regna Lavini Dardanidae venient . . . sed non et venisse volent. But Aeneas has now heard the very word of fate: he has obtained all he asked—the direct *confirmation* of his destiny by Apollo himself.

All this, however, is but preliminary to the next part (4). It is not the dreadful *prophecy* that Aeneas needed to hear (non ulla laborum, o virgo, nova mi facies inopinave surgit) but how to get to his father—*ire ad conspectum cari genitoris*. The divine accolade has now been delivered; fate has spoken; the over-arching imminence of the Latin War has once more been made manifest. It is time for the *furor* to quiet and the 'still small voice' to speak. Here, just as in the very different story of Elijah at Horeb, the thunder and fury of the 'divine' presence give way to a silence (cessit furor et rabida ora quierunt) which is the climax of the scene, a climax made all the more impressive by the deliberate contrast with the preceding commotion. The voice is *now* that of the Sibyl herself: she is still a *sacerdos* but is no longer a mere mindless mouthpiece of the god; now she is once more the august guide and conscience of the hero; she can dispense with the god's *afflatus* that constituted, as it were, her credential, and speak, as Aeneas requested, with her own voice (ipsa canas oro). There is no antithesis or mixture of roles here; the Sibyl speaks with the god's voice and then with her own; she acts as *vates* and as guide; but both functions express the same essential relation to the god, to fate and to Aeneas.[1]

But Aeneas in his request for admission to the underworld (103–23) dwells far more on his own affection for Anchises than on the *mandata patris* (116) or the commands of Jupiter. He who has undergone so many ordeals, is now ready for the great-est of all, but it is not fate; it is love and filial piety that motivate him. He also sees in such morally dubious and highly personal exploits as those of Hercules,[2] Orpheus, Pollux and Theseus,

---

[1] Cf. J. H. Waszink, 'Vergil and the Sibyl of Cumae' (*Mnemosyne* (1948), pp. 43–58). He sees a conflation of three Sibyls (Cumae, Troy and Cimmeria mentioned by Naevius, Piso and Varro respectively), but the point is: why and with what purpose did Virgil 'conflate' or 'contaminate' his sources? The Sibyl is perfectly comprehensible, indeed dramatically inevitable, in terms of Virgil's own narrative.

[2] 123: 'quid memorem Alciden?' The distinction between Aeneas and these others is made clear in Charon's speech at the crossing (388–97) and in the Sibyl's reply (399 f. nullae hic insidiae tales). Aeneas, *unlike them*, is a *pietatis imago* who

the proper precedents for his undertaking: et mi genus ab Iove summo. His point of view is obviously *pious* and praiseworthy but he quite fails to grasp the unique difficulty of his projected *catabasis* and, especially, its unique relation to fate. The Sibyl's first words touch the heart of the issue:

126   Tros Anchisiade, facilis descensus Averno—
               noctes atque dies patet atri ianua Ditis—
               sed *revocare gradum* superasque *evadere* ad auras,
               hoc opus, hic labor est.

Death is easy: the return from death—resurrection—is the hard thing. There are therefore two conditions for success in this ordeal: the passport, the golden-bough that only *he who is fated* (si te fata vocant) can pluck; and the *piacula* (sacrifice of black cattle) that he must perform for Misenus whose sudden death has polluted the whole fleet (150). In other words, there are *ordinary death* (Misenus) and *life from death* (the golden bough); the one is the *facilis descensus*, a thing easy even for the profane; the other is the reward of very special purification, *opus* and *labor*.

The last part (5) of the Preparation Section contains the execution of these two commands or conditions. The fact that Sibyl foresaw Misenus' death (or knew of it before Aeneas could) confirms her words about the as yet undiscovered bough and connects the two conditions in one process of fulfilment. Thus Aeneas is led to the bough while he supervises the cutting of wood for Misenus' pyre. Meanwhile (*interea*, l. 212) the Trojans go on with preparations for the funeral, perform the appropriate lustrations: finally Aeneas (with the bough) rejoins them and erects the imposing tomb. *After this* (l. 235) he sacrifices the *piacula* (black cattle) to Hecate, Erebus, Dis and Proserpina. And the sacrifices are potent. The groaning of the ground, the motion of the woods, the howling of dogs, signal the arrival of Hecate herself. At that, the Sibyl warns back the

carries the *fatalis virga*. The *piety* and the *fatality* of his *catabasis* put him in a quite different category. This distinction becomes even clearer in the seventh book when the parallel with Heracles (Euripides' Heracles) is carried further: Aeneas, unlike Heracles, cannot be made mad by Juno's (Hera's) agent (Allecto, Lyssa). Heracles' underworld journey just precedes his terrible madness: Aeneas' *catabasis* has given him a divine invulnerability to such infection. It is Turnus, not Aeneas, who is made mad and, even then, only by the release of his own *furor* for which he is, therefore, rightly held responsible. Cf. pp. 324 f. below.

other or *profane* Trojans (procul o procul este profani) and guides Aeneas on his way to the underworld.

It seems plain on the face of it that the death and burial of Misenus are an integral part of the preparation. When the Sibyl says of the dead Misenus:

152   sedibus hunc refer ante suis, et conde sepulchro,
         duc nigras pecudes, ea prima *piacula* sunto

she is obviously referring to the black cattle as purificatory offerings for the death (Misenus') which has polluted the fleet: this sacrifice is really meant to be part of the burial ceremony. Later, however, the black cattle are sacrificed directly to Hecate and the underworld gods without *apparent* reference to Misenus (243 f.). The conclusion is almost inescapable that Misenus' polluted death is a symbol of the soiled mortality common to all the *profane* (those who have not been purified and initiated into the mystery that protects them from death or gives them life from death) and that Aeneas, both by the piacular sacrifice and by the power of the life-giving branch, is made ritually pure and capable of withstanding death. In another sense, perhaps, Misenus' death is itself a sacrifice (but, unlike Palinurus', a sacrifice to Hecate and the infernal powers) and represents the exchange of a life for a life: his own life for that of Aeneas.[1] The bough, of course, is the regenerating plant of the mysteries and fertility cults. We need not here rehearse all the folklore and ethnographical data as to revivifying plants or trees (like, e.g. the mistletoe to which the golden bough is actually compared in l. 205). The main and crucial point is that the whole passage recalls an initiation or mystery with both sacrificial purification and the offsetting of mortality by a magic life-giving talisman.[2]

But what needs to be insisted upon is the delimitation of the magic. The golden bough is a *fatalis virga*, metallic, unique, and

---

[1] Fletcher (Virgil, *Aeneid VI*, 1941) interprets rightly here: Norden, ad loc., would separate the *piacula* of this line (153) from the burial-injunctions preceding. The 'erroneous' mixture of the *piacula* (actually a *catabasis* ceremony) with Misenus' burial, he attributes to Virgil's imitation of Circe in the *Odyssey*. But we simply cannot ignore the obvious sense of the line. Norden did not see that Virgil *intended* the connection of the *piacula* with Misenus.

[2] Cf. Norden, ad loc. and Kerenyi (*Hermes*, 66 (1931), pp. 411–41), but especially Servius ad v. 136: licet de hoc ramo qui de sacris Proserpinae scripsisse dicuntur, quiddam esse mysticum adfirment . . . ramus enim necesse erat ut et unius causa esset interitus: unde et statim mortem subiungit Miseni: et ad sacra Proserpinae accedere nisi sublato ramo non poterat.

cannot be broken off by any but the appointed few (the divine-men) who are fated to carry it.[1] Aeneas and the Sibyl *alone* are not profane: all the rest are warned back from the approaching *numen* of Hecate. Aeneas' initiation, his *catabasis* and reascent, are thus special signs of his heroic and divine status, and of the *pietas* which, here as before, is the human side of fate. He is fated to pluck the bough but he also influences the gods and even fate itself by his unique devotion to Anchises. What we come back to again and again in this book is the heroic ordeal: the Sibyl, like a conscience, is ever reminding Aeneas of the courage it requires: *nunc animis opus, Aenea, nunc pectore firmo.*

II. *The descent: the Mythological Hades* (264–547)

The plan of the Underworld that this book clearly pre-supposes is relatively simple but of great symbolic significance. We can represent it approximately thus:

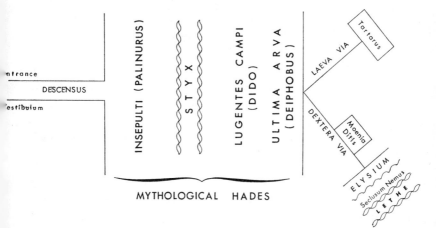

The river Styx separates the *insepulti* from the *sepulti*. Between the Styx and the fork in the road (ubi se via findit in ambas, 540) lies the *mythological Hades* proper (as we might call it) which is essentially the same as that of Homer and obviously reminiscent of it, though Homer of course does not actually take Odysseus *through* it, as Virgil takes Aeneas. The fork goes two ways (left and right), to Tartarus and Elysium respectively. The centre of Hades, as Virgil seems here to envisage it, is at

---

[1] See note, on p. 220.

U

the palace of Dis (with its great Cyclopean walls) not far along the right hand road. Beyond this and deep in Elysium is the secluded grove and valley of the river Lethe where Anchises and Aeneas review the souls awaiting rebirth: this is clearly the *philosophical Hades*. Actually Elysium proper and Tartarus play a minor role in the book: it is the mythological Hades and the Lethe valley that take up by far the most space (284 and 214 lines respectively or 498 altogether out of a total of 638, after the Preparation Section) and clearly hold the centre of attention.

The essential symbolism here is quite unmistakable.[1] The mythological Hades represents Aeneas' past in the reverse of the temporal order: here he meets first Palinurus, second Dido, third Deiphobus (a hero of dying Troy). Virgil thus recalls Books 5, 4, 2 in that order. The Homeric setting of these heroes (Palinurus, Dido, Deiphobus) does not in the least diminish their predominance. But it does account for their preoccupation with the *past*: they, like the shades that met Odysseus, are simply ghosts of their former selves, reliving their days on earth with no apparent future or occupation beyond one of empty recollection. They can therefore stand for the dead past that Aeneas leaves behind him. It is very different with the souls of the philosophical Hades: they have no ostensible past (so far as we are explicitly told) and will in any event forget their past when they quaff the Lethe water before their approaching reincarnations. They obviously stand only for the *future*. When, therefore, Aeneas passes from the mythological Hades (before the road fork) to the Lethe valley he is also passing from past to future, from death to new life.[2] It is his ultimate identification of himself with the future that constitutes the psychological meaning of his resurrection (as we shall see). But it is relatively easy to grasp the significance of his viewing of the future. What is much more difficult to understand is the effect upon him of the past, or why his passage through the past was apparently deemed by Virgil to be an essential preparation for his experience of the future.

[1] Cf. here my article, 'Three Problems of Aeneid 6' (*TAPA* 90 (1959), pp. 165–79). Norden, in his commentary, was so concerned with the sources and the religio-philosophical schematism of Virgil's underworld that he quite missed its literary, poetical and even Roman meaning.

[2] An analogous distinction of past and future is made in Book 8, the 'correspondent' of 6 in one of the two schemes of correspondence of books according to which Virgil designed the *Aeneid*. Cf. p. 217 above and pp. 331 f. below.

At any rate, it seems clear that Virgil conflated two quite different conceptions of the life after death (roughly the Homeric and the Platonic) in order to indicate the two times— the past and the future—with which his hero was effectively concerned. Virgil was seemingly not interested in reconciling the obvious contradictions between the two conceptions. The Homeric shade fixed, so to speak, in an unchangeable past or moment of the past, has almost nothing in common with the souls of the Myth of Er and with their busy forward-looking life of punishment, instruction and reincarnation. Nor is it helpful to reconcile the discrepancy by ingenious hypotheses. What we must find out first is Virgil's purpose in using the inconsistent systems or why he wanted to juxtapose past and future in this rather odd way.

(*a*) (264–94). The first part of Aeneas' ordeal in the mythological Hades may be called his encounter with unreality. Our first impression of Hades is one of vacuity and emptiness:

268   Ibant obscuri sola sub nocte per umbram
            perque domos Ditis *vacuas* et *inania* regna.

The shades of the *vestibulum* or entrance are horrible personifications—*Senectus, Metus, Fames, Egestas*—or traditional Monsters, Centaurs, Chimaeras, Gorgons and Harpies. But Aeneas is warned by the Sibyl to put up his sword: they are merely thin bodiless things, hollow images that flit about; to fight them is to fight shadows. This is really much like the dream world of the third book: it is dangerous only to him who thinks it so.

(*b*) (295–383). There is in fact no real difficulty in the descent to the Styx. The true ordeal begins at the river and the crossing. Here sincere emotion replaces empty fantasy; here are no unreal monsters but dead human beings. First of all, the pathos of the dead, especially the young and immature dead, is enhanced by their numbers: quam multa in silvis . . . lapsa cadunt folia. But the most striking thing to Aeneas is the pathos of the unburied, those who strive so vainly to cross the Styx and yet must remain for a hundred years on the hither bank. When he learns their sad lot from the Sibyl, he is temporarily overcome by this insight into the stern law of the underworld:

331   Constitit Anchisa satus, et vestigia pressit
            multa putans, sortemque animi miseratus iniquam.

But the pathos of the *insepulti* as a whole is reinforced by the instance of Palinurus (337–83). Virgil in fact is not primarily concerned with the *insepulti* but with Palinurus himself—that is, with Aeneas' own past—but he deliberately sets the individual within a general context. Palinurus is a faithful friend and servant of Aeneas but is nevertheless bound by the same law that governs all the unburied. His conversation with Aeneas is obviously designed to lead up to his final request: that Aeneas should, as it were, smuggle him across the Styx:

370   da dextrum misero et tecum me tolle per undas.

Palinurus makes this bold suggestion—for it is offered only on the supposition that Aeneas is in touch with the divine will, *numen divom*—at the end of an account of his own pathetic death. It is quite clear that his story here does not gibe with the corresponding part of Book 5 (this is a discrepancy that Virgil would certainly have ironed out in revision)[1] but the important point is that Palinurus' death was in accordance with the plan of the gods in both versions (in 5 Neptune and Venus co-operate in his death; in 6 Apollo's prediction is made good). That either he or Aeneas can now change the divine law is obviously an impious, if unconsidered, idea; the Sibyl answers before either can speak:

373   unde haec o Palinure *tibi tam dira cupido*?

The gods act in their own way and in accordance with Fate, as the Sibyl now reminds Palinurus (desine fata deum flecti sperare precando). He cannot disobey the law of the *insepulti*: nevertheless his *pietas* toward Aeneas will be remembered and divine prodigies will bring about his burial: for all time his name will be connected with the site of his tomb. This lesson in both divine law and divine clemency, in the inexorability and the justice of fate, is obviously meant primarily for Aeneas. The Sibyl in answering Palinurus, instructs Aeneas. He begins to see the inexorability and the justice of his own destiny.

The episode is the first of three modelled on or, more accurately, developed from, scenes of the eleventh *Odyssey*. Palinurus corresponds to Elpenor, as later, Dido corresponds to Ajax and Deiphobus to Agamemnon. But the difference between Elpenor

[1] See Appendix 9, pp. 417 f.

and Palinurus is far more important than the similarity: the religious significance of the unburied state, the special meaning of Palinurus' death, the divine motivation of his burial, above all the tension between his human desire and the inexorable law that binds him—all are lacking in Homer.

(c) (384–416). All this has been preliminary: Aeneas has, however, had his first lesson in the rigid rules of the place and of the fate that governs it. He now crosses in Charon's boat after the Sibyl has stilled Charon's objections by pointing out that Aeneas is no Hercules, Theseus or Pirithous, engaged on some questionable exploit, but a *pietatis imago* who carries the *fatalis virga*. Here, as before, *pietas* is the obverse of *fatum*.[1]

(d) (i) (417–49). We pass quickly by Cerberus (whom the Sibyl easily pacifies with a soporific morsel) into the region of the true or central Hades where the dead have taken their proper position and will apparently remain forever in gloomy reminiscence of their former lives. We see first the prematurely dead—infants, the falsely condemned, suicides—and then come to the fields of mourning (lugentes campi) where

442   quos durus amor crudeli tabe peredit
         secreti celant calles

and where, among the other victims of love, is Dido herself. Obviously, as with Palinurus before, the general scene is depicted only as background to a specific individual in Aeneas' past.[2] But Dido is a far more important part of that past and Aeneas' encounter with her is invested with just as great a burden of meaning as his later encounter with Deiphobus, the symbol and image of his lost Trojan homeland.

(d) (ii) (450–76). In one sense the Dido episode of this book, like that of Palinurus and the Deiphobus episode to come, is a reminiscence of the eleventh *Odyssey*: Dido, like Ajax, preserves a haughty silence; Aeneas, like Odysseus, cannot be forgiven. But this undoubted reminiscence is also most striking evidence of the fundamental difference between Virgil and Homer. The Ajax of the *Odyssey* was no vital part of Odysseus'

---

[1] See pp. 286 f. above and n. 2, p. 286.

[2] Paratore (*Virgilio*, 3rd edn., 1961), pp. 357–8, supposes the whole Dido episode (ll. 450–76) to be a later insertion! But the whole point of the 'mythological Hades' is to introduce these three major scenes each of which has its appropriate 'model' from *Odyssey* 11. On Paratore's theory of the *Aeneid*, cf. Appendix 9.

past and he makes no other appearance in the whole poem. He is but one of several ghosts that meet Odysseus. Nor is Odysseus especially bothered by Ajax's behaviour. He might, he says, have followed him to Erebus and talked him out of his anger but he preferred to stay where he was and chat with the other shades. Virgil, however, took the essential ideas of an hostility persisting after death and of silence as its most effective expression, and made them into an intense drama of the relation between a man's present and a man's past, and of what happens when a man confronts his past.

The episode starts with a quite un-Homeric simile, that of a man who sees or thinks he sees the new moon rising through the clouds:

451   Quam [i.e. Didonem] Troius heros
       ut primam iuxta stetit adgnovitque per umbras
       obscuram, qualem primo qui surgere mense
       aut videt aut vidisse putat per nubila lunam.

This is taken from Apollonius (*Arg.* IV. 1477–80) who so describes Lynceus' vague vision of the long-lost Heracles. But Virgil applies it to a quite different end: it is not the uncertainty of Dido's presence that he primarily wishes to convey (for she does, after all, emerge from the obscurity as Heracles did not) but, rather, the feelings of a man who cannot quite believe his own eyes or accept the sudden removal of doubt as to what he has feared, but not certainly known. This idea is conveyed by his tears and by his very first words:

456   infelix Dido, verus mihi nuntius *ergo*

So then it was true! Now for the first time he realizes what he had done. He tries to explain: it was against *his* will he left her; he was then, as now, the hapless agent of the gods:

461   sed me iussa deum quae nunc has ire per umbras
       per loca senta situ cogunt noctemque profundam,
       imperiis egere suis.

Nor could he have believed that she would do such a thing. But Dido will make no answer: she averts her gaze and keeps a rock-like silence. Then she quickly withdraws to the spot where she and Sychaeus have been forever rejoined. Aeneas can only follow her into the distance with his weeping eyes: the encounter is brief because she will not permit it to be prolonged.

This passage assuredly compresses much in very little space. Its great importance, for the book and for the poem as a whole, is its revelation of the irrevocability of the past. Here Aeneas sees both what he had done (and did not yet realize) and *what he cannot undo*. His attempt at explanation, at reconciliation, is rejected and rejected in a manner that is far more cutting than any of Dido's tirades in the fourth Book. She, indeed, does not so much reject as ignore Aeneas; she has in effect reverted to her past life with Sychaeus and deliberately put Aeneas out of her consciousness. But this very act, especially her rock-like silence, is of course also an expression of irreconcilable hatred—the hatred into which her wounded love has now turned. She is far beyond the possibility of being moved by Aeneas' tears or sympathy. He, for his part, had quite failed to realize the full depth of her passion; he now sees that it has not only killed her, but fixed her in an unappeasable, unalterable enmity both to himself and to that phase of her life in which he had been concerned. Now he sees that he can never hope to smooth out the part of his past that Dido represents, to ease his troubled conscience by receiving her forgiveness. He can only accept the *fait accompli*. Up to now, Dido represented in some hidden sense a guilty hindrance, an emotional counter-weight to the destiny he so reluctantly followed: he *now* sees that there is no way back, that he cannot ever come to terms with a past that rejects him, that he cannot have his cake and eat it—have Dido's forgiveness, the easing of his own guilty conscience, *and* his Roman destiny. He must accept the full penalty that his *culpa* of 4 has exacted, and, in mature acknowledgement of past weakness, go on toward his future destiny.[1]

(*d*) (iii) (477–547). The next phase of his journey through the mythological Hades is also the last: the *ultima arva* to which dead heroes and, above all, his dead Trojan comrade, Deiphobus, are assigned. Deiphobus represents a quite different aspect of his past from Dido. He is the human image of dead

---

[1] Cf. T. S. Eliot (*What is a Classic?* (1944), p. 21) on this episode. His comments that Dido acts 'as Aeneas' conscience would expect', that 'what matters most is that Aeneas does not forgive himself' are I think quite true and very well put. But it is this act of confrontation that shows Aeneas where he stands with Dido as he could not have been shown otherwise, i.e. without this *special* traumatic experience.

Troy, of all that Aeneas had lost and left and to which he most of all desired to return, as his first words in the epic (terque quaterque beati) and his later words to Dido (4. 340 f.) had so pathetically shown. Here again the contrast with Homer is significant: Agamemnon in the *Nekuia* (*Odyssey* 11) is the 'model' of Deiphobus in much the same sense that Ajax is the model of Dido. But in the *Odyssey* the contrast is between the two homecomings, between the good Penelope and the wicked Clytemnestra, between the fortunes of the two heroes themselves. Agamemnon's evil *nostos* is, so to speak the foil, the contrast to Odysseus' successful *nostos*, both here and elsewhere in the *Odyssey* (e.g. in the speech of Zeus at the council of the gods of Book 1 and at the arrival of the suitors in Hades in Book 24). Deiphobus is, on the contrary, the symbol of all the violence and treachery that attended the destruction of Troy—the very proof, so to speak, that Aeneas can never go home.

Deiphobus is seen as part of a company of dead warriors, Trojans and Greeks, who still retain their former shapes and equipment:

484   tris Antenoridas, Cererique sacrum Polyboeten
        Idaeumque etiam currus, etiam arma tenentem.

But they are reliving a past which is dead and gone. Their volatile and fragile bodies cannot withstand the challenge of a real man: when the Greek shades see Aeneas, they tremble, flee and raise a feeble cry (vocem exiguam). The unsubstantialness of this dead world reinforces the impression of its unreality: this past is but empty nothing. Deiphobus himself exhibits only the horror of his ignominious and treacherous death: he is so dreadfully mangled (laniatum corpore toto) that Aeneas can hardly recognize him. His story recalls everything that was wretched and ignominious in the fall of Troy. Even so his only occupation is remembering it: et nimium meminisse necessest. Yet Aeneas cannot tear himself away from this sorry replica of his past. Had the Sibyl not intervened, he would have spent all his limited time in idle reminiscence with him: et fors omne datum traherent per talia tempus. But he has now come to the fatal fork in the road, the line of demarcation that ends the land of the past, the mythological Hades, and points on to the future. He must proceed, as the Sibyl insists: nox ruit Aenea:

nos flendo ducimus horas. And it is here Deiphobus who comes to his friend's aid:

544   'ne saevi magna sacerdos;
               discedam, explebo numerum, reddarque tenebris;
               I decus, i, nostrum: melioribus utere fatis'.
               Tantum effatus et in verbo vestigia torsit.

The symbolism is plain beyond any possibility of doubt. Aeneas, even though he sees the emptiness and desolation, the ignominy and futility of his Trojan past, cannot quite break away from it. He lingers in it at the very moment and turning point that divides the past from the future. But his weakness, his false nostalgia for the past, is cured by his very experience of it. Deiphobus, in himself turning his back on Aeneas, has done all the past can do for the future and shown, in the clearest way, that the living future is the past's only proper continuation; even to *him* it is Aeneas, *decus nostrum*, not the pitiful shades of dead Trojans, who now represents the glory of Troy.

The difference between Dido's and Deiphobus' partings with Aeneas must not be neglected. Dido's presence and behaviour come to Aeneas as a shocking experience: his very inability to prolong the encounter constitutes its sting. This is the hostile, guilty past that he now knows can never be assuaged but only accepted. On the other hand, Deiphobus is, after all, the image of Troy and, in this sense, of Aeneas' own nostalgic goal. That Deiphobus himself should second the Sibyl and take the initiative of parting, *should turn his back*, is the clearest sign of where Aeneas' and Troy's true destiny now lies—in the future, in Rome. Aeneas has thus endured his greatest ordeal, that of re-encountering his past and leaving it behind him. Not until he had faced and left the unappeased guilt and empty nostalgia of his old self, could he be ready for the realities of his future.

III *and* IV. *Tartarus and Elysium* (545–678)

These sections deal with Tartarus and Elysium proper. Both places are set between the mythological Hades (which ends at the *ultima arva*) and the Lethe valley where Anchises is. Both are summarily treated and constitute an obviously secondary part of the narrative. But they both illustrate one important point that Virgil is plainly concerned to make: the rule of justice by which all human life is bound—the sure allotment of punishments and rewards. Aeneas had just seen the futility of a false attachment to the past: he now sees the stern morality that judges the past, the inexorable law to which the dead are held accountable:

618   Phlegyasque miserrimus omnis
           admonet, et magna testatur voce per umbras:
           'discite iustitiam moniti et non temnere divos.'

But Tartarus is exactly countered by Elysium where the good shades receive their reward. Here are patriotic heroes, chaste priests, pious prophets, discoverers of new arts—all who by merit have made themselves memorable: quique sui memores aliquos fecere merendo. Aeneas has thus been brought from the personal and particular to the general, to the rule that subsumes all past actions and individuals in one iron principle of justice. This is also a necessary preparation for his future: he sees now that human weakness is without excuse, that there is no exception.

In an aesthetic or literary sense, of course, the interlude between the fork in the ways and the Lethe Valley is designed to raise and heighten the narrative tone—to give greater depth and seriousness to the action. We pass from the personal pathos of the mythological Hades to the almost impersonal majesty of Tartarus and Elysium: we are so prepared for the solemn philosophy and idealism of Anchises. But Virgil carefully avoids putting too much emphasis on what is, after all, an interlude and especially avoids dissipating the effect of that 'schedule of destiny', that rigid time-table against which Aeneas' hesitation and reluctance in the preceding scene with Deiphobus have been so saliently delineated. He does not visit Tartarus but only *hears about it* from the Sibyl: though her account is fairly long (66 lines), it does not unnecessarily delay the action itself. On the other hand, the deposition of the bough at the citadel of Dis (635–6) and their journey through Elysium proper (666–78) are described with a brevity that indicates the Sibyl's haste to get on to Anchises. Now that the bitter journey through the past has been accomplished, now that Aeneas has finally been goaded to the point of actually achieving it, too much time has been lost, too much is yet to be done, to permit any delay. The harsh part of the ordeal is now over. The terrible passport is delivered, for its work has been done; Aeneas has now survived death, survived the emotional pull of the re-encountered past, and is ready for the future and for resurrection.

V. *The Philosophical Hades* (679–892)

(a) (679–702). Here in the Lethe Valley, the *seclusum nemus* so carefully separated from Elysium proper, Aeneas finds Anchises wholly engaged in viewing and enumerating the vast company of the souls (his *nepotes*, the future Romans) about to go up again to the light above—*lustrabat studio recolens*. Anchises is here what he had so suddenly become at the end of Book 2, the aged survivor of Troy converted by Jupiter's omens into the ancestor and prophet of Rome. He, concentrated on the future, on his *nepotes*, is the decisive contrast to Dido and Deiphobus. They represented the past in which Aeneas had so longed to linger despite the rigid schedule of his destiny. Anchises represents his future, points it out to him, enlists once more, but now decisively, his *pietas* in the Roman destiny to come. We now see how much Anchises has been the 'conscience' of Aeneas, how this re-encounter represents the climax of Anchises' reiterated actions as the ever-insistent father image: his words—

690   sic equidem ducebam animo rebarque futurum
       tempora dinumerans, nec me mea cura fefellit.
       quas ego te terras et quanta per aequora vectum
       accipio! quantis iactatum, nate, periclis!
       quam metui ne quid Libyae tibi regna nocerent!

—express a concern that Aeneas has only too keenly experienced:

695   Tua me, genitor, tua tristis imago
       saepius occurrens haec limina tendere adegit.

But this re-encounter is no mere renewal of a human tie. When Aeneas actually tries to embrace the shade of his father, it repeatedly slips from his grasp:

700   Ter conatus ibi collo dare bracchia circum;
       ter frustra comprensa manus effugit imago,
       par levibus ventis volucrique simillima somno.

For Anchises' role is not to restore the past himself as a real father on earth—all *that* is vanished forever—but to point out the future, to redirect Aeneas' feelings from the time that is gone to the time that will come.

(*b*) (703–51). Before the heroes are 'shown' and named, Aeneas is given an explanation of reincarnation itself. The souls at the bank of Lethe (qui complerint agmine ripas) obviously recall the souls at the Styx (huc omnis turba ad ripas effusa ruebat); here as there, Aeneas asks for an explanation of the sad phenomenon. Why should these celestial spirits long for human bodies?

721   quae lucis miseris tam *dira cupido?*

The question is crucial. Aeneas is not merely anxious; his whole emotional being is revolted. To one so filled with the sadness and bitterness of life, this desire to live again seems all but incomprehensible. Anchises' answer (722–51) is of course only a restatement of very well-known doctrine: much has been written of its sources but there is really little here that Virgil could not have gotten from the Myth of Er and countless reflections of this and other Platonic myths in middle-platonic and neo-pythagorean writings. The dualism of body and soul, the contamination of the soul by the body, the necessity of a long post-mortem purgation, eventual reincarnation with temporary oblivion of former existences, were all part of a very well established ideology. Virgil's primary reason for using it here was to provide an explanation of the show of future Roman heroes. Just as Homer's (the Mythological) Hades gave him a frame for Aeneas' past, this gave him one for Aeneas' and Rome's future. Any attempt to find consistency in this double-faced conception of the after-life, this combination of mythological and philosophical sources, is obviously quite futile: Virgil's underworld is an emotional and psychological, not a consistently logical whole. But the philosophy is *also* an answer to Aeneas' question and from this point of view it has a decided relevance to the mood of the moment and of the whole book.

The 'answer' is in one sense disappointing. We are given no *reason* for the whole procedure of reiterated reincarnation save that the god ordains it (deus evocat). We are not told (as we are in Plato, in middle and neo-platonic philosophy, and in Indian treatises on *samsara*) that its end and *raison d'être* is an eventual spiritual perfection or union with the divine.[1] The purpose of Anchises' philosophical disquisition is not in fact *religious* so much as it is patriotic and Roman. The solemn philosophy seems to be used only because it reflects the majesty of Rome as Homeric mythology could not. Nor does Virgil have any inkling of a philosophy in which concrete history, particularized temporal events, are in themselves the necessary preliminaries of a religious *eschaton*. He uses platonic dualism—a philosophy in which the body and all its temporal-material conditions are heavily discounted—in order to validate an essentially *historical* scheme of values. It is to Rome, Augustus, the *imperium sine fine* that he points as the goal, the true meaning of human action and *pietas*. His gods, or the stoic fate they symbolize, have a Roman orientation. He is not apparently at all concerned with the subsequent or post-Roman reincarnations of these heroes, although the platonic scheme logically demands it. But the rigorous moralism of the philosophy does reflect and reinforce the moralism of Rome:

739   Ergo exercentur poenis veterumque malorum
       supplicia expendunt: aliae panduntur inanes, &c.

The new Roman souls are products of a severe purification:

742   infectum eluitur scelus aut exuritur igni;
       quisque suos patimur manis.

Each suffers for his own sins, endures his own appropriate purgation.[2] The Roman hero is no ordinary man but a purified soul. He has died to live again but not to live again the old impure life. So too, by analogy and example, does Aeneas here undergo death and purification in order to be reborn as another, a truly Roman hero.

(*c*) (752–892). Anchises' speech that points out and briefly characterizes the future heroes of Rome, is, as has often been remarked, a *logos parainetikos* or *protreptikos*, a hortatory address that uses examples (*paradeigmata*) to reach formal moral conclusions at the end of each division or section (principally at

---

[1] Cf. Norden, pp. 10–48. There is a good discussion of Orphic-Pythagorean doctrines of the after-life in W. K. C. Guthrie, *Orpheus and Greek Religion* (2nd edn. (1952), pp. 148–93).
[2] Cf. Norden and Fletcher, ad loc. 'Each of us endures his own purgatory, the purging of his own spirit' probably comes close to the real sense of l. 743.

806–7, 847–53; secondarily at 822–3, 832–5).[1] There are three *major* divisions or sections:

1. (756–807): Romulus and Augustus
2. (808–53): The Greatness of Rome
3. (854–86): Marcellus

Essentially, the last two sections point toward or anticipate the Iliadic *Aeneid*. The famous and crucial definition of Rome's moral purpose (*Excudent alii*, &c., 847–53) and the description of Marcellus as the very type of heroic Roman sacrifice, are, as it were, the texts on which the last six books of the poem are based. The first section (756–807), on the contrary, points the present moral toward which Aeneas has been directed throughout the whole of his underworld journey. The strictly 'pre-Roman' stage of Roman history (the Alban kings, the older Italian cities) is followed by a panegyric of Rome's founder, Romulus, and of Rome's *other* founder, Augustus:

791   Hic vir, hic est, tibi quem promitti saepius audis,
           Augustus Caesar, Divi genus, aurea condet
           saecula qui rursus Latio regnata per arva
           Saturno quondam . . .

And Augustus is represented as greater than another hero of Rome—Hercules, or even than Bacchus, in his universal domain and glory. He is in other words the divine man, the *theios-aner*, who by his deeds achieves divinity. He is thus the last of a trio of *theoi-andres* connected with Rome: Hercules and Romulus have preceded him but by no means excelled him in glory. For he will restore peace to a world at war, restore the *Saturnia regna*, the age of gold. Aeneas is obviously one of this series, a fourth, he also designed to be a *theios-aner*. His mission, his duty are thus now and for all time, clear:

806   Et dubitamus *adhuc* virtutem extendere factis,
           aut metus Ausonia prohibet consistere terra?

The *adhuc* clearly implies: *until now* there may have been room for hesitation and recalcitrance; can there be any longer in the face of such *exempla virtutis?* Here Aeneas has finally seen the true *telos* or goal, finally realized what it means to be the Augustan prototype. There can be no further faltering.

[1] See Norden, ad loc.

With this moral (806–7) the major purpose of the sixth *Aeneid* is accomplished: Aeneas has been finally brought out of the past, to moral duty and his future. He accepts at the hands of his father and conscience, his now unmistakable personal destiny. But the show continues: this is not anticlimax but foreshadowing of what is to come, an indication of what it really means to be a Roman hero and thus a key to the future account of the Roman hero in action (Books 7–12). The second division of Anchises' speech (808–53) depicts the Roman kings after Romulus, Brutus with the heroes of the early Republic, and the great men of Rome's prime (the Scipios, Mummius, Aemilius Paulus, the *Fabii*, the great *Cunctator*). The unfortunate opponents of the Civil War, Pompey and Caesar (826–35), are skilfully put in the middle of the list, as if apparent exceptions to an otherwise undivided patriotism. The moral of 847–53 (*Excudent alii*, &c.)[1] is thus given the aspect of an appeal to the pre-civil-war Rome, as re-embodied, so to speak, in the Augustan present. We shall revert to this moral in the context of the Iliadic *Aeneid*: it of course gives added power to Aeneas' reborn *pietas*, generalizing the lesson of all the *exempla* that have preceded.

The Marcellus passage, though obviously subsequent to his death in 23 B.C., is no mere appendage. Virgil would almost certainly have conveyed the same idea through another *exemplum*, had not Marcellus died when he did. (It is even possible he reworked an earlier draught after Marcellus' death.) For he did not wish to close on a note of triumph and exultation.[2] His last word is characteristically one of *humanitas*, of the human price of empire and the lesson in moderation that this imposes:

870   Nimium vobis Romana propago
        visa potens, superi, propria haec si dona fuissent.

Marcellus thus prefigures the similar heroes of the last six books: Pallas, Lausus, Euryalus, Camilla. The ordeal of empire is based on sacrifice, especially sacrifice of the young. Otherwise, the destructive influence of *hybris*, inhuman pride, could not have been avoided. We shall see, later on, how the

---

[1] See the discussion of this on p. 314 f. below and esp. n. 1, p. 314.
[2] See chap. viii, pp. 391 f. below.

Iliadic *Aeneid* depends for much of its substance and vitality on the Marcellus motif. Aeneas is now prepared to face and accept the tragedy of his mission. What in the last analysis makes the *Aeneid* so much more than a piece of Roman propaganda, is its mitigation of success by accepted tragedy. The Marcellus ending is in this sense typically Virgilian (as are also the endings of Books 4, 10 and 12).

It is only after all this that Anchises gives Aeneas explicit directions for his conduct in Latium (888–92): *quo quemque modo fugiatque feratque laborem*. This is no otiose addition but a necessary return to the theme for which this book and the whole Odyssean *Aeneid* is preparatory: the Latin War. *Now* the *question* of line 806:

> dubitamus adhuc virtute extendere viris?

has become sober *fact: incendit . . . animum famae venientis amore* (889).

VI. *The reascent: the two gates* (893–901)

Aeneas leaves the underworld through the ivory gate (the gate of false dreams, *falsa insomnia*) rather than through the gate of horn (the exit of true shades). The reason for this preference has been often, and perhaps vainly, discussed.[1] He is clearly not a shade. Is his underworld experience nothing then but a false dream? Perhaps the best explanation that can be given is that *falsa insomnia* is a phrase here used to suggest that his experience is not waking reality or literal truth. The whole thing is in the deepest sense enveloped in mystery. There can be no doubt of its reality for Aeneas' understanding of himself and of Rome. But he had, as it were, gone out of ordinary time, out of the factual present, to encounter the past and the future, the dead and the yet-to-be-born. The encounter demanded a realm of experience beyond experience, a realm cognate with both death and sleep. At the end of 5 we saw how death came to Palinurus in the guise of sleep: here Aeneas escapes death through the gate of sleep. Both the gate of dreams and the gate of death (true shades) are set side by side: perhaps, then, Virgil

---

[1] Cf. again my article cited above (p. 290) where various theories of the two gates (Everett, Highbarger, Rolland, Brignoli, &c.) are briefly summarized and discussed.

is suggesting that sleep, like death, can communicate the secrets of an underworld into which no waking consciousness can enter and which, therefore, never quite gives up the *literal* or *full* truth about itself.

So closes the book that completes and ends Aeneas' preparation for Latium. It sums up the whole Odyssean *Aeneid* while laying the basis for the whole Iliadic *Aeneid*. In its combination of recollection and prophecy, of past and future, it recalls some other great works of imagination and perhaps most powerfully the last movement of Beethoven's *Ninth Symphony*. Here also the preceding themes are recapitulated immediately before the introduction of the final major theme (the *Hymn to Joy*). But this book is best taken for what it is, though it is suggestive that both Virgil and Beethoven, in perhaps their greatest single achievements, each strove for a supreme effect by an almost identical technique.

We can now grasp the total design of the whole six books. The psychologically continuous narrative corresponds at all points to an elaborate symbol-structure. Neither can be really separated from the other, but it is perhaps useful here, as before in our analysis of the Dido episode, to consider them apart before trying to grasp their complex unity. The essential narrative is in itself quite simple. We first encountered Aeneas at a moment of despair and acute nostalgia. This was gradually overcome as he experienced the calming of the storm, the recovery of his ships and men, and the generous hospitality of Dido. But the recovery was premature, and ironically deceptive. The passing of the empathetic and psychological initiative from Aeneas to Dido (ll. 712 f.) was in itself a sign of something very wrong. And his narrative, so ironically set in the very middle of the love story, makes clear what was wrong. The omens at the end of Book 2 had marked a change in all Aeneas' ideas and expectations, a change that he could neither understand nor emotionally encompass. The one sure *pietas* that he could and did understand and encompass, was that toward his father Anchises. Anchises, on the other hand, had really been converted, had felt and known that his life had been prolonged for one divine purpose. His initiative in Book 3 was thus as necessary to Aeneas as his death was unnerving. Aeneas as yet had neither the experience nor the knowledge to support

x

his new Roman *pietas* alone. He was still emotionally 'dependent' on his father. But after his father's death this dependence could mean only weakness and vulnerability. His conscience was now no match for Eros. Hence the almost immediate transition from the death of Anchises to the union with Dido in the cave.

We only regain empathetic contact with Aeneas when we see him appalled at Mercury's message, bewailing his fate, yet eager to do quickly what do he must. The ensuing tragedy of Dido takes place by itself while Aeneas is off, planning his departure, sleeping on his ship, or sailing the high seas. He does not grasp its meaning either for Dido or for himself. Even the 'miraculous' return to his father's grave is to him but the opportunity for a pious anniversary. Most of the fifth book is to Aeneas, as to the ordinary reader, a pleasant interlude of games. It is only at the terrible crisis of the ship-burning that the hand of the fates is seen to have been constantly at work. The women, the weak, the faint-hearted could never have borne the Latin wars: the loss of four vessels and the founding of Acesta are the fateful corollaries of this fact. But, above all, it is Aeneas' own lack of preparation for Latium that is made evident as we see him once more brought face to face with apparent disaster: *fatorum oblitus*. This is the cue for Anchises' appearance: it was time for Aeneas to *return* to his father. What the first five books tell us, in other words, is the extent to which Aeneas is dependent on Anchises and cannot stand alone without him. Even the gods (Mercury) cannot supply from without what is lacking within.

The sixth book had thus to be the solution of a profound psychological problem: how to establish in Aeneas a firm and *independent pietas*. It is solved not merely by the re-encounter with Anchises but, first and perhaps foremost, by the re-encounter with Dido and with his lost homeland, Troy. For these obviously are the two elements in his past that effectively dispute his acceptance of the future: the home to which he has always, in his heart of hearts, wished to 'return' and the loved woman, the *eros* figure, that represented his most powerful substitute for home. In meeting these and finding them irreconcilable or both impotent and wretched, he found in effect that the past had nothing in it that could hold him further. He was then prepared for the future: once he sees it in something of its true sweep and colour—sees it as vivid emotional reality and not as vague portent or ambiguous prophecy—and, once he fully identifies his *pietas* toward Anchises with his *pietas* toward Rome, his spiritual regeneration is finally accomplished. He is now able to stand alone: Anchises will no more trouble him in dreams nor will Mercury need any more to remind him of his duty. But of course we do not realize this new Aeneas *in action* until the books to come.[1]

In this sense the Odyssean *Aeneid* is a narrative that can in part be analysed in Freudian or other psychological terms. But it is not necessary to do this. What Virgil was trying to describe was how a *Roman* hero, an Augustan prototype, could emerge from both the normal man and the Homeric hero he originally had been. How was it possible to leave all the past, all the familiar attachments, behind and devote oneself to a new and unknown future? It was both a stroke of genius and an evidence of profound (though probably inarticulate) psychological insight to answer the question in terms of a son's devotion to his father. By making Anchises both a father and a semi-divine agent of Fate, Virgil was able to give human meaning to an otherwise inhuman or incomprehensible development. For Anchises unites two *pietates*: a normal, human *pietas* toward the past (his own toward Troy and Aeneas, Aeneas' toward him) and an absolutely extraordinary *pietas* toward the future. But Aeneas could not really comprehend the dual role of Anchises until he had actually encountered him in the underworld with the future Romans. And he could not have encountered him there unless he had also undergone a kind of death—the death of his old Trojan and erotic self. Only then was he really open to the vision of reincarnation and only then could he himself rise to the upper world as the very different hero of the Iliadic *Aeneid*.

The most common misunderstanding of the *Aeneid* is to take Aeneas' *pietas* as a mere product of fate, a mere reaction to external force, and thus to deny any internal development or maturation of his character. The fact, however, is that the 'action' of fate in the first six books is external only to the degree

---

[1] This is a crucial point. Thus those like Pöschl who see no change in Aeneas' character will interpret the last six books very differently. See particularly my discussion of the two crucial incidents of the eighth book (Tiber vision, omens) on pp. 332 f. and 339 f. below.

that Aeneas shows internal weakness or failure. It is not Mercury's intervention in Book 4 or Anchises' intervention in Book 5 that make Aeneas finally and fully *pius*: what makes him finally *pius* is, rather, his 'conversion' by Anchises in the underworld. The point, in other words, of the climactic sixth book is to show how Aeneas found *for himself* the steadfast *pietas* that could dispense with further divine warning. This in fact is just the kind of *pietas* that Aeneas does show throughout the Iliadic *Aeneid*.[1]

Thus there assuredly is development of character in the poem but it is not precisely identical with that in Shakespeare or the modern novel. Aeneas does not, like Macbeth or Natasha Rostov or Lydgate in *Middlemarch,* undergo a process of growth or degeneration that we can mark stage by stage as it goes on over time. His reaction to the initial sea storm is not materially different from his reaction to Dido or the burning of the ships: he is in all these cases a man whose *pietas* is subject to collapse under strain. Nor is he even very different when he re-encounters Dido and Deiphobus in the underworld. The important fact, however, is that he does undergo an experience of death and resurrection or its psychological equivalent, and emerges from the underworld as a new man.

Furthermore, we are not meant to envisage this event as a pistol-shot 'conversion' that has no effective relation to what has preceded. On the contrary, the sixth book is carefully prepared for by all that has gone before it: we see in it the consequences of Anchises' change of attitude in 2 and of his death in 3, of Dido's death in 4 and of the ship-burning in 5. Without these preliminaries, Aeneas' experiences in the underworld would have been meaningless and futile. In short, the 'conversion' of Aeneas in 6 is effective precisely because of its climactic relation to the whole preceding narrative. This is perhaps not *development* in the strict sense; but it is certainly *change*; it certainly leaves Aeneas a very different person from what he originally was. He begins as a man whose *pietas* has to be reinforced from without; he ends as a man whose *pietas* is his own, internal, possession.

This psychological narrative is accompanied and, so to speak, punctuated by a quite intricate symbolism. The most obvious

---

[1] See esp. pp. 332, 339 and 364 f. below.

aspect of the symbolism is of course the divine machinery—the gods. What differentiates Virgil's use of the gods from that of Homer or, indeed, all the later writers of Homeric epic, is, as we have already partially seen in our discussion of the Dido episode, his quite unique method of correlating his divine with his human actions or, more precisely, with his human psychology. Juno, as the opponent, the enemy, of both Aeneas and his *fatum*, provides the outer stimulus that corresponds to and excites the inner response, as in the initial sea-storm, the storm at the cave, the burning of the ships. The physical reality, the outer coercion, is of quite minor significance. The introductory storm is, as we have seen, proleptic and paradigmatic: the physical violence is not and is not meant to be decisive or paramount; not only is the storm calmed as quickly and as mysteriously as it is raised, but the reaction it excites in Aeneas is not primarily a response to outer danger but to an inner despondency seizing on the storm as its excuse or occasion for overt utterance. But the first storm really looks ahead to and anticipates the second: that by which Juno drives Dido and Aeneas to the cave. Here divine action (both Venus and Juno) obviously corresponds to an inner, human event: the *physical* rain and thunder are only the setting, not the cause of the guilty amour. Again, the ship-burning is an act of despair and weariness: Juno and Iris make the latent overt, but the human motivation is very plain. The violence and *furor* of Juno always re-echo or, more exactly, correspond to a *human* violence and *furor*.

So too, the interventions of Jupiter and the other warnings of Fate always look ahead to a human result. Divine revelation and warning are alike conceived in terms of exciting the appropriate inner response. It is made quite clear that Troy is destroyed and that Aeneas is saved by the gods' own decree. A revelation (the omens of Book 2) is essential to start the process, to excite the human response. But the revelation is not made so explicit as to preclude uncertainty and an almost endless search for the clear truth. Even the warning that sends Aeneas from Dido toward Italy is not meant to be decisive: the spirit that can endure the Latin War is not to be instilled from without. (Where the gods in fact send Aeneas is to Sicily and Anchises, not Latium.) But the warning does reveal the inability of Aeneas to 'stand alone', to dispense with the active presence of the father he had lost. Thus we are prepared for the wonderful synthesis of the human and divine sectors of the poem in the Anchises vision of the fifth book: he is at once Anchises, the father, and the exact equivalent of Mercury in 4—the fully authorized messenger of Jupiter. The way is then open to the *catabasis* and show of Heroes: the fated future *shown to* Aeneas *by* Anchises. The clarity of the revelation corresponds to the decisiveness of the moment (the moment just before the landing in Latium) and to the readiness of Aeneas, which is symbolically indicated by his crossing of the line between past and future when he leaves the *arva ultima* of the mythological Hades. By undergoing the crucial ordeal of death, of the loss of his old self, he has finally put on the 'new man' of Roman destiny.

The symbolic element of the narrative, however, includes much more than gods and oracles. We find also sheerly miraculous or supernatural episodes that are not in themselves an essential part of the divine machinery. The trickery of Venus and Cupid in the first book, the adventures of Book 3 (Polydorus, the Harpies, Achaemenides), the portrait of *Fama* in Book 4, above all the Hades of Book 6, reflect something of the wonder-world of the *Odyssey* and the *Argonautica*. Here, *with one great exception,* the outer supernatural mirrors natural or human emotions: the *horror* of impious crime (Polydorus), the *dread* of what is uncanny, mysterious and monstrous in the future (Harpies), the intense *loneliness* of the thwarted *nostos* (Achaemenides), the *awesome transition* from secret to public guilt (Fama), the pathetic *ordeal* of recovering and facing the past (the Mythological Hades). All these marvels correspond to the mood of Aeneas or the reader at the time they appear: without this correspondence they would be as emotionally incongruous as they are actually incredible.

The difference here between Virgil and the 'objective' Greek epic (Homer, Apollonius) is very instructive. Apollonius, for example, does not hesitate to make the Harpies physically vulnerable and to associate them with the favourable prophecy of Phineus. Virgil, on the contrary, presents them as invulnerable monsters, and their spokeswoman, Celaeno, as a hellish fury who converts true prophecy into an ominous threat. The episode is thus symbolic of Aeneas' whole attitude toward prophecy and the future at the crucial moment when he has just begun to realize how remote and strange the goal of his journey actually is. We can see the same difference between the quite tangible Cyclopes of Homer and the weird monsters of the Achaemenides episode, between the Odysseus' chatty conversations with the ghosts and Aeneas' dramatic encounters with Dido and Deiphobus in locales that so graphically reflect and intensify their psychological impact upon him. But what we may call the atmospheric blending of the supernatural with the psychological in these episodes is, of course, possible only because they themselves belong to a pervading motif-structure that connects all levels of the poem (cf. our discussion in chap. iii), and are described in the subjective, the empathetic-sympathetic style that really assimilates everything to one emotional tone and purpose.

The great exception to what we have just said is the show of Heroes. This is obviously much more than the symbolic reflex of a psychological state, much more than an evocative correspondence of inner and outer experiences. For it is primarily *revelation*, revelation of what could not otherwise have been known or experienced. Here Aeneas finally learns to live for the future, to accept the future as that which determines his *pietas* and his destiny. And here therefore Virgil finally completes his picture of the Roman and Augustan hero, the divine-man who devotes his life to the service of future history and so renounces the motivations and goals of his Homeric past. But even such revelation is psychologically 'placed': it would have been jarringly incongruous had it come before Aeneas had been emotionally prepared for it.

The difference between Virgil and Homer, or between Virgil and all previous epic, whether Antimachean or Choerilan, is indeed enormous. This is primarily because his essential theme is, as we have seen, Roman-Augustan and not Homeric, because the *Aeneid* is basically a narrative version of the ideas he had already set forth in the *Eclogue Book* and the *Georgics*. But the Homeric motifs, none the less, are an essential element of the poem. On the one hand, they give the story of Aeneas an epic resonance such as only Homer could call forth. On the other hand, their very difference from Homer, their intentional reversal of Homer, creates a unique effect of pathos. The Roman hero is a man without a true *nostos*, a man who is mainly kept from his goal by his own nostalgia and passion, a man whose very immunity from real, external danger (the fact that Jupiter and fate are so manifestly on his side) accentuates his inner struggle for piety. He is indeed no Odysseus. This is why his odyssey is so strangely moving.

CHAPTER VII

THE ILIADIC *AENEID*

THE second half of the *Aeneid* is strikingly different from the first. The change of model—the substitution of *Iliad* for *Odyssey*—is but a symptom of another and deeper change. The psychological and subjective emphasis of the first six books is gone: Aeneas is no more engaged in inner struggle, in the hard task of his remotivation, but in a great war with very tangible human opponents. His *pietas* has been established: we now see it demonstrated in action. In this sense the Iliadic *Aeneid* is the obvious climax of the epic; Aeneas' struggle with the Latins is a *maius opus* and with it a *maior rerum ordo* begins. But in another sense, the Iliadic *Aeneid* contains or seems at first sight to contain an element of anticlimax: we have been so prepared for the great test in Latium, so assured of Aeneas' success, so instructed in the designs of fate, that the actual result seems all but discounted in advance. The interest of the hero's bitter, personal struggle for self-mastery is, for at least many moderns, far greater than that of the tangible narrative of a battle whose outcome is certain. Nor does Virgil seem to make it easy for us: he now presents Aeneas as a quite static figure, unchanging and foursquare in his *pietas*, while it is his opponents, Turnus above all, but also Lausus, Camilla and even Mezentius, who struggle with pathetic heroism in a most unequal combat with fate. Nor does Virgil share with Homer any particular zest for battles or the incidents of battle: he does not in fact hide his aversion to war or his strong preference for peace; all his own tastes and values seem to contradict and discount his martial subject. What then are we to think of the Iliadic *Aeneid*? It is really a *maius opus*, the true climax of the epic, or is it not?

But the answer to this question and the main key to Virgil's purpose has been already given us in the sixth book. Obvious as in one sense it is, it has often been overlooked, as the curious variety of attempts to 'explain' the Iliadic *Aeneid* to modern sensibilities have repeatedly exemplified. The moral that interprets and sums up the heroic *exempla* of the Roman past is stated in the famous lines:

847   Excudent alii spirantia mollius aera
       (credo equidem), vivos ducent de marmore voltus,
       orabunt causas melius, caelique meatus
       describent radio et surgentia sidera dicent:
       tu regere imperio populos, Romane, memento
       (hae tibi erunt artes), pacisque imponere morem,
       parcere subiectis et debellare superbos.

The Roman, though he may lack the *arts* of Greek culture, has one great art that is his very own: that of ruling the peoples in one empire and of imposing on them the *habit of peace* by conquering the haughty and sparing the humble.[1] This ideal is thoroughly un-Homeric and, on the whole, un-Greek. It is certainly true for Homer that the chief virtue (the ἀρετή) of the hero is shown in his *aristeiai*, his great feats on the battlefield. The question of the justification of war—of the opportunity for the *aristeiai*—is not raised except in the most particular and superficial sense. The notion that war is only permissible as an instrument of pacification, of universal good government, was of course quite beyond Homer's ken as, indeed, it was beyond that of anyone who could not envisage humanity as a single society or order for which actual rulers could be held responsible. In any event, it certainly presented a problem for a poet who was concerned to exemplify it not only in an heroic epic but in an avowed imitation of the *Iliad*.

The bearing of the passage just cited on the Iliadic *Aeneid* has often been missed because its concrete applications have not been seen. After all, the only way to conquer the haughty is by battle and all battles are much alike: this has perhaps been the usual view of the matter. But the battles of the Iliadic *Aeneid*

---

[1] Cf. Norden, ad loc. I do not, however, think these famous lines are just a comparison of the Greek βίος θεωρητικός with the Roman βίος πρακτικός. Virgil, I think, uses *artes* (the Greek τέχναι) in a somewhat Pickwickian sense, as if to say: the arts, Roman, are not your forte; your business is to rule—call that your *art* if you will. The real implication is that ruling is *not* an art in the Greek sense but a moral achievement. The Romans are above *art* because they have character like that of the heroes who have just been described. Cf. G. Radke (*Gymnasium* 64 (1957), pp. 176–7) who stresses the connection with Q. Fabius Maximus, the *cunctator* (Fabius refused to participate in the plundering at Tarentum, thus illustrating the principle of *parcere subiectis*). I would also mention the story of Camillus in the fifth book of Livy (especially his behaviour toward the people of Falerii: cf. 5. 27. 6 Sunt et belli, sicut pacis iura, iusteque ea non minus quam fortiter didicimus gerere).

are in fact most unusual and the point of view from which they are described and the conduct of the fighters is described, is more unusual still. For the Latin War is seen by Virgil as a simply horrible instance of *furor* or *violentia* on a social scale. It is not only war but civil war, war between destined fellow-citizens and in fact actual fellow-citizens whose *foedus* or plan of union has been impiously disrupted. It is Juno's final and most horrible attempt to thwart fate and it leads to a terrible perversion of human character, both Latin and Trojan.

Aeneas' *pietas* comes out not only in his opposing such violence by fighting it with all necessary courage, but in the *way* he opposes it, in the way he fights and treats his enemies. His is the *humanitas* that sees war as a terrible necessity and a means to its negation, peace. The desire for battle-glory (*aretē* in this sense) or for plunder, the satisfaction of revenge and hatred, the sheer lust of conquest, is, with one apparent exception, conspicuously absent from his conduct. And it is this which in the last analysis gives him the moral superiority that justifies his military superiority over Turnus and the Latins. He is surrounded and seemingly eclipsed by the exploits of both Trojans and Latins: he is absent from Book 9, very inconspicuous in Book 11, while in Books 10 and 12 he shares the stage with Turnus, Mezentius, Pallas, Lausus, and others. What gives him pre-eminence, despite all the competing figures, is his immunity from the moral failure that fatally stains the conduct of the rest. Unlike Turnus, Nisus, Euryalus or Camilla he does not succumb to the lust of plunder. Unlike them also, he does not manifest any eagerness for fighting, except when dominated by a special emotion such as his affection for Pallas. Unlike them, he regrets and sorrows over the war. He alone thinks throughout of the peace to be gained. He alone realizes the true *pathos* of the *Marcelli*, the noble young doomed to premature death, and thus pays the price of peace with some sense of its magnitude. He alone avoids the sin of *hybris* and feels the sadness of success.

Seen in such a light, the Iliadic *Aeneid* is very far from an anticlimax or a mere tale of events already predicted and of a victory already guaranteed. In the Odyssean *Aeneid*, the *pietas* that Aeneas achieves with such difficulty is basically an acceptance of his own role as the servant of the Roman future.

But not until the Show of Heroes does he really gain any concrete notion of what that future will be or what it really means to be a Roman. Now his problem ceases to be merely one of his own remotivation; of internal struggle with his own individual passion and nostalgia—and becomes, instead, one of leadership, of action, of exemplifying in a great war the *social* meaning of *pietas* or, still more, of *humanitas*. We are now to see how the Roman could do what no one else, certainly no Greek, had done, that is, actually achieve true peace—proleptically at least the ecumenical peace of Augustus—by setting a new standard of humanity. Whatever the culture of the Greeks (and Virgil sweepingly grants its superiority in his *excudent alii*) they had not solved the problem of peace because they lacked the moral prerequisite of a solution.

What gave Aeneas this prerequisite was the ordeal—the ordeal of the Odyssean *Aeneid*—by which his *humanitas* was changed from an element of weakness to an element of strength. In the first six books, Aeneas is certainly humane: he is touched by the 'tears of things' when he views the sculptures of the Juno temple in Book 1; he weeps over Dido; he is moved by the work of Daedalus, &c. But such humanity is compounded with a self-pity that even verges on despair. He pities the Trojan dead because they are at rest and he is not; he sees in the rising walls of Carthage the disturbing evidence of his own remoteness from his goal; he bids a reluctant farewell to Helenus' New Troy because *he* has no such home. In the mythological Hades of the sixth *Aeneid*, he lingers or tries to linger over the pathetic remnants of his past in a 'humanity' of feeling that temporarily displaces any sense of his destiny and of its rigid schedule. But all this is now changed: in the Iliadic *Aeneid* his humanity is never exercised at the expense of his duty. He fights well because he feels it his duty to fight well, but he fights without the violence and cupidity that make war an end in itself or an expression of irrational *furor* indifferent to any peaceful or rational purpose. The obverse of *debellare superbos* is always for him *parcere subiectis* because the final aim is *pacis imponere morem*. To this line of conduct there are exceptions, as we shall see, especially when Aeneas is humanly angered or grieved, but even the exceptions are related to his *humanitas*, his love and pity for Pallas, the great Marcellus figure. At no point, however, does he falter in fighting because of his *humanitas* or exult in the fighting because of sheer *furor* and blood-lust; it is, instead, the combination of *virtus* with *humanitas* that gives him strength and makes him the only hero of the Iliadic *Aeneid* who looks ahead from war to peace, who is able to see in his present foe a future fellow-citizen and Roman. The Augustan meaning of all this is, of course, obvious: we now realize that the 'reborn' hero is a truly Roman hero who stands in the great line that includes Hercules, Romulus and Augustus but who is particularly the Augustan prototype because he, like Augustus, brings peace not only to a world at war but to a *civitas* divided against itself in fratricidal conflict. Here, in short, Aeneas finally emerges as the divine man or 'saviour' of the *Eclogues* and *Georgics*.

The plan of the Iliadic *Aeneid* is itself evidence of the general purpose just described. There are two books of introduction (7, 8) in which the infernal, impiously violent character of the war and Aeneas' role as the divine man, *theios-aner*, designed by fate and his own *pietas* to counteract such violence, are firmly set forth. The last four books then show the violence and the man at work. Their essential aim is to illustrate Aeneas' combined *humanitas* and *virtus* by contrast with the *furor* of both friends and foes. The main Iliadic theme (the parallelism of Achilles-Hector-Patroclus with Aeneas-Turnus-Pallas) is carried by the two major or even books (10, 12) and contrasts the two main heroes, Aeneas and Turnus. The minor or odd books (9, 11) contain, as their central pieces, two great episodes of heroism (a Trojan and a Latin) that establish another sort of contrast with Aeneas: the contrast between his mature *humanitas-virtus* and the immature combination of *virtus* with the battle fury and lust of plunder, with the *caedis cupido* that finally dooms even such heroes as Nisus, Euryalus and Camilla.

But the factor that gives continuity and climax to the whole story is the development of Turnus' character after he has been removed from battle by Juno in Book 10. In one sense Book 12 is a repetition of all that went before, made necessary only because Turnus was not permitted to face Aeneas in the crucial conflict of the tenth book. But, as we shall see, the avoidance of their encounter in 10 is necessary to motivate Turnus' *voluntary* seeking of the encounter in 12. When he *decides* to sacrifice himself 'for the many', the peace and union of Trojans and

Latins are assured. Thus, as we shall see, Virgil solved the problem of 'retardation' (the deferring of the climactic duel of the main heroes), as Homer did not.

The purpose and consequent structure of these books thus account for the fact that their use of empathy and of symbolism is so different from that of the Odyssean *Aeneid*. The empathetic 'spot-light' is no longer on Aeneas mainly but on several Trojan and Latin figures and most positively on Turnus. One of Virgil's primary objects is to show *furor* in the mass and in several different individuals and, above all, to show the inner conflict it arouses within such individuals. The opponents of Aeneas are anything but villains or mere *exempla* of violence: they are not only Latins or Italians, whose virtues for obvious reasons must be insisted upon, but human beings whose tragedy is accentuated by their virtues. Even Mezentius, the worst of all, is really glorified in his sacrificial death. But they are nevertheless unable to control their inner *furor* and when they do repent, repent too late. The conflict in their psyches is itself a sign of their malaise. It is indeed the very absence of such inner conflict that makes it unnecessary for us to read Aeneas' mind as we did before. He shows a steadfastness that contrasts favourably with the changing and turbid emotions of Turnus. Yet we see enough of his mind, especially at certain pivotal moments, to understand the difference between him and the others, especially Turnus. Thus the main action is by no means physical, even though there are so many battles, but really a conflict of motivations and it accordingly brings out the essential quality of the divine man who embodies the heroic virtues of Hercules and Romulus and most of all the pacificatory virtues of Augustus.

No one can escape noticing how differently the gods behave in the Iliadic *Aeneid*. The initial action of Juno is of course the climax of her activity in the whole epic: it is the great test of the hero besides which the storms off Africa and at the cave or the ship-burning were merely preparatory. Against this is set the action of Venus in Book 8 but, much more, the investment of the hero with the whole future of Rome, not as a show to be passively witnessed but as a burden to be actively borne into battle. Just as Book 7 gives *furor* a social meaning and magnifies the threat to Aeneas into a general attack on the whole Trojan-Latin destiny, so 8 identifies Aeneas with the *Roman* past and future and with Rome's social significance as the opponent of all violence that threatens peace. Venus for once acts like the goddess who had heard the prophecy of Jupiter (Book 1) and now sees in Aeneas the incarnation of Rome's destiny.

The rest of the poem (Books 9–12) might almost be called, at least from the divine viewpoint, the tragedy of Juno, though in the end she is reconciled to Roman victory. Juno now tries, not so much to damn Aeneas as to save Turnus from his fate, but in fact her interventions (especially her crucial intervention in Book 10, which is repeated *via* Juturna in Book 12) only compel him to the insight that his fate is unavoidable. Aeneas, on the other hand, needs no further warning or instigation from Jupiter: the latter actually declares in the gods' council of Book 10 that he will not interfere but let the fates find their own way. In both cases—for both Turnus and Aeneas—the essential decisions come from within; Juno can but defer the outcome; Venus at best helps to cancel the work of Juno. In the end the sub-fates withdraw and the Dirae indicate clearly enough the will of Jupiter. Turnus has no chance, once he has come up against Aeneas (i.e. his fate), but he need never have brought himself to this pass. Acceptance or rejection of fate is free but it is precisely through this freedom that fate works. The divine machinery of the Iliadic *Aeneid* is a most impressive attempt to depict in symbolic terms the inextricable union of free will and predestination. We see the individual and social and demonic aspects of violence brought face to face with *pietas* and humanity, and we see that Fate is finally on the moral side because the moral forces have in fact already put themselves on the side of Fate.

The plan of Book 7 indicates its purpose fairly clearly:

I. Arrival of Aeneas and the Trojan *foedus* with Latinus (1–285)

    (*a*) Arrival of the Trojans in Latium (1–36)
    (*b*) The history of Latinus and Lavinia: the oracles (37–106)
    (*c*) The omen of the tables (107–47)
    (*d*) The Embassy to Latinus (148–285)
        (i) Arrival of Trojans (148–94)
        (ii) Speeches of Latinus and Ilioneus (195–248)

(iii) Latinus grants hospitality; the Trojans return to Aeneas (249–85)
II. The mission of Allecto (286–571) = 286 lines
   (*a*) Juno's wrath (286–322)
   (*b*) Her charge to Allecto (323–40)
   (*c*) The visit to Amata (341–405)
      (i) First stage of *furor*: Amata exhorts Latinus (341–72)
      (ii) Second stage of *furor*: Frenzy of the women (373–405)
   (*d*) The visit to Turnus (406–74)
      (i) Allecto as Calybe (406–44)
      (ii) Allecto in *propria persona* (445–74)
   (*e*) Ascanius and the deer (475–539)
   (*f*) Departure of Allecto (540–71)
III. Mass Violence and the Muster of the Italian Clans (572–817)
   (*a*) Latin fury and withdrawal of Latinus (572–600)
   (*b*) Juno opens the gates of war (601–40)
   (*c*) The muster (641–817)

The book contains two long sections of equal length (285 or 286 lines): the auspicious arrival and reception of the Trojans by Latinus, and the terrible mission of Allecto. Clearly this is a deliberate imitation in reverse of Book I:

I. The Storm (1–304)
II. Arrival at Carthage and favourable reception by Dido (305–642)

There Juno's storm precedes the reception by Dido; here the reception by Latinus precedes Juno's war. Otherwise the parallelism is almost exact: Juno, there as here, is attracted by the unwelcome sight of the happy (*laeti, laetum*) Aeneidae or Aeneas; there as here she soliloquizes on her thwarted spite (7. 286 f.; 1. 34 f.). The two speeches are even similarly structured. Again, in the Embassy to Latinus, Ilioneus is the spokesman as he was before to Dido. Even the gifts of Aeneas to Latinus correspond to his gifts to Dido. Again we are given a brief history of Latinus and Lavinia, as we were, in 1, of Dido: each precedes the general encounter or embassy.

It is thus clear that Virgil has planned this book to correspond to 1, but *with a difference*. For this starts what he calls the *maius opus* and marks the beginning of a *maior rerum ordo*. It is in every respect a more imposing order than that set into motion by the storm of the first book. For the war that Juno and Allecto inaugurate cannot stop until the end of the epic itself: it thus must follow and reverse the mood of the auspicious embassy. Here there can be no proleptic introduction, briefly revealing Juno's fury and then letting it subside in order to commence a new tragedy on a low key. The purpose of the preliminary hospitality is only to reveal the fury and *impiety* of the force that disrupts it. The fates intended and intend the union of Latinus and the Trojans, of Aeneas and Lavinia; the war is against the intention of Jupiter:

10. 8   abnueram bello Italiam concurrere Teucris.
          Quae contra vetitum discordia?

And on a quite human level, Latinus had already committed the Latins to the *foedus* with Aeneas:

7. 260   dabitur, Troiane, quod optas.

Both Juno and Latinus realize exactly what is happening:

7. 313   Non dabitur regnis (esto) prohibere Latinis
          atque immota manet fatis Lavinia coniunx:
          at trahere atque moras tantis licet addere rebus,
          at licet amborum populos excindere regum.

And these words of Juno are as it were reflected in Latinus' acknowledgement of the sacrilege:

595   Ipsi has sacrilego pendetis sanguine poenas,
          o miseri.

The war is thus the most horrible of all wars, a *civil* war, a conflict between acknowledged kinsmen and co-citizens, and a *sacrilegious* war because it is undertaken against the will of Jupiter and his oracles, and because it involves from the start a flagrant breach of hospitality and a plighted *foedus*.

The introduction (1–285) also, of course, provides a dramatic contrast with, and hence heightens the effect of, the sombre and terrible Allecto episode. But it gives us as well a sense of the divine peace in nature itself and in that wonderful Italy, the cosmic mean, the *Saturnia tellus*, of the Second *Georgic*. After the death and burial of Caieta, after the ominous passage by Circe's abode, the Aeneidae come in the first flush of dawn

Y

(*iamque rubescebat radiis mare*: their first sight of Italy is here recalled—3. 521 f.) to a place where a miraculous calm suddenly descends upon them. They look up and see a mighty grove:

30   Hunc inter fluvio Tiberinus amoeno
                 verticibus rapidis et multa flavos harena
                 in mare prorumpit; variae circumque supraque
                 adsuetae ripis volucres et fluminis alveo
                 aethera mulcebant cantu lucoque volabant.

The peaceful, happy scene corresponds with the relief and *joy* of the arrival: *laetus fluvio succedit opaco*.

This mood of happy arrival at the homeland—of peace after the long labours of the sea—is mixed with the sense of fate, of watchful beneficent providence. The miraculous hush of the winds is the first sign; we are next shifted to Laurentum and told of the omens and prophecies that decree an *externus vir* for Lavinia and a blessed union of peoples in the mighty empire to come. We are shifted back to Aeneas and see how the table-eating omen at last assures him of his actual arrival in Latium. Finally the two groups, Latins and Trojans, are brought together in an atmosphere of predestined and almost effected union. Then and only then, does Juno appear.

Juno now plays her last and strongest card: she is now counterfate at the moment of final decision. The difference between her intervention in Book 1 and her intervention here is carefully underlined. The failure of heavenly or earthly means is what makes her turn to hell itself: (312) flectere si nequeo superos, Acheronta movebo. She no longer uses the Homeric Aeolus (a minor sea-god interested in getting a handsome wife) but the hellish monster, Allecto. She no longer raises a physical and quite external handicap (the sea-storm) but the very spirit of discord and hatred who works *internally* by breathing her venom into the human breast. For it is no longer possible to *divert* Aeneas from his goal or *discourage* him from reaching it: what is now necessary is to disrupt social peace and concord by criminal war (*Dissice compositam pacem, sere crimina belli*), the beneficent design of heaven by infernal rebellion against it. The violent element is not simply *compared* to social revolution or sedition, as was the storm in Book 1; Allecto is herself the very essence of such things.

Allecto is thus the key symbol of violence and *furor*, of all that opposes *pietas* and *humanitas* in the Iliadic *Aeneid*. She sums up the images of violence that have gone before and adds to them new qualities of infernal vengeance and fratricidal hate and most of all a *tragic* note, the note so completely absent from the purely Odyssean sea-storm of Book 1. In one sense Allecto is a strange composite of disparate things: the ancients found her disconcertingly un-Homeric. Macrobius (*Sat.* V. 17, 1 ff.) remarks that since Virgil had no model in Homer for the beginning of a *war*—the *Iliad* describes only one incident in the tenth year of the siege of Troy—he was free to employ the incongruous potpourri of motifs that we find: the tame stag and its sequel, the bringing of the greatest of goddesses down from Heaven and the greatest of furies up from Hell, the snakes, the chaste matrons in bacchic orgy, &c. Would, adds Macrobius, he could here have found some Greek source for this part of his narrative too! But such criticism quite misses the point. The Allecto episode is indeed a mixture of motifs and sources and labours under the complexity of its ingredients; it decidedly lacks simplicity or cleanness of contour. But it is a wonderful study in mass emotion with a real unity of sweep and tone. Unlike Macrobius, we must not try to visualize it but rather take it as an *emotive symbol* designed to set the key of the whole epic that follows.

Allecto is in fact a combination of two major motifs—the *Discordia* of Ennius and the *Lyssa* of Euripides' *Mad Heracles*.[1] Ennius' *Discordia* (*Annals* 7) was the goddess of Discord or Strife who opened the gates of War at the start of the Punic War:

Vahlen 266 f.   Postquam Discordia taetra
            Belli ferratos postes portasque refregit.

And she is also mentioned by Virgil in the next book (8) as one of the terrible participants in the battle of Actium (scissa gaudens . . . Discordia palla). This is the social aspect of Allecto, the sower of civic and military violence (335 f.). But

---

[1] The Ennius passage (given below) is cited by Horace, *Ser.* 1. 4. Cf. the discussion of Heinze, 182–93; E. Norden (*Ennius und Vergilius*, 1915), esp. 1–40, 153–73; E. Fränkel, 'Some Aspects of the Structure of Aeneid VII' (*Journal of Roman Studies*, 35 (1945), pp. 1–14). I have been stimulated by all these authors and others: essentially, however, the views expressed are my own.

Allecto is also the *Madness* of Euripides. Her identity with his *Lyssa* (in the *Heracles Mainomenos*) is at least sixfold: she is (1) sent by Juno (Hera), just after the hero (Heracles, Aeneas) has emerged from the underworld (2), to turn a joyous escape into a terrible tragedy (3). She is the virgin child of Night (*Heracles* 834, 844; *Aeneid* 7. 331) and a snake-haired Gorgon (4). She is hated by the gods above and below (5), and her frenzy is likened to Bacchic possession (6). As Lyssa, therefore, Allecto is the inspirer of madness in the individual: she works the terrible will of the implacable goddess who is determined to ruin the divine hero (*theios aner*) just at the moment when he has escaped his final and greatest ordeal (the underworld adventures of Hercules and Aeneas). The great difference between Euripides' Lyssa and Virgil's Allecto is that the former makes the divine man himself mad whereas the latter works only on his enemies or more exactly, on his potential allies and kinsmen. *Aeneas is threatened not by his own madness but by that of others.* Furthermore, Euripides' Lyssa wholly distorts and deranges the mind and spirit of Heracles so that he is in fact the quite unwitting agent of his own ruin. There is no such displacement of reason or will in Turnus, Amata and the Latins.

Allecto is thus, as Discordia-Lyssa, the *symbol of individual furor raised to a social dimension.* There is no real inconsistency between the two, because the individual emotion is quite naturally represented as the predisposing cause of the social: the mob is but the single person writ large. She is very similar to Fama (Book 4) who also converts private passion into public response. But Allecto (here quite unlike Lyssa but like Fama and particularly the Iris of Book 5), only takes advantage of an emotion *already present*: as Eduard Fränkel has well observed, Allecto's visits to Amata and Turnus are each carefully divided into two parts in such a way that the emotional feeling of the first, is intensified and made public in the second. Amata is at first quite moderate in her complaints to Latinus (they are in fact the reflection of her already strong bias toward Turnus): it is only when he rebuffs her that the venom is represented as taking effect and that she begins her *simulated* Bacchic orgies. She clearly knows exactly what she is doing: at no point has she lost control of her mind; at no point changed an original motivation. It is much the same with Turnus: he is utterly indifferent to Allecto's persuasions when she is disguised as the aged crone Calybe and only approaches *furor* (*arma amens fremit*, &c.) when Allecto reveals herself as the Erinys she is. But Turnus likewise is predisposed to Allecto's point of view: it is his natural masculine contempt for elderly female advice that makes him resist at the first; but his response is technically 'sane' at both times. Virgil's intention here seems quite clear: Allecto symbolizes the fury within the human heart that is ever ready, given the proper motivation, to burst into flame and overwhelm the more rational part of the soul. But there is no madness in the strict sense and no diminution of moral responsibility.

Virgil shows great skill in the way he depicts Allecto as a motivator of *internal* feeling or more exactly as an externalized image of such feeling. Ovid in the Ino narrative of the *Metamorphoses* (4. 432 f.) used Virgil's Allecto as the model for his Tisiphone but the difference is very revealing. Tisiphone is an amusing hobgoblin, perfectly visualized and quite articulate, and thus without symbolic suggestiveness. Virgil avoided this kind of *overt* and pictorial allegory: nothing is done to make us *visualize* Allecto beyond the mention of snakes—she is simply described as a Tartarean monster with a changing multiplicity of faces, shapes and aspects (324-9). She does not even reply to Juno's command (340) but goes silently about her work.

The episode is designed to grow crescendo-wise to a crashing climax. Each of its three main sections—Amata, Turnus, the deer —is climactically arranged, and the three parts themselves are climactically arranged within the whole structure. For Virgil's intention is to show how individual feeling rises to mass emotion and, finally, to open warfare. Allecto's multiple and changeable personality shifts at each stage to express the increasing scale and intensity of the violence. First she chooses an easy victim, the *woman* Amata, whom she does not even confront but merely leaves to the venom of *one* snake. Amata, in turn, rouses the *women* (she has no effect upon Latinus) in a mock Bacchanalian revel. We are as yet quite far from physical or martial violence: Amata, in the first of four pivotal similes, is likened to a *top* that *boys* whip on in their play: *stupet inscia supra inpubesque manus*, mirata *volubile buxum*. The juvenile character of the image suggests the preliminary scale and tone of the scene—*women* engaged in a pseudo-ritual whose frenzy is not yet overt violence.

To Turnus, Allecto's approach is quite different. Making no headway as the aged Calybe, she (like Callimachus' Demeter) shifts to her own terrible shape so that Turnus is truly terrified at the sight; she rolls her *flaming eyes* (*flammea lumina*), the snakes rise from her head, she hurls her torch at his breast. Now he is truly *amens* and *furiosus*:

461   Saevit amor ferri et scelerata insania belli,
        ira super

and (in the second major simile of the episode) is likened to a vessel of boiling water. He now rouses his warriors *to arms*. We have thus progressed from frantic women to men preparing for war: mass action and battle itself is the next stage. Allecto now picks not a queen or a prince but children and a tame deer: she is concerned at this point not with human motivation but a *casus belli*, and one whose pathetic insignificance will contrast most sharply with its horrible sequel.[1] She herself develops this incident into actual conflict by sounding the *pastoral horn* from the roof of the royal stable (Tartaream intendit vocem). The whole countryside is now aroused. The inflamed rustics rush to attack Ascanius and his fellow hunters and the other Trojans come to their aid. The battle is (in the third simile) likened to *waves that gradually increase in size and violence* as the wind grows (paulatim sese tollit mare, &c.). With the first deaths, the war becomes an accomplished fact.

This is the extent of Allecto's interference but it is not the climax of the action. Juno dismisses her (552 f.) and herself takes charge: ego . . . ipsa regam. This dismissal and the further fact that Juno herself, not Allecto (Discordia), opens the gates of War, have been much discussed. Why did Virgil depart from Ennius at this point? The answer seems on the whole clear enough: the war is too considerable to be left to a subordinate agent entirely; Juno alone must finally declare it and thus take on herself the ultimate responsibility for Allecto's acts. Allecto could begin it: it has now reached a magnitude far beyond the

[1] Here the theme of innocence perverted, of children and simple rustics driven, despite their intentions and nature, to violence, is fittingly made to constitute the climax of the Allecto episode. Cf. the muster and my remarks on it, p. 329 below.

scope of any being save that of the primary Counter-Fate figure itself. Thus this last, Junonian, phase of the action is also its true climax. Now the embattled shepherds, now Turnus and his warriors, now the sons of the mothers caught up in Amata's bacchic rout, have merged their voices in a universal demand for war:

583   Ilicet infandum cuncti contra omina bellum,
        contra fata deum, perverso numine poscunt.

The wave simile is fittingly applied to all these forces as they finally batter in unison against the opposition of Latinus. He is the great rock against which the storm breaks (simile of 586–90) but his resistance is finally vain:

591   Verum ubi nulla datur caecum exsuperare potestas
        consilium et saevae nutu Iunonis eunt res,
        multa deos aurasque pater testatus inanis
        'Frangimur heu fatis' inquit 'ferimurque procella!'

Here Virgil has taken the 'inverted' simile of the storm in Book 1 (the agitated waves compared to civic tumult) and turned it back to its simpler and more usual form: the men are now like waves that sweep away the last obstacle in their course. The wild tide engulfs all scruple and piety, all regal prerogative. Now (601 f.) at last Juno performs the office that Latinus has abdicated and herself opens the gates of War: ferratos rumpit Saturnia postes. The Jupiter prophecy, that closed the storm episode of Book 1 with the spectacle of impotent Fury shut behind the closed gates of this same temple, has here been reversed. Anarchy and war, sacrilege and fury, have finally burst all their bonds.

In this climactic episode Virgil has obviously drawn on every device and motif that could give cumulative effect to the idea of destructive, anti-social fury, and to its infernal, counter-fatal character. The four great similes mark the three stages of the crescendo and the climax: *whipped up* (1), *boiling* (2), *progressively surging* (3) emotion that finally *breaks against its barriers* (4) and seethes uncontrolled upon its course. But they are only part of a complicated motif-complex. Allecto, as it were, embodies all the motifs of *violence* and *fury* in Books 1, 2 and 4. The snakes of Laocoon (and of Book 2 in general) with their bloodshot eyes, the destructive fire of dying Troy, the bacchic frenzy of unhappy

Dido, the mysterious formlessness and self-magnification of *Fama*, even the wounded deer to which Dido was compared and the ominous hunt in which she participated, are all reproduced or suggested. Allecto sums up the horror of Troy's fall and Dido's tragedy, the tonality of all that is serpentine, fiery, bloody, tragic, dark and irrational. But she more than *sums up*: she introduces a quite new dimension of evil, the evil of social violence (*discordia*) in which the individual inflames the mass and the mass the individual. Aeneas, back from the underworld, now meets the infernal on earth. It is no unreal fantasy or feeble ghost that he meets but a demon in the terrible shape of fratricidal war.

The recall of Book I in particular brings out the uniqueness and the special note of this new phase of the epic. The *storm* (I. I–304) is, as we have seen, a balanced composition built around the contrasts of storm and calm, Juno and Venus, *furor* and *pietas*. Here (in Allecto) there is no effect of balance but of progressively increasing imbalance; no evenly matched opposition of two forces but the sweeping victory of one. This is shown again and again as the motifs of the earlier *storm* episode are deliberately recalled: it is not (in Book I) until Neptune has calmed the waters that they are compared to a seditious mob; the emphasis is on the peace-making deity and on his human analogue, the peace-making statesman. Then, when Venus appears to balance Juno, we are ready for Jupiter's prophecy of Augustus and the Augustan containment of furor, the closing of the Janus-temple, on which the episode concludes. But the Allecto episode introduces the wave and sea similes only to mark its crescendo and climax (the rising waves, the storm breaking on the rock, Latinus yielding to the *procella*) and ends with *Juno* triumphant and *herself* throwing open the gates. The old statesman, Latinus, is utterly unable to control the mob. Virgil, in short, has tried by the pointed contrasts to indicate the wholly new scale and intensity of the *furor* at work here. There can be no stopping of it now until it has been met and mastered head-on in an action that cannot end or even pause until the final victory has been won.

This is shown also in the flamboyant muster of Italian tribes that ends the book. The peculiar note of this scene, that which makes it seem so oddly different from its Homeric counterpart, is the blending in it of patriotic pride in old Latin virtue and humane disapproval of Latin *furor*. There is indeed a distinct note of pity, a sense of the tragedy of primitive virtue perverted. The key to Virgil's intention here is the way in which he begins and closes the muster. The muster is led by Mezentius, the *contemptor divom* who is closely followed by his noble son, Lausus:

649   quo pulchrior alter
            non fuit excepto Laurentis corpore Turni
653   —*dignus patriis qui laetior esset*
        Imperiis, et cui pater haut Mezentius esset.

The same motif is repeated at the end where Turnus with his terrible Chimaera crest:

787   tam magis illa fremens et tristibus effera flammis
        quam magis effuso crudescunt sanguine pugnae

and his shield depicting the metamorphosis of Io

790   iam saetis obsita, iam bos

is followed by the young and graceful Camilla with her golden *fibula*, quiver and pastoral staff. Noble youth is the pathetic victim of impious *furor*; Latin innocence is sacrificed to a bad cause. Turnus is not represented as an evil man simply: but his *fury* entailed as one of its worst consequences, the scrifice of his Latin followers to his own passions and ambitions. He and Mezentius were, in Virgil's eyes, doomed by a just fate: it was very different with the innocent youth they had enlisted in their cause.

The rest of the Italians are seen in much the same light: they are unsophisticated primitives whose courage is put to a very bad use. We see their crude violence (Aventinus and his bristling lion's skin, the Tiburtians like Centaurs crashing through the woods), their rural, barbaric equipment, their simple Arcadian life and their tragic fate (as of Umbro 756 f. and Virbius, 776 f.). Violence—violence in its very worst form, the disruption of a divinely ordained *civitas*, has now enlisted Latin *virtus* in its service. The time has come for Aeneas to prove what he can do against it, and, on the divine level, for Venus to show her hand against Juno and for Fate itself to make its will known. This is the function of Book 8. The imbalance of forces in Book 7 is so great that a whole book is needed to restore a proper equilibrium.

The plan of Book 8 is itself the main key to its meaning:

I. The Preparations for Rome (1–101)
    (*a*) Events in Latium (1–17)
    (*b*) Aeneas' dream and response to it (18–80)
    (*c*) The voyage to Rome (81–101)
II. The First Day in Rome: The Arcadian and Herculean Past (102–368)
    (*a*) Reception by Evander (102–183)
    (*b*) Hercules and Cacus (184–305)
    (*c*) Arcadian Rome (306–368)
III. The next Night: Making the Arms (369–453)
IV. The Second Day in Rome: the Present (454–596)
    (*a*) Evander accepts the alliance (454–519)
    (*b*) The Omens (520–40)
    (*c*) The departure (541–96)
V. The Second Day in the Valley near Caere: The Augustan Future (597–731)
    (*a*) Arrival (597–607)
    (*b*) The shield (608–731)

The meaning of this remarkable book has often been misunderstood [1] because its basic unity of design has not been clearly seen. It has one major theme: Aeneas is the divine man (theios-aner) of Roman destiny whose mission is to defeat impious *furor*, the *furor* represented by Allecto and the Latin war. He stands in a present that is framed by a past and a future: the Arcadian Rome whose *theios-aner* was Hercules and the future Rome whose *theios-aner* is to be Augustus. All three symbolize the eternally Roman struggle of *pietas* and *humanitas* against savage and barbaric violence, against the force represented by Cacus, Mezentius and Antony. Aeneas, in witnessing and celebrating the anniversary sacrifices to Hercules, in himself accepting leadership in the struggle against Mezentius and the Latins, in bearing away the shield whose central panel

---

[1] Cf. esp. W. Warde Fowler, *Aeneas at the Site of Rome* (1917); Franz Bömer, 'Studien zum VIII Buche der Aeneis' (*Rh. Mus.* 92 (1944), pp. 319–69); Cartault, pp. 633–4. I have found Cartault most suggestive here (esp. his view that the shield is to Pallanteum as a great drama is to the 'empty theatre' in which it is about to be enacted). No one, to my best knowledge, has yet grasped the true unity of the book (esp. the significance of the three days).

depicts the battle of Actium, finally realizes in very deed the role that was paradigmatically pointed out to him in the sixth book. We now see both the Latin War and Aeneas' part in it within the full perspective of Roman history. The shield and armour constitute Venus' answer to Juno and Allecto but they are an answer only because Aeneas is himself the man of destiny and of *humanitas*—the man ordained both by fate and his own piety to conquer human violence and overcome the demonic powers.

The three *theoi-andres* are set within three separate eras, each represented by a different place or time: Hercules belongs to the Arcadian Rome or Pallanteum of the first day, the day kept sacred to him; Aeneas conducts his present business only in the morning of the second day (the day after the sacred festival) when, though the scene is still Pallanteum, his concern is no longer with the Arcadian, Herculean city of the past but with the impending war; finally the Augustus-shield is received and studied only in the very special atmosphere of the remote Caere-vale, a region quite withdrawn from either Arcadian Rome or the present war preparations (e.g. from Caere itself, the Etruscan ally of the moment). The parallelism with the sixth *Aeneid* is, of course, explicit and indeed essential to a full understanding of the book's action and structure. The introductory part (I) recalls the intervention of Anchises and the summoning of Aeneas by him at the end of Book 5; the First Day in Rome (II) recalls the *mythological Hades* of Book 6; the Second Day in the Caere-vale (V) recalls the Lethe-valley and Show of Heroes. The past and future of *Rome* in this book are thus compared to the past and future of *Aeneas* in Book 6. The major point of difference between the two books is that the section on the present (IV) in this book has no parallel in 6. The reason of course is that the main point of this book (8) is to *join* Rome's past and future to its present, to represent Aeneas as the *active* successor of Hercules and *active* prototype of Augustus. And this also accounts for the differences of atmosphere and plan: as in 6, 8 demarcates times or eras by spatial means and by quasi-miraculous devices (such as the prophetic shield) but 8 is no *descent* into an underworld, no kind of dream or vision, no *psychological preparation* for heroic leadership, but rather the direct assumption of it: it marks the moment when the passive spectator or endurer becomes the active possessor of his history. Hence the mixture of reality and unreality, of immediacy and remoteness, of exigent present and faraway past or future, that gives this book its peculiar and uniquely fascinating character.

I. *The Preparations for Rome* (1–101).

We start with a brief review of events in Latium (1–17) and then turn at once to Aeneas:

18   Talia per Latium. Quae Laomedontius heros
       cuncta videns magno curarum fluctuat aestu,
       atque animum nunc huc celerem, nunc dividit illuc
       in partisque rapit varias perque omnia versat.

The transition here is important because Virgil wants to avoid at all costs the impression that the events inaugurated in 7 have stopped or that there can be any cessation of the military action. The simultaneity of Books 8 and 9 is essential to Virgil's purpose here and in 9 itself (as we shall see). Aeneas at this point was obviously uncertain as to his course of action but only a very powerful motive (such as the Tiber vision) could have induced his withdrawal from the Trojan camp by the Tiber mouth: he knew only too well that Turnus and the Latins would not wait for him to return. Unless we share his sense of crisis, of supreme tension, we cannot understand his situation at all.

The mood of Aeneas in these lines (18 f.) has been taken by some commentators [1] to amount to a reversion to the despair of *terque quaterque beati* or to his *forgetfulness of the fates* after the ship-burning. But there is not in fact the slightest indication that Aeneas was here registering anything more than an almost inevitable concern at the state of affairs. The war had abruptly ended his all but completed *foedus* with the Latins. Though he knew the fates and had been told of the war several times (Helenus, the Sibyl, Anchises), he could not be expected to have been secured by prophecy from all suffering or perturbation. The fact that he foresaw the future in a general, imprecise way did not mean that his day-to-day conduct was settled

---

[1] E.g. Constans, pp. 269–71. His attempt to refute Heinze (p. 276) on this point seems to me quite mistaken.

beyond the necessity of action, reaction and emotional involvement. The relation between fore-knowledge and free-will is here, as always, enigmatic and ambiguous: but had Aeneas greeted the new threat of war without some regret, pain or inner turmoil, he would have ceased altogether to be human. Yet the difference from his reactions in the Odyssean *Aeneid* is unmistakably clear: he now expresses no despair; he now receives no human advice (like that of Nautes), no direct *warning or reproof* from an emissary of Jupiter (as Mercury in 4, Anchises in 5), but only the *guidance* of the *local* stream god, Tiber.

Furthermore the simile (22 f.) by which Virgil represents his mood is very revealing in itself. It is taken from Apollonius' famous description of the wavering Medea (*Arg.* III. 758–60). In her amorous indecision, she is likened to a quivering sunbeam reflected on the walls of a room from a vessel of dancing water. But Virgil not only gives the simile a nocturnal tone by adding the moon's light (aut radiantis imagine lunae) but pictures the beam striking the elaborate ceiling (*laquearia*) of an obviously Roman house (25: summique ferit laquearia tecti). He follows this with the lines:

26   nox erat et terras animalia fessa per omnis
       alituum pecudumque genus sopor altus habebat

which also recalls not only Apollonius on Medea but Virgil himself on Dido (4. 80 f., 522 f.)—they are isolated from all other creatures by their inability to sleep. But Aeneas is here only the careworn and sober Roman statesman (the solitary night vigil in the lofty Roman mansion is suggested by the *laquearia* and the moonbeam) who does in fact, though belatedly, get to sleep; his anxiety is great but responsible and obviously not overpowering.

Yet it is certainly true that the passage and the ensuing Tiber-vision in some sense recall his anxiety and Anchises-vision of the fifth book (cf. 5. 700 f. with 18 f. here). The great difference is that the Tiber-god here outlines a very different mission from that of Book 6. Aeneas is now given immediate advice for an immediate crisis: it will also lead him back to the past and on to the future but this is not the primary or ostensible purpose of either Aeneas or the god. We are far removed from the mood of either Books 5 or 6.

II. *The First Day in Rome: The Arcadian and Herculean Past*
(102–368)

The Tiber-god's advice now leads Aeneas to Rome: the
voyage up the river takes place in a romantic and mysterious
calm. The remoteness and strangeness of the journey are
stressed: the very waters and woods are surprised (91–92).
Finally the humble city of Evander is sighted; the difference
between *then* and *now*, between the primitive beginnings and the
later wealth is particularly emphasized:

99   quae *nunc* Romana potentia caelo
         aequavit, *tum* res inopes Euandrus habebat.

Aeneas finds the Arcadians celebrating the *dies sollemnis* of
Hercules (102 f.). He is, however, most courteously received
by Evander, who renews with the son his old and great friendship with the father, Anchises: Evander thus becomes the
Anchises-surrogate of the Iliadic *Aeneid*, who receives by transference, something of the filial *pietas* that Aeneas had exhibited
so strikingly in Book 6. All therefore promises to fulfil Aeneas'
hope of alliance and aid. But the day itself admits of no actual
business; that must be put off till the morrow. Meanwhile
(*interea*) Aeneas must join in the annual rites which it is unlawful
to defer (quae differre nefas).

Thus Virgil *sets apart* Aeneas' first day in Rome for the celebration and recollection of the past and of Hercules in particular.
The Cacus story that Evander tells Aeneas is the legend or myth
that illustrates Hercules' character and *aretē*. It represents but
one of the many exploits in which he had worsted powers of
irrational, immoral violence (288–302), such as the terrible
snakes of his cradle, the centaurs Hylaeus and Pholus, the wild
bull of Crete, the Nemean lion and finally Typhoeus and the
Hydra:

298   Nec te ullae facies, non terruit ipse Typhoeus,
        arduus arma tenens; non te *rationis egentem*
        Lernaeus turba capitum circumstetit anguis.

But Cacus is important because he is the local monster and
because his defeat made Hercules a divine man of Rome. The
story itself (115–275) is, in form, an *aition* or explanation of an
altar (*ara maxima*) and rites that were of great importance in
Augustan Rome, but the rites themselves are clearly subordinate

to the figure of Hercules in Virgil's mind.[1] His worship, as Livy tells us, was the only foreign cult allowed by Romulus, *iam tum immortalitatis virtute paratae . . . fautor*. The art by which, according to Horace, the man who was just and tenacious of principle, could imperturbably withstand the dangerous violence of mobs, the face of threatening tyrants, the thunder and the lightning, was one that Pollux had shared with Hercules and Hercules with Augustus (*Carm.* III. 3. 1 f.). Hercules in short had defeated all the monsters because they did not find him *rationis egentem*. He is the heroic opponent of anti-social *furor* and *violentia*.

The Cacus story is thus an example of the conduct by which man can become divine and by which Hercules himself became the true predecessor of Aeneas, Romulus and Augustus. It is an old tale that we find also in Dionysius and Livy [2] but it has been significantly altered by Virgil to fit his purpose here. Livy's Cacus is only a thieving herdsman, Dionysius' a mere robber; Virgil's is a true *monstrum*, a son of Vulcan, a forbidding, inhuman, infernal creature who is the terror and curse of the whole countryside. On the other hand, Virgil converts the old bucolic Hercules of the original myth into the saviour (σωτήρ) who deserves human reverence and gratitude for his deeds (*meritos . . . honores*). Accordingly Virgil changes the motivation of Cacus: he is not attracted by the mere beauty of the cattle but acts from sheer wickedness, *ne quid inausum aut intractatum scelerisve dolive fuisset*; his *impiety* toward Hercules is stressed. The whole story is lifted from an earthy, bucolic to an heroic, divine level: Virgil thus eliminates all petty details as to Hercules' weariness, sleep, counting of the cattle, &c., and devotes his attention exclusively to the terrible combat. His great innovation in the story was to make Cacus flee to his

---

[1] The best monograph on Cacus is that of Friedrich Münzer, *Cacus der Rinderdieb* (*Progr. Basel*, 1911), which Heinze summarizes (p. 485, n. 1). Neither, however, seems to have realized the symbolic meaning of Cacus here. Hermann Schneff ('Das Hercules-abenteuer in V's Aeneis', *Gymnasium* 66 (1959), pp. 250–68), however, has seen this point though he, like other commentators, overemphasizes the narrowly political reference. There is, of course, a vast literature on Hercules' status as a Roman θεῖος ἀνήρ. Cf. Livy I. 7 and Horace *Carm.* III. 4. 65 f. in addition to 3. 1 f. quoted in the text. Hermann Fränkel (*Miscellanea G. Galbiati = Fontes Ambrosiani* XXV, vol. i (1951), pp. 127–8) could well have been less tentative in stating, 'This analogy [i.e. that of Hercules and Augustus] seems to have been the main reason for Vergil to insert so elaborate a rendering of the Cacus legend.'

[2] Livy I. 7. 4–9; Dionysius Hal. I. 38. 4 f.

cave and shut himself in it by an immovable stone. Hercules was accordingly able to get at him only by the superhuman exploit of tearing off the earth and rocks that formed the top of the cave. The consequent rent in the terrain, from which the monster's horrid fumes came belching forth, could be aptly compared to the very opening of Hades (243-246):

> non secus ac si qua penitus vi terra dehiscens
> infernas reseret sedes et regna recludat
> pallida, dis invisa, superque immane barathrum
> cernatur, trepident immisso lumine manes.

The lines recall those of *Iliad* 20 (61 f. Hades' fear lest Poseidon by his earthshaking exploits expose the underworld to the light of day), and most especially the cave by which Allecto had returned to the underworld (7. 568 f.): *specus horrendum . . . saevi spiracula Ditis . . . ruptoque ingens Acheronte vorago.* Thus the Hercules who exposes and throttles the fire-breathing monster in his infernal lair becomes the symbol of enlightened *vis temperata* (he is the man who is *non rationis egens*) and its victory over the infernal powers that Allecto represents.

The story, however, still retains a bucolic nuance. Hercules is still a herdsman of sorts and Cacus a cattle thief. The rustics at the story's close gape with naïve curiosity at the *informe cadaver*. The ensuing dance of the Salii has the flavour of a rural ceremony: *populeis adsunt evincti tempora ramis*. The story is thus suited to a simple society in which cattle-keeping gods are completely at home. The theme of simplicity and noble *paupertas* (as opposed to a later and degenerate luxury) is a major motif of this part of the book. This is the life that made Rome great:

Georgics II. 532   Hanc olim veteres vitam coluere Sabini
                        hanc Remus et frater, sic fortis Etruria crevit
                        scilicet et rerum facta est pulcherrima Roma.

Aeneas now takes on, as it were, the aura of Hercules as he likewise accepts and appreciates the noble primitivism of this Arcadia.

The walk that Aeneas takes with Evander, from the Tiber bank near the Aventine (the site of the *antrum Caci*) to the humble *casa Evandri* on the Palatine, now sets this Arcadia in the perspective of its own past even while it evokes so powerfully the Roman future. The moral that applies to both is that of the destructive effect of irrational violence and greed: *belli rabies et amor . . . habendi* (327). Evander's Pallanteum is at once the golden mean, the primitive, virtuous Arcadia, and the empty theatre that is to be filled with so much glory and so much temptation to repeat the excesses of the ruined civilizations of the past.

Virgil's impression of Arcadian Rome must have been much like that of the eighteenth-century tourist we see in a Piranesi print. Pallanteum is a rural village but all around are the *virum monumenta priorum . . . disiectis oppida muris . . . reliquias*, the relics of civilizations which grew out of the ruins of the golden age (*aurea saecula*) and were in turn ruined by their own vices. Saturn had civilized a primitive race, a *genus indocile ac dispersum montibus altis*, but his civilization had been corrupted by avarice and the *belli rabies*. This is of course a lesson for the *aurea saecula* that Augustus is to restore (6. 791 f.). Pallanteum is the empty interim between two civilizations and between two golden ages, and it is itself a partial *exemplum* of golden age virtues. The sheep that wander in the forum, the wild thickets that cover the Capitol are a contrast with both Roman power and Roman luxury.

All this constitutes the peculiar tonality of this section of the book. In this waning day that has been set apart for rural ceremony, in this locale that is filled with the aura of Hercules, that is surrounded by the remains of the past yet awaits in its emptiness the infinitely greater future, we fall into a mood of twilight nostalgia, of pity for the departed civilizations, of foreboding for the civilization that is so greatly to surpass but so much to endanger the *aurea mediocritas* of this Arcadia.

The section closes on a moment that sums up the meaning of the whole scene. Aeneas is finally brought to Evander's humble *regia* on the Palatine. Evander tells him that Hercules before him had entered here and that he must now follow that divine example:

364   aude, hospes, contemnere opes et te quoque dignum
         finge deo rebusque veni non asper egenis.

Virgil is of course referring to the studied simplicity of Augustus' own 'palace' at this time (cf. Suetonius, *Augustus* 72) but the essential purpose of the lines is to indicate the simplicity (the

z

contempt for mere wealth) that the three divine men have in common. In their opposition to the rage of war, to greed, to all violence of heart or appetite, they are together illustrations of the great Roman ideal. But Augustus is not directly mentioned: this day (Section II) is set apart for the past, for Hercules; Aeneas here sees and follows a past ideal, a past *exemplum*. Yet everything mutely anticipates what is to come: the empty theatre must be filled; Hercules is but the bucolic predecessor of more glorious followers.

III. *The next Night: Making the Arms* (369–453)

The arms-making occupies the night that separates Aeneas' two days in Pallanteum and thus serves to demarcate the interval. This is important because this interval spells the difference between two quite different times and aspects of the story— between the Arcadian, Herculean past and the exigent present of the Latin War. Furthermore, the scene keeps us in mind of the destiny which is crowding Aeneas at an ever accelerated pace. It is this very night (as we shall see)[1] that the Trojans at the camp are keeping anxious vigil and the Nisus-Euryalus episode occurs. Every moment that Aeneas is away from Ascanius and his men is of crucial importance. This motif is now reflected in the urgency of the arms-making itself. It thus begins:

369   Nox ruit et fuscis tellurem amplectitur alis.
        At Venus haud animo nequiquam exterrita mater
        Laurentumque *minis* et *duro mota tumultu*.

Again, the rising of Vulcan at dead of night like a poor woman pressed by necessity to turn night into day (the Apollonian and Homeric simile is here used with a quite new emphasis on the necessity or urgency of the work, *noctem addens operi*) and his commands to his assistants (Tollite cuncta ... coeptosque auferte labores ... praecipitate moras) reinforce the same motif which we see expressed once again in the early rising of Evander and Aeneas himself on the next morning (455 f.).

The Homeric coloration of the episode (the use of the 'deception of Zeus' from the *Iliad*) does not seem quite in keeping with

---

[1] Cf. p. 343, below.

the rest of the book. Virgil obviously wanted to fill the night interval with events (as we have seen) and could not, like Homer, describe the legend on the shield as it emerged in the process of manufacture. Aeneas himself must see the legend when he gets the completed shield. This episode does, however, indicate Venus' concern for Aeneas and prepares us for the following parts (IV, V) of the book.

IV. *The Second Day in Rome: The Present* (454–596)

The urgent *presentness* of this part is indicated at the very start:

463   Hospitis Aeneae sedem et secreta [Evander] petebat
         sermonum memor et *promissi muneris* heros.

The *promissum munus* obviously refers to Evander's words of the previous day:

170   lux cum primum terris se crastina reddet
         auxilio laetos dimittam opibusque iuvabo.

The interval of religious ceremony, of concentration on Hercules and the past, is over, and the hard task of the moment overshadows everything else. Evander (470–513) now explains the situation: Aeneas is the predestined leader from abroad whom the Etruscans are awaiting. He is thus appointed by fate to be the opponent of the terrible tyrant Mezentius and of his protector, Turnus. The present thus in effect repeats the past: the struggle of the divine man is still with furious and impious enemies who defy the laws of men and gods alike. Aeneas, like Hercules, has come from abroad to protect an innocent people from such destructive violence.

Evander finally adds that he will supply 200 horses of his own *and his son Pallas*:

515   sub te tolerare magistro
        militiam et grave Martis opus, tua cernere facta.

This is the great moment of the book. Aeneas is temporarily saddened by the near prospect of war and, above all, by the charge just laid upon him by Evander:

520   Vix ea fatus erat, defixique ora tenebant
         Aeneas *Anchisiades* et fidus Achates
         multaque dura suo tristi cum corde putabant.

Warde-Fowler [1] has rightly called attention to the significance of *Anchisiades* here. As later at 10. 822, the epithet recalls Aeneas, *the son:* there he thinks of Lausus' father; here of Evander. He now sees that he is taking on a responsibility to a father for his son and that his *pietas* toward Anchises and indeed something like Anchises' *pietas* toward himself must be reflected in his new relationship to Pallas and Evander. But to this is also added a presentiment of the future, as if Aeneas were already anticipating the Marcellus-like fate in store for Pallas: multa . . . dura putabant. But before he can quite compass such thoughts, the omens come:

522   putabant,
          ni signum caelo Cytherea dedisset aperto.

The contrast of the imperfect indicative *putabant* and the pluperfect subjective *dedisset* tells the story of surprised interruption, the unexpected sign breaking his mood of saddened realism.

The omens themselves (the thunderbolt, the bray of Tuscan trumpet . . . *mugire per aethera clamor*) transform the whole scene. The moment is surely one of the most wonderful in the *Aeneid*, one of the places in Virgil where the touch of genius seems most authentic. It unites a whole complex of motifs: Evander, Pallas, Aeneas, Anchises, the Etruscans, Venus, the War, the Arms. It recalls the omens of Book 2 (cf. 2. 692 and 8. 520) and thus the original motivation of the whole epic. Aeneas' response (so unlike that of the other time) is immediate: he recognizes his mother's promise and thus the full significance of the moment (she had promised the arms *si bellum ingrueret*) [2] and so he fits the very words of the *terque quaterque beati* passage into this new context:

538   quam multa sub undas
          scuta virum galeasque et fortia corpora volves,
          Thybri pater! poscant acies et foedera rumpant.

So have events been reversed! Aeneas is now at last the determined hero. Let them demand their battle, break their treaties; he is ready.

There can thus be no excuse whatsoever for taking these lines as another evidence of Aeneas' 'wavering' at a crisis, or as a

---

[1] *Aeneas at the Site of Rome*, p. 88. Cf. n. 1 on p. 359.
[2] We have no prior word of this promise. Probably Virgil would have supplied it in the revised version. Cf. Appendix 9.

recurrence of his weakness in Books 1, 4, and 5.[1] His 'hard thoughts' are humane in the best sense of that word. But the mood of sad foreboding (which does not in the least affect his determination) is momentarily broken by the encouraging signs. It recurs in a moment when he prepares to depart and Evander now quite clearly forebodes the fate of Pallas:

578   Sin aliquem infandum casum, Fortuna, minaris.

The boy, as he leaves in all the brilliance of his cloak and painted armour, is likened to Lucifer rising from the ocean (588 f.). The simile suggests, of course, the setting of Lucifer as well: what has now risen so brightly is destined soon to set in the darkness of death.

V. *The Second Day in the Valley near Caere: The Augustan Future* (597–731)

Aeneas has now seen the past and its great *exemplum* (Hercules) and accepted his role in the *present* struggle against impiety and violence. The omens have given divine sanction to his enterprise. They have also pointed his way toward the future. He now proceeds toward his predestined Etruscan allies. But here, as in the Elysium of Book 6, he finds in a *secluded valley* (in valle reducta) his parent (Venus this time, not Anchises) and is once more shown the future under parental auspices. It would have quite spoiled the contrast of times and moods that makes this book so rich and complex, had Aeneas received the arms on the site of Rome or in any spot that was already connected with his own past or present.

The shield that he now takes from Venus contains seven tableaux on the periphery and a central section depicting the great triumph of Augustus over Antony at Actium. We need not here re-discuss the vexed question of its arrangement: it is assuredly *not* to be reduced to any one plan that can be visualized. The important thing is its main theme which is the constant opposition of *virtus, consilium* and *pietas* to the forces of violence in all Roman history. We see the kindly she-wolf licking the twins *Mavortis in antro*; the unscrupulous rape of the Sabines composed and atoned for by a solemn treaty; the treachery of Mettius Fufetius and its punishment; the Roman

---

[1] As do V. Pöschl in *Festschrift Regenbogen* (1952), pp. 135–43 and R. Salenbauch, unpublished Freiburg diss. (1952).

defence against Tarquin, Porsenna and the Gauls; the *religio* of
the Romans (Salii, Luperci, etc.) and the judgement of the dead
in Hades (the impious Catiline, the pious Cato). Everywhere
violence is defeated, evil is punished, *religio* observed. All this
is but the setting of the greatest of struggles between Roman
pietas and barbaric *violentia*. Augustus *cum patribus populoque
penatibus et Magnis Dis* is opposed to all the evil gods and powers:

698   Omnigenumque deum monstra et latrator Anubis
         contra Neptunum et Venerem contraque Minervam
         tela tenent, saevit medio in certamine Mavors
         caelatus ferro, tristesque ex aethere Dirae,
         et scissa gaudens vadit Discordia palla,
         quam cum sanguineo sequitur Bellona flagello.

And the book ends with the triumph that Augustus has won
over the far-flung barbarians, all the *rationis egentes*.

These then are gifts so fashioned that with them Aeneas
need not shrink from engaging the haughty Laurentians or
fierce Turnus (613 f.): in wearing this armour and carrying this
shield into battle he literally takes on his own shoulders the
famam et fata nepotum (731). He has become, after Hercules and
before Augustus, the divine man of Roman destiny, the divine
opponent of Allecto and all that she symbolizes. The eighth
book has now answered the seventh and all is ready for the
battle itself; the opposed forces, ideals and destinies have finally
been arrayed against each other. Aeneas in the sixth book had
seen *himself* in retrospect and in comparison with future Roman
heroes: he now sees and accepts the past and the future of a
civitas, a whole society. He first stands in the 'empty theatre'
and then carries off with him its visible completion, the active
life of Rome at peace and in war. For the shield depicts actions
and events, not a procession of figures. It is Rome's history and
Rome's destiny. It is at once Aeneas' protection and responsibility.

With Book 9 the war actually begins: Allecto was but a
symbolic prelude. Now while Aeneas is off in Pallanteum and
Etruria (atque ea diversa penitus dum parte geruntur, 9. 1),
Turnus and the Latins, at Juno's urging, attack the Trojan
camp. The simultaneity of Books 8 and 9 is thus stated and is,
as we have seen, an essential part of Virgil's plan: the war, once
begun, cannot stop or wait; the tension must not be permitted

to drop until at least Aeneas and Turnus have met or are given the opportunity to meet in battle. There are, however, difficulties in Virgil's scheduling of events that make any rigidly consistent order impossible. Iris (10) tells Turnus that Aeneas has already proceeded to Etruria and Turnus himself (148) refers to Aeneas' 'Volcanian arms' though Nisus (196) speaks of bringing a message to Aeneas at Pallanteum. Virgil was thus not consistent in his times.[1] On the other hand, the clear demarcation of two days and a night in both books seems to indicate that Virgil wants us to accept the parity of days and events, as follows:

	8	9	10
First Day	Trip and Reception at Pallanteum	Battle (ships)	
First Night	Arms-making	Nisus-Euryalus	
Second Day	Pallanteum-Caere-Etruria	Battle: Turnus in Camp	
Second Night			Aeneas at Sea
Third Day			Aeneas at the camp

But Virgil's timing is not exact: the reader is meant to get only a general sense of simultaneity. Whether or not Virgil would have eliminated the contradictions in revision is, of course, an insoluble question. What clearly happened is that, though he fully intended the simultaneity, he in fact assumed in some places that 9 was subsequent to 8 in time as well as in order of books. For, as we shall see, it was essential that Turnus, to some degree at least, should know and understand the events of Book 8.

But we cannot explain 9 simply in terms of the simultaneity. It is obviously an intermediate 'odd' book (like 11 or like 3 and 5 in the Odyssean *Aeneid*) that is meant to separate the greater events of 8 and 10 from each other. Both 9 and 11 (for the most part) [2] avoid the central Pallas theme which is so crucial in

---

[1] The matter has been thoroughly discussed by Krokowski (*Quaestiones Epicae*, Prace Wroclawskiego Towanzystwa Naukwego, Seria A. Nr. 46, 1951) who has shown the defects of previous chronologies (e.g. Heinze, p. 342; Büchner, p. 390). But all such attempts at precise, consistent times are quite futile.

[2] The dead Pallas is conspicuous at the beginning of 11 but he (or his memory) do not determine the outcome as in 10 and 12 or foreshadow the outcome as in 8.

Books 8, 10 and 12. Nor do they decide any aspect of the war except indeed its indecisiveness and futility in the absence of Aeneas. But the two books (9, 11) do each present us with a great episode of youthful heroism (Trojan in 9, Latin in 11) that together are obviously meant to bring out, by contrast, aspects of Aeneas' character. Furthermore, they correspond in other ways: in 9 the Trojans are attacked and their camp is besieged; in 11 the Latins are attacked and their city, Laurentum, is finally put under seige. The real difference between them is that 11 marks a definite development in the narrative (it clearly brings out the effect of the Latin defeat in 10, and prepares us for the final showdown in 12), whereas 9 is altogether preliminary and ineffective. The action could really quite as well have started with Aeneas' arrival in Book 10.

The true meaning of 9 is in fact only brought out when we realize its relation to 5. In the scheme described above (p. 217) Book 7 is at the centre and is surrounded by corresponding Odyssean and Iliadic books:[1]

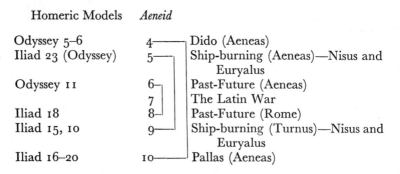

Homeric Models	*Aeneid*	
Odyssey 5–6	4	Dido (Aeneas)
Iliad 23 (Odyssey)	5	Ship-burning (Aeneas)—Nisus and Euryalus
Odyssey 11	6	Past-Future (Aeneas)
	7	The Latin War
Iliad 18	8	Past-Future (Rome)
Iliad 15, 10	9	Ship-burning (Turnus)—Nisus and Euryalus
Iliad 16–20	10	Pallas (Aeneas)

Book 8, as we have seen, shows us Aeneas taking possession, so to speak, of the future *promised* him in 6. Book 9, in a somewhat analogous way and as we have already seen (p. 273 above), shows the Trojan heroes (Ascanius, Nisus-Euryalus, Mnestheus) engaged in the reality (war) that they had anticipated in simulacrum (games) in 5. But the great difference between 5 and 9 is the absence of Aeneas and presence of Turnus. This is particularly brought out in the ship-burnings of both books: in 5 Aeneas is disheartened by the event even though its corollaries (the

---

[1] See Appendix 9, esp. for a discussion of the special role of Books 5–9.

miraculous saving of all but four ships, the founding of Acesta, concentration of the good fighters) are really essential preparatives for the Latin War. In 9, Turnus is *not* disheartened by the miraculous prevention of his attempt to burn the ships but breathes a *fiducia* which is not only belied by all the signs but indicates his irrational *furor* and resistance to fate. Again, just as 5 re-emphasizes the weakness of Aeneas in 4 and thus necessitates the *catabasis* of 6, 9 brings out Turnus' *failure* to appreciate the events of 8 and thus prepares us for his fatal despoiling of Pallas and his ignominious withdrawal by Juno in 10. The important point to be made here is that 9 reveals the character of Turnus and prefigures his fate and that the incident of the ship-burning is the touchstone that shows at once his similarity to and his difference from Aeneas.

The absence of Aeneas from the book is thus the primary clue to its function. We not only see the character of Turnus when he is forced, as it were, to play the role of Aeneas in a deliberately parallel situation. We see also what is lacking in even Trojan heroism when Aeneas is not on hand to guide it. Both sides (Trojan and Latin) together reveal the impotence of mere violence and even of heroism when it is touched by violence. The pious Aeneas is thus conspicuous *in absentia*. As a result his dramatic reappearance in Book 10 is prepared for: we not only feel by contrast what he is; we anticipate and are prepared to understand the significance of what he will do.

The plan of this book, as of the others, reveals its primary emphasis and functions:

I. Introduction (Juno-Iris-Turnus) (1–24)
II. The episode of the ships (25–158)
    (*a*) Turnus' attack and attempt to fire the ships (25–76)
    (*b*) The metamorphosis of the ships (77–122)
    (*c*) Turnus' *fiducia*: withdrawal at night (123–58)
III. The Euryalus episode (night) (159–502)
    (*a*) Introductory (159–75).
    (*b*) The resolution of Nisus and Euryalus (176–223)
    (*c*) The scene with Ascanius (224–313)
    (*d*) The raid on the Latin camp (314–66)
    (*e*) The death of Nisus and Euryalus (367–449)
    (*f*) The mother's grief (450–502)

IV. Fighting at the walls and *aristeiai* of Turnus (503-89)

V. Ascanius and Numanus (Remulus) (590-663)

VI. The fighting at the gate (664-818)

    (*a*) Pandarus and Bitias open the gate (664-90)

    (*b*) Turnus overpowers the Trojans (691-777)

      (i) Fighting at the open gate (691-721)

      (ii) The gate reclosed (722-77)

    (*c*) The Trojan recovery, Turnus withdraws (778-818)

Here an initial episode centred on Turnus (1-158) is balanced by a final Turnus episode (664-818) of almost exactly the same length (155 lines). In between is the massive Nisus-Euryalus story (344 lines) and two brief sections (Turnus' *aristeiai*; the single exploit of Ascanius). The book, in short, is divided almost evenly between Turnus (400 lines) and Nisus-Euryalus (344). Some attention (*pace* Book 5) is paid to Ascanius (conspicuous by his father's absence) and other Trojan heroes (especially Mnestheus) but these hardly dispute the pre-eminence of the major themes. Each is a theme of unsuccessful enterprise and ultimate failure and each marks, in its way, a conspicuous contrast with the Aeneas theme. But the two themes are also very different: the difference is not primarily one between Latin and Trojan but one between mature and immature patterns of abortive heroism. We see almost exactly the same contrast in Book 11 where the one side is again represented by Turnus and the other by a Latin figure, the young heroine Camilla. But here (in 9) the two contrasting themes gain much of their meaning and point from their parallelism with the corresponding themes of 5.

Turnus is urged by Juno *via* Iris to attack the Trojans in Aeneas' absence. But, frustrated by the Trojan refusal to come out and do battle (Aeneas had told them not to leave the walls of the camp), he attempts to fire the ships, which are then, at the instance of Cybele and Jupiter, turned into sea-nymphs. This is obviously a terrible portent, a clear indication of the gods' will, but Turnus' *confidence* is not shaken:

123   Obstipuere animis Rutuli; conterritus ipse
      turbatis Messapus equis, cunctatus et amnis
      rauca sonans revocatque pedem Tiberinus ab alto.
      At non audaci Turno fiducia cessit.

The meaning of Turnus' *fiducia* here is shown in the ensuing speech by which he tries to minimize the purport of this fearful event. He is not, he declares, terrified by the fates (Nil me fatalia terrent—133). The fates and Venus have in fact been satisfied by the *mere landing* of the Trojans while he, Turnus, has his own counter-fates:

136   Sunt et mea contra
       fata mihi, ferro sceleratam excindere gentem
       coniuge praerepta.

The sophistic character of such an argument is obvious and it is compounded by another: Troy can be punished all over again because it hates the whole female race. He then taunts the Trojans in words of sarcastic *superbia*. He boasts that he is more than a match for Aeneas' Volcanian arms, his Etruscan allies, his confidence in walls that did not save Troy before.

It is clear from this speech that Turnus' reliance on Juno is mixed with a haughty pride which blinds him to reality. He knows the facts (even all the events in Pallanteum and Etruria), actually sees the hand of fate at work in the miracle, yet refuses to admit its evident meaning. His *fiducia* is thus not a warranted confidence but the destructive *superbia* that precedes a *nemesis*.

And this impression that we get from his words is fully borne out in his deeds. He is courageous and, in a sense, noble-hearted, but battle-mad: he is likened to a *wolf* prowling around a sheepfold (ille asper et *improbus* ira saevit, l. 63), an eagle seizing his prey (563 f.), and again a wolf seizing a lamb (565 f.) or, finally, a lion at bay (792 f.). When he learns that Pandarus and Bitias have rashly opened the gates to the camp, he rushes to the spot *immani concitus ira* and kills five Trojans in succession. This *furor* is precisely what explains his failure: had he at this moment, when through Trojan folly he had been admitted within the walls, paused to reopen the gates and bring in the Latin army, he would have won the war then and there. But his blood-lust made him miss the supreme chance:

756   Diffugiunt versi trepida formidine Troes:
       et si continuo victorem ea cura subisset,
       rumpere claustra manu sociosque immittere portis,
       ultimus ille dies bello gentique fuisset;
       sed *furor* ardentem *caedis*que *insana cupido*
       egit in adversos.

It is *furor* and *caedis insana cupido* that undo him. His violence is both morally reprehensible and tactically stupid. The initial *fiducia* that made him despise the miracle of the ships thus foreshadows and prefigures his folly in this battle within the walls that closes the book.

What the ship miracle meant, of course, was that the Trojans no longer needed ships because they had in fact reached their predestined home. Here, as in the other ship-burning episode, Juno's intervention had resulted in the fulfilment, not the obstruction, of fate. But here both Juno's and Turnus' intention is almost immediately reversed, and Turnus, quite unlike Aeneas, is only emboldened by the reverse; his *furor* is that of a deliberate opposition to fate and it is, ironically, through this very failure to face and see consequences, that he defeats himself. The similarity between him and Aeneas in Book 2 (before the omens) is striking: he here, like Aeneas there, is motivated by a terrible *dolor* (duris dolor ossibus ardet, l. 66) and *ira* (ignescunt irae, l. 66) that blind him to what he does. His emotional handicap is not the doubt or despair that afflicts a man struggling with a new motivation (the Aeneas of 5), but a terrific *aidōs* or warrior's dread of anything that diminishes his battle-glory: when *that* is tainted or put in doubt, the result cannot but be the most shattering of psychological upheavals. Turnus, in short, is a truly Homeric hero, an Achilles who cannot endure an inferior position.[1] It is not Lavinia (coniuge praerepta, l. 138) but himself that is at the centre of his motivation.

The difference between Virgilian and Homeric values is brought out, of course, by the constant shadow of the Homeric model: the ship-burning episode here recalls (though only in the most general way) that of *Iliad* 15. Furthermore, this book corresponds in a vague sense to *Iliad* 1. 221 f. on to 16. 316 f. (the period of Achilles' absence from the battle). Turnus in fact is, for plot purposes, a blend of Hector and Achilles: he has something of the Achillean *menis* or wrath but also the Hectorian role of Aeneas' main opponent. The important point, however, is that Turnus' Homeric *aretē* is unfavourably compared to the *virtus-humanitas* of Aeneas. Similarly the other great episode of the book, the Nisus-Euryalus tragedy, is a Virgilian *Doloneia* and, again, the 'imitation' gives poignance to the difference.

---

[1] For a diametrically opposite view of Turnus, cf. Pöschl, esp. 153 f.

The *Nisus-Euryalus* shows the tragedy of two youths who possess *virtus* of a high order but are overcome at the supreme test by the excessive, irrational violence of the one and the desperate *eros* of the other. The ironical juxtaposition of the good and the bad in their natures is brought out when Nisus first mentions his resolve to penetrate the Latin lines and bring a message to Aeneas:

184   Dine hunc ardorem mentibus addunt,
        Euryale, an sua cuique deus fit *dira cupido*?

The *dira cupido* is here double-edged: it is meant to be a noble desire for true glory; it becomes an ignoble lust for blood and booty and an *eros* that destroys itself. In the end Nisus' question is answered: his *cupido* is not divine but very human. When the two plunder the Trojan camp, Nisus is no longer the somewhat sentimental rhetorician but an unfed lion ravaging the sheepfolds (impastus . . . *plena leo per ovilia turbans*) in his *mad hunger* (*vesana fames*). Euryalus commits no less slaughter, pathetic darling of Nisus though he may be. Yet he quite lacks Nisus' maturity of judgement:

353   breviter cum talia Nisus
        (Sensit enim *nimia caede* atque *cupidine ferri*)
        'Absistamus' ait 'nam lux inimica propinquat;
        Poenarum exhaustum satis est, via facta per hostis.'

Here we have the bad sense of *cupido*, the sense in which it was used of Turnus in 760: *caedis insana cupido*. In consequence, of course, Euryalus, delayed and slowed by his booty and revealed to the enemy by one part of it, the gleaming helmet of Messapus, is captured by the Latins (galea . . . Euryalum prodidit immemorem, 373 f.) before Nisus is even aware of what has happened.

We then see and feel the situation from the standpoint of the now isolated Nisus. The plot here provides Virgil with a wonderful opportunity for empathetic identification with a character.[1] We literally share the *dolor* which makes Nisus reckless of everything but Euryalus:

---

[1] See chap. viii (p. 388 f.) for a further discussion of this episode. It is, among other things, a fine example of Virgil's subjective style with its psychological continuity, empathy and sympathetic 'editorialism'. Compare the account of this on pp. 388 f. and in chap. iii, pp. 88 f.

425   nec se celare tenebris
         Amplius, aut tantum potuit perferre *dolorem*.

His love for Euryalus has indeed turned out to be a *dira cupido*.
His is a *Liebestod* but a *Liebestod* marked by utter forgetfulness
of his resolve and his manifest duty to deliver the message.

Yet Virgil at this juncture takes occasion to intrude on the
narrative *in propria persona*:

446   Fortunati ambo! si quid mea carmina possunt,
         nulla dies umquam memori vos eximet aevo,
         dum domus Aeneae Capitoli immobile saxum
         accolet imperiumque pater Romanus habebit.

He here shows that he admires their heroism in spite of all the
reservations he has so far expressed. The devotion of Nisus and
his tragic grief is a forecast of the affection and grief of Aeneas
for Pallas in Book 10. But the similarity *also* brings out the
difference. Nisus and Euryalus, like Turnus, have failed in their
enterprise through a *cupido* that was not noble or was, at the
least, extremely ambiguous. We now look back at Book 5 and
recall the *dolus* by which Nisus tripped Salius and gave the
victory to Euryalus: *Salius . . . ereptum . . . dolo reddi sibi poscit
honorem* (5. 342). The triumph of Euryalus' *lacrimae decorae* by
which, in spite of Salius' just protest, he carried off the prize
is here (in Book 9) made tragic: we still admire the devotion of
Nisus to Euryalus but we now see the result to which Euryalus'
excessive eagerness for prize or booty had led him and, above
all, what fateful possibilities the unreckoning *eros* of Nisus held
in reserve. Virgil's admiration for the pair does not in the least
conceal the qualitative difference between their heroism and
that of Aeneas.

So from every direction we return to the cardinal fact that
Aeneas is absent. It is his absence that provides the opportuni-
ties as well as the frustrations of this book. Turnus because of it
has no real competition but is still betrayed by his fury and
misses his great chance. Nisus and Euryalus are motivated by
it to plan a splendid enterprise but are finally beaten by their
bad *cupido* and miss the glory that their good *cupido* envisaged.
Ascanius can only show his spirit in one adventure (the killing
of Numanus): otherwise his enhanced importance is exhausted
in his fruitless patronage of Nisus and Euryalus:

312   Multa patri mandata dabat portanda; sed aurae
         Omnia discerpunt et nubibus inrita donant.

The mature *pietas*, the wise *humanitas* of the divine man is lacking, and, without it, there can be no effective decision. Even
the courage of Mnestheus and the other Trojan opponents of
Turnus was necessitated only by the danger to which the rash-
ness of Pandarus and Bitias had unnecessarily exposed them.
Aeneas had told the Trojans to stay within their camp and his
advice is completely justified in the event; their disregard of it
would, in fact, have been quite disastrous if Latin folly had not
come to their aid.

    In the next book Aeneas returns and all but wins the war.
It is only by the intervention of Juno and her timely removal of
Turnus from the battle, that the general conflict can be continued. This great reversal of the tide of events is motivated by
human feeling, by Aeneas' *pietas* toward Pallas and Evander.
Here his actions and feelings almost exactly reverse those of the
structurally analogous Dido episode.[1] In the greatest crisis of
the Odyssean *Aeneid*, Dido was the object of an affection that
threatened his mission and his destiny. In this corresponding
crisis of the Iliadic *Aeneid*, Pallas is the object of a *pietas* that not
only coincides with Aeneas' destiny but supplies the emotional
power that Aeneas needs to realize it. In the fourth book,
Aeneas was acting against his conscience and father image,
Anchises. Here, in avenging Pallas and Evander, he is devoting
himself to an Anchises-surrogate, an image of *pietas* that had
already taken on an unmistakably Anchisean coloration.
The death of Pallas is a tragedy of sorts—Pallas is the great
Marcellus figure of the poem—but, like Marcellus himself, he
is also an *exemplum virtutis* who in dying rouses the very forces
that bring victory. On the other hand, this book *also* corresponds
to 4 in much the same sense that 5 corresponds to 9: as 4 and 5
revealed Aeneas' unreadiness for Latium and the war there
(hence the necessity for the further and final ordeal of 6), both
9 and 10 reveal Turnus' unreadiness for the final conflict with
Aeneas. Not until he is prepared to accept his fate can he be
permitted to meet Aeneas. But 10 is the book that decides
Turnus' fate: after his killing and despoiling of Pallas, he has

---

[1] See pp. 217 f. and p. 344 f. above.

no further effective choice but to encounter Aeneas on the field of battle and there undergo his inevitable death.

The structure of the book is again the key to its meaning.

I. Introductory (1–259)
    (*a*) The concilium deorum (1–117)
    (*b*) The Trojans beseiged (118–45)
    (*c*) Aeneas: the Etruscan tribes and leaders (146–214)
    (*d*) Aeneas and Cymodocea (215–59)

II. The battle up to the death of Pallas (260–509)
    (*a*) The arrival of Aeneas (260–75)
    (*b*) The landing and first battle (276–361)
        (i) Turnus' reaction to Aeneas' arrival (276–86)
        (ii) Aeneas and the landing (287–307)
        (iii) *Aristeiai* of Aeneas (308–44)
        (iv) General engagement and stalemate (345–61)
    (*c*) *Aristeiai* and death of Pallas (362–509)
        (i) Pallas exhorts the Arcadians to fight (362–78)
        (ii) *Aristeiai* of Pallas (379–404)
        (iii) Pallas and Lausus (405–38)
        (iv) Contest of Pallas and Turnus and Pallas' death (439–509)

III. The battle after the death of Pallas (510–908)
    (*a*) *Aristeiai* of Aeneas: his victory; the siege raised (510–605)
    (*b*) Juno deceives and saves Turnus (606–88)
    (*c*) The contest of Aeneas with Mezentius and Lausus (689–908)
        (i) *Aristeiai* of Mezentius (689–746)
        (ii) The battle evened: stalemate (747–61)
        (iii) First contest of Mezentius and Aeneas (762–90)
        (iv) Battle of Aeneas and Lausus; death of Lausus (791–832)
        (v) Mezentius' grief and return to battle (833–72)
        (vi) Second contest of Mezentius and Aeneas; death of Mezentius (873–908)

Everything, it is evident, turns on Pallas. His death inspires the new ardour of Aeneas (in Part III) which, on the one hand, makes Juno withdraw Turnus in order to save him, and, on the other, decides the whole battle. The final contest with Mezentius does not really stop the élan that had already given Aeneas the victory by line 605. But though the book is indecisive in the sense that the final contest of Aeneas and Turnus remains to be fought, all the factors that will determine its outcome have been established. The contrast of Turnus' behaviour toward Pallas with Aeneas' behaviour toward Lausus is what shows the moral superiority of Aeneas and justifies the fate of Turnus. In a broader sense, it is Aeneas' attitude toward friends and foes in this book that wins him the victory and puts him on the side of both morality and fate.

The importance and purpose of the book is indicated by the *concilium deorum* with which it opens. The fact that it is here and only here in the poem that Virgil depicts such a *concilium* is of course an indication of the central significance of the book. Here the relation of Jupiter (fate) to the sub-fates, Juno and Venus, and, particularly, his relation to the human characters of the epic is finally made clear. Jupiter begins the council by denouncing the war: the struggle of Rome with Carthage has indeed been fated but this war is contrary to his express design: abnueram bello Italiam concurrere Teucris (8). He therefore urges that peace be made at once (placitum laeti componite foedus, 15). These words then introduce a vehement debate between Venus and Juno: Venus reviews Juno's past opposition to Aeneas and seemingly despairs of the present; all she wants now is to save Ascanius. Juno, in turn, defends Turnus and the Latins and blames the Trojans' troubles on Aeneas and themselves. Jupiter then settles the argument by what *seems* to be a deliberate abdication of authority. Since, he says, a *foedus* between Latins and Trojans cannot be re-established due to the discord of the two goddesses, he will leave the issue of the battle to the fortune of the day, without prejudice toward either side (nullo discrimine). The designs of each will correspond to his toil and his success:

III   sua cuique exorsa laborem
          fortunamque ferent. Rex Iuppiter omnibus idem.
          Fata viam invenient.

Do these words really mean that Jupiter has resigned all direction of events?[1] In that case why and how will the *fates find a way?* The obvious answer is that Jupiter is here distinguishing between two meanings of fate and of his own will; one is the

---

[1] Cf. Cartault (715, 720–1) who describes the council as 'un fiasco complet'.

ultimate outcome or result such as the eventual destruction of Carthage by Rome or the eventual *foedus* of Latins and Trojans; the other is the detailed attainment of this result, the means by which it is effected, the way in which seemingly disparate and opposite forces are made to contribute to one end. The interference of the sub-fates, especially of Juno, has deferred the establishment of a *foedus* (it cannot be made *now* as Jupiter somewhat provocatively suggests) but not deferred it permanently. For the fates always *find a way*. But this way need not be (and in fact is not) one that precludes or denies human freedom, the toil and the deserved success or failure of human undertakings (exorsa). Aeneas' *pietas* and his temperate wisdom and humanity are not fated: nor is Turnus' *furor*. (That he missed his great chance in the battle within the walls of the camp was his own fault.) Destiny is not independent of human will or effort. This idea, as we have seen, is implied throughout the *Aeneid* (otherwise *pietas* would not have been a moral achievement at all) but here it is explicitly stated. And it is explicitly stated because this book is, so to speak, 'set apart' as the *locus classicus* of the idea, the one place where the right and wrong sides declare themselves most unambiguously as responsible for their good and bad fortunes.

The human actions which thus determine the outcome, the actions through which the fates find their way to their intended result, are the two great encounters in which Turnus and Aeneas face the noble Marcelli of each side—Pallas first and Lausus, second—and the second encounter is made possible, is, so to speak, 'set up' by the first. All the mass action, the battle as such, is determined by these encounters. Juno likewise is guided by the prior decisions and actions of the heroes, Turnus and Aeneas. It is, as Jupiter sarcastically tells her, not Venus but Aeneas' *vivida bello dextra* and *animus ferox patiensque pericli* (609–10) that have put Turnus in the strait from which Juno only temporarily saves him. The concatenation of events here is relatively easy to see even though the critics have only too often ignored it.

Aeneas' reappearance after the final night journey by sea from Etruria (260–75) is one of the dramatic high-points of the epic. The suspense built up by his long absence from the scene in Book 9 is now used with maximum effect:

260   Iamque in conspectu Teucros habet et sua castra,
stans celsa in puppi, clipeum cum deinde sinistra
extulit ardentem. Clamorem ad sidera tollunt
Dardanidae e muris.

He is here with his wonderful shield: Virgil uses with great
éclat the simile applied by Apollonius to Jason.[1] Aeneas is like
the bane-bringing star Sirius or—as Virgil himself adds—like a
red comet in the night: both foretell bad news, such as Aeneas
undoubtedly is to the Latins.

But this dramatic arrival does not in itself settle anything.
Turnus' *fiducia* still holds strong (276). And Aeneas' initial
aristeiai (which continue to 344) do not prevent the battle soon
being dead-locked (345–61). Virgil obviously wished to introduce Pallas before giving Aeneas his due: with line 362 (*at parte
ex alia*) we turn to another part of the battlefield, where Pallas
is leading the Arcadians. The next lines (to 410) are filled with his
aristeiai and they are much more impressive than those of
Aeneas just recounted. But in line 411 Halaesus again intervenes
(he had been one of the first Latins to check the initial élan of
Aeneas): he is killed by Pallas in the latter's greatest and last
feat of arms, but is immediately succeeded by Lausus, *non caede
viri tanta perterrita Lausus . . . sinit agmina*. Thus a great battle
between Pallas and Lausus seems inevitable and everything
attests its fitness and equality:[2]

433   Hinc Pallas instat et urguet,
hinc contra Lausus, nec multum discrepat aetas:
egregii forma, sed quis Fortuna negarat
in patriam reditus.

But this battle is not permitted to take place. On the divine
level, Jupiter forbids it because the two are soon to meet their
fates under greater foes (438). Yet the divine will does not in the
least determine the human: it is Turnus' own desire that makes
him put Lausus aside and select Pallas as his and *only* his proper
opponent—*soli mihi Pallas debetur* (442–3). His arrogant *fiducia*

---

[1] Cf. *Arg.* III. 956–61. Apollonius compares Jason to the brightness and beauty of
Sirius: but Medea's 'love-sick' (δυσίμερον) 'care' (κάματον), i.e. her anguish of the
moment, to the woe it brings on the sheepfolds. But there is no sense of *future* doom
in his simile: this is Virgil's own contribution. Virgil also used Homer (*Iliad* 5. 4 ff.
and 22. 25 ff.) but the red comet is his own.
[2] This part was quite misunderstood by Heinze (p. 226).

and *caedis cupido* is shown above all in his heartless wish that Evander himself were at hand to see what was going to happen (443)—words that Virgil pointedly characterizes as *superba*. The inequality of the contest is evident to all, not least to Pallas as he turns his eyes over Turnus' huge body (corpus per ingens). Pallas' simple reply to Turnus ('It is you or I. My father is equal to either outcome. Enough of threats.') is a fitting rebuke, the answer of courageous modesty to boastful power. The ease with which Turnus kills Pallas (the lion and the steer, 454–6) is of course further evidence of Turnus' superior strength. The contest in fact is meant to be unequal; and thus to enhance both the *virtus* of Pallas and the *superbia* of Turnus. For it is not so much Pallas' death as its setting that is significant. As Jupiter remarks to the grieving Hercules: each man has his day in the shortness of time, *sed famam extendere factis, hoc virtutis opus.* The significant thing is that it is precisely to such divinely warranted *virtus* that Turnus shows the contempt of his arrogant nature: he leaves the body for Evander to see and bury (his meaning surely is that if Evander could not witness the contest, he could at least witness its result) but brutally despoils it of the ponderous belt, the belt on whose medallions was impressed a *nefas*, the slaughter of the fifty sons of Aegyptus by the Danaids (fitting booty for the breaker of a marriage treaty!).

The whole episode is thus designed to exhibit Turnus' *culpa* and character. Virgil even intervenes editorially to point the moral:

501   Nescia mens hominum fati sortisque futurae
          et servare modum, rebus sublata secundis.

A time will come when Turnus would give much to have sent back Pallas' body unspoiled! (503–5). It must, however, be carefully noted that Turnus' ignorance of his fate and fortune (501) is equated with his inability to be moderate in his hour of success (502). It is in short his *inhumanitas* that condemns him. He does not recognize the *virtus* of an enemy and by exulting in the grief of the bereaved father,[1] he shows also his contempt for human suffering and *pietas*.

---

[1] Note here the premonitory use of this motif—contempt for a parent's grief—in the close of the Nisus-Euryalus episode when the Latins exhibit the impaled head of Euryalus to his aged mother (9. 462 ff.).

It is now and only now that Aeneas begins to fight with decisive effect. The difference between his earlier *aristeiai* (310–44) and those that follow the death of Pallas (510 f.) is carefully emphasized.[1] The earlier exploits were baldly and succinctly described: stravitque Latinos ... Lichan ferit ... Gyan ... deiecit leto ... (hasta) volans clipei transverberat aera Maeonis ... hasta fugit servatque cruenta tenorem. It is all quite routine fighting: it is almost the weapons rather than Aeneas that kill. But in 510 ff. the personal involvement is intense: he snatches up four youths to immolate to the shades of Pallas (518 f.); he disdains all *commercia belli* since, as he tells Mago, Turnus had already done away with them by killing Pallas (531 f.); his contempt for Tarquitius (557 f.), for Lucagus and his brother (575 f.), for the priest Haemonides (537 f.), is that of a man driven out of himself by a *dolor* that overwhelms his previous nature. Here, indeed, Aeneas shows no mercy to the enemy but his motivation is the very antipodes of that of Turnus. What moves him is both *pietas* toward Evander and affection toward Pallas:

515   *Pallas, Evander* in ipsis
          omnia sunt oculis, mensae, quas advena primas
          tunc adiit, dextraeque datae.

The mensae (the guest-friendship) and the sworn *fides* represent the *pietas* but these are emotively reinforced by his deep feeling for Pallas: Pallas ... sinistro adfixus lateri (160–1). In one sense Aeneas' fighting at this juncture seems quite devoid of his usual *humanitas*; in another it is the very symbol of it—a completely human reaction to the *violentia* that breaks treaties, despises filial piety, and wreaks its fury on the dead. It is not mercy toward the *impii* that Virgil wants or approves: debellare superbos is in itself a harsh thing and the fact is not disguised. But Aeneas is not driven by battle-lust (caedis cupido) or the mere wish for military glory. *Once his sword is hot* (ut semel intepuit mucro, 570), he fights like the hundred-armed Aegeon. But for the heating of his sword is required the stimulus of a great grief and wrong.

The effect of the new spirit in Aeneas is soon evident. By 604–5 the siege is raised and the Trojans victoriously leave their

---

[1] Cf. Conway, *Virgilian Age*, pp. 135–6 who well notes the change in Aeneas' mood.

camp. All that remains to clinch the victory is the quick and apparently certain defeat of Turnus by the triumphantly irresistible Aeneas. But Juno intervenes and withdraws Turnus, tricking him into the pursuit of a phantom Aeneas. When he discovers the ruse, he is alone at sea on the ship in which he had expected to bring a craven and fleeing enemy to bay. Ignorant as he is of his real danger (666), he can only feel a sense of overwhelming shame. He wants the earth to gape open for him, the ship to fall into rocks or shallows

679   quo neque me Rutuli nec *conscia fama* sequatur.

Thrice he tries suicide, thrice to leap into the water and swim back to the fighting: always Juno stops him and at last returns him to his own city and his father Daunus. Juno had in fact been defeated by Turnus' brutality and its reaction on the spirit of Aeneas. All she could do was to bend before the storm and save her favourite from the consequences of his own actions. Truly the fates had found their way!

Turnus was indeed saved from a quick death, but only at the cost of shattering damage to his ego. Virgil did not, like Homer, leave the rescue to the moment of the hero's imminent defeat in actual combat (as with Hector in the twentieth *Iliad*). By making Juno save Turnus *before* he could meet Aeneas, Virgil put the emphasis not so much on Turnus' martial inferiority to Aeneas as on his desertion of his friends and allies in their hour of need. And it is just this sense of desertion, the consciousness of having saved himself at the expense of others, that from now on constitutes Turnus' great problem.

All that is now left for Aeneas to do is to dispose of the terrible Mezentius. When the latter appears, he asserts himself with such *aristeiai* that, for the moment, the battle is once more brought to a standstill. But this is of course but dramatic preparation for the final contest of the book. Just as Pallas had carried all before him until he came up against Lausus and Turnus, so now Mezentius' very success brings him to Aeneas. The contest, however, seemed to be quickly decided since Mezentius' spear missed Aeneas and Aeneas' spear penetrated Mezentius' groin: it looked as if Aeneas could have finished him off quickly with the sword. But Lausus had seen and deeply felt his father's mishap:

789   ingemuit cari graviter genitoris amore
           ut vidit, Lausus, lacrimaeque per ora volutae.

Lausus now inspires another of Virgil's editorial apostrophes but this time before rather than after the action. Virgil, from the very start, wishes to direct our attention to the importance of the event and to indicate the tragic nobility of Lausus: mortis durae casum tuaque optima facta.

Everything that now happens is the exact reverse of the Pallas-Turnus encounter. Aeneas does not displace another and more equal opponent in order to fight Lausus: Lausus instead initiates the fight as he darts between Aeneas and Mezentius. Aeneas, even in this moment of his frustration and grief, tries to warn off his ill-matched foe:

811   quo moriture ruis maioraque viribus audes?
           fallit te incautum *pietas tua*.

His recognition of Lausus' filial *pietas* is the second great reversal of Turnus' behaviour toward Pallas. But Lausus of course presses on: nec minus ille/exsultat demens (812). Aeneas is now forced to fight and, for that matter, his own ire is raised in the heat of contest (813). He does not yet grasp the nature and nobility of Lausus. But when he turns to look at his victim's body, his mood completely changes:

821   At vero ut voltum vidit morientis et ora,
           ora modis *Anchisiades* pallentia miris,
           ingemuit graviter miserans dextramque tetendit
           et mentem patriae subiit pietatis imago.

Anchisiades is of course the key word.[1] The man of *pietas* (the *son of Anchises*) now recognizes a true image of his own *pietas* in his enemy. His first thought is to do what he can for such nobility and devotion:

825   quid tibi nunc miserande puer, pro laudibus istis
           quid *pius* Aeneas tanta dabit indole dignum?

All he can actually do, however, is to hand the body *unspoiled* to Lausus' comrades and thus return it to the shades and ashes of his ancestors:

---

[1] The significance of *Anchisiades* here was first pointed out by La Cerda in his commentary, ad loc. Cf. also Conington, ad loc. and Warde Fowler, *Aeneas at the Site of Rome*, p. 88, and our note on p. 340 above.

827   arma quibus laetatus habe tua teque parentum
             manibus et cineri, si qua est ea cura, remitto.

He himself summons Lausus' battle-companions and helps
them to raise the body from the ground. Thus in every respect
his conduct is the antipodes of the conduct of Turnus. The moral
justification of his final victory is here.

The book ends with the 'return' of Mezentius to the battle.
The self-sacrifice of Lausus has finally caused the terrible tyrant
and *contemptor divom* to recover his moral perspective and repent
—too late—of his past misdeeds. He sees that he has spoiled his
son's good name by his crimes (851) and he regrets above all
his own survival. But he will not survive long

855   nunc vivo neque adhuc homines lucemque relinquo:
             sed linquam.

The mixture of shame and grief in his soul is depicted in one of
the most remarkable lines of the whole *Aeneid*:

871   uno in corde pudor mixtoque insania luctu.

His death now comes quickly: indeed he is not only wounded
but pinned under his dead horse. Aeneas, of course, cannot
spare him (the past cannot be obliterated by this 'deathbed
repentance'), but it is much that Mezentius himself has been
driven to recognition of his crimes and of the only possible
satisfaction yet left him, the death which he accepts so willingly:
iugulo ... haut inscius accipit ensem/undantique animam
diffundit in arma cruore.

This 'return' of Mezentius is of course the pointed obverse
of Turnus' non-return. Turnus by his unnecessary and brutal
treatment of Pallas had created the new spirit that had given
Aeneas the victory. He had then left his allies and companions
to face the new Aeneas and die for his own cause in his absence.
But the self-sacrifice and the *pietas* of his followers had not yet
brought Turnus, as it here had brought Mezentius, to a sense
of his own violence and folly. His suffering is still that of a man
whose ego has been terribly bruised, whose *conscia fama* has been
unbearably stained: there is no element of *pietas* or self-sacrifice
in such brittle egoism. But the death of Mezentius, with which
the book ends, both prefigures the fate and indicates the moral
problem of Turnus. It is in a sense a substitute for his own death,

for the 'logical' end of the battle with the defeat of the main opponent of Aeneas, but it is also and more significantly an earnest of what is to come.

Aeneas, on the other hand, is now established as the man whose *pietas* is both a human emotion and an expression of true humanity. He avenges Pallas and Evander (so far at least as the absence of Turnus permits); he appreciates the *pietas* of Lausus toward Mezentius. And in so doing he puts himself on the winning side. It is precisely through *his* emotions, his *actions* that the fates find their way. This is obviously Virgil's intention and, to a quite significant degree, he fulfils it. But he has not, for all that, fully overcome the discrepancy between the Homeric fighter, the almost Achillean hero, that Aeneas is in the latter half of the book, and the humane, Augustan hero that Aeneas is also supposed to be. It is not at all that Aeneas is a sort of 'pacifist' who yet fights; it is rather that Aeneas' shift of mood after line 510 seems somehow excessive, that the picture of Pallas lacks the emotional connotations required to explain his supposed hold on Aeneas. Evander is too new and too remote a character to play the role of Anchises and Pallas is too much of a fighter himself (he has killed too many) to excite all the sympathy that we are clearly expected to feel at his death. The tenth book, in short, is almost too Homeric to justify its anti-Homeric moral. Emotionally we share the shame of Turnus, the *pietas* of Lausus, the repentance of Mezentius, more than we share the pathos of Pallas or the righteous wrath of Aeneas. But we must, I think, finally admit that Virgil here brought off a *tour de force*, for all the reservations we may want to make. He had tried to show and in considerable degree had actually shown how a man could fight with all that was in him and yet preserve an essential humanity in which utter devotion to his own was mingled with respect for his enemy. The idea may seem to us limited—it is certainly far from Christian—but it is a distinctly new note in epic.

The eleventh book is the bridge between the decisive battle of 10 and the final victory of 12. But it is, to say the least, a curious bridge. The best clue to its meaning is its structure:

I. Trojan section (1–202)

   (*a*) Aeneas at the bier of Pallas (1–99)

   (*b*) The Latin burial; embassy to Aeneas (100–38)

(*c*) Evander's mourning (139–81)
(*d*) The Trojan burial (182–202)

II. Latin section (203–444)
    (*a*) Latin grief, accusation of Turnus (203–24)
    (*b*) The embassy returns from Diomedes (225–95)
    (*c*) Speech of Latinus (296–335)
    (*d*) Speech of Drances (336–75)
    (*e*) Reply of Turnus (376–444)

III. The attack on Laurentum (from Latin viewpoint) (445–915)
    (*a*) The Trojans are coming (445–85)
    (*b*) Dispositions for battle; Turnus and Camilla (486–531)
    (*c*) Diana and Opis (Camilla's girlhood) (532–96)
    (*d*) The first engagement and battle (597–647)
    (*e*) *Aristeiai* of Camilla (648–724)
    (*f*) Death of Camilla (725–867)

        (i) Tarchon, Arruns (725–67)
        (ii) Death of Camilla (768–835)
        (iii) Punishment of Arruns (836–67)

    (*g*) Rout of Latin cavalry (868–95)
    (*h*) Withdrawal of Turnus: siege of Laurentum (896–915)

If we disregard the first two parts (1–444) and consider only the second half (445–915), the parallelism with Book 9 is striking. Here, as there, initial (445–531) and concluding (896–915) sections on Turnus enclose a tragedy of heroic, youthful valour. Camilla obviously corresponds to Euryalus: she is his Latin counterpart. Her story, however, is much more closely connected with the main plot and the reason is clearly her relation to Turnus, already prefigured in their joint entrance at the end of the muster in 7. Turnus also acts very much as he did in 9. His bold design (the ambush of Aeneas) is frustrated by his premature withdrawal just before Aeneas' arrival. But this is caused by his loss of self-control at hearing of Camilla's death. Here as in the final fighting of Book 9, he is defeated by his own *furor*. But here, unlike 9, the *furor* is due to his own rage at his recurrent inability to help his supporters in their hour of need and especially his failure to help such a heroine as Camilla.

In this sense 11 definitely prepares us for the *foedus*, the agreement to decide the issue by personal combat with Aeneas, that begins the next book. The arrangement of the two *Aeneids* is in this respect quite parallel:

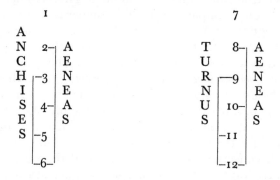

3 and 5 are the Anchises books; 9, 11 are the Turnus books; 6 and 12 are the books in which the two sets of figures (Anchises, Aeneas/Turnus, Aeneas) share the stage in a final, decisive encounter.

Much more important, however, is the correspondence of 11 with 3 in the scheme (p. 217) of concentric parallels based on the centrality of 7. Book 11 takes Aeneas from the scene of crucial action (10) to the scene of his *final* triumph (Laurentum). It thus exactly reverses the movement of 3, from Troy, the place of *initial* defeat (2) to Carthage, the place of crucial action (4). Furthermore, while 11 begins with the obsequies of Pallas and concludes with Aeneas' arrival at Laurentum, 3 ends with the obsequies of Anchises and begins with his departure from Troy. But these superficial correspondences point to a much more fundamental one: the respect in which both 3 and 11 bridge the psychological gaps between 2 and 4 and between 12 and 10 respectively. Without 3 and its events (above all its revelation of Anchises' initiative *and* his death) the behaviour of Aeneas in 4 would be unintelligible; without 11, the change of motivation in Turnus between 10 and 12 would be far less cogent and natural.

We need not comment in detail on the Camilla episode. Its purpose is roughly the same as that of the Nisus-Euryalus—to depict a youthful hero betrayed by immaturity and lust for plunder. The contrast she makes with the mature *pietas* of Aeneas is here (as in 9) quite different from that made by the *furor* or inhumanity of Turnus. Camilla is a most appealing and sympathetic heroine. Her romantic upbringing in the wilds —she is a true child of nature—shows its effects in her actions.[1] She is at once simple and terrible, naïve and ferocious. Her easy deception by Aunus' son and her fierce revenge upon him, illustrate admirably the two sides of her nature. She is finally betrayed by her woman's love for finery and her primitive desire for spoil: *femineo praedae et spoliorum amore* (782). Her tragedy is thus fatally in character. Her self-confidence (sui . . . fiducia . . . forti, 502), her defiant exposure of the breast, her rusticity, her *cupido caedis*, her femininity—all combine to make her an easy prey for the sly Arruns. But in defeat she is utterly self-forgetful, concerned only for Turnus and the war. Her faults are clearly less than those of her leader—her death once more brings out his responsibility for such useless sacrifice of noble life—but her primitivism is, in the last analysis, a most ambiguous and fatal thing. Yet Virgil, in making the parallel between her and the Trojan youths of Book 9, has shown, as clearly as he knew how, the tragedy of *civil* war and the *humanitas* that looks beyond the battle lines to peace.

The great problem of the book, which no commentator or critic seems ever to have taken seriously, is the bearing of Turnus' behaviour in 10 on his motives and actions here. How did the searing experience of his withdrawal by Juno, his abandonment of his friends in the very crisis of the battle, affect him now—what difference did it make to his whole character and future? This is indeed the question with which Virgil is concerned in the first two parts (1–444).

The first part (1–202) is centred on the Trojans and Aeneas. Little or no stress is put on the *victory* of the previous day: Aeneas, to be sure, erects a *tropaeum* but pays the scantest attention to it; he is concerned only with the sad task of burial (22 f.). Above all, the body of Pallas must be sent back to Evander. Aeneas' farewell to Pallas (41 f.) and the ensuing departure of the funeral cortege, is one of the great scenes of

---

[1] Clearly ll. 532–96 are an integral part of the book. The account of Camilla's childhood gives us the perspective in which we are meant to view her battle performance: brought up 'without a woman's care' by her father in the wilderness, she is really a woman who is not a woman.

the poem; the most moving part of it is the last tribute that Aeneas speaks over the body:

96   *Nos alias hinc ad lacrimas* eadem horrida belli
      fata vocant: salve aeternum mihi, maxime Palla,
      aeternumque vale.

These words recall his farewell to Helenus in Book 3:

493   Vivite felices, quibus est fortuna peracta
      iam sua: *nos alia ex aliis in fata vocamur.*
      Vobis parta quies.

But the effect is quite different: in 3 Aeneas was nostalgically contrasting his own bitter circumstances with Helenus' contentment and peace; here he is only describing the hard task he has yet to finish; the humanity now comes from strength, not weakness. This is shown by the *actions* that follow the *words*:

98   Nec plura effatus ad altos
      tendebat muros gressumque in castra *ferebat.*

There is no hesitation here: the imperfects show Aeneas on his way back to his hard duties almost before the words of farewell have ceased to vibrate.

Obviously this is a man whose resolution is no less than his *humanitas*. When the Latin envoys arrive, requesting a truce for the purpose of burying their dead (100–38), he not only grants it, but adds: equidem et *vivis* [pacem] concedere vellem. He has no quarrel with the Latins: it is the Latins and Turnus who quarrel with him. But it would have been fairer for Turnus *alone* to have fought with him:

117   his mecum decuit concurrere telis:
      vixet, cui vitam deus aut sua dextra dedisset.

This proposal was of course more than acceptable to Drances, the Latin spokesman, since, among other things, Drances was Turnus' domestic enemy. But in any event, Aeneas is here represented as a responsible and humane leader who both deplores the war and is willing to end it by his own courage. The burden of decision and responsibility now rests on Turnus.

We are thus made to see Turnus in the light of Aeneas' *virtus-humanitas*. We return to the Latins (204 f.) and see their grief as they light the innumerable pyres for the dead of the previous battle. The mothers and wives of the war-dead spontaneously echo Aeneas' challenge:

217   dirum exsecrantur bellum Turnique hymenaeos;
ipsum armis ipsumque iubent decernere ferro,
qui regnum Italiae et primos sibi poscat honores.

And Drances (220 f.), of course, re-echoes their sentiments. At this moment the arrival of the ambassadors with the unfavourable response of Diomedes to the Latin request for aid in the war (225 f.)—he indeed recommends that they come to terms with Aeneas—now gives solid support to the peace party. Latinus accordingly urges conciliation, but his proposal (302–35) hardly meets the situation, since, as Drances at once remarks, he omits the pivotal factor: Lavinia. No promise of land or material help can avail if the marriage question remain unsettled.

But Latinus was obviously trying to placate Turnus. He thus passes over the embarrassing absence of Turnus from the crisis of the battle, and the consequent catastrophe of Lausus, Mezentius and the Latin army. He avoids recriminations:

312   Nec quemquam incuso: potuit quae plurima virtus
esse, fuit; toto certatum est corpore regni.

In all this part, the contrast between the Trojan preoccupation with Pallas and the Latin silence about Lausus and Mezentius is eloquent indeed.

Drances, however, is not only the analogue of Polydamas in the *Iliad*, the giver of sound but unpleasant advice, but the embittered rival of Turnus who, for quite personal reasons, is not in the least hesitant to reveal the unpalatable truth. He refers to Turnus' flight (*fugae fidens*, 351) and urges him to admit defeat:

365   Miserere tuorum
pone animos et *pulsus abi.*

This obvious reference to the shameful disappearance of Turnus from the previous battle (Book 10) is what draws from Turnus the remarkably eliptical words:

392   pulsus ego? aut quisquam merito, foedissime, pulsum
arguet, Iliaco tumidum qui crescere Thybrim
sanguine et Evandri totam cum stirpe videbit
procubuisse domum atque exutos Arcadas armis?

haud ita me experti Bitias et Pandarus ingens
et quos mille die victor sub Tartara misi,
inclusus muris hostilique aggere saeptus.

No one can fail to note here the *omission* of all that happened
in the battle *after* the death of Pallas and the compensatory
emphasis on the prior battle (before Aeneas' arrival) within
the walls. Turnus wholly by-passes the main issue, the Latin
defeat and his own responsibility for it, and dwells on the
indecisive contest of two days back *and* on his own killing of
Pallas. He must have known by now the consequences of that
act and the new spirit of victory it had fostered in Aeneas. His
implication is: 'You can't blame me for being deceived by the
phantom Aeneas. But look what I did do!' [1] This failure to face
reality, above all to face the deaths of Mezentius and Lausus and
his own implication in their fates, obviously argues a very
uneasy conscience, an egoism that cannot bear to mention
or hear mentioned the terrible wound that it has received. His
speech is a desperate effort to save his reputation and prestige
by ignoring what has really undermined them.

But there is another and even more ominous element in this
most revealing speech of Turnus: fear. He argues that Latin
despondency is unjustified by their numbers and resources
(419 f.). He lists the heroes (Messapus, Camilla) that remain. [2]
(Note again the eliptical reference to Lausus and Mezentius).
Finally he refers to Aeneas' challenge. *If* indeed the *Trojans*
(note the plural) want to fight him alone, he will not refuse
(434 f.). Such an eventuality, however, is *put in the conditional* as
a kind of corollary of Latin timidity and cowardice. The actual
challenge of Aeneas is dismissed in the curiously off-hand
words:

442   'Solum Aeneas vocat': et vocet oro.

Thus Turnus quite refuses to face his own responsibility for the
lost battle and the war. 'Vobis animam hanc soceroque Latino
... devovi', he declares, as if indeed Latinus wanted such

---

[1] Cf. Servius ad loc: hoc vult intelligi, non posse dici merito pulsum eum, qui in
sequendo hostem bella deseruit, aperte autem hoc dicit: potest merito credi qui
pulsus sit is cuius tot extant tropaea? Here Servius is better than most commentators but he still misses the implications of Turnus' words.

[2] There is possibly a reference to Mezentius' and/or Lausus' death in ll. 416 f. If
this is so, Turnus certainly wrests it to his own uses. Mezentius is *fortunatus* in his
death since it kept him from seeing the despair and cowardice of the Latins (ne
quid tale videret procubuit moriens).

sacrifice or recognized Turnus as his rightful son-in-law. But Turnus deliberately confuses his own egoistic desires with the *bona communia* (435) and thus evades Aeneas' *personal* challenge. The *vocet oro* of line 442 in effect puts it off and leaves Aeneas to take the initiative, even though Turnus surely knows that Aeneas has already done so in his words to Drances and the Latin embassy. It is clear that Turnus has in fact not the least desire to fight Aeneas in single combat and *therefore* wants the war to go on. When the news of Aeneas' approach from the camp is announced in the council (445 f.), Turnus rushes to arms with the remark: cogite concilium et pacem laudate sedentes:/illi armis in regna ruunt (460 f.). Obviously he seizes the opportunity to stop debate and continue the general war and thus to leave Aeneas' challenge unanswered and unacted upon. It is therefore impossible to avoid the conclusion that Turnus is really birking the main issue. His defensive and truculent speech conceals a large element of fear.

We can therefore imagine the mood of Turnus *after* the defeat and death of Camilla. As if in fated repetition of the events of 9 and 10, Jove's will and his own *furor* (note once more the parallel action of the human and divine elements of the poem) make him abandon the ambush at the very moment of Aeneas' approach:

> 901 Ille furens (et saeva Iovis sic numina pellunt)
> deserit obsessos collis, nemora aspera linquit.
> Vix e conspectu exierat campumque tenebat,
> cum pater Aeneas saltus ingressus apertos
> exsuperatque iugum silvaque evadit opaca.

The clear implication is that Turnus had just missed his great and final opportunity for military victory.[1] Neither the place nor the time could be recovered. It was already too late to wait and engage the enemy outside the walls (912 f.) and this locale was obviously quite devoid of the advantages of the ambush in the woods. Here as in the battle within the walls of 9, Turnus defeats himself by his own lack of self-control. But in

---

[1] This point has been strangely missed by most commentators. Büchner (397) attributes Turnus' retreat to the *strategic* consequences of Camilla's death; Cartault (p. 806) to the cavalry defeat. But this is *not* what Virgil says. It was too late for Turnus to fight at l. 912 but this was some time after he had withdrawn from the ambush. Even so he wanted (at 912) to fight, though cut off by the dusk and when his *strategic* situation was considerably worse.

this case the *furor* comes from a virtual repetition of his *furor* in 10: the doubly wounded ego of a hero who *again* had managed to be absent in the hour of need and decision. Ironically, it is precisely Camilla's death that ruins his plans by the very remorse it excites.

Obviously Virgil wished to end his epic with the death duel of the two heroes. Thus Turnus' frustration in 9, 10 and 11 (and especially in 10 and 11) is an essential part of the plot or scheme of the Iliadic *Aeneid*. In 9 Aeneas is absent and Turnus cannot use his absence to win a clear-cut military victory. In 10 he is decoyed away by Juno. Here in 11, as we have now seen, he just misses his chance to fight Aeneas at the ambush. At first sight Virgil seems to solve the problem of 'retardation'—of deferring the final contest of the heroes—in a way quite like that of Homer. But the real difference, for all that, is profound.

In the *Iliad* Achilles' wrath keeps him out of the battle until the twentieth of the twenty-four books. Patroclus' death, to be sure, occurs in Book 16 but Books 17–19 intervene before Achilles can actually return: the fight over Patroclus' body, the notification of Achilles, the making of the armour, take up the interval. But in 20 Achilles does appear in all his might and fury and even encounters Hector (when the latter cannot over-look the killing of his brother, Polydorus). Hector, however, is saved when Apollo intervenes, wraps him in mist and carries him off the field. But this episode does not seem to matter par-ticularly to either the plot or to Hector's motivation. What finally moves Hector to await Achilles by the walls and accept battle, is his *aidōs* or shame over an *earlier* episode. As he explains in Book 22 (99–130), he feels that in rejecting Polydamas' wise counsel (to avoid Achilles, leave the plain and withdraw into the city: it is given for the last of three times in Book 18), he was responsible for many Trojan deaths and had in fact 'ruined' the Trojan host. He cannot avoid Achilles now if he is to face the Trojan men and women any more. He does not have much hope of success since he knows and acknowledges that Achilles is his superior. Like a true Homeric hero, he sacrifices his life to his *aidōs*.

In the *Aeneid*, Turnus' wrath does not keep him from battle with Aeneas—quite the contrary. His first chance at Aeneas comes in 10, and he is very eager for it. But he is not saved from certain death in a combat already under way (as in *Iliad* 20): Juno and the reader know that Turnus could not have stood long against the enraged Aeneas of this book but Turnus does not. He pursues in fact what he believes to be a fleeing Aeneas (10. 647) and is quite ignorant of the true situation (ignarus rerum, 10. 666). He simply feels himself shamed by his withdrawal from the battle. But by 11 he has had opportunity to learn the true circumstances of the battle: he now not only avoids the bitter recollection of Mezentius and Lausus but tries to defer Aeneas' personal challenge, and instead, continue the general war. The fact that he plans an *ambush* for Aeneas (the very opposite of an open contest) is a tacit indication of his feelings (furta paro belli, 11. 515). Thus Virgil's apparently slight modification of *Iliad* 20 (the substitution of the phantom Aeneas *before* the two heroes can meet for the mist that separates the Homeric heroes *after* they have met) changes the whole plot and in fact converts a physical into a psychological sequence of events. Turnus' problem, *after* the rescue and battle of 10, is to accept Aeneas' challenge knowing full well its probable result. But the very fact that the actual contest with Aeneas had not as yet been inaugurated, that Turnus' heroic reputation had not as yet been put to real proof, allowed him with some probability to argue and act as he did in 11. But with his failure there, compounded as it was by Camilla's death and the practical vindication of Drances, he had no further alternative but to accept the challenge.

In other words, the real problem of the epic after Book 10 is the problem of Turnus' motivation: he must, as Virgil sees it, be brought to face Aeneas voluntarily and even despite the aid of Juno and (later) Juturna. For he is meant to be both *furiosus* and *heroic*. His fury first takes the form of impious rejection of the fates and a declared *foedus*, then turns to a desperate and half-unconscious struggle to preserve at the same time both his warrior's pride and his own life. This is why he seeks to generalize the conflict and put at least a large part of the blame on others. But he is not really a coward and when he sees that he must finally choose, choose in effect between life and honour, he chooses honour. Unfortunately his choice comes too late, and after he has sacrificed too many other lives to his own pride and fury. And this fact must be clearly demonstrated, if Aeneas himself is to remain the great combination of *virtus* and *humanitas* that he is supposed to be. These conditions explain the chief pecularity of the last book (12), that is, explain why it is so largely a repetition of what has gone before. The repetitive character of the book can best be shown by a brief outline of its plot:

I. The Ratification of the Truce (1–215)
   (*a*) Arranging the truce (1–133)
   (*b*) Juno and Juturna (134–60)
   (*c*) Ratifying the truce (161–215)

II. The Violation of the Truce (216–467)
   (*a*) The breaking of the truce (216–323)
   (*b*) *Aristeiai* of Turnus (324–82)
   (*c*) Curing of Aeneas' wound; his return to the battle (383–467)

III. The withdrawal of Turnus (468–696)
   (*a*) *Aristeiai* of Aeneas and Turnus (Juturna as Metiscus) (468–553)
   (*b*) Aeneas' attack on Laurentum (suicide of Amata) (554–613)
   (*c*) Turnus comes to himself and returns (614–96)

IV. The Combat of Aeneas and Turnus (697–952)
   (*a*) First phase of the combat (697–790)
   (*b*) Intervention of Jupiter (the Dirae; Juturna departs) (791–886)
   (*c*) Final phase of the combat (887–952)

Here Section I in effect repeats the *foedus* of Book 7; Section II repeats the immediately following disruption of the *foedus* (also in 7) by Juno, Allecto and Turnus himself; Section III repeats the withdrawal motif of Book 10. In other words it takes the first 696 lines of this book to bring Turnus to the point where (but for Juno's intervention) he should have been in Book 10 and could have been in Book 11 (had he taken seriously the challenge delivered by Aeneas to the Latins in ll. 115 f.). But the repetition is nevertheless essential to the psychological drama and its climax. Virgil could not let Turnus and Aeneas fight 'in cold blood' right after the *foedus*. In that case the emotional value and even the moral significance of the final conflict and the death of Turnus would have been largely lost.

But far more fundamental is the fact that the repetitions of the book have much the same meaning as those of Book 6 and indeed correspond [1] to them: here Turnus, as there Aeneas, repeats in rapid sequence the crucial steps that have brought him to his present ordeal and so finally realizes the absolute necessity of going beyond them to the true and final test that he has so far avoided. The actions and motivations of the past are no good: Turnus now sees this as he had not seen it before. Alternatively, the justice and inevitability of Aeneas' cause receives a quite new clarity and emotional colour. And as with the men, so with the gods. Juno likewise, with Juturna's co-operation, repeats the moves of her old game: the breaking of the *foedus*, the withdrawal of Turnus. But these too are no good any more and they are defeated not only by the opposition of Jupiter and fate but pre-eminently by the spirit of Turnus himself. In his last supreme act, he breaks through the shield of divine protection to defend his own honour. He has of course no real chance against Aeneas but he should have known this long ago. In his final agony he sees that Jupiter is against him, and that his case is hopeless, but he sees it too late. He had already rejected his chance for mercy; the proof of this is the Pallas loot he still flaunts on his shoulder.

The book opens with Turnus defeated and forced to make good on his past promises; he can no longer put off the duel with Aeneas. So he is now the *wounded lion at bay*:

4   Poenorum qualis in arvis
        saucius ille gravi venantum volnere pectus
        tum demum movet arma leo, gaudetque comantis
        excutiens cervice toros fixumque latronis
        impavidus frangit telum et fremit ore cruento:
        haud secus accenso gliscit violentia Turno.

This remarkable simile is taken from the *Iliad* (20. 164 f.) where the lion is likened to the wrathful Achilles who had just returned

---

[1] See chap. viii, p. 391 f. below and Appendix 9. The correspondence of books in the 6–6 Scheme (1 with 7, 2 with 8, 3 with 9, &c.) is not as significant as the correspondence of books around the central book 7 (6 and 8, 5 and 9, &c.), but, of course, 6 and 12 as the two final books of the Odyssean and Iliadic *Aeneids* have a special importance.

to battle. But, as Pöschl [1] has pointed out, the wound has no such direct application to Achilles as it has to Turnus: Achilles is no stricken hero, but Turnus is indeed such and is in fact already doomed to his death. The wounded doe, to which Dido was compared in the fourth book, is suggested and, probably, deliberately so. But Turnus—and this is the difference between him and the amorous Dido—is no doe, but a lion. In his extremity of frustration, it is his *violence* that asserts itself: gliscit violentia. We see this again in the simile of the bull (101 f.) *his agitur furiis veluti cum . . . taurus*, &c., a passage that directly recalls the fierce bulls of the *Georgics* (III. 220 ff.).

This 'wounded' Turnus will have none of Latinus' conciliatory advice. He has now reached the point of choice between life and honour (letum . . . sinas pro laude pacisci, 49) but he has still only scorn for his opponent (longe illi dea mater erit, &c.) and refuses to admit, at least publicly, his own inferiority. To the more affecting plea of Amata, he says much the same thing in other words: there is no denying his grim destiny (neque enim Turno mora libera mortis, 74) but it is not yet time for forebodings; his own challenge at least, will not please the 'Phrygian tyrant'. The fury of Turnus here takes the form of a haughty contempt: Aeneas is to him the effeminate Phrygian (semiviri Phrygis, 99) with curled and scented hair. But it is the contempt that conceals his 'wound'; the violence that rises from frustration and latent fear.

The fear emerges finally at the very moment of the *foedus* when he and the other Latins finally see the full scope of the danger, the inequality of the contest to which he is now exposed: *at vero Rutulis impar ea pugna videri* (216). Turnus' appearance (tabentesque [2] genae et iuvenali in corpore pallor, 221) accentuates the inequality. We get here the impression that it is not just the Latins but Turnus himself who dreads the result (for to what was his pallor due?). The intervention of Juturna (at Juno's behest) clearly reflects a prior human motivation (it is the same as with Iris in 5, Allecto in 7). The Latins *want*

---

[1] Pp. 183 f. But I cannot accept Pöschl's theory of Turnus' original *innocence*, i.e. that he was originally motivated by his own sense of the gods' (esp. Juno's) support. Juno is surely not the primary cause of his *violentia* and *furor*: any more than fate is *primarily* responsible for Aeneas' *pietas*.

[2] *Tabentes*, the reading of the MSS a [2], c, the *deteriores*, Bentley and Hirtzel (Oxford text) here seems to me better than the *pubentes* of the main MSS.

to break the *foedus*; they are ready in their hearts for the demonic suggestion. When the disguised Juturna asks: (229) *Non pudet, O Rutuli, pro cunctis talibus unam obiectare animam?* she but makes explicit the implications of Turnus' defensively fierce reply to Drances in the previous book. Why should the numerically superior party accept such a vicarious sacrifice? The answer, of course, is that it is only Turnus' quite personal *furor* that has made the Latins fight against their own real interests and their solemn undertakings. But unlike the rather impromptu *foedus* in Book 7, this *foedus* is attended with every circumstance of religious solemnity. A repetition of their original sacrilege will only be more overt and reprehensible and presumably all the richer in collective suffering. Their pity for Turnus comes much too late. It is just this sense (which Virgil conveys so powerfully) of a misguided desire to repeat the past *when the lessons of the past should have been learned*, that gives this book its peculiar tone.

The true feelings of Turnus are clearly shown when the violence begins. He welcomes the sacrilegious disruption of his plighted *foedus*:

324   Turnus ut Aeneam cedentem ex agmine vidit
         turbatosque duces, *subita spe fervidus ardet.*

The contrast with Aeneas, who, disarmed as he was, still tried to restrain his own men from the impious combat (313 f.) and was then wounded for his pains, is carefully drawn.[1] Turnus' fury is now brought out in an elaborate simile in which he is likened to 'bloody Mars' with his fierce *comitatus*:

335   circumque atrae Formidinis ora
         Iraeque Insidiaeque.

And his *aristeiai* bear out his fury: his cruelty toward Eumedes (359 f.), his suspension from his chariot of the gory heads of Amycus and Diores (511 f.), and, above all, his cruel slaughter of the modest and peaceful Menoetes (517 f.), are more than ordinary exploits of battle. Virgil's intention is to show how unnecessary and destructive his violence now was.

So far then everything has been done to show the culpable violence of Turnus, the outraged innocence of Aeneas. But of

---

[1] This is, of course, the supreme exhibition of the 'reborn' Aeneas' ability to meet the most discouraging circumstances with resolute courage. The fact that (l. 400) he is *lacrimis immobilis* describes an emotion, not a change of resolution.

course the violence has no more success than before: indeed, in this rapid tempo of repetition, the turn in the tide comes quickly and all but irresistibly. It is enough for the wounded Aeneas to show himself once more in the battle in order to panic the Latins:

446   Vidit ab adverso venientes aggere Turnus,
        videre Ausonii, gelidusque per ima cucurrit
        ossa tremor: prima ante omnis Iuturna Latinos
        audiit adgnoscitque sonum et tremefacta refugit.

Turnus' withdrawal from the new onset of Aeneas is now ostensibly the work of Juturna (who displaces his charioteer Metiscus and assumes his shape) but Turnus is not really deceived. We see this in his revealing statement when, after reaching the outskirts of the battlefield, he hears the distant echo of terrible conflict at the centre: this is his first intimation of the siege of Laurentum and the crisis of the capitol. Now when Juturna, still playing the charioteer's role, tries to urge him yet further off, he recognizes her and reproves her with the words:

632   o soror, *et dudum adgnovi*, cum *prima* per artem
        foedera turbasti teque haec in bella dedisti,
        et nunc *nequiquam fallis* dea.

It is thus at last plain to him that he has only repeated his former humiliations: once more he has missed the crisis of victory and defeat, once more abandoned his own in their hour of need. But this time he can only blame himself. He had been in fact the accomplice or at least the half-conscious accomplice of Juturna (632 f.). Now at last he sees his true situation:

643   Exscindine domos (id rebus defuit unum)
        perpetiar, dextra nec Drancis dicta refellam?
        Terga dabo et Turnum fugientem haec terra videbit?
        Usque adeone mori miserum est?

The whole speech (632–49), from which these words come, marks the turning point of the Iliadic *Aeneid*. Here Turnus not only recognizes the real shame of his attempt to evade the duel with Aeneas but rejects the aid of the counter-fates as well. Virgil, of course, now accumulates the evidences of what has happened in Turnus' absence: the crisis of the siege, the suicide of Amata, the isolation of Messapus and Atinas—all while he had been driving his chariot 'through the empty grass'. But this news only accentuates the decision he had already made. His tragedy is that he came to the decision too late—that he deferred it until another impious violation of a solemn agreement, another round of unnecessary slaughter, another abandonment of his own comrades to useless destruction, had already taken place. But it is just this sense of fatal repetition, the repeated reduction of his efforts to the same result, that brings him self-awareness. He finally sees that he has once more ruined everything by his own violence. But this time all avenues of escape (especially escape from his own self-knowledge) are closed.

His motivation is now set forth in two tremendous lines:

666   aestuat ingens
uno in corde pudor mixtoque insania luctu
et furiis agitatus amor et conscia virtus.

The first line (667) is a repetition of 10. 871 when the mood of Mezentius, as he returns to his last battle and his death, is described. For in both cases the *shame* (pudor) and the maddened grief are the same.[1] But Turnus is also (668) driven by his love for Lavinia and his consciousness of his own heroism, of that valour he still has and must now show. As for his love, this is no easy thing to understand, since Virgil has quite deliberately relegated it to the background; he could hardly make Aeneas too overt a disrupter of mutual passion. But it is clear that Turnus' *amor* is but one element of his wrath: it is the prospect of dispossession by the *externus*, the slur thrown on his own heroic glory, in short the slight to his *ego*, which also makes him so eager to fight for Lavinia.[2]

But the last word in these lines is the *virtus*—*conscia virtus*: Turnus has after all a sense of his own worth, of his own courage and righteousness. In the final showdown, he will sacrifice himself to his friends and companions, to all the Latins whose leader he has been and for whose sins he must now make atonement:

694   me verius *unum*
pro vobis foedus luere et decernere ferro.

---

[1] The reference back to Mezentius is of course intentional: Mezentius is a 'surrogate' for the absent Turnus. 10. 872 (not in the main MSS. *MPR* or even in the first hand of γα) is surely an interpolation.   [2] Cf p. 348.

These lines measure the shift that has taken place from the former words of Juturna in which Turnus tacitly concurred: non pudet . . . Rutuli, pro cunctis . . . unam obiectare animam? (229–30). So Turnus, of his own accord, moved now by a *virtus* that contains at least an element of repentance and self-sacrifice, returns to face Aeneas and certain death.

Two problems confront us at this point. To what extent is Turnus' *culpa* a product of Juno and Juturna, a misplaced confidence in the counter-fates? And why did Virgil set such store on Turnus' voluntary return and his finally deliberate self-sacrifice?

The dependence of Turnus on Juno (and to some degree, Juturna) has been viewed by some [1] as the essential cause of his whole tragedy. He is a good man misled by Juno, by a genuine but mistaken belief in counter-fate. Such a view, in my opinion, misconceives both the character of Turnus and the role of the gods in the epic. Juno and her creatures never displace human responsibility and freedom: even Allecto only reinforces or gives demonic significance to motivations already present. Turnus' violence is in fact his own and is even self-defeating in a way clearly contrary to Juno's intention. She certainly would, for example, have preferred him to take advantage of his strategic situation at the close of Book 9 instead of wasting it through blind *furor* and blood-lust. But Juno herself is short-sighted: she even defeats herself by forcing Turnus to the point where he voluntarily relinquishes her (or Juturna's) protection and accepts his fate. She could get him away in Book 10; she perhaps co-operated with his own anguish to make him miss Aeneas at the close of 11; she could encourage Juturna to break the *foedus* and protect him in 12. But all this was at the cost of his heroic *virtus*: when he finally realized the fact (as he did in the scene just described) neither Juno nor Juturna had any more power over him. They had in fact driven him to resist fate; then, when through his own *furor* (9) and brutality (killing and plundering of Pallas in 10) he had lost his great opportunity and finally roused the fighting spirit of Aeneas, they had tried to save him from the consequences of his own acts at what, as he finally saw, was the price of his own honour.

---

[1] Especially by Pöschl, 153 ff.

In fact it is through Turnus' own character and will that both Juno and Juturna are finally defeated. The tragedy of Juno and Juturna consists in their inability to realize anything but failure, and above all their inability to help those whom they love. In the case of Juno, we do not feel this so particularly since Juno's status is ambiguous: she is both the opponent and the spouse of Jupiter (both the symbolic counter-fate and the Homeric Hera) and she has, for religio-historical reasons, to be finally reconciled to Roman victory. But Juturna, who (for this very reason) takes Juno's place in the twelfth book, is a truly tragic figure whose very immortality is frustrated by her failure to save her brother. The splendid simile (473 f.) in which Juturna, as charioteer, is likened to a swallow or swift darting about the pools and empty porticoes and bringing tidbits to its young:

474   pinnis alta atria lustrat hirundo
        pabula parva legens nidisque loquacibus escas,

surely conveys a sense of her quasi-*maternal* concern for Turnus. This is why the conflict of her divinity and her humanity is so affecting at the end:

879   cur mortis adempta est
        condicio? possem tantos finire dolores
        nunc certe, et misero fratri comes ire per umbras!

This brings us back to the question of Turnus' death. Why did Virgil insist on Turnus' voluntary *acceptance* of his death, his final repudiation of Juturna and the counter-fates? The answer assuredly is that Virgil wanted to depict Turnus as a true hero, however violent or *furiosus* he might otherwise be. Even Mezentius, as we recall, had been given the opportunity to 'repent', to show himself at the last a father who appreciated too late the *virtus* of his son. Much more so with Turnus; as the leader of the Latins, he could not be represented simply as a villain or a coward. But beyond this, his very return to himself, the final belated dawning of a sense of duty to others— ut primum discussae umbrae et *lux* reddita menti—represented a necessary precondition of peace between Latins and Trojans. Up to this *lux*, Turnus had never seen the true iniquity of his actions, his maleficent sacrifice of the many to the one who was himself, his mad attempts to defy the will of Jupiter. His voluntary return to battle, to the duel with Aeneas, had thus an aspect of beneficient sacrifice: the sinner atoning with his own life for the sin of the many and for his own sin, the Latin enemy helping to lay the foundation of a new, permanent *foedus* between Trojans and Latins.

But it is still the case that the *Aeneid* does not end with the *reconciliation* of the heroes but with Aeneas' impassioned killing of his beaten enemy. The final contest (part IV) falls into three sections—a first phase in which Juturna and Venus cancel out each other's efforts (Juturna restores Turnus' sword, Venus releases her son's spear); a second phase in which Jupiter finally intervenes and sends one of the terrible *Dirae* to clear the scene of Juturna and warn Turnus of his approaching doom; and a third in which Turnus, recognizing the overt hostility of Jupiter, loses all power of effective resistance and falls an easy victim to Aeneas' spear. Virgil here makes no attempt to represent the contest as even: Turnus is finally brought against a quite irresistible fate. As he says to Aeneas:

894   Non me tua fervida terrent
          dicta, ferox; di me terrent et Iuppiter hostis.

But Virgil is not here concerned to display Aeneas' *aretē* and martial prowess in this moment of final decision: once Turnus has accepted fate, it is fate that he receives; the sphere of freedom and voluntary effort, of human action, has now entirely coalesced with the sphere of destiny, of Jupiter. We can, if we like, think of the *Dira* as a sort of symbol of Turnus' foreboding conscience, the voice that tells him his end has come, and hence causes his dream-like languor and inability to put forth his strength any more, but it is better on the whole to think of the *Dira* as the sign of ineluctable fate itself. All the opposition of counter-fate, all human effort has led or been led to this point: there indeed fate takes over but only as the last touch on a destiny that has already been shaped.

The last *human* decision to be made in the epic is thus not who should win but whether the victim should be spared. We must give the lines in full:

938–952   Stetit acer in armis
          Aeneas volvens oculos dextramque repressit;
          et iam iamque magis cunctantem flectere sermo

coeperat, infelix umero cum apparuit alto
balteus et notis fulserunt cingula bullis
Pallantis pueri, victum quem vulnere Turnus
straverat atque umeris inimicum insigne gerebat.
Ille, oculis postquam saevi monumenta doloris
exuviasque hausit, furiis accensus et ira
terribilis: 'Tune hinc spoliis indute meorum
eripiare mihi? Pallas te hoc vulnere, Pallas
immolat et poenam scelerato ex sanguine sumit.'
Hoc dicens ferrum adverso sub pectore condit
fervidus; ast illi solvuntur frigore membra
vitaque cum gemitu fugit indignata sub umbras.

It is indeed fitting that Turnus really carry out the sacrifice that he contemplated from the moment when he checked Juturna and turned back to Laurentum and Aeneas. His death is the act of atonement that brings the peace.

It is not the reconciliation of the two heroes but the union of Latins and Trojans that is here essential: Turnus must pay for his past, for the violence that he has not even yet overcome (he still wears the belt of Pallas) but, in paying for it by his own voluntary act, he finally achieves the union of the two peoples. Virgil could not have shown this by making Aeneas the victor in a true fight: he therefore all but eliminated the fight (it is really the *Dira*, not Aeneas, that defeats Turnus) and attributed Turnus' death to that *pietas* of Aeneas toward Pallas which the sight of Turnus' booty, the infamous belt, had once more brought back to vivid actuality. Turnus' appeal for pity toward *his* father Daunus (934) was meeting an apparently favourable response from the pious son of Anchises (fuit et tibi talis Anchises) when it was utterly extinguished by this evidence of callous indifference to another father and son. Aeneas finally saw that it was too late for Turnus to get mercy; he had shown no mercy to Pallas; and Aeneas, as Pallas' destined avenger, had an obligation that greatly overshadowed any *humanitas* he might wish to display toward his beaten foe. Thus does Turnus in the end pay for his sins, does earn, with his death, the peace that his indignant spirit had in life so violently rejected. The last words of the poem fittingly concern him.

Is Aeneas therefore neglected? Does his pre-eminence suffer from Virgil's concentration on Turnus? The answer is assuredly negative: Aeneas stands out, more than ever before, as the one hero who has subjected his own desires to a social purpose, who wins because he has put courage and toil—duty—above success: when he tells Ascanius

435   'disce, puer, virtutem ex me verumque laborem,
         fortunam ex aliis.'

he reveals, as it were, the secret of his heroism. He is the divine man (theios aner) who combines *virtus* with *humanitas* while Turnus is simply the Homeric hero who, to the very end, flaunts the trophies of his arrogant past. His final act of partial repentance and sacrifice cannot wipe out his predominant role in the whole epic: this is why he is truly a tragic character who can only buy honour with death.

The end of the *Aeneid* is certainly not Christian. There is no reconciliation or forgiveness in the Christian sense. Aeneas is still a man who takes vengeance in blood, who can be driven to ferocity by the very recollection of Pallas. But this too is an aspect of his humanity. His feeling for this great Marcellus figure is really an index not only of his *pietas* but of his deep sympathy for defeated heroism, the death of the noble young. We saw this in his encounter with Lausus, the great paradigmatic contrast to Turnus' savage disposal of Pallas. We see it more generally in the pathos that invests even such flawed heroisms as those of Nisus and Camilla (Aeneas, we feel sure, would have shared or did share the sentiments that Virgil expresses about them). We see it *socially* in his concern to end the war without further useless sacrifice of Trojan or Latin lives. We can make what we will of the noble deaths of Mezentius and Turnus but Virgil, at least, does not forget their brutal and senselessly repeated sacrifice of others—of whole societies— to their own selfish desires. To be an Achilles or a Hector was assuredly enough for Turnus or enough until it was too late. But Aeneas was a wholly different hero, whose *aretē* consisted not just of *virtus* but of *humanitas* and *pietas* as well. His preference of *virtus* and *labor* to *fortuna* expresses what is perhaps the most important and moving idea of the whole poem—and this is the necessary sadness of success, the notion that Rome never could have fought its way to permanent greatness had it not felt so deeply the toil, the grief, the melancholy cost of the struggle.

This is the reason, at least the most fundamental reason, why fate was finally on its side.[1]

Aeneas thus stands for a new idea in history, the idea that *violentia* and *superbia* can be controlled, that a just *imperium* can be established, that universal peace can be a fact as well as an ideal. The Greeks were far too clever to understand this: since they never could make a durable empire, they tended to see human behaviour in either tragic or Machiavellian terms. *Humanitas* was but a theory; brutal self-seeking the hard reality; *hybris* the normal result of power; *aretē* a species of egoism.[2] To all this kind of thinking, the Romans opposed their humanity and *pietas*, their goal of *pacis imponere morem*. This was something new—not perhaps new as an abstract idea but new as a practical ethic, a pattern for warfare and government. Virgil shows us how new it could also be in poetry. Here, as in politics, history had turned a corner.

[1] Cf. 6. 870 f. *Nimium vobis Romana propago/visa potens, superi, propria haec si dona fuissent* and p. 303 f. above.

[2] Here the comparison of Livy and Thucydides is very instructive. The tendency of many moderns to prefer the 'realism' of Thucydides to the 'moral rhetoric' of Livy begs the whole question at issue, i.e. it assumes the falsity of the Roman thesis that citizens with the right character and *doctrina* can literally change the course of 'realistic' history.

CHAPTER VIII

CONCLUSION

T HERE is no need for elaborate summary. The novelty of Virgil's work should now be clear. He had no real precedent for the *Aeneid*. Horace in the *Ars Poetica* had drawn a picture of what a real epic should be and had said in effect that the only proper model was Homer, not some disunified string of adventures or κλέα, not another *Thebais* or *Argonautica*, and, above all, not History in epic clothes (the fatuous ambition of the *Choerili* in Greek or the *Enniades* in Latin), but a unified poem in the high style with real heroes and gods. He thus discarded the whole post-Homeric past without really conveying any idea of how such an astounding return to Homer himself could be accomplished. And Virgil, as a poet schooled in neoteric and Alexandrine *doctrina*, was certainly well aware that the Greek critics for whom he had most respect had long given up Homeric epic as a possible medium of effective poetry.

There were in fact two readily available alternatives, each of which seemed equally forbidding. He could write another *mythological* epic out of the storehouse of Mycenaean or heroic legend, or he could write another *historical* epic on a Roman or Augustan theme, a *Bellum Actiacum* for example. The one type was simply anachronistic and impossible for a true poet. The other seemed to be even less promising, a hopeless mixture of two worlds and styles, of *vera* (history) and *falsa* (myth), a putting of urbanized Romans into Mycenaean clothes and armour.

So Virgil did not begin with Homer but with imitations of Theocritus and, on a much greater scale, with a didactic poem on agriculture. These seem, at first sight, to constitute a very strange road to epic. But it would be hard for us now to imagine a better one, given Virgil's traditions and his particular problem. For what both *Eclogues* and *Georgics* reveal, or at least reveal if we look beneath their rather smooth surfaces, is a curious duality, a startling difference between form and content. The *Georgics*, for example, is in appearance and proclaimed intent, a poetical treatise on crops, vineyards, cattle, sheep, and bees; in short, a *De Agricultura* in verse. Actually, as we have seen, it is an Augustan poem on the revival of Italian and Roman society after the Civil Wars: its agricultural contents are the symbolic counters of an intricate ideological pattern that is also poetically alive. Virgil had given a quite new meaning, a thoroughly contemporary meaning, to the didactic form.

This is the light then in which we must look at the *Aeneid* if we are really to understand it. Virgil used Homer here, much as he had used Hesiod, Nicander or Aratus in the *Georgics*. In other words Homer gave him a form, something of a style, a great deal of content, but not the essential idea or meaning, not the ideological *truth* he wanted to convey. He saw (I would suspect very early in the game, though we can never be certain) that he could not directly *Homerize* modern or historical material or, in other words, write of Augustus as if he were really the associate of Hector, Achilles and the gods on Olympus. Hence his question was: how can I use the Homeric counters as effective *symbols* of Augustan realities? Or even more specifically: how can I put the basic Augustan schema of the *Georgics* into such symbols? The great difference of course was that Homer had written of human beings, not of soils, cattle, and bees. It was the difference, in other words, between human and non-human symbols. Or, even more exactly, it was the difference between symbols and more or less *exemplary* men and women. It was in this way, as I conceive it, that Virgil looked at the problem, though we cannot of course draw too many conclusions as to how far he consciously articulated it to himself.

At any rate the *Aeneid* makes sense when seen in this perspective. Aeneas is, in effect, an Augustan type—a *divine man*, not necessarily copied after the Emperor himself but embodying the Augustan ruler-ideal—who emerges out of Homeric society and, in virtue of his emergence, imposes upon a more primitive but still quasi-Homeric society a defeat that is the means to unity, peace and civilization on the Augustan plan. But he does this only because he *becomes* Augustan, that is, because he is 'reborn' at the crisis of his career by the acquisition of an historical perspective which includes Augustus and the Augustan *pax Romana*. Only so can he bring the civilized future to bear upon the primitive or Homeric present in which he, as *dramatis persona,* is supposed to stand. In this sense we can partially describe the *Aeneid* as the creation of Roman civilization out of Homeric barbarism. It is not, however, so much the contrast of the Homeric and Augustan eras in themselves that Virgil is interested in, as the contrast of human ideals and motivations: he is, in short, concerned with Aeneas as the opposite and opponent of such men and women as Dido and Turnus and, perhaps above all, as the man who overcomes the Dido and Turnus inside himself.

It was not, in theory at least, too difficult to devise a *plot* that would carry Virgil's ideological, Augustan meaning. The Homeric motifs had to be recast and united to Roman legend, the Augustan present had to be introduced by prophecy and prophetic scenes, the role of the *Nekuia* had to be wholly transformed, &c. But all this was more a matter for ingenuity than poetical genius. The real problem was to make the plot function in a poem. This meant the achievement of credibility by creating the right poetical atmosphere or, more exactly, the directing point of view that would give poetical unity to such an intricate and necessarily artificial mixture of ideas and motifs. Here was where Virgil's subjective style and psychologically continuous narrative became of paramount importance. Had he envisaged his plot in the objective manner of Homer and Apollonius and told it as a simple narrative of real people and real events, he would surely have accomplished only a grotesque failure. Actually, as a Roman, Virgil inherited a kind of subjective style (in the sense that I have set forth in chap. iii), but he certainly added a quite new dimension to what he got from Lucretius or Catullus or others. So far as we can tell, he alone employed the kind of sustained empathy that permitted a psychologically continuous narrative. But it was above all his combination of empathy with editorial 'sympathy' that gave him control over his Homeric material, enabled him to *correlate* mythological symbols with psychological events and made possible his marvellous transformation of epic conventions. It is on his 'subjective style' in short that his whole intricate structure of symbols and motifs depends. Without this, his plot *per se* would be a curiously artificial thing, a flimsy paste-and-scissors job that could not create or sustain any sort of poetical illusion.

But we must not therefore assume that the whole *Aeneid* is an operatic *trompe l'oeil*, an artificial combining of Homeric and Augustan elements by various stylistic tricks. The Virgilan empathy and sympathy are quite real: he really does see into and feel with the hearts of his characters. He really does see his world in deeply emotional terms, really does transform Homeric motifs and similes into evocative symbols of his own feelings and thoughts. Truth can be subjectively as well as objectively conveyed. Virgil is not false because he is not Homer.

It is worthwhile even at this point to recall quite specifically what Virgil's blend of empathy and sympathy does to his symbols and exemplary characters. Let us take two examples: one of animals from the *Georgics*, one of a youthful hero from the *Aeneid*.

In *Georgics* I (351–514) there is, as we have seen above (chap. v), a long concluding section on *The Signs of Things to Come*. This is actually part of the 'Days' section of this Hesiodic-ally planned work. The Farmer's calendar is set by the sky-gods themselves: it is a sign of the cosmic sympathy by which man and nature are united in mutual reciprocity. But there are also signs of unseasonal events that are not part of the calendar. These are arranged climactically in an order that goes from weather signs to signs of historical events and catastrophes such as the death of Caesar in which the book culminates. The basic idea throughout is the supreme sensitivity of nature, each part of which is sympathetic to the other. Man by his crimes and perver-sities (*fas versum atque nefas*, 505) can upset the order of nature: conversely, a divine man, like Octavian, can restore it (500–1).

It is this idea or, more exactly, *feeling* that guides Virgil's description of the birds who foretell the coming of good and bad weather. His Greek model here is Aratus' *Phainomena* (932 f.). By comparing the two we can see how Virgil transformed a quite pedestrian and quite objective piece of natural history into a highly emotional expression of cosmic sympathy, climactically structured so as to reach at the end a Roman and Augustan dénouement. It is the little extra details of Virgil that spell the difference.

Aratus' sailor (935–6) merely fears to be caught; Virgil's furls his wet sails (373); Virgil's swallow (377), unlike Aratus' (944), is *arguta*, shrill; Virgil's frogs, unlike Aratus' (947), *sing their old complaint* (378); Virgil's ants leave not, as in Aratus, their *hollow nest* (956), but their *penetralia tecta*; Virgil's crows are not like Aratus' (965), a mere flock but an *army with serried wings* (382). Virgil's birds play in the streams and vie in splashing each other in their *vain desire to bathe* (385–6); Aratus' birds only smite the water with their breasts (945). Aratus' lamp merely sputters (979): in Virgil it is the girl plying her nightly task who *sees* it sputter (390). More careful analysis would go far beyond these superficial observations and indicate how every feature of the Virgilian passage (the selection made from Aratus' indiscriminate list, the diction, metre, use of tenses, periodization, sequence) conforms to the divergences indicated above. For Virgil has given sentient life and a point of view to the oxen, swallows, frogs, ants, cows and water birds of Aratus: what was a catalogue of weather signs has somehow been brought alive and in the process tinged with human feeling.

Then in lines 393–423 Virgil rises in a wonderful crescendo from halcyons and pigs, to owls and crows. Here he suggests by his allusions to metamorphosis myths (Ceyx-Alcyone, Nyctimene, Scylla) a more direct and emphatic humanization of the animal: Alcyone, Scylla, Nisus, &c., never quite displace the birds they represent but Virgil's empathy just exceeds that which would be appropriate to mere birds. Then, in the climactic description of the crows (410–14), Virgil suggests the *humanitas* common to all nature:

412   nescio qua praeter solitum dulcedine laeti
       inter se in foliis strepitant: iuvat imbribus actis
       progeniem *parvam dulcisque* revisere nidos.

He seems in one sense to contradict this by the physical explanation of lines 415 f.—he denies that the animals can be said to possess true *ingenium*—but the impression left is that of a common bond of sympathy in all nature:

422   hinc ille avium concentus in agris
       et laetae pecudes et *ovantes* gutture corvi.

It is precisely such empathy—such a subjective style of exposition—that enables Virgil to unite his Hesiodic didactic, his stoic cosmology, and his Augustanism in one harmonious poem. He assimilates all his subject matter, no matter how insignificant and how animalistic, to a common feeling-tone that seems with apparent ease to cover the enormous gap between owls and crows, on the one hand, and Roman history—the civil wars, Octavian—on the other. To a considerable extent Lucretius displays a similar empathy in some of his descriptions of nature, especially animal nature, but he never uses the empathy, as Virgil does, to achieve a unity of tone, a real fusion of didactic and poetical elements, of theory and feeling. For in the last analysis Lucretius' primary purpose is didactic and Virgil's is not.

An example of how Virgil gives emotional vitality to his exemplary characters is the Nisus-Euryalus episode of *Aeneid* 9. It seems plain that the episode is essentially paradigmatic, a Trojan *exemplum virtutis* designed to balance or be balanced by the Latin *exemplum virtutis* (Camilla) of *Aeneid* 11. Nisus and Euryalus are not clear-cut characters in their own right so much as types of youthful devotion and sacrifice. The story is carefully arranged to make a point, to put Nisus' *Liebestod* before us in all its dramatic force and pathos. It we compare it with the tenth *Iliad* (Doloneia), which in some sense it is meant to recall, the difference between Virgil's *exemplary* and Homer's merely *narrative* intention is quite apparent. What, however, gives Virgil's *exemplum* its emotional power is precisely the empathy by which Virgil has made us (his readers) share the feelings of Nisus (esp. from l. 386 on) and share his own feelings as the sympathetic narrator. His use of the remarkable Catullan simile—the flower cut down by the huge, insensitive plough—is here a key to his poetic achievement:

433   Volvitur Euryalus leto, pulchrosque per artus
           it cruor inque umeros cervix conlapsa recumbit:
           purpureus veluti cum flos succisus aratro
           languescit moriens, lassove papavera collo
           demisere caput.

The simile is inserted in the very thick of the action. It is preceded by

431   viribus ensis adactus
           transabiit costas et candida pectora rumpit,

and followed by:

438   At Nisus ruit in medios solumque per omnis
           Volcentem petit.

So Virgil's pause here, to mark by the simile the shock and
meaning of the event—his sense of the beauty ruthlessly cut off,
of Euryalus as the tender flower brutally crushed, takes us at
once into his own world of feeling that is also in some sense that
of the protective lover, Nisus himself. We thus can proceed with
little sense of discontinuity from the apparently descriptive
conclusion:

444   tum super exanimum sese proiecit amicum
       confossus, placidaque ibi demum morte quievit

to the overt editorializing of

446   Fortunati ambo! si quid mea carmina possunt,
       nulla dies umquam memori vos eximet aevo,
       dum domus Aeneae Capitoli immobile saxum
       accolet imperiumque pater Romanus habebit.

In the end the episode is assimilated to Roman history, to the
ideology of Roman patriotism, but the connection is poetically
possible only because of the sympathy between Nisus, Virgil,
and reader that has already been established.

We cannot deny poetic truth to a poet who felt and wrote
this way. But there is of course a broader problem that we have
hardly touched upon so far in this book. That is the justification
of Virgil's 'ideological' viewpoint, the extent to which his poetry
may or may not be vitiated by his Augustan 'propaganda', if
indeed we can use so unkind a term without question-begging.

First of all, it seems quite plain that Virgil was himself a
convinced Augustan. He was clearly inspired by his theme: he
believed in his own 'ideology'. He really saw in Augustus the
type of man who could bring peace out of fratricidal war, order
from anarchy, self-control from selfish passion, in a sense, an
'age of gold' from an age of iron. He also saw in Rome the
paradigm and goal of all historical activity, in Roman *pietas*,
virtus, and *consilium* the only hope of peace and social order,
of humane behaviour associated with strong government.

Our own judgement of such a vision is qualified by our
knowledge of the later empire and of Rome's 'decline and fall',
by our experience of Christianity and of the whole modern
world. Even Augustans, however, were able to see certain flaws
in the picture: the very idea of a return to rural, Italian simplicity or of the revival of antique morality, had a distinctly

'propagandistic' flavour like the studied republicanism and simplicity (e.g. the *princeps*' simple, Evander-like dwelling on the Palatine!) of Augustus himself. Ovid, at least, was keenly aware of the gap between Augustan words and Augustan deeds. The old neoterics around Valerius Cato, the unfortunate Gallus, the decapitated Cicero—the victims and the embittered survivors of Octavian's rise to power and all who later brooked his wrath—had a case which was to find belated expression in the stoic 'Republicanism' of Lucan, Tacitus and many another.

But there is also a very good case to be made for Virgil's Augustanism. He had lived through a period of great violence which seemed at one time likely not only to end all peace at Rome and in Italy but the Roman world imperium itself. The last of the dissident leaders, Antony, may not seriously have proposed to 'orientalize' the empire, but he surely must have seemed an unwelcome alternative to Augustus. I do not myself believe that there was ever a real question of replacing Rome by an oriental capital (a rebuilt Troy) but Rome, in the relative ruin of a century of civil war, must have been very uncertain of its future. All this Augustus changed. That he at least tried to effect some sort of moral reform could hardly have been a discouraging sign. He was of course tainted with the proscriptions and other unsavory incidents of his rise to power, yet, judged on a contemporary standard, he must have seemed far preferable to others, not least to his embittered republican opponents. There was, in short, hope where there had been despair. And, after all, this hope was justified by the centuries' duration of the Roman empire, Augustus' own foundation.

But Virgil's Augustanism was based on more than Augustus. We can, I think, look upon his conception of the 'Augustan Hero' as a kind of hopeful prophecy, his elucidation of an ideal which represented Rome's best and true reason for being. The Greeks, for all their culture, had not known how to keep any peace among their cities or their fellow citizens. Their view of life was tragic or sophistically realistic or anti-politically religious: they offered no hope to the world; when and where they were not subjected to authoritarian masters, they could only continue the parochial quarrels which made their 'freedom' as intolerable to themselves as it was to their neighbours. Thus it was not unreasonable to hold that Rome's mission was to rule and by ruling (by checking the disturbers of the peace, the warmakers) to maintain a just and humane world order. But Virgil did more than say this: he gave poetical vitality, a whole new sensibility to the Augustan doctrine of empire.

But every ideology is bound to be a terrible oversimplification of life. The Augustan ideology revealed in the *Aeneid* is no exception to this rule. The fated triumph of Roman *pietas* and *humanitas* over foreign *furor*, *violentia*, *indignus amor*; the moralism of the whole story, the ethnocentric pride, the shallow eschatology (*imperium sine fine dedi!*), all this is hard, very hard for the modern reader to take! But it is only one aspect of the *Aeneid* and of Virgil. Aeneas is not just an image of *pietas*, Turnus not just an example of *furor*, Dido not merely a portrait of *indignus amor*. The most remarkable fact about the poem, perhaps, is its treatment of the victims: the two great action books, 4 and 10, end with the tragic deaths of Dido and Mezentius; the whole epic ends with the death of Turnus. And these deaths are certainly not invested with the colour of mere triumph—the gloating of the conqueror over the conquered—but almost entirely with the pathos, the tragic pathos of defeated heroism. It is especially noteworthy that Virgil describes at length the last agony of Troy and says nothing of the Trojan triumph at the end: we know that it has taken place, that Latin resistance has ended with Turnus' fall, but the last word of the epic is about Turnus, not about Aeneas or his victory or the joy that the Trojans must have felt at the happy conclusion of all their toil and suffering. It has even been difficult for many readers of Virgil to understand this: hence the fruitless and perverted attempts to complete the *Aeneid*! All of which points to the pivotal importance of *humanitas* as one of the two essential elements of the poem. In addition to Virgil's obvious moralism —the quite clear-cut victory of the 'good' over the 'bad' cause— there is his humanity, his feeling for what is humanly admirable in the 'bad' characters and for what is humanly blameworthy in the 'good'. Yet such feeling does not destroy the realism that sees and accepts the final dichotomy of the two.

What I mean is perhaps most apparent in the two books (6, 12) in which Virgil sums up the two *Aeneids*. The *Aeneid*, as we have seen, is both a dual epic (a combination of two sub-epics, each based on a different Homeric model) and a single epic based on the correspondence of the books that diverge in both directions from Book 7. We can in fact see *two kinds* of parallelism between the books:

(Centre)	7	1 (Beginning)	7	(Beginning of Iliadic *Aeneid*)
(Trojan Victory)	12	2 (Trojan Defeat)	8	(Rome offsetting Troy in 2)
(Transitional)	11	3 (Transitional)	9	(Transitional)
(Pallas Tragedy)	10	4 (Dido Tragedy)	10	(Pallas Tragedy)
(Transitional)	9	5 (Transitional)	11	(Transitional)
(Future)	8	6 (Future)	12	(Same recapitulative structure as 6)

Thus Books 6 and 12 correspond, especially in the fact that they recapitulate what has gone before: each repeats or recalls the most significant events of the preceding five books. And this repetition is, in each case, designed to precede and lead up to a decisive, new stage of the action in which the hero concerned (Aeneas, Turnus) finally realizes and fulfils his true destiny. But their two destinies are very different and it is precisely this difference to which the designed parallelism of the books invites our attention.

In one sense Aeneas is the 'good' opposite of the 'bad' Turnus: he is *pietas* and *humanitas* versus *impietas* and *violentia*. Indeed the very fact that in Book 12 Turnus once again breaks a solemn engagement (the *foedus*) and once again deserts the main battle and his companions at the hour of their greatest need, enhances the moral superiority of Aeneas. But Virgil does not emphasize this obvious point anywhere near so much as a quite different one. We are vastly more impressed by the fact that Turnus finally comes to himself and heroically defies Juturna's efforts to save him: the repetition of his past experiences is what finally opens his eyes to the choice he has so far avoided, the choice between death and dishonour. Virgil is far too realistic and too moral to let Turnus off at this last

moment (his end is both fated and deserved) but he nevertheless gives him the chance by which he can redeem himself and
meet his death with heroic magnificence.

It is therefore clear that Virgil had no intention of cheapening
the quality of Turnus or diminishing the poignance of his
tragedy. Yet he is a very different hero from Aeneas, and Virgil
has also made *this* clear. In Book 6 Aeneas, too, had recapitulated
the bitterest moments of his past: the *dolor* of Troy's treacherous
destruction, the terrible separation from Dido. But the effect of
this recapitulation was not an heroic acquiescence in his doom
but the very reverse: the opening of the road to Rome. The
difference in the two destinies is surely not to be accounted for
solely in terms of fate, of one man's destiny to failure, another's
to success. It is also true that Aeneas had learned by experience,
had ceased to be the furious warrior or reckless lover he had
once been, whereas Turnus had learned only enough to play,
at the last possible moment, the role of a tragic hero. In a word,
he was *not* a man twice-born. It is in the end not Turnus but
Aeneas who is humane, who can see the human side of his
enemy. And it is in the end Turnus' tragedy that it is precisely
his persistent lack of humanity—the brutality that the Pallas-
belt symbolized—which undoes him. Virgil pities Turnus, gives
him his full heroic due, but recognizes also that his fury can lead
nowhere but to death. For Virgil's *humanitas* does not in any
sense negate his moral realism: he will not let Turnus or even
Mezentius die without a tribute to their heroism, but he will
not spare them.

It is just this unromantic combination of humanity with
moral realism—of justice with sympathy—that gives the 'ideology' of the *Aeneid* its balance, its fluidity, its richness and complexity of texture. There are tears for Dido, for Nisus and
Euryalus, for Camilla, for Mezentius and Turnus: yet they all
pay the penalty for their own excesses. There are also tears for
Marcellus, Pallas, and Lausus: these are examples of a much
higher order of self-sacrifice who also must die. But Aeneas is
the *hero* in that he looks beyond such tragedy to a peace that
will in some sense overcome it and, at the least, serve to
mitigate it.

In a word: Virgil is a civilized poet. By comparison Homer is
primitive or barbarous. This fact has usually been admitted in

greater or lesser degree but usually also with the implication that Homer is *therefore* the greater poet. We need not in fact debate either Homer's primitivism or his poetical magnitude in order to doubt that such a view of poetry is really just to Virgil. What I have tried to suggest in this chapter and in the whole book is that this view is not just, that Virgil's greatness consists precisely in his ability to make civilization poetical.

APPENDIXES

APPENDIX 1

(ON CHAPTER I: LITERATURE ON VIRGIL'S LITERARY BACKGROUND)

I have derived most help on the Hellenistic epic from Wilhelm Kroll's article 'Das Historische Epos' (*Sokrates*, 70 (1916), pp. 1–14), but also from Kinkel (*Epicorum Graecorum Fragmenta*), Powell (*Analecta Alexandrina*), Susemihl (*Geschichte der Griechischen Literatur in der Alexandriner Zeit*, 1891) and articles in PW. On Ziegler's monograph, cf. Appendix 2. A good monograph on Hellenistic Epic is, to the best of my knowledge, still a *desiderandum*. There is a good review of recent literature on Callimachus and Apollonius by Hans Herter (Bursian, *Jahresbericht*, 1937 and 1944–55). In general Herter's view of the 'quarrel' seems to me correct as opposed to the arguments of Walter Allen, Jr. (*TAPA*, 71 (1940), pp. 1–26) and F. Wehrli (*Hermes* (1941), pp. 14–21). On Apollonius and Theocritus, cf. Appendix 3. On Ennius, Lucilius and the lesser Roman writers of epic, cf. the footnotes ad loc. My discussion of the *poetae novi* has been more influenced by Luigi Alfonsi's *Poetae Novi* (1945) than by any other work. The dates of Parthenius and his relation to the Cinnas are difficult points, but his general influence and doctrine are clear. Cf. esp. Martini (*Parthenii*, &c. = *Mythographi Graeci* II. 1 *Suppl.*) *Reliquiae* 4, 27, *Testimonia* 1, 3, 4, 6, 7. On the effect of Parthenius on Cinna and the *poetae novi*, cf. Alfonsi's excellent treatment, pp. 56–72. The *Ciris* is, almost certainly, non-Virgilian, very likely a work of Tiberian date (cf. Rudolf Helm, 'Ein Epilog zur Cirisfrage', *Hermes*, 72 (1937), pp. 78–103). But it is valuable for its revelation of lost neoteric material, especially of Calvus' *Io* and Cinna's *Zmyrna*. Cf. here, especially, W. Ehlers, 'Die Ciris und ihr Original' (*Mus. Helv.* 11 (1954), pp. 65–88). The *Ciris* contains the very rare *Bistonis* (*Ciris* 1. 65) also used in the *Io* (Morel, Calvus, frag. 11) and the rare word *tabis* (254) recorded by Charisius (cf. Morel, Cinna frag. 10) as an *hapaxlegomenon* from the *Zmyrna*. Besides, the agreement of the *Ciris* with the plan of the *Zmyrna* as set forth by Ovid (*Met.* 10. 298 f.) and Antoninus Liberalis (XXXIV) is decidedly impressive. On the whole the partial dependence of the *Ciris* on the *Zmyrna* seems certain. For the influence of Catullus' *Peleus and Thetis* on the *Ciris*, cf. Vollmer (*Sitzungsberichte Bayer. Akad. Phil.-Hist. Kl.* (1907), 365 f.) and Bellinger (*TAPA*, 53 (1922), 73 f.).

HISTORICAL EPIC

The estimate of Historical Epic given in the text runs directly counter to that given by Konrat Ziegler in a short (55 pages) but often cited monograph, *Das Hellenistische Epos* (1934). This monograph has made a considerable impression. Thus A. S. F. Gow (*Theocritus* I, 1952, p. xxii) accepts Ziegler's arguments ('as K. Ziegler has convincingly shown'), though others (e.g. E. A. Barber) show more reserve.

Ziegler's arguments are almost all of the supposititious kind since (save for the *Argonautica* and possibly the fragments of Ennius' *Annals*) only the merest scraps of lines and brief references to names and titles remain of the Hellenistic epic (the same can also be said of Antimachus' *Thebais*). Ziegler's thesis, in brief summary, is that the Callimachean attack on long epic has produced a wholy mistaken *communis opinio* as to its vogue and importance. The actuality, according to Ziegler, is that the Callimachean 'banning' of long epic was very short-lived and had little effect after the third century; but that the revival of Callimachean principles by the Romans of Sulla's time established the present tradition as to the worthlessness of Hellenistic epic, a tradition according to Ziegler that is wholly false ('Das traditonelle Urteil ist schief und falsch', p. 9). Aside from the epigoni of Theocritus (Moschus, Bion, &c.) the epic dominated the period between the late third and early first century before Christ. Ziegler cites here the various names of epic poets recorded and the records of various historical, historical-mythological, and mythological epics. But all this mass of material is now lost, practically without trace. This is why Ziegler seeks to 'recover' it by elaborate and (to me) quite unconvincing hypotheses.

So Ziegler takes Ennius' *Annals* as a more or less faithful representation of the historical Hellenistic epic: a kind of Ῥωμαϊκά to be set against Rhianus' Μεσσηνιακά. (I think Ziegler's assumption here is quite arbitrary.) On the question of the nature of this epic *before* Choerilus of Iasos Ziegler is extremely sketchy (Cf. pp. 23–25): he assumes that the introduction of the Homeric divine machinery into historical epic came in with the deified Hellenistic rulers (Alexander and his diadochi). But the coming of the Roman *imperium* 'naturally' spelled a loss of interest in the Hellenistic court and regional epic. After, however, the 'Kallimachos-Renaissance' of the first century B.C., Virgil 'returned' to Hellenistic epos (Virgil knüpft an den Stil des grossen hellenistischen Epos an, in Virgil und in nachvergilischen römischen Epos lebt es fort, p. 30). There were three fundamental reasons for the disappearance of Hellenistic epic (p. 37): (1) the 'Atticism' which condemned all 'post-classical' literature; (2) the Roman and also modern superiority to the fate and deeds of the conquered (though actually the Hellenistic monarchs were long

unaware of their 'fate' and were equally as 'proud' as their victors);
(3) the 'partisan' judgement of Callimachus on all that did not
conform to his 'new' style. Ziegler, however, sees no reason why in
fact Hellenistic epic did not reflect the actual greatness and
heroism of the age as seen by its kings and participating Greek
states. Hence he draws an analogy: just as the little poems
of Callimachus and Theocritus correspond to Hellenistic miniature art and Hellenistic 'Genrekunst' (e.g. the child in Callimachus' Artemis hymn and the child-statues), so Hellenistic epic
must have corresponded to large Hellenistic sculpture like the Pergamum
frieze. If the grand style existed in art, it must have existed in literature. We can thus extract from Ennius, Nonnos, and Hellenistic
grandiose sculpture an idea of what, e.g. the Attalid epic (and of
course other Hellenistic epic) was like. Pergamum may in fact have
been the antipodes of Alexandria, pitting so to speak its Homeric
epic against the discontinuous narrative of Callimachus.

All this is of course a tissue of conjecture. But is it plausible conjecture? It seems to me that the principal fallacy of Ziegler's whole
argument is his assumption that an age of great deeds and great
monumental sculpture must have been reflected in great epic. He
notably pays little attention to Apollonius' Argonautica (the one
actually surviving Hellenistic epic) or to the strictly mythological
(i.e. non-historical) epic. But the thesis that the Hellenistic historical
epic must somehow correspond to the 'heroism' of Hellenistic history
seems to me thoroughly false: epic is the product or natural literature of an 'Heroic age', not of an age of prose; the parallelism that
Ziegler draws between the Hellenistic epic poets and historians
(e.g. Timaios, cf. Ziegler, pp. 30–31) is thus quite misleading. In
the second place, the assumption that Ennius really gives us an
accurate idea of Hellenistic epic seems to me also false: here Ziegler
quite leaves out of account the all-important difference between a
relatively new people (writing a new literature in a new tongue) and
the 'post-classical' Greeks, as well as the marked difference between
Greek and Latin literature in general. In the third place, the sculp-
tural analogy seems to me obviously unsound: can we, for example,
say that the historical epic of Silius Italicus corresponds to the
'greatness' of Roman historical sculpture such as that on the column
of Trajan? Finally the statement that Virgil 'revived' the Hellenistic epic ignores not only Virgil's 'Callimachean' origins but all that
differentiates the Aeneid from Ennius' Annals, Apollonius' Argonautica
or Homer himself! In short, Ziegler ignores the whole problem of
anachronism, i.e. the fact that epic was strictly the product of the
heroic age and that it, like all other past literary forms, could only
be successfully 'revived' under highly special conditions and by a
commanding genius. But is there any evidence that Choerilus of
Iasos or such Attalid poets as Leschides and Musaios were geniuses?
We have here not merely the sentence of oblivion but the evident
contempt of such tradition about these epics as has reached us. To

attribute this oblivion and contempt merely to the conquest of the Greek Diadochi by Rome is obviously unconvincing: plenty of Roman epics (both in Greek and Latin) also failed to survive. And finally: why did the Romans of Sulla's time and later take Callimachus so seriously? Why did some (at least) of Callimachus, Theocritus, and the epigrams survive? Why of the epics did only the *Argonautica* survive and constitute the model of Varro of Atax and Valerius Flaccus? The answers seem not so obscure. Only in a very special environment and under favourable circumstances was a really cogent criticism and a really effective revival of poetry at all possible. Alexandria and Sullan Rome are the exceptions to a generally low literary level. But posterity has not cared to preserve the mediocre and worse: of *epics* the *Argonautica* was alone good enough to survive. Where Ziegler comes closest to being right in his monograph is in his insistence on the relative popularity of Hellenistic epic *in its own time*: the better poetry, then as now, constituted an exception to the rule of mediocrity.

We know that Callimachean poetry did not enjoy an undisputed supremacy in the Hellenistic Age: thus all the papyri of Callimachus are relatively late and are post-Ptolemaic. He had also many critics (even after the *Telchines*). For the general level of Hellenistic poetry after the third century was not high: the Romans of the first century B.C. were the first poets of sufficient ability to hew effectively to the Callimachean line.

APPENDIX 3

APOLLONIUS AND THEOCRITUS

The true importance of this question (Theocritus' supposed use of Apollonius' *Argonautica* in Idylls 13 and 22) has not, I think, been even yet appreciated. If indeed it is the case (as I shall here contend) that Theocritus 'corrected' Apollonius in these two idylls, then these are the *only* two instances in which we can actually see the difference between the *continuous poem* (ἓν ἄεισμα διηνεκές) and the short epos (ἔπος τυτθόν) of Callimachus' definition, and thus discern the practical meaning of Callimachus' criticism. Callimachus' *Hecale* is still too fragmentary a base for valid conclusions and it is not, in any event, the direct analogue of anything in a contemporary epic of the sort that Callimachus attacked. There are two main problems here: (1) the factual question as to whether or not Theocritus did use Apollonius (in these two idylls) or vice versa and (2) the question of Theocritus' literary purpose (if he did *in fact* 're-do' Apollonius).

1. The abundant literature on the factual question need not be cited since it can be found in A. S. F. Gow's *Editio Maior* of Theocritus, vol. ii (1952), p. 583 and, even more fully, in Hans Herter's elaborate review of Apollonius literature from 1921–55 (Bursian, *Jahresbericht*, 1944–55). The four works (aside from *Herter*) with which

I am principally concerned and which I shall hereafter refer to simply by the last name are: *Gow* in *C.Q*. 1938, p. 10–17 and 1942, p. 11–18; *Wilamowitz, Die Textgeschichte der Griechischen Bukoliker (Philologische Untersuchungen*, XVIII, 1906), pp. 174–99; *Perotta*, 'Studi di Poesia Ellenistica' (*Studi Italiani di Filologia Classica* (NS IV), pp. 85–280); and *Pfeiffer*'s *Editio Maior* of Callimachus (II, xli–xliii).

The case for asserting Theocritus' use of Apollonius has generally rested on the similarity of plot (esp. in the Hylas episode) and on certain verbal similarities (esp. the use of the wild-beast simile in Theocritus 13. 62 f. and *Arg*. I. 1243–7). In general it is fair to say that it has not yet convinced the specialists in this field (e.g. Pfeiffer and Herter). I think, however, it is possible to adduce new arguments that ought to put the question beyond reasonable doubt. It will be noted that there are in fact two questions here: (1) is there enough evidence to show that one used the other (whoever was prior)? and (2) is there evidence to show *who* was prior, if the answer to (1) is affirmative?

(1) So far as I can tell, quite insufficient attention has been given the fact that Theocritus' two idylls (13, 22) are clearly related and show, in fact, a *designed correspondence*. In Apollonius' account of Hylas (I, 1221 f.) there is of course mention of the spring to which Hylas goes for water and where he meets the (single) nymph but it is described only by one adjective, καλλίναος, 'fair-flowing'. In his account of the Amycus-Polydeuces contest, the fight takes place on the beach (II. 36) and there is no spring at all. But in Theocritus 13 we have a 4-line *description* of the spring (39–42) with specific mention of the vegetation around it (rushes, celandine, maiden-hair, celery, dogs-tooth). Again in 22, there is a 7-line description of the spring (ll. 37–43) also with specific mention of vegetation (pines poplars, cypresses, flowers). In both idylls the central figures (Hylas, Dioscuri) wander apart from the other Argonauts to find the spring (at a distance from the beach) and there encounter, alone, its fateful denizens (the three spring nymphs, Amycus). Their desire to drink or get water from the spring is the cause of what follows (Hylas' abduction, the fight). The parallelism is indeed striking and would seem to point clearly toward a designed correspondence or reciprocity between the two idylls. Here Theocritus has not only used two episodes *that are directly contiguous* in the *Argonautica* (end of Book I, beginning of II) but has indicated by the elaborate parallelism that he is quite aware of a connection or relation between them. Surely the chance of Theocritus' taking the two from the *Argonautica* (where they exist side by side) is very much greater than the chance of Apollonius' happening to find precisely these two contiguous episodes in Theocritus. But this is an argument for the priority of Apollonius only if we assume that Theocritus did not use *another* source, i.e. another *Argonautica* in either prose or verse. But it certainly is a very powerful argument against treating *Idylls* 13 and 22 differently: that is, it is hardly conceivable that Theocritus would

have used Apollonius' story of Hylas and then ignored the immediately ensuing story of Amycus and Polydeuces when he was clearly relating the one episode to the other in his mind. If any one thing is clear, it is the deliberate parallelism of the two idylls.
(2) In *Odyssey* 22. 298 f. we find the suitors, under attack by Odysseus and Athene, described as follows:

Τῶν δὲ φρένες ἐπτοίηθεν
οἱ δ'ἐφέβοντο κατὰ μέγαρον βόες ὣς ἀγελαῖαι·
τὰς μὲν τ' αἰόλος οἶστρος ἐφορμηθεὶς ἐδόνησεν
ὥρῃ ἐν εἰαρινῇ ὅτε τ'ἤματα μακρὰ πέλονται.

To this one Homeric passage, both Apollonius and Theocritus have made no less than *four different* allusions:

1. Apollonius' simile of the bull stung by the gadfly (I. 1265 f.).
2. Apollonius' reference to the nymph's emotion:

τῆς δὲ φρένας ἐπτοίησεν/Κύπρις (1232–33).

3. Theocritus' reference to the spring-nymphs' love (13. 48):

πασάων γὰρ ἔρως ἁπαλὰς φρένας ἐξεφόβησεν

4. His reference to Heracles grief: παῖδα ποθῶν δεδόνητο (13. 65) (which immediately follows the one simile that corresponds to one of Apollonius' similes (*Ap.* 1243 f.; *T.* 62 f.)).

Thus it is hard (almost impossible) to ascribe both Apollonius' and Theocritus' use of this one Homeric passage to mere coincidence. Here both Apollonius and Theocritus use Homer but *select different things* from Homer in a way that is hardly conceivable unless one of them had directed the other's attention to the Homeric passage. Did then Apollonius force Theocritus back to Homer or vice versa? It seems to me that the former (the priority of A.) is very much more probable (even if we disregard the argument from the springs presented just above). What Apollonius took from Homer (the consecutive phrase φρένες ἐπτοίηθεν and the simile, at least in part) is much more obvious than Theocritus' quite subtle borrowing. Theocritus deliberately preferred to use Homer's ἐφέβοντο (in the active and with the more normal omicron) with φρένες even though Homer (followed by A.) connects φρένες with ἐπτοίηθεν; but Homer connected the suitors themselves (οἱ δέ) with ἐφέβοντο. Again Theocritus rejects the gadfly simile (since he, having no Polyphemus, needs only one simile) but uses Homer's word for the gadfly's bite (ἐδόνησεν) applied in the perfect passive to Heracles. Gow first made this point (as to ἐδόνησεν and δεδόνητο) but did not see that it derives its force from the word's (δονέω) position in the *one* Homeric context of which both A. and T. made so much use. Nor did Herter see this when he criticized Gow's argument.

The big question here is obviously: how do A. and T. actually use Homer? Here Perotta has made a contribution that has often been disregarded. He points out quite correctly that, when both poets use Homer, T. always varies his imitation while A. does not. Thus: Theocritus 13. 36 ὕδωρ ἐπιδόρπιον/Apollonius 1. 1209 ποτιδόρπιον/Homer Od. 9. 234 and 249 ποτιδόρπιον; Theocritus 59 ἀραιὰ δ᾽ἵκετο φωνά/Apollonius 1249 μελεὴ δέ οἱ ἔπλετο φωνή/Homer Il. 17. 696 θαλερὴ δέ οἱ ἔσχετο φωνή; Theocritus 70 ὁ δ᾽ᾇ πόδες ἆγον ἐχώρει/ Apollonius 1264 ᾗ πόδες αὐτὸν ὑπέκφερον ἀΐσσοντα/Homer Od. 15. 555 (wrongly attributed to Iliad in Perotta, p. 87) τὸν δ᾽ὦκα προβιβάντα πόδες φέρον and Od. 3. 496 (again wrong reference in Perotta) τοῖον γὰρ ὑπέκφερον ὠκέες ἵπποι. But the best instance of T.'s variation of Homer (as against A.'s direct imitation) is in the one simile they have in common (Arg. I. 1243 f.; T. 13. 62 f.). Here A. follows Homer (Od. 6. 130) in putting the emphasis on the sheep (μήλων) which a wild beast (θὴρ ἄγριος) attacks. He changes Homer only by generalizing the beast (Homer has λέων ὀρεσίτροφος) and leaving out the other animals (cattle, deer) incidentally mentioned by Homer as also the lion's prey. Theocritus, per contra, takes the phrase ὠμοφάγος λῖς from another Homeric passage (Iliad 5. 782), eliminates the sheep and introduces a single fawn (νεβροῦ φθεγξαμένας). He thus leaves out the whole business of the beast's attempt to enter the sheepfold which Apollonius slightly expanded after Homer (Arg. I. 1246–7; Od. 6. 134; also Iliad 11. 548 f.). It seems quite plain that Theocritus has chosen the single fawn as far more appropriate for Hylas than the sheep in the guarded sheepfold. He has also reduced the five-line Homeric simile to two, whereas Apollonius has kept it at its full Homeric length.

It is fairly easy to see that Apollonius was the first to go to Homer (his imitation is all but literal) and was then subtly corrected by Theocritus' far more eclectic and sophisticated use of Homer.

We need not linger over various other considerations that have led such men as Pfeiffer to question Theocritus' use of Apollonius here. It is clear, for example, that an early dating of Theocritus 13 and 22 (Gow originally put them at 275/4) is impossible since Apollonius copiously imitated the Aitia of Callimachus and the Aitia can hardly be put much back of 275. But there are none but the most hypothetical reasons to put these idylls so early and Gow now admits (Theocritus II, p. 591) that they may well belong some ten years later. We can thus put the Aitia (1st edn.) about 275, the Argonautica (or its first two books) a little before 265 and the two idylls a little later. In any event, the chronological order (if not the exact dates) is clear. There are not equally clear verbal parallels between Apollonius and Idyll 22 but obviously 22 is so closely related to 13 (see above) that they must be taken together. This is what Wilamowitz (who was convinced of Theocritus' use of Apollonius in Idyll 13) did not see.

2. But what was Theocritus' intent in re-doing Apollonius? Some (e.g. Blumberg and Erbse, cf. citations in Herter) seem to see only a complimentary reference. To this we can only say that both T.'s

doctrine and his actual performance are sufficient indications of his
critical or critical-polemical purpose.

The general position of Theocritus in the great literary dispute of
his time is set forth specifically in a famous passage in the *Thalysia*
(7. 37 f.). Simichidas—the narrator and presumably intended to
represent Theocritus himself—meets the goatherd-poet Lycidas to
whom he describes his own poetic ideal. 'I too', he declares, 'am
the clear voice of the Muses' (*Μοισᾶν καπυρὸν στόμα*) 'though no
match for Sicelidas of Samos or Philetas.' This speech is designed
to provoke an opinion from Lycidas (*ὡς ἐφάμεν ἐπίταδες*) and
has the intended effect. Lycidas' estimate of Simichidas (Theocritus)
which follows, is thus clearly sought and repeated as the judgement
of a friend and elder colleague: it is obviously the view which
Theocritus accepts as an accurate description of his own poetic aim
and achievement. Lycidas says he gives Simichidas his stick (i.e
invests him with his own poetic 'mantle') because Simichidas-
Theocritus is a 'sapling fashioned by Zeus entirely for truth' (*πᾶν ἐπ'*
ἀλαθείᾳ πεπλασμένον ἐκ Διὸς ἔρνος). This praise is then *explained*
in terms of the opposite type of poet:

> ὥς μοι καὶ τέκτων μέγ' ἀπέχθεται ὅστις ἐρευνῇ
> ἶσον ὄρευς κορυφᾷ τελέσαι δόμον Ὠρομέδοντος
> καὶ Μοισᾶν ὄρνιχες ὅσοι ποτὶ Χῖον ἀοιδόν
> ἀντία κοκκύζοντες ἐτώσια μοχθίζοντι.

For hateful to me is the builder who ventures
To make his house high as the top of Oromedon
And those birds of the Muses who senselessly
Waste their time crowing against the poet of Chios.

In other words *truth* in poetry is to be preferred to senseless rivalry
of Homer. The former is the proper occupation of the real poet; the
latter is only a bombastic pretence whose futility is manifest. But
what exactly does Theocritus mean by *truth* aside from the negative
quality of refusal to 'rival' or imitate Homer? It is clearly something
within his own capacity, as Homeric epic is not. At the end of 22
after referring to the glory brought to all the Achaeans by Homer he
characterizes his own contribution to the fame of the Dioscuri:

> ὑμῖν αὖ καὶ ἐγὼ λιγεῶν μειλίγματα Μουσέων,
> οἷ' αὐταὶ παρέχουσι καὶ ὡς ἐμὸς οἶκος ὑπάρχει,
> τοῖα φέρω.

To you also I bear the sweet strains of the Muses
Clear voiced, such as they give and such as mine house
provides me.

But we can only determine what Theocritus' conception of poetic
truth or *ἀλάθεια* was, what the stores in his *house* actually were, by
seeing what in fact he did to the Homeric pretentions of Apollonius.
Here we need not repeat our general discussion in the text (pp.

13–15). But there can be little doubt of what T.'s ἀλάθεια meant: it is the *truth* for which and by which the relatively clumsy narratives of the *Argonautica* were transformed by Theocritus into little master-pieces of sentimental and realistic description. These masterpieces, however, were achieved at a rather high price: the surrender of both the *ethos* and the narrative continuity of Homeric epic. Heracles and Polydeuces are no longer heroes moving in an heroic and divine atmosphere: the disparity between their traditional mythical status and the Alexandrine personalities with which Theocritus has invested them is endurable only when they are removed from the context of sustained narrative and glimpsed as it were in an isolated tableau most artfully prepared to produce a bare moment of illusion. Theocritus' Heracles is a sentimental pederast; his Polydeuces is a skilful young boxer contending with a stupid and arrogant 'strong man'. Both are effectively stripped of social environment: the others, Argonauts and Bebrycians in each story, count for nothing in the narrative proper. The spotlight falls on Heracles and Hylas alone; on the Dioscuri and Amycus by themselves. All the concrete detail in which the two idylls are so rich, is concerned either with the physical locale (the two springs) or the *moment* of sentimental or realistic emphasis: Heracles' sense of loss and separation from his beloved; the courtesy, skill and sportsmanship of the young Poly-deuces in his victory over the uncouth Amycus. It is by this isolation and asymmetry (i.e. the physical removal of the main characters from their companions and the reduction of the mythical narrative context to a bare summary) that Theocritus reduces or eliminates the intrinsic incongruity of his 'modern' or 'contemporary' use of myth. Otherwise the sentimental eroticism of Heracles, the clever boxing technique of Polydeuces, would form a grotesque contrast with both the traditional conceptions of those heroes and the whole heroic era to which they traditionally belonged.

A little consideration will show how impossible it would have been for Apollonius to have followed Theocritus' methods even if he had had Theocritus' idylls before him, as Theocritus in fact had the *Argonautica*. Apollonius could not have isolated the characters in Theocritean fashion without utterly relinquishing the continuity of the narrative; he could still less have asymmetrically curtailed the preceding and succeeding narratives. But what is more important, he could not have ventured upon such modernization of character: he had to take quite seriously the heroic and semi-divine status of Heracles and the Dioscuri; and he had, above all, to associate them with his other heroes. He could not possibly hope to recapture the natural simplicity by which Homer could represent an Odysseus as *both* man and hero, both humanly real and epically dignified. The clumsiness of his narrative was thus not just a matter of defective genius. Where he had some scope for the description of a 'modern' or 'Euripidean' theme, as in the love-scene of the Third Book, he showed great narrative skill and even more than that. But this very instance is extremely revealing: he, like Theocritus, could only make effective poetry out of the 'truth' which he saw and felt—i.e. the truth of his own time and milieu—and he consequently failed quite badly when he dealt with a quite alien time and milieu. His characters in such a case became wooden and unconvincing; his narrative, disunified and awkward.

Perhaps the most striking single difference between the two authors is in their use of simile. In the *Hylas*, Theocritus' similes and simile-like descriptions reveal a modernity and homeliness which thoroughly fits the familiar-sentimental theme: in the Dioscuri his avoidance of simile in the pugilistic passages is obviously determined by the very realism of his narrative. But in both episodes of Apollonius, the use of the formal, Homeric simile produces only a pseudo-archaic and poetically jarring impression. The comparison of Heracles to a fly-maddened bull, the three similes by which he tries to give decent length to his description of the boxing, are at once too conventional to achieve an effect of Homeric simplicity, too inaccurate and malapropos to express any genuine contemporary feeling. On the other hand, Apollonius could not have preserved the tone and ethos of epic, had he used the homely similes of the Hylas or avoided all similes in the manner of the *Dioscuri*. Here again we encounter the difference between a contemporary and an anachronistic style—between one who expresses his own personal sensibility and one who has sacrificed this to recapture a sensibility which is remote and alien.

So the contrast between the ἀλάθεια of Theocritus and the pretentious style of the Homerides—between, specifically, Theocritus and Apollonius—is quite clearcut. It is in fact difficult on almost every ground to believe that Theocritus was not here referring to Apollonius. For one thing, consider how *all* the differences between Apollonius and Theocritus represent a *concentrated* as opposed to a *diffused* narrative: thus in the *Hylas*, Theocritus omits Polyphemus, increases the number of nymphs in the spring from one to three (so generalizing and reducing a competing love element; his whole emphasis is on *Heracles' love for Hylas*), leaves out the oar motif, merely mentions Telamon, eliminates the whole problem of the relation of the other Argonauts to Heracles by putting on him alone the entire onus of 'desertion'. In the Dioscuri, the *omission* of the gauntlets and the warfare with the Bebrycians and the *addition* of a distant spring alike serve to isolate the main characters and concentrate the story.

Apollonius was certainly not referring to Theocritus. To suppose this is to credit Apollonius with a lack of aesthetic perception that does no justice to his very real abilities. We cannot indeed conceive how Apollonius could have written these episodes *after* the Theocritean versions: very likely he would have omitted them altogether or greatly shortened them. Even if he could not (as a good Alexandrian) have turned his back on the *truth* of Theocritus, he could hardly have turned it on the epic model and the epic style. For the ἀλάθεια

of Theocritus was inconsistent not only with epic style but with any
symmetrical or true narrative and with any heroic or heroic-
divine conception of life. Indeed these two aspects of high classical
literature—its narrative integrity and its heroic-mythical subject-
matter—were but two facets of a single style with which the Calli-
machean-Theocritean style had no point of congruity.

APPENDIX 4

(ON CHAPTER III: LITERATURE ON VIRGIL'S STYLE)

The analysis of Virgil's style in this chapter, has, to the author's best
knowledge and belief, been only vaguely anticipated in former work
on the subject. Undoubtedly, Heinze came closest to it and it is to
Heinze's great book that this chapter is most indebted. Cf. especially
his discussion of *emotion* in the *Aeneid* (362 f.), of Virgil's *subjectivity*
(370 f.), the *continuity* of his narrative (379 f.) and his pages on
Virgil's *style* (169–70, 362–73). In his later book, *Die Augusteische
Kultur* (2nd edn. 1933), pp. 141–56, he gave perhaps the best formula-
tion of his ideas on the whole matter. Yet he curiously stopped short
of either close linguistic analysis or analysis of what I have called
Virgil's 'motif structure'. He quite failed to see the essential symbolism of the *Aeneid*. Norden in his great commentary on *Aeneid* 6
unfortunately relegated the bulk of his stylistic analysis to *Anhänge*
at the end of the book: thus, despite the acuteness of his account
of Virgil's metric, placing of words and periodic structure, he
avoided the crucially important analysis of actual passages in their
true setting within the continuity of the poem. The fact is that,
because of their date, both Heinze and Norden did not attempt a
strictly literary-critical analysis. Other stylistic studies (cf. the excellent short bibliography of Perret) have done much the same thing.
The great exception here is Pöschl, to whom I am (after Heinze) most
indebted, especially in respect to his treatment of Virgil's similes and
symbols. But his book is very eclectic and, above all, limited by its
method—its emphasis on the *characters* of the *Aeneid*, as opposed to its
structure. I have used the major commentaries (Heyne, Henry,
Conington, Norden, Pease, &c.) but not with much profit for
stylistic analysis as such. Here I owe a much greater debt to modern
English and American criticism than to classical scholars. On the
comparison of Virgil and Apollonius of Rhodes, I have found no
previous work of very great help (cf. the works of Hugi, Bozzi, &c.,
cited by Herter, *Bursian*, 1944–55). By and large this field (stylistic
analysis of the *Aeneid*) is much more of a *terra incognita* than one would
think and I am acutely aware of how much, how very much,
remains to be done. On the difference, for example, between the
style of the *Georgics* and the *style* of the *Aeneid* I have said nothing

except for a few remarks in Appendix 7. In chapters vi–vii I have
been more concerned with the general structure of the *Aeneid* than
with style. All I have really done or tried to do is to indicate a
method and give some *samples*.

APPENDIX 5

(ON CHAPTER IV: LITERATURE ON THE *BUCOLICS*)

After Paul Jahn (*Die Art der Abhängigkeit Vergils von Theokrit*, 1897–9)
had summed up the usual nineteenth-century view of the *Eclogues*
(as essentially an *imitation* of Theocritus) Gunther Jachmann ('Die
dichterische Technik in Virgils Bukolika', *Neue Jahrb. Klass. Alt.* 25
(1922), pp. 101–20) inaugurated a quite new approach, in some
respects anticipated by A. Cartault (*Étude sur les Bucoliques de Virgile*,
1897), but really quite different from anything preceding. Jachmann
saw the utterly non-Theocritean spirit and style of the poems. But
the major work (though indebted to Jachmann) is Georg Rohde's
dissertation, *De Vergilii eclogarum forma et indole* (*Klass. Phil. Studien* 5,
1925) to which should be added the remarkable review of it by
Friedrich Klingner (*Gnomon* 3 (1927), pp. 576–83) and the brief
book of Erwin Pfeiffer (*Virgils Bukolika*, 1933). All other work on the
style of the eclogues (esp. of *Eclogues* 8 and 2) is, in my view, quite
secondary. In the discussion of 8 I am most indebted to Rohde and
Pfeiffer but diverge from them at essential points, specifically in my
view of the climactic structure of the eclogue, the contrast of past and
present and the interpretation of the ending. In my treatment of 2 my
principal difference from Rohde and Klingner (as also from Büchner,
Hubaux, Kappelmacher, Helck, Cartault, Stégen) is in the interpretation of the 'second lament' (ll. 55 f.) and the contrast between
lines 8–13 and 66–68. In other words, my treatment is intended to
bring out the dramatic structure of these two eclogues and hence
their major difference from both Theocritus and the neoteric epos.

On the arrangement of the *Eclogue Book*, cf. the survey of former
views in Büchner, 236–7. The principal expositor of the view I have
here argued for is undoubtedly Paul Maury ('Le Secret de Virgile et
l'Architecture des Bucoliques', *Lettres de Humanité* III (1944), pp.
71–147). Unfortunately Maury's brilliant (in my view) analysis of
the general 'architecture' was largely obscured by his very dubious
attempt to find a numerical key to the book in the 'Pythagorean
numbers' 333 and 666 (supposedly indicating Caesar and Gallus
respectively). But Lawrence Richardson (*Poetical Theory in Republican
Rome* (1944), p. 121) had postulated much the same order on purely
aesthetic grounds. On alternative theories of the sixth eclogue (e.g.
Franz Skutsch, Jachmann, van Berchem, Zeph Stewart: references in
J. B. Evenhuis, *De Vergilii Ecloga Sexta Commentatio*, Groningen diss.,

1955, and Stewart, *Harvard Studies Class. Phil.* 64 (1959), pp. 179–205) I need not say much: their basic error, in my view, is to ignore its obvious (to me) chronological plan. The only major problem of the eclogue is, really, the Gallus (Grynaean grove) insert, but this, by itself, is certainly not intended to destroy the obviously temporal structure of the Silenus song as a whole.

APPENDIX 6

(ON CHAPTER V: LITERATURE ON THE *GEORGICS*)

Büchner (243–5) has surveyed the recent literature on the *Georgics*. To this should be added: Guy Le Grelle, 'Les Premières Géorgiques, Poème Pythagoricien' (*Les Études Classiques* 17 (1949), pp. 139–235 *plus* inset supplement) and Perret (his chapter iii on the *Georgics* is extremely suggestive). It is fair to say that the most important single thing done on the *Georgics* in recent times is the short study of Erich Burck, 'Die Komposition von Vergils Georgika' (*Hermes* 64 (1929), pp. 279–321). Burck was really the first to discard the prevailing custom of analysing the poem into isolated bits and 'digressions' and to seek for the basic lines of its inner movement, to comprehend it as an 'organic whole' (ein organisches Ganzes). To this analysis Büchner has added (his discussion of the *Georgics* is far and away the most valuable portion of this monograph). Will Richter's 1957 Commentary is also helpful at certain points (less so at others). Yet it is still true that the *symbolic structure* of the poem has been most inadequately treated, when not ignored (on this, cf. the penetrating remarks of Wolfgang Schadewaldt in the anthology *Aus Roms Zeitwende*, pp. 80–88). The contrapuntal arrangement of the *Aristaeus-Orpheus* was admirably discussed (in an article that, unfortunately, had but little influence) by Georges Ramain (*Revue de Philologie* 48 (1924), pp. 117–23) and referred to by F. Klingner ('Catulls Peleus Epos', pp. 74–75; cf. the reference above on p. 208) as analogous with with the *Peleus-Thetis*. Unfortunately he has not yet published his promised discussion of the *Aristaeus-Orpheus*. I have not found the various attempts to find an intricate balance of strophes or verse-groups (Witte, Magdalena Schmidt) very useful for understanding the poem: Le Grelle's article (based entirely on the first book) seems to me to combine a rather shrewd content-analysis with rather fantastic speculation (astral numbers, &c.). By and large I think it fair to say that this great poem has been admired rather than understood: this is the primary reason why the meaning of the contrast of books (esp. 1 and 2), the animal symbols, and the *Aristaeus-Orpheus* has been so often missed.

APPENDIX 7

THE ENDING OF *GEORGICS* IV

The *vitae* state that Virgil composed the *Georgics* in seven years which would give us the dates 37 to 29 or 37–36 to 30–29. We are told also that the complete *Georgics* was read to Augustus at Atella just after his return from the Actian victory (post Actiacam victoriam: *Vita Donati* 27). This would most probably be just before the triumph of August 12–14, 29 B.C., but almost certainly, not later (cf. N. Pulvermacher, *De Georgicis a Vergilio retractatis*, diss. (Berlin, 1890), pp. 1–30). But Servius (*ad ecl.* 10. 1) tells us that the entire second half (a medio usque ad finem) of the Fourth *Georgic* was changed after Gallus' death, the *laudes* of Gallus being replaced by the Aristaeus story (or, *ad Georg.* IV. 1, by the Orpheus story). Since Gallus committed suicide in 27 or 26, this would put the *Aristaeus* (or *Orpheus*) in 26–25 or even later. The issue is important because on it hinges the question as to whether the *Aristaeus-Orpheus* was written before or after the sixth and possibly also the first and second books of the *Aeneid*. The whole problem of the relationship of the two poems (*Georgics* and *Aeneid*) is thus very much affected by our answer to it.

Basically my whole chapter on the *Georgics* is an argument (both overt and tacit) for the unity of the poem and for the pivotal place of the *Aristaeus-Orpheus* in that unity. Much the same reasoning also underlies George Duckworth's article, 'Virgil's *Georgics* and the *Laudes Galli*' (*AJP*, 80 (1959), pp. 225–37) which I received only after completing the text of my *Georgics* chapter as it now stands. But Büchner and, independently of him, Will Richter (*Georgika*, 1957) have argued for a considerable revision of the second half of the Fourth *Georgic* and particularly for the priority of the *Aeneid* (1, 2, 6) in those passages of the two works where influence one way or another is certain. Richter says flatly (p. 12): 'Daruber hinaus ergibt die Vergleichung von mehreren Stellen derselben Buchhälfte [i.e. the *Aristaeus-Orpheus*] mit gleichlautenden Stellen der Aeneis eine kaum zu leugnende Priorität der Aeneis-formalierungen'. I think myself that the exact opposite is true.

The argument hinges mainly (if not exclusively) on five passages of *Georgics* IV and their doublets or analogues in the *Aeneid*. The first is *G.* 418–23 and *Aeneid* 1. 159–69. Here Büchner and Richter agree in supposing that the *harbour* of the *Aeneid* is the original and has been converted into the *cave* of the *Georgics*. Thus, according to Büchner, in the lines:

A. 161   frangitur inque sinus scindit sese unda reductos
G. 420   cogitur inque sinus scindit sese unda reductos

frangitur becomes *cogitur* only 'because there is nothing before the cave which breaks the waves'. In *G.* 422; *A.* 159–160:

G.   intus se vasti Proteus tegit *obice* saxi
A.   insula portum/efficit *obiectu* laterum, &c.

the *obice* is for Büchner a vague recall of the precise *obiectu laterum*. As a whole the cave has no significance for the narrative like that of the harbour of the *Aeneid*. In the latter the force of the waves is broken by an island: they are literally split into segments that finally wash themselves away in remote inlets. None of this is true or necessary in the cave of the *Georgics*. So in effect runs the argument of Büchner and Richter (in part at least this seems to go back to Kläre Mylius' Freiburg, 1946, unpublished dissertation: 'Die wiederholten Verse bei Vergil.').

Now it is quite clear here that both passages derive primarily from the harbour *and* cave of the 'old man of the sea' Phorkys in *Odyssey* 13. 96 f. But the one emphasizes the harbour; the other the cave. The reason for the harbour is obvious (it is part of the 'calm' that follows the 'storm') but so also is that for the cave. This is the refuge to which the sea-god Proteus betakes himself with his seals during the heat of the day. Also, like the cave of Polyphemus which Virgil too has in mind, it is just the place where their 'theft-conscious' master would conceal them during his siesta. This is why, like Polyphemus, he blocks the exit with a rock (obice): compare Cacus and his great stone—emuniit obice postis. In short, it is a true sea-*cave*. The waves do not *break against* an island (frangitur) but are forced (cogitur) by the winds into its mouth and then disperse in quiet among its labyrinthine recesses. It is also a good place for Aristaeus to hide—*in latebris aversus a lumine*—since he is not, like Menelaus in *Odyssey* 4, protected by a seal-skin.

But the main thing to note is the much greater length, complexity and emotion of the *Aeneid*. (Comparison with its Odyssean original is also most instructive.) The whole passage (ll. 159–69) has a passionate and strenuous tonality. The waves do not merely crash on this island breakwater: vast cliffs also threaten (minantur) the sky, bristling woods lower (imminet), while, in partial contrast, sweet waters, seats of living rock, mark the cave, the home of the nymphs. We get the impression of mysterious power, the wildness of nature turned magically into peace and security. The *aequora tuta silent* of line 164 is set between the *vastae rupes* around then and the *silvis scaena coruscis* above them. All the inanimate objects (unda, rupes, nemus, vincula, ancora) have strongly emotional verbs: frangitur, minantur, silent, imminet, tenent, alligat. Finally, the climactic arrangement is evident: first the harbour itself, then the rocks around (hinc atque hinc) and the quiet interior (intus). The anaphora of the close (non vincula ... non ... ancora) emphasizes the security, the calm that has come to the weary ships (fessas ... navis).

The style of the *Georgics*, by contrast, is simple and quiet: the *cogitur* lacks the strength of the waves outside. The line (421): *deprensis olim statio tutissima nautis* comes almost as an aside, a descriptive pause: its initial spondees and pauses have a calming effect. And it is a brief passage: there is no need for more than an indication

of the locale, certainly no need for high epic emotion. We are dealing
with seals, a dark quiet cave, a calm cool sleep in the middle of the day.

The question therefore that we must ask ourselves is: would Virgil
contract and tone down the *Aeneid* passage or, on the contrary, would
he expand and intensify (fill with epic emotion) the *Georgics* passage?
Which is the most natural progression? Obviously the question cannot
be answered on the basis of one comparison. But exactly the same
situation confronts us in *G.* 374 f. and *A.* 1. 700 f. Compare these
two passages:

> *G.* 376   Cyrene, manibus liquidos dant ordine fontis
>   germanae, tonsisque ferunt mantelia villis

> *A.* 701   dant manibus famuli lymphas Cereremque canistris
>   expediunt tonsisque ferunt mantelia villis

Here the placing of *dant*, the substitution of the verb *expediunt* for the
neutral noun *germanae*, the addition of a third clause to the *Georgics*
passage tell their own story: it is the difference between the typically
Odyssean reception of Aristaeus by his exotic sisters in the undersea
palace and the tense, expectant, dramatic meeting of Tyrian and
Trojan in Dido's banqueting hall. And again even in the difference
of:

> *A.* 705–6   ministri
>   qui dapibus mensas onerent et pocula ponant

and

> *G.* 378   pars epulis onerant mensas et plena reponunt
>   pocula

the much greater tension of the *Aeneid* comes through. With this
goes the greater amplitude of the epic: thus in *Aeneid* 5. 77 f., the one
line libation speech of Cyrene (*G.* 380–1) is expanded to four. *G.*
352, of the piquant blonde, Arethusa:

> prospiciens summa flavom caput extulit unda

is transformed into the majestic picture of Neptune calming the
waves:

> *A.* 1. 126–7   prospiciens summa placidum caput extulit unda

(Büchner sees here only a 'playful' re-doing of the *Aeneid*!). In all
these instances, the *Aeneid* is stylistically distinct from the *Georgics*:
the language of the latter has been lengthened and complicated,
given greater emotional tone, a quite new dignity and force. It is very
difficult indeed to imagine the process reversed, the amplitude cut
down, the tone lowered, the complicated and tense made simple and
relaxed.

But, of course, the style of the *Aristaeus* is, as we have seen (p. 197f.),
far less emotional and empathetic than that of the *Orpheus*. What
of that? We turn at once to the decisive lines in which Virgil describes
the innumerable dead:

G. 473   quam multa in foliis avium se milia condunt,
              Vesper ubi aut hibernus agit de montibus imber.
A. 6. 309   quam multa in silvis autumni frigore primo
              lapsa cadunt folia aut ad terram gurgite ab alto
              quam multae glomerantur aves ubi frigidus annus
              trans pontum fugat et terris immittit apricis.

Here we must note, first of all, that the *Georgics* passage recalls not only the cranes of *Iliad* 3. 2 f. but the cranes of *Georgics* I. 374 f. or the bees of the preceding half of this book (IV. 18, *vesper ubi*, &c.). The difference between the two descriptions (in the *Orpheus* and *Aeneid* 6) is of course obvious: in the *Orpheus*, what is emphasized is the thronging of the shades *cantu commotae*; in the *Aeneid* it is the chill touch of death (the touch that takes the leaves in autumn or sets the birds migrating). In the first, there is a contrast between the song and the host of volatile, wretched *umbrae*. In the second, the *newness* of death (the crowd at the river), the pathetic *insepulti* are stressed. The ideas of *cold* (frigore primo, frigidus annus) and *descent* (lapsa cadunt, ad terram gurgite ab alto) are insisted upon. This is quite different from the *Orpheus* situation where *vesper . . . aut agit imber* connotes the effect of the song—that which *drives* the shades from the lowest recesses of Hades (Erebi de sedibus imis) to take part in the dance.

Here again the *Aeneid* is much fuller and more epical (four lines for two, the solemn anaphora, *quam multa . . . quam multae*, the explanatory *ubi* clause, &c.) and seems an almost obvious *expansion* of the *Georgics*. The leaves in which the birds gathered are now expanded (doubtless after Bacchylides and Homer) into a simile of their own and the birds' evening reunion or taking of refuge from the winter storm becomes a massive migration.

The priority of the *Georgics* passage is practically certain since it clearly refers to a clustering of birds in the *leaves* of a tree or trees, not in woods (silvis) as such (the visual image is of a tree covered with the birds). But when Virgil used it for the *Aeneid* he developed the bare *foliis* (quam multa in foliis) into a complete leaf-image (such as that in Homer-Bacchylides) and then expanded the *Georgics* image into one of winter migration; the gathering in the leaves thus merged into the more general: quam multae *glomerantur* aves. Since it is certain that the one passage influenced the other, it is all but certain that this expansion, the subtle development of *quam multa in foliis* and the consequent generalization of the bird-gathering, must come later. That Virgil would break up and re-fuse the two similes of the *Aeneid* into the single simile of the *Georgics* (leaving *foliis* as a sort of uneasy remnant of the original) is exceedingly hard to believe. Actually the phrases *in foliis* and *agit de montibus imber* had been in his mind since his writing of *Georgics* I. 412–13 (about the crows):

              nescio qua praeter solitum dulcedine laeti
        inter se *in foliis* strepitant: iuvat *imbribus actis*
        progeniem parvam . . . revisere, &c.

Then the three identical lines (G. 475–8, A. 6. 306–8) are transposed
(in relation to the simile) because in the *Orpheus*, the *movement* of the
dead; in the *Aeneid*, their *pathos* is of primary importance. The shifting and subtle changing of G. 474 (tardaque palus, &c.) into A. 438
(tristisque palus, &c.) expresses, of course, the difference between the
lethargic and unresponsive environment of the dead to whom Orpheus
sings and the *sad* lot of the suicides. But *tardaque palus* is really more
native to the *Georgics* than *tristisque palus* is to the *Aeneid*: it is much
easier to envisage *tarda* becoming *tristis* than vice versa.

The difference in scale and mood between *Georgics* and *Aeneid* is
perhaps best of all brought out by the lines that describe the partings
of Orpheus and Eurydice (496 f.) and of Aeneas and Creusa (2. 775
f.). The much greater length and coldness of Creusa's words do not
suit an Aeneas *lacrimantem et multa volentem/dicere* (A. 790–1) as
Eurydice's brief farewell does an Orpheus *prensantem nequiquam, et
multa volentem dicere* (G. 501–2). Orpheus' short spasmodic emotion-
ality, his reckless passion and grief could hardly have originated in
this cold scene where Creusa, like Wordsworth's Laodamia, reproves
her 'rebellious consort'.

To sum up, the style of the *Aeneid* is quite different from that of
either the *Aristaeus* or the *Orpheus*. To suppose that the former (the
Aristaeus-Orpheus) preceded the latter (*Aeneid*) is to imagine an almost
incredible reversal of form, much the same in effect as would be
Milton's reversion from the manner of *Paradise Lost* to that of *Comus*
and *l'Allegro*. But the kind of thing that Virgil did to these passages of
the *Georgics* is exactly what we might expect of a man who was trying
to raise neoteric and hellenistic material to epic, Roman and Augustan dimensions. And just as important: to read the *Aristaeus-
Orpheus* as a simplified *Aeneid*, as a retroactive effort thrown off by a
poet engaged on a difficult and utterly different masterpiece, is to
miss its own point and poignance.

There is thus no reason to date the *Aristaeus-Orpheus* later than 30/29
except indeed the Servian testimony as to a revision after 27/26 and
certain difficulties in a few parts of the text (the curious 'introduction',
lines 281–314 on Egypt, the second introduction at line 315, the
deficient line 530, the two *bougoniae*, one Egyptian, one Greek). These
difficulties, however, are real and do point to at least some minor
revising or changing. Furthermore the Egyptian or proto-Egyptian
elements (the introductory 281–314, the obvious Homeric connection of Proteus with Egypt, the traditional Egyptian or Libyan
provenience of Cyrene) do suggest that Gallus was, somehow or
other, brought in by their means. But a complete revision—a
substitution of 250 or more lines of *laudes Galli* in the present
Aristaeus-Orpheus—is incredible and false to the spirit and balance of
the *Georgics* as a whole. Probably Virgil had praised Gallus (the actual
laudes could hardly have exceeded those previously allotted to
Augustus or Maecenas, i.e. 10–20 lines at most) as the ruler of Egypt
or in the glory of his Egyptian office: the subsequent disgrace and

death of his friend *in Egypt* would have, therefore, made the praise particularly objectionable, not only to the Emperor but also to Virgil's own good taste and concern for Gallus' memory. The situation was thus quite different from that of the sixth or tenth eclogues which refer only to his *poetry* of many years back. What the occasion accordingly demanded was an excision not only of the *laudes* (almost certainly restricted to a very small number of lines) but also of some part at least of their otherwise pointless Egyptian setting. A good guess is that the awkwardness of the Egyptian introduction, the otiose character of the double *bougonia*—Egyptian *and* Greek—and the somewhat unnatural removal of the Homeric Proteus from Egypt to Thessaly, are all due to the fact that Virgil, after Gallus' death, shifted his locale from Egypt to Greece and did so by making only the most hasty and—for him—awkward changes. The obvious truncation of line 530 (*At non Cyrene* with no verb: we can of course see the sense but it was not Virgil's habit to be so ungrammatically elliptical) and the obvious difficulty of relating lines 285 f. to lines 315 f. point *not* to a wholesale revision (that would have smoothed everything out) but only to a few hasty changes and omissions (of probably not more than 20–30 lines *in toto*, i.e. the omission of the *laudes* with their immediate Egyptian context, the substitution of a Greek for an Egyptian terrain at ll. 317, 365–73, 387 and some omission *and* addition at ll. 530 f.). Servius, of course, greatly exaggerated the changes: but there is no reason to take him too literally, as numerous other evidence makes clear. The important point is that the poem was always *substantially* the same as it is now and should be, with relatively unimportant reservations, dated with the rest of the *Georgics* at or slightly before 30/29.

APPENDIX 8

(ON CHAPTERS VI AND VII: LITERATURE ON THE *AENEID*)

I have made some use of Heinze, Pöschl, Cartault, Perret and Büchner (cf. exact citations on p. xiii) as well as of the commentaries (esp. Conington, Pease, Norden, Warde-Fowler). By and large, however, these chapters were (originally) written quite independently of any of them, except Heinze and Pöschl (with whom both explicit agreements and explicit divergences are usually indicated in the footnotes). In general I have gained far more from recent Virgilian scholarship in French and German than from that in English or Italian (an exception is Conway, some of whose observations, especially on *Aeneid* 6 and 10, have been most helpful to me). I have two very definite convictions: (1) that in respect to the *Aeneid* as a whole (just as in respect to Virgil's style) there is still no book or general treatment that has anything like the importance

of Heinze's great work; and (2) that the defects of Heinze's analysis
(due in large part to his date: his book is a work of nineteenth-
century scholarship though appearing at the very beginning of the
twentieth) have not yet been made good. Recent advances in the
criticism and analysis of Virgil have concerned the *Bucolics* and the
Georgics rather than the *Aeneid* (esp. the work of Burck for the
Georgics; of Rohde, F. Klingner and Maury for the *Bucolics*).

The great achievement of Heinze was his almost definitive
demonstration that Virgil's narrative *technique* was utterly un-
Homeric and had indeed a *psychological* and *dramatic* emphasis
different from that of all Greek epic of which we know (though
Heinze did not carry out a comparison of the *Argonautica* with the
Aeneid comparable to his comparison of Homer and *Aeneid*). But he
failed to indicate the actual structure of the *Aeneid* (except at certain
special points) and, above all, failed to see what Virgil's *technique*
really meant and accomplished, viz. that it was part of a new
narrative style and of a 'symbol structure' by which traditional
Homeric motifs were given contemporary Augustan values and in
which *therefore* an obsolete genre and subject-matter (the mythical-
legendary basis of epic) could be made into a great epic of civilization (cf. chaps. iii, viii above). Heinze's failure to perceive the true
structure of the poem was due, in part, to his deference to Norden,
whose commentary on Book 6 was in preparation when Heinze was
writing. But, of course, Heinze would not have by-passed the sixth
book even for this reason, had he really seen its pivotal position in
the poem. Even so, Heinze *did* see that the sixth book was a crucial
element in the hero's psychological preparation for the Latin War:
here Pöschl, it seems to me, has most unwisely rejected Heinze.

But, most fundamentally, Heinze's tendency to see the *technique* of
the *Aeneid* as a *separate element* that could be demonstrated by more
or less isolated examples and comparisons supplemented only by
generalized topical discussions, greatly restricted his view of the
whole problem. This, however, is a limitation peculiar to Heinze's
time. But it is curious that no successor of Heinze was able to make
good his defects (those of, after all, a great pioneer work). Stylistic
analysis on the one hand, has remained largely confined to special
points (metre, vocabulary, sentence-structure) that never quite
touch the style *as such*; general treatments of the *Aeneid* (e.g. W. F. J.
Knight, Tenney Frank, Rostagni, Paratore, Prescott, Rand) have
remained, largely, impressionistic, either heavily dependent on quite
unprovable theories (e.g. a theory of Virgil's poetic development
based on the *Appendix Vergiliana* or some particular hypothesis as to
the *Aeneid*'s composition) or largely devoid of any clear sense of the
major questions and problems that needed to be answered (e.g. the
relation of the *Aeneid* to previous post-Homeric epic). The best of
such general treatments are, in my view, those of Cartault and, to
a lesser degree, Constans, but I think it is also fair to say that, except
for a good number of excellent observations and comments, they

mark no clear and decisive *advance* over Heinze and introduce no real reformulation of the essential problems.

Here Pöschl, is, in my view, unique: thoroughly aware of the extent to which Heinze avoided a true literary-critical analysis, he attempted to supply the deficiency at a few points of great significance, especially in respect to the symbolism and Virgil's ability to create 'atmospheric' effects. Pöschl's book, however, is episodic and, in large part, also impressionistic; for instance, it avoids a structural approach and by and large confines itself to Virgil's characterizations (Aeneas, Dido, Turnus in particular). Its rejection of the idea of 'psychological development'—its acceptance, in other words, of the curious dogma that no ancient writer understood 'development of character'—is, in my view, its greatest positive defect, for this largely inhibits an understanding of the poem's structure (esp. of Book 6, again neglected). But, for all that, the excellence of Pöschl's work is thrown into relief by Büchner's extensive monograph: the latter's treatment of the *Aeneid* is systematic, is concerned with structure, and shows an admirable understanding of Heinze's work but, instead of completing it along the lines Pöschl had adumbrated, it virtually ignores Pöschl and contributes little or nothing to our understanding of the poem's symbolism or 'ideology' (the treatment of Book 6 is especially disappointing).

In many ways the most suggestive approach to the *Aeneid* is that *adumbrated* rather than *executed* by F. Klingner in Germany and by J. Perret in France, i.e. the approach *via* the *Bucolics* and *Georgics* (cf. here esp. Klingner's essay 'Die Einheit des Virgilischen Lebenswerkes' in *Römische Geisteswelt*, 1956). I cannot accept without very serious reservations the 'mathematical' approach to the *Aeneid* (esp. its analysis in terms of the 'golden section') illustrated by George Duckworth ('Mathematical Symmetry in Virgil's *Aeneid*,' *TAPA*, 91 (1960), pp. 184–220) and based on Le Grelle's analysis of *Georgics* I (cf. Appendix 6). The positive results of Duckworth's analysis (e.g. 'proof' of the 'genuineness' or Virgilian authorship of the *Culex* and of the 'deliberateness' of the half lines) seem to me to bear against the analysis itself. On the other hand, many of the 'golden sections' do coincide fairly well with the natural divisions of the poem as revealed by careful content analysis and show (as I see it) that Virgil did often compose in carefully balanced episodes. But, in my view, mathematics must be introduced only as a final and rather minor supplement to a discussion of content. It is to be hoped that Duckworth will eventually relate the two.

APPENDIX 9

(THE COMPOSITION OF THE *AENEID*)

There has been much discussion of the development (Entstehung) of the *Aeneid*, though it has not attained to anything like Homeric or biblical proportions. The fact is, of course, that the *Aeneid* is the consciously and carefully planned work of *one* author, writing in a highly literate era and society: there is no possible comparison with the *Iliad* or the *Pentateuch*. Nevertheless ever since Frederick Conrads published his *Quaestiones Virgilianae* in 1863, there have been repeated attempts to show that the *Aeneid* underwent serious changes (both in general plan and in detail) during the process of its composition. The most important of these are probably (1) that of Noack (1892) who claimed that there was an 'erste Aeneis' consisting of Books 1, 2, 4, 6 to which was later added an Iliadic supplement (7–12) and the other odd books; (2) that of Sabbadini (1900) who thought the third book was originally writ ten inthe third person and was the first book of a primitive Aeneid in which the present books (or their equivalents) followed the order 3, 5, 1, 2, 4; (3) that of A. Gercke (1913) who thought the last six books were older than the first six and that there were in fact six stages of the poem's composition, the changes being in part motivated by Virgil's conversion from an Epicurean to a Stoic position; and (4) the present theory of Paratore which sees the original kernel as 8 (where Virgil reveals his rejection of the Epicureanism he had, according to Paratore, shown in his earlier work) whereupon 6 (minus the Dido and Marcellus parts), the Latin War books and 2, 4 followed in about that order. The so-called *Odyssean* books (1, 3, 5) are, for Paratore, latest of all. Paratore thinks it was only very late in the game that Virgil adopted the Homeric model; even the shield in 8 is basically Hesiodic not Homeric. Paratore's pupil, Giovanni D'Anna (*Il problema della composizione dell'Eneide*, 1957) has now conflated Paratore's views with those of Sabbadini.

I cannot here attempt to deal with these theories, to say nothing of various alternatives and modifications that have been proposed (there are good résumés with bibliographical data in Büchner, 405–6, Pease, 56–59, and, for recent material, G. D'Anna, op. cit.). Since, however, this book has assumed throughout that the *present Aeneid* (as we have it) reveals a most carefully designed and wholly coherent plan, I feel it necessary to say a little about the assumptions that underlie all these theories.

1. It seems to me quite impossible to suppose that Virgil ever *planned* the even books without the odd. The alternation of major and minor, or graver and lighter books, was an essential principle of his aesthetic. An order such as Noack's 1, 2, 4, 6 would clearly destroy the salience and effect of 2, 4, 6. Furthermore Virgil had *already* used this principle of alternation in the *Georgics* (cf. above, p. 151) and, to some extent at least, in the *Eclogue Book*.

2. It likewise seems to me impossible that he could ever have conceived the *Iliadic* witho utt he *Odyssean Aeneid* and vice versa. Without the balanced scheme that we have, the whole point of 6, its relation to the previous books and the succeeding books, would be lost. Above all, perhaps, the obvious correspondence of books 7 and 1 would make no sense. Juno's supreme effort (Allecto, &c.) implies a

previous record of failure: flectere si nequeo superos, Acheronta movebo, cf. p. 322 f. above.

3. It seems clear (cf. pp. 216–217 above) that he followed, in part at least, the scheme of the *Eclogue Book* and designed 7 to be in some sense the centre with planned correspondence between 6 and 8, 5 and 9, 4 and 10, &c. He also followed a 6–6 scheme (cf. p. 392), as is obvious. This plan of a work in two parts or halves with overlapping correspondences is common also to both *Eclogue Book* and *Georgics* (cf. pp. 216–217 and pp. 217–218). There is no reason at all to suppose that Virgil did not have it in mind when planning the *Aeneid*.

The *Aeneid*, however, is admittedly an unfinished or unrevised work and contains certain minor but unmistakable inconsistencies that would presumably have been corrected, had Virgil lived to do so. Paratore (*Una nuova ricostruzione del De Poetis di Suetonio*, 1950) has attempted to minimize the authenticity of the famous statement in the *vita* that Virgil wrote first a prose outline in twelve books and that he then composed the poem *particulatim* (*Vita Donati* 22). I am not convinced by Paratore's arguments: but it is hard, in any event, to imagine Virgil writing in any other way. He planned the poem *as a whole* and then wrote it piecemeal. Obviously this made for some inconsistencies and inequalities. There were the famous *tibicines* or rough transitional sections, the half-lines, &c. Even aside from chronological considerations (e.g. the reconciling of the *septima aestas* of 1. 755–6 with that of 5. 623–6) which really do not bother the reader at all, there are a number of points which show that certain parts or books preceded others in order of composition. Thus the table-eating omen of 7. 107 f. is there connected with a prophecy of Anchises though it is the main burden of Celaeno's dread speech at 3. 245 f. There is a discrepancy between the thirty white pigs of 3. 389 f. and 8. 36 f., 81 f.; there is the much more important discrepancy about Palinurus between Books 5 and 6; there are the disturbingly different roles of Helen as told by Deiphobus in 6 and witnessed by Aeneas in 2; there is the absence of Venus in 3 though Aeneas has already said in 1 that his mother showed him the way (1. 382); there is the recollected prophecy of Venus (8. 534) that we had not heard of before; there do seem to be some (though very slight) difficulties about the use of the first and third persons in Book 3. Most of these difficulties are accounted for (it is a great excess of zeal to argue them all away as some would do) if we assume that much of 3 and 5 was written quite late (i.e. after 1, 6, 7, 8) and that the necessary retouches in the other books (to bring them into accord with the later ideas) had been left to the uncompleted revision. The Helen passage in 2 is really a proof of this: obviously Virgil was dissatisfied with the passage and marked it for eventual omission and replacement (this is why Varius and Tucca actually did omit it: there is no reason to doubt Servius here, ad loc). He clearly preferred to let the Deiphobus account stand as it was in Book 6 and saw that he therefore had to remedy a discrepancy. We cannot be sure whether

he wrote the Helen lines in 2 before or after the Deiphobus lines
(though 6 seems to be earlier) but we can reasonably surmise that
Virgil had done one or the other and was later concerned to reconcile the contradiction. (Even if we deny the authenticity of the Servian
lines omitted by the main MSS. we must still postulate an omission
that would have had to be made good.) It is also quite possible that
he wrote a few lines of 3 in the third person and later changed them,
but this does not in the least imply the extensive revision postulated
by Sabbadini.

   In short all the discrepancies are quite minor or (as in the case of
Helen) obviously tentative and slated for emendation. The important
thing, by contrast, is the massive evidence for meticulous planning of
the 12 book ensemble, such as e.g. the careful correlation of 7 and 1,
9 and 5, 8 and 6, 10 and 4, 12 and 6; the innumerable cross-referen-
ces (especially true of 6 and 8, 5 and 9); the recapitulative character
of 6 and 12; the careful dovetailing of Anchises and Venus in 1–6 so
that neither should intrude on the other; the remarkable use of 2 in 5;
the carefully elliptical quality of Helenus' prophecy in 3; and indeed
the whole argument of this book!

   Any reasonable theory as to the order in which Virgil wrote the
books of the actual poem (as opposed to those of the prose outline)
must necessarily be tentative but ought clearly to be based on utterly
different premises from those of Noack, Sabbadini, Gercke, Paratore,
&c. Virgil had in mind a plan (the essential Odyssean-Iliadic plan)
in which certain books were of pivotal significance. We can see this
from the overlappings in his two main schemes of 'correspondence'
(cf. p. 217 and pp. 312, 344) between the books:

A (based on 7 as centre)		B (based on correspondence of each half)
7	1	7
12	2	8
11	3	9
10	4	10
9	5	11
8	6	12

In other words: 7 and 1, 10 and 4 correspond *in both schemes*. The
first set (7, 1) are obviously the introductions of the two main
sections (*Odyssean, Iliadic*); the second set (4, 10), the main action
books (the great tragedies: Dido, Pallas) of each section. Equally
important to Virgil, however, would be 6 and 12 the concluding
books of each section; of only slightly less importance, 8, the indispensable pendant to 6.

From another point of view the *Aeneid* obviously falls into three distinct parts: the main action books of the *Odyssean* part (2–4); the main action books of the *Iliadic* part (10–12); and the *Interlude* of books that prepare Aeneas for actual combat in Latium (5–9). In 5 the Latin War, *for the first time*, becomes of over-riding concern (the founding of Acesta, the ship-burning, the Anchises summons— hence indirectly the games, the one non-Odyssean episode of the first part—all look ahead to the coming war); in 6 Aeneas is steeled for the future in Latium; in 7 the war is symbolically inaugurated; in 8 Aeneas takes over Arcadian-Etruscan leadership and assumes the shield; in 9 his very absence from battle bears witness to his indispensable importance and prepares us for his grand entry in 10. W. A. Camps (*C.Q.* (1959), pp. 53–56) has called attention to the special character of these five books (5–9). They reveal *five* successive counterparts of Homeric originals (Games, Nekuia, Catalogues of Heroes, Shield, Doloneia: Camps has omitted the ship-burnings); the Roman theme is here emphasized as nowhere else with specific mention of characteristic Roman institutions (Troius Lusus, Sibylline Books, Janus Temple, Ara Maxima, &c.); and, the five Homeric motifs are each given a specific Roman application. Above all, of course, Aeneas and Augustus come together in these books and in them also the victory of Actium triumphantly emerges (cf. Propertius).

The reason for the peculiarity of Books 5–9 is surely obvious. These are the books that join the other two parts (2–4, 10–12)—the main action parts (esp. Books 2, 4, 10, 12)—to each other, by uniting the two great themes of the *Latin War* and the *theios aner* and, Homerically, by uniting the Odyssean and Iliadic motifs: the Iliadic *games* of 5 anticipate the Iliadic *aristeiai* of 9; the ship-burning of 5 anticipates the ship-burning of 9; the futuristic climax of the Odyssean *Nekuia* (6) anticipates the futuristic climax of 8 in the *Iliadic* shield; finally the Iliadic proem (7) recapitulates and repeats (in reverse) the Odyssean proem (1, esp. 1. 1–304). But of these five intermediate books, 6 is assuredly the most pivotal in that *in it* the Odyssean hero is 'reborn' and converted into the Iliadic *theios-aner*.

Now it is reasonable to suppose that Virgil would first try to grapple with the more pivotal books before tackling the less pivotal: thus 6 (most of all), 1 (at least 1. 1-304), 7 and the main action books (4, 10) followed closely by the other great action books (2, 12) and the Augustan 8, would seemingly be the first to engage his detailed attention. We know in fact that he did read 2, 4, 6 to Augustus probably shortly after Marcellus' death in 23 (*Vita Donati*, 31–33); that 1 is probably very early (since it does *not* mention the epithet *Augustus* and seems to refer only to the *first* closing of the *portae Belli* by Octavian, cf. W. F. Friedrich, *Philologus*, 94, 1940, pp. 164 f.); that Propertius (about 25 B.C.) knew of the first lines of the *Aeneid*, of the poem's Iliadic intent and its praise of Augustus' victory at Actium (cf. Propertius II. 34. 61-66). To suppose (with, e.g. D'Anna) that Propertius' line: nescio quid maius nascitur Iliade

EE*

(66) means that *only* the *Iliadic* books then (25 B.C.) existed, is not merely to press the literal meaning of *Iliade* much too closely but to ignore the rather obvious reference to Aeneid 1. 1–7 in:

> II. 34. 58   qui nunc *Aeneae Troiani* suscitat arma
> 59   iactaque *Lavinis moenia* litoribus.

The main reason for thinking that 6 was one of the books which first seriously engaged Virgil's attention is the very strong presumption (argued above in Appendix 7) that the identical lines or the very slightly altered lines of the *Orpheus* song in *Georgics* IV belong to, or even slightly before, the year 30–29 and thus indicate Virgil's pre-occupation at the start of the *Aeneid* not only with the death-resurrection theme (as a pivotal element of his Augustan 'ideology') but with much of its *ethos* and poetical ambience. Furthermore the *Aristaeus* shows also points of congruity with *Aeneid* 1 and 2 (cf. Appendix 7).

It is thus, for several reasons, probable that Books 1 and 6 are very early compositions (in at least a preliminary form) though there is no good basis for supposing that Virgil *necessarily* wrote 6 before 2, 4. We cannot be *certain* either that he wrote 2, 4 before 8, 10, 12, but 2, 4 do show signs of greater finish and were the books selected for reading to Augustus. It would be more natural for Virgil to write them before the others. *But we must always bear in mind Virgil's eclectic method of composition* (nihil in ordinem arripiens, *Vita* 24) *and the fact that a quite detailed plan preceded the actual writing of each book.* In any event, any reasonable theory of the poem's composition indicates once more its original unity. Virgil grasped from the start the pivotal role of 6, the idea of a combined *Odyssey-Iliad* (with two proems), the notion of a central Augustan section surrounded by Odyssean and Iliadic 'action books' (2, 4, 10, 12), the arrangement of the books in two contrapuntal schemes (A and B on p. 418) and the general distribution of content between the even and odd books (major themes in the even; minor in the odd). Everything points to the scope and exactitude of his original plan. Beside the massive evidence for this, the relative unimportance of the 'inconsistencies' is remarkable especially when we bear in mind that the poem was, after all, unfinished.

GENERAL INDEX

TEXTS AND PASSAGES DISCUSSED